MW00906966

THE
METAPHYSICS
OF SELF AND
WORLD

THE
METAPHYSICS
OF SELF AND
WORLD

*Toward a Humanistic
Philosophy*

E. M. ADAMS

Temple University Press • PHILADELPHIA

Temple University Press, Philadelphia 19122
Copyright © 1991 by Temple University
All rights reserved
Published 1991
Printed in the United States of America

The paper used in this publication meets the minimum requirements
of American National Standard for Information
Sciences—Permanence of Paper for Printed Library Materials,
ANSI Z39.48-1984 ∞

Library of Congress Cataloging-in-Publication Data

Adams, E. M. (Elie Maynard), 1919–
    The metaphysics of self and world : toward a humanistic
philosophy / E. M. Adams.
        p. cm.
    Includes bibliographical references and index.
    ISBN 0-87722-784-5
    1. Humanism. 2. Metaphysics. 3. Humanities. 4. Civilization,
Modern—1950– 5. Civilization—Philosophy. I. Title.
B821.A425   1991
144—dc20   90-39479

For Phyllis

CONTENTS

PREFACE

We form our identity and live our lives in terms of the humanistic culture—the language of selfhood, morality, art, religion, and the humanities; but we, in the modern age, do our serious thinking in our efforts to know and to understand things in terms of the naturalistic conceptual system of modern empirical science. Thus, as Ernest Gellner says, "our identities, freedom, norms, are no longer underwritten by our vision and comprehension of things" (*Legitimation of Belief*, 1974, p. 207).

Many have tried, and still do, to trim our humanistic culture and to validate its indispensable aspects in terms of the scientific method and the naturalistic world-view it presupposes. But confidence in this approach may be waning. Some conclude that we cannot integrate the culture and ground it in a unified world-view; that, while we must accept the scientific way of defining and understanding the world, the humanistic culture must remain soft, without ontological support. The only ground it can have, they say, is history; that is, the way of life of a cultural community and the culture embodied in it are the products of an evolutionary process and need no other warrant. Others conclude that what is true of the humanistic culture has to be true of the scientific culture as well. The only warrant any sector of the culture can have, they say, is its survival in the ongoing cultural process. While reason may resolve some problems internal to the way of life of a cultural community, reason itself, according to this view, is internal to the particular culture and can gain no critical perspective from which it can hold the culture accountable to an independent principle or reality. Those who share this view abandon the quest for an integrated culture and a unified world-view; and they either discredit philosophy or re-define its mission.

This work is an attempt to provide a full-fledged humanistic view of persons and society and a humanistic world-view as a way of solving the modern human identity crisis and the cultural antinomies occasioned by the disjunction between the way we must think in living our lives and the way we have become accustomed to think in our search for knowledge and understanding of the world.

Although the work is self-contained and stands alone, I think of it as the last in a trilogy. The first was *Ethical Naturalism and the Modern World-View* (1960, 1973) and the second was *Philosophy and the Modern Mind* (1975, 1985). In all three works I have been concerned with the upheavals and dislocations in the culture and the resulting human identity crisis occasioned by the rise of modern science and its natu-ralistic world-view.

I began *Ethical Naturalism and the Modern World-View* in the 1950s with a thorough commitment to modern naturalism. My intent was to find a naturalistic but realistic theory of ethics that would not be vul-nerable to the kinds of criticism that had been brought against classical ethical naturalism and that had given rise to emotivist and good-rea-sons theories. But in the course of my efforts I ran into insuperable difficulties. At the same time I was engaged in a series of studies on phenomenalism and physical-object language. In that work, I came to embrace, on the basis of criticism of the sense-datum theory, a semantic (intentionalistic) theory of sensory experience and a realistic theory of physical-object language. I then asked similar questions about emotive (affective and conative) experiences as I had asked about sensory expe-riences, and I became convinced that emotive experiences were inten-tionalistic also. This development gave rise to new insights into an alter-native realistic value theory, which I worked out in some detail in the book. But I knew that there was a lot more work to be done. My whole naturalistic world-view had been shattered.

In *Philosophy and the Modern Mind* I undertook a comprehensive philosophical critique of modern Western culture. The emphasis was on the philosophical perplexities grounded in the logical tensions be-tween the humanistic dimension of the culture and the prevailing natu-ralistic assumptions about knowledge and reality in our scientific/tech-nological age. I examined, and found wanting, our best philosophical defenses of naturalism, especially with regard to value, ethics, meaning, and the mental; and I concluded that the antinomies of our modern culture could be resolved only on the basis of a realistic philosophy of the humanities.

In the present book the results of the first two studies are brought forward and further advanced, but the emphasis is no longer on criticism of modern naturalism (although it is not entirely absent); rather the focus is on taking humanity and the humanities (and the whole humanistic dimension of the culture) seriously in our efforts to restore coherence in the foundations of the culture and to achieve a unified world-view in terms of which we can make sense of our humanity, the social world, and all sectors of the culture. The work is a study in the philosophy of the humanities: It is a philosophy of humanity, a philosophy of culture, and a philosophy of social reality; and it explores the metaphysical implications of these for a coherent world-view and for our efforts to comprehend ultimate reality.

In Chapter 1 I explore the human identity crisis in modern culture. In Chapter 2 I consider the humanities, their plight in our scientific/technological age, and their proper role in cultural criticism and in the life of the culture. Value and meaning are the basic and most distinctive categories of humanistic discourse. In the course of Chapters 2 and 3 I bring forward and explain the realistic theory of value language I have developed in earlier works; and in Chapters 3, 4, and 5 I develop a realistic theory of meaning and the mental, a humanistic theory of knowledge, and an account of the semantic and knowledge-yielding powers of the human mind that validates a realistic interpretation of humanistic discourse and underwrites an objectivist interpretation of the culture in general. In Chapter 6 I argue for a humanistic view of minds and persons in conjunction with a realistic theory of logic and ethics; and in Chapter 7 I develop a humanistic view of social reality and the normative structure of society. In the final chapter, after an extensive summary, I explore the implications of persons and the social world for a humanistic view of ultimate reality and the role of religion and theology in the human quest for understanding.

In this work I have used certain conventions that need explanation, although they are not uncommon in philosophical literature. I have used quotation marks for two purposes other than for quotations: (1) to convert a word, phrase, or sentence into a name of itself when I wish to mention it rather than to use it; and (2) for "scare quotes," as here illustrated, to warn the reader that the word or phrase is being used in a somewhat unusual or special sense. I have also used italics for two purposes other than for titles of books and journals: (1) to convert a word, phrase, or symbol into a name of the concept or proposition that it conveys as distinct from the word, phrase, or symbol itself; and (2) to emphasize a word or phrase or to place the emphasis on a particular word or phrase to determine the meaning of the sentence. The reader can determine from the context the use being made of quotation marks or italics in a particular instance.

I have made use of ideas and material from previously published papers, most of which were developed from this project as it was in progress. These include "Philosophical Grounds of the Present Crisis of Authority," *The Southern Journal of Philosophy* 8 (Summer and Fall 1970): 129–42; "The Humanities and Their Role in Modern Life," in *Images and Innovations: Update '70s,* ed. Malinda R. Maxfield (Spartanburg, S.C.: Center for the Humanities, Converse College, 1979), 16–31; "Philosophical Education as Cultural Criticism," *Teaching Philosophy* 3 (Spring 1980): 1–11; "Persons and Morality," *Philosophy and Phenomenological Research* 42 (March 1982), 384–90; "Categorial Analysis, Meaning, and Ultimate Reality," *Ultimate Reality and Meaning* 5 (March 1982): 8–22; "The Concept of a Person," *The Southern Journal of Philosophy* 33 (Winter 1985): 403–12; "The Accountability of Religious Discourse," *International Journal for Philosophy of Religion* 18 (Spring 1985): 3–17; "The Human Substance," *The Review of Metaphysics* 39 (June 1986): 633–52; review of John J. McDermott's *Streams of Experience: Reflections on the History and Philosophy of American Culture* in *The Review of Metaphysics* 11 (September 1986): 134–35; "Taking the Humanities Seriously," *The World and I,* a publication of *The Washington Times Corporation* (December 1987): 689–700; "Human Rights and the Social Order," *The Journal of Value Inquiry* 22 (1988): 167–81; "An Examination of the American Way of Life," *The World and I* (October 1989): 589–97; "The Individual and Society: A Response to the Conservative Critique of Liberalism," *The World and I* (January 1991); "The Meaning of the Twentieth Century," *The New Rain* 1 (1990). I am grateful to the editors of these publications for permission to draw on these articles.

My intellectual debts have been accumulating through the years. At this point many of them are too hidden to be traced and the others are too numerous to recall. But I do want to acknowledge my debts to William Lycan, Warren Nord, John Pauley, Jay Rosenberg, Richard Smyth, and David Weissbord, who have discussed with me parts of this work or papers in which many of the ideas developed here were first expressed; and especially Seth Holtzman, who has worked over the entire manuscript with me. I owe a special debt to the participants in my 1989 NEH Summer Seminar for College Teachers on Metaphysics, Morality, and Moral Theory: Charles C. Crittenden, Carlton Fisher, Marcus B. Hester, Deryl J. Howard, James S. Kelly, James F. Peterman, Gregory P. Rich, Terrence L. Moore, George E. Scott, Katheleen Wallace, May A. Webber, and Robert Baxter Westmoreland. They challenged me on many points in this work and forced me to rethink some of them. Readers and editors for Temple University Press offered suggestions and corrections that have made this a more readable book, with fewer blemishes. I owe special thanks to Jane Cullen, senior acquisitions editor. She is an author's delight; it has been a pleasure to work with her.

I dedicated the first book of this trilogy to my mother and father, Bessie Callaway and Wade Hampton Adams, and the second to my son and daughter, Steven and Jill. I dedicate this book, the culmination of my life's work, as I did my very first book, to my wife, Phyllis, who has been the love and inspiration of my life for more than fifty years. From these five dear people I have learned more about humanity and what it is to be human than from all others.

THE
METAPHYSICS
OF SELF AND
WORLD

CHAPTER 1

Self and World: The Problem

We are reflective, critical beings. Unlike tigers, each of whom lives the life of the tiger, we define our lives: We live under a concept of who we are. We live under an inner imperative for our experiences, actions, and lives to be meaningful and fitting for us as human beings and as the individuals we are; and we live under an inner imperative to be consistent and correct in our experiences and beliefs and to place the realities we know in the world in a way that would make them intelligible. Reflective, critical living of the human sort requires that one be a self unified under a normative self-concept* that embraces these imperatives and that one have a world unified under a conceptual frame of description and explanation.

One's normative self-concept is both constitutive of oneself and the basic organizing and governing idea of the life one lives. It is embedded in a conceptual system that is grounded in, and is constitutive of, one's experiences as a reflective, critical agent in an intersubjective society with a shared culture. Here the whole gamut of human experiences is in play: somatic sensation, external sensory perception, desire, feeling, emotion, intention, self-awareness, reflective awareness, expression perception, act perception, person perception, the "you" experience, the "we" experience, and so on. In short, the normative self-concept that unifies one's self and integrates one's life is part of, and presupposes, a team of concepts grounded in, and constitutive of, one's humanity. This conceptual system includes our personal, social, mental,

*A concept is normative if a statement containing it as its predicate entails an imperative or "ought" judgment.

agency, semantic, logical, epistemic, value, moral, aesthetic, and cultural concepts. These concepts are rightly called "humanistic."

The descriptive/explanatory conceptual system in terms of which we define an ordered world and seek to describe and to place in the world what we experience and count as real may include our humanistic concepts or some extension of them. If so, we have a humanistic metaphysics. Most religious world-views have been generated in this manner. This team of concepts grounded in selfhood is the source of all theistic and idealistic metaphysics. But there is the possibility in the human condition for the development of an independent, non-humanistic, world-defining, descriptive/explanatory conceptual system. Some intellectuals in ancient Greece entertained this possibility, but only in modern times has a civilization seriously embraced a non-humanistic world-view. The full human consequences of such a world-view are not yet known, but it is clear that something deep within human beings rebels against it.

Civilization consists of two fundamentally different kinds of enterprises. We are engaged in human, cultural, and social development: in organizing, sustaining, enriching, motivating, and directing our own lives, our institutions, and our societies. Here we seek the kind of knowledge, understanding, and general culture that will shape our identity, establish our relationships as human beings in the world, and nurture, enrich, empower, and guide us from within. We also try continually to reconstruct and to control the material conditions of our existence to our advantage. So we seek the kind of knowledge and understanding of things that will further this enterprise—knowledge and understanding that will give us increased power to make, to change, and to control things. These two kinds of on-going activities, human development and control of our material conditions, are in response to fundamental human needs. Although they are intermeshed and mutually supporting in many ways, they are distinct approaches, each having its own objective and method. There is a constant tension between them within any culture. This tension is likely to produce philosophical perplexities and errors in our ways of thinking about ourselves and the world.

Philosophical error in our cultural ways of thinking about the world could systematically mislead and defeat us in our efforts to understand and to cope with reality. Error in our philosophical ways of thinking about the physical world could impede or thwart us in our efforts to cope with the material conditions of our existence. If the subject matter were that of persons and the social world, philosophical error could even pervert us as human beings, derange our culture, deform our institutions, and give rise to pathological social conditions; it could be devastating for civilization, even for humankind.

In most societies prior to the modern age, humanistic concerns about the inner constitution and dynamics of persons and society were dominant. Perhaps this was partly so, not for genuinely humanistic reasons, but because the road to power lay in social organization and the control of people. There were heavy investments in the glorification of God and kings, saints and heroes, and in maintaining a consensus, although often imposed, about the proper place and duties of all. Moral, political, aesthetic, and religious values, although often bent in the service of special interests, were kept in the forefront of the culture. They played a major role in shaping the lives of the people, the institutions of the society, and the intellectual life of the culture.

In a humanistic culture, whether free or controlled in its development, the humanities and their modes of thought are at the forefront of intellectual life. As the term indicates, the humanities study humanity and all that is human, but not in the external way in which modern science studies human and other phenomena. Science, as we understand the term today, seeks knowledge of the factual and causal structures of its subject matter in a way that will give us manipulatory power over it. The humanities seek to understand and to critically assess experience, life, culture, and society in terms of the categories of subjectivity, meaning, and value as well as those of existence and factuality; they seek the kind of understanding and critical judgment that is relevant to inner development, inner strength, and inner direction on the part of individuals, institutions, and societies.

The humanities are, first and foremost, the critical memory, the reflective awareness, the interpreter, the critic, and the integrator of the culture and of the life and society that generate and embody it. Without the collective memory and judgment that history provides, our collective self-consciousness would be so truncated that we would not be a civilized society and individuals would be severely limited in their possibilities. Without art, Proust insisted, we know neither ourselves nor others, and we are left with only a "terminology for practical ends which we falsely call life."[1] And without humanistic analysis, interpretation, and criticism of art and its history, we would not understand the truth that art reveals.

Ethical criticism and normative social and political thought are so much at the center of the humanities that none of the major humanistic disciplines can disengage itself from these functions. Religion, as a humanistic discipline, studies the language, symbol systems, and practices that our own and other historical communities have developed to give expression to, and to structure, their religious consciousness—their interpretations of, and attitudinal responses to, themselves as human beings in the world. The theology of a religion takes its departure from the narrative, literary, artistic, symbolic, and creedal expressions of the religion. Operating in humanistic categories, it attempts to give a coherent, systematic conceptual interpretation of the truth about humankind and the world embodied in the religious culture and to defend it against, or to reconcile it with, the truth recognized in other dimensions of the culture.

Philosophy subjects the whole culture to partial and total criticism to expose and to correct false philosophical assumptions in the makeup of the cultural mind and thereby eliminate their pernicious effects throughout the culture and the life of the people; it tries to move the culture toward reconstruction of its intellectual foundations to achieve a coherent and defensible view of humankind, culture, and world that would make for a healthy culture, a well-formed society, and human well-being.

And of course the humanities include the study of language, composition, rhetoric, grammar, art forms, logic, and critical thinking, which are of the first importance in the development and enlargement of our human powers.

The great revolution in Western civilization, indeed in world history, occurred in Europe in the early modern period. It was occasioned by a shift in priorities—a shift in emphasis from humanistic to materialistic interests and values. The emphasis on moral and spiritual values gave way to a dominant concern for control over, and exploitation of, the material conditions of our existence. This gave rise to a new social order and a new culture. Greater emphasis was placed on the production of economic wealth, and new institutions arose for more efficient production and management of this wealth.

These changes gave rise to renewed interest in the physical sciences and brought about a profound reformation in them. Scientists progressively liberated themselves from the intellectual framework that had been generated from within the earlier humanistic orientation and developed their own naturalistic conceptual system. This new conceptual frame of description and explanation was grounded in refined sensory observation under a governing concern to understand things in a way that would make manipulatory control of them possible. Language that could not be funded with meaning from within this approach was progressively eliminated from the descriptive/explanatory conceptual system of science.

In this reformation of the conceptual system in terms of which scientists identified and interpreted their subject matter and sought to render it intelligible, the basic questions that framed and guided their search underwent a radical change in meaning. "What?" "How?" and "Why?" demanded not only new answers but new kinds of answers. The answers to a "What is *X*?" question were restricted to predicative sentences (the "*X* is *F*" type). No longer were answers allowed in terms of the features or properties the thing in question *ought to have* or *ought to come to have*; nor were answers tolerated in terms of the features or properties the thing *must have*. Also a restriction was placed on allowable predicates in predicative sentences; value and modal predicates, for example, were eliminated. "Description," which literally means a written account of something, took on a new meaning; it came to mean a strictly *factual* account, free of modal and value concepts. Indeed, the concepts of *fact* and of *the factual* were radically transformed. "Fact" had meant that which was done, that which was completed, that which was no longer in the process of becoming, that which was no longer to be conceived in terms of what it was to be but solely in terms of what it already was actually. And with actuality conceived independently of normativity and value and even necessity, "fact" came to mean simply what is contingently the case, what exists but might not have been at all, or the way something is but might have been otherwise.

With these changes, the concepts of natural kinds and objective essences were in trouble. With the elimination of modal concepts from descriptive language, no longer could we take certain features or properties of a thing to be essential or *necessary* properties of it in an objective sense; no longer could we say that there were properties that a thing ought to have, and that to the extent it did not have them it was a defective specimen of its kind. No forces were recognized in nature that could do this kind of grouping. Such matters were regarded as language dependent, as relative to our grouping or classificatory principles. Concepts were no longer judged in terms of correctness or truth but in terms of their usefulness.

Also "how" and "why" questions demanded new kinds of answers. With descriptive language limited to purely factual discourse, the concept of causation was in trouble. Some have insisted that this concept is entirely bogus and should be eliminated from scientific discourse, except for heuristic purposes. In any case, the elimination of normative sentence forms and value predicates from descriptive language radically transformed the concept of causation. Only existences and factual structures were taken to be involved in causal processes. The concept of final causes was eliminated from the conceptual system. Ends in nature were no longer recognized. Change was no longer conceived as becoming, as the actualization of potentiality; the degree of actuality of a thing was no longer taken to be a measure of its perfection. The dynamics of the universe were no longer regarded as working for the realization of what ought to be. So the concepts of explanation and intelligibility were radically transformed. "How" and "why" questions had to be answered in terms of contextual and antecedent or elemental existential and factual conditions and in terms of non-normative (and some would say non-necessary) laws or generalizations. Teleological, functional, and holistic explanations were eliminated, except as a manner of speech.

The continuing success of the new science in providing an expanding knowledge-base for extending our mastery over nature deepened and spread the commitment to the new priorities and to the new intellectual approach. Western civilization, and, in time, the modern world, became defined by commitment to material progress and the modern scientific way of understanding things.

While pure scientists are motivated, for the most part, by intellectual concerns, it is no accident that the results of their labors feed technology. The framework in terms of which they define their problems and seek intelligibility has been forged by a cultural perspective defined by the quest for manipulatory power over our environment. Whereas classical cultures were generated by a dominant concern with what reality requires of human beings and how we can understand ourselves and the world in a way that would further the human enterprise conceived in these terms, modern Western culture has been generated by a dominant concern with how we can impose our will upon the world by manipulatory action and how we can understand the world in a way that would further the human enterprise defined in this manner.

Although belief in progress is not entirely a modern phenomenon, it was never a dominant idea in any civilization before the Enlightenment. Increasingly in the West since the seventeenth century, belief in general human progress has been grounded in faith in the advancement of knowledge and power through science and technology. Not only could nature be conquered and poverty and disease eliminated, but, with the banishment of ignorance and superstition by the light of scientific knowledge, peaceful living in a progressive social order would be in the reach of all.

Even humanistic ways of understanding and thinking about persons and the social world have yielded, to a large extent, to behavioral and social science. We have heard a lot of talk about mind control, technology of behavior modification, and social engineering. We have attempted to bring human beings, their behavior, and their culture and social institutions under the categories of modern scientific thought; otherwise this whole area would remain beyond the reach of our ways of progress and would be unintelligible in terms of, and a challenge to, the dominant framework of thought our civilization has developed for making sense of the world. There have been widespread movements, political and otherwise, dedicated to conquering and controlling human behavior and social change through scientific knowledge in much the same way we have tried to conquer and to control nature. This is often the approach in psychotherapy, educational psychology, and social reform-and-control movements, especially among Marxist socialists and right-wing dictators.

Progress through science and technology was the driving faith of Western civilization throughout the eighteenth and nineteenth centuries and well into the twentieth. Indeed, it is still alive in many quarters, but it seems to be eroding in spite of the amazing success of science and technology and great improvements in the material conditions of human existence and the educational and cultural benefits for nearly everyone. "Clearly," Robert Nisbet says, "the idea of progress can breathe only with the greatest difficulty, if at all, in a civilization as bedeviled as our own Western civilization at the present time by irrationalism and solipsism."[2] When the identity of the twentieth century is finally fixed by future historians, Nisbet claims, the abandonment of faith in the idea of progress will be seen as one of its chief attributes.[3]

The decline of faith in the idea of progress has many causes, not the least of which are increasing cultural contradictions and uncertainties. "To be modern," Marshall Berman says, "is to experience personal and social life as a maelstrom, to find one's world and oneself in perpetual disintegration and renewal, trouble and anguish, ambiguity and contradiction: to be part of a universe in which all that is solid melts into air."[4]

Science, by its very nature, is skeptical and questioning. It is not very comfortable with certainties. At best, it deals in probabilities and constantly puts its tentative conclusions to new tests. In its progress, it multiplies its questions and generates uncertainty about its own most solid accomplishments. Witness the dissolution of the Newtonian world-view, the displacement of Euclidean geometry in relativity theory, the Heisenberg uncertainty principle, and the questioning of traditional logic by virtue of quantum theory. No one expects even the best scientific theories of today to be viable in their present form for very long. And serious questions are being raised from within science itself about the limits and the objectivity of scientific knowledge.

On the practical side, there are increasing doubts and uncertainty about the values we seek, fear of unforeseen consequences of actions based on advanced scientific knowledge, concern over the extent to which we may be disturbing the universe, and fear of the power scientific knowledge places in human hands.

Furthermore, as we bring human beings and social and cultural phenomena under the scientific conceptual system and thus tuck them in the world as it is delineated in scientific categories, we find them and the normal human world rent from their humanistic intellectual foundations. Indeed, the humanistic conceptual system in terms of which our normative self-concept is formed and in terms of which we organize and direct our lives and our society is rendered suspect.

The results of the divorce of our descriptive/explanatory and humanistic conceptual systems under the influence of materialistic values in modern Western civilization have been devastating. Among them are insolvable philosophical perplexities about the humanistic conceptual system and persons and the social world; disenchantment of the world; a severe human identity crisis; tendencies toward moral confusion, anomie, social atomization, alienation, collapse of authority, and loss of inner strength; and, in reaction, the rise of conservatism, anti-intellectualism, irrational ideologies, authoritarianism, increased dependence on coercive power, and the like. Some cultural critics have succinctly and dramatically summarized these results with the phrases "the death of God"[5] and "the abolition of man."[6]

The basic fact of life in the twentieth century is that, at the very time we have the greatest power over nature and the most challenging opportunities in human history, we find ourselves confused about fundamental matters. We are caught up in patterns of thought and ways of understanding the world that make it difficult for us to know who or what we are, what we ought to be, and what we ought to do. While we know more than ever before about how to make things and how to control the material conditions of our existence, we are confused about our self-concept as human beings, about how to educate and to organize our feelings, aspirations, desires, judgments, and activities, and about how to empower and to govern ourselves both as individuals and as societies. The roots of these problems are deep in our culture and in our history.

Ever since humanistic concepts were eliminated from our descriptive/explanatory conceptual system and thus from our view of ourselves as human beings in the world, value language has been problematic even in its action-guiding role. Practical rationality becomes a matter of means-ends reasoning and is elevated to the level of a science in decision theory. Conventional ethics is widely regarded as the pressure of the power structure of society on the individual, and thus as something for individuals to liberate themselves from. The only authentic ethics for one becomes an expression of one's wants, preferences, and choices.

According to Robert Bellah and his collaborators in *Habits of the Heart*,[7] there are two dominant images of character in our society today: the image of the manager as one who singlemindedly uses all available resources in profit-making; the image of the therapist as one who thinks only in terms of the organization of the feelings and preferences of a subject in ways that the subject will find personally satisfying.

The mode of rationality of the manager is utilitarian efficiency in the pursuit of a given end. The mode of rationality of the therapist is "expressive" individualism. For the therapist, there are no objective principles or norms to which one is responsible; the mode of dealing with others in one's private life is communication based on complete honesty about one's feelings, wants, and expectations. Bellah and his colleagues find, from their studies of a sample of successful middle-class Americans, that typically such Americans lack a language or conceptual system in terms of which they can validate their feelings, preferences, basic choices, and life-styles.

"When science seemed to have dominated the explanatory schemas of the external world," they say, "morality and religion took refuge in human subjectivity, in feeling and emotion. . . . Nonetheless, theologians and moralists believed feeling had some cognitive content, some access to the external world. . . . But with the emergence of psychology as an academic field—and, even more important, as a form of popular discourse . . . the purely subjective grounding of expressive individualism became complete."[8]

Alexander Solzhenitsyn, in his famous Harvard speech in 1978, attempts to point out the effects of modern Western culture on persons and society.[9] He speaks of the fragility, weakness, and spiritual exhaustion of the West; of its moral poverty, destructive and irresponsible freedom, and defenselessness against criminals; of its loss of bearings, and loss of civic courage; of the decline of the arts and lack of great leaders. With regard to the effects of the culture on persons, he speaks of the weakening of human personality; the pursuit of happiness in a morally inferior sense; lack of spiritual development; paralysis of humankind's noblest impulses; lack of voluntary self-restraint; depression, passivity, and perplexity on the part of intellectual leaders; and hastiness and superficiality as the psychic diseases of the twentieth century.

Daniel Bell, in discussing the cultural contradictions of modern Western civilization, talks about the disjunctions between our subjectivistic normative culture, the techno-economic order, and the political order.[10] He thinks that by virtue of these contradictions our civilization is on a self-destructive course. His solution for our cultural and social problems is the revival of the "sacred" in which to anchor our culture and to provide some stability and intersubjectivity to our values. The resurgence of fundamentalist religion seems to be in line with this prescription, but it may not be quite what Bell had in mind.

Roberto Unger claims that the organizing and governing ideas of modern Western civilization, although they proved liberating and energizing in the early modern period, have generated a whole nest of contradictions and antinomies and that our subjectivistic individualism is destructive to both selfhood and the social order.[11] However, he thinks that two results of modern thought must be accepted: There are no intelligible essences and no objective values. His prescription for our psychological and political pathologies is the establishment of an organic society in terms of which the identity of individuals could be formed and an "objective" ethics made possible. But he does not make it very clear how we, from within our subjectivistic individualism, can establish an organic society in terms of which subjectivistic individualism could be overcome. Ethical values could not guide and motivate us in the creation of such a society; neither could such a society have any meaningful ethical justification. Rather the "objective" ethics would be grounded in the new human form generated by life in the organic society. This might overcome the disjunction of orders of which Bell writes or even the antinomies of our modern culture on which Unger focuses. But it places the social order beyond ethics and thus beyond reform under the guidance of ethical criticism. In this regard, Unger embraces the conservative position that society is the source of ethical principles but not subject to ethical criticism.

Alasdair MacIntyre, in an assessment of our culture,[12] argues that our civilization has undergone a catastrophic change that destroyed the context in terms of which classical moral discourse had its meaning. There was a time, he says, when moral judgments made objective truth-claims, and people could reach a moral consensus by rational means. This, he contends, is no longer the case. In modern liberal individualism, the individual self has been stripped of its classical identity in terms of a natural telos and social roles and relationships. The result is a self without a normative structure, and thus ethics is deprived of an objective foundation. In our time, MacIntyre says, the emotive theory of ethical discourse is correct. Ethical judgments only express the feelings, preferences, or choices of the speaker and are used to influence the feelings, preferences, and choices of others. MacIntyre has no hope of reestablishing a metaphysics of final causes and natural ends. His solution, like that of Unger, calls for us to reject modern individualism and to regain the identity of the self in terms of only social roles and relationships and in this way give normative content to selfhood. Only then can the "objectivity" of morals be restored. MacIntyre extols an ethics of virtue and condemns an ethics of rights. The ethical substance resides in the social order, not in the individual; and the moral virtues prepare the individual for his or her social roles and relationships. The classical liberal view that ethics provides the grounds for judgment on, and reform of, the social order to make it suitable for individuals is rejected, or at least undermined and deemphasized.

Here again we see the move toward conservatism as the attempted correction of our modern subjectivistic individualism. There is no probing to the deeper intellectual developments in our culture that produced our subjectivistic individualism and undermined the ethical foundations of the social order. It seems that the most basic foundations of modern Western civilization must be brought into question and critically examined.[13] This means examining the priorities that define our culture-generating stance and the fundamental conceptual system in terms of which we define what is real and seek to understand the world.

The world as it is present to us from within our modern scientific conceptual system is one dimensional. It consists of the structure of existence and factuality and the kind of causality that is possible within it. It has no value or meaning dimension. In such a world there is no teleological causality. There is no interiority: no normativity and no subjectivity. There are no rational processes. Nothing is right or wrong, correct or incorrect. The world, according to the modern scientific world-view, has none of these things, unless, of course, they can be shown to involve only the categories of existence, factuality, and naturalistic causation. In such a world, ontologically speaking, there is no categorial room for persons, social structures, or cultural entities. Insofar as these are recognized at all, they are regarded as reducible to, or explainable as, complex physical systems.

This is not simply an abstract, intellectual problem. The naturalistic world-view is embodied in deep assumptions that pervade our culture, especially the major intellectual disciplines and our educational system. The intellectual banishment of persons and social phenomena to the realm of appearance, folklore, or superstition leads to spiritual problems and the drying up of the cultural support system for both human beings and the social order. Without a hospitable and supporting intellectual vision, persons and the social world cannot flourish for long; indeed, they might perish entirely.

The conflict between humanistic and materialistic values and their influences on the culture is deeply rooted in the human condition and pervasive in all cultures. But nowhere and never before has the conflict been so accented as in modern Western civilization. This is because only in modern Western civilization have materialistic values played such a dominant role in shaping the intellectual life and the higher culture. The result has been to raise doubts about, or to put in jeopardy, the areas of the culture in terms of which we define our identity, find meaning for our existence and the lives we live, organize and govern our lives and our society, and empower ourselves from within. The contradictions, paradoxes, and antinomies generated by the conflict between these two perspectives as they contend with each other in defining our world-view and in forming the intellectual foundations of modern culture have set the agenda for modern philosophy ever since the seventeenth century.

The major schools of modern philosophy represent alternative ways in which philosophers have tried to solve these profound and deeply disturbing philosophical problems in the foundations of modern Western civilization. Descartes is considered the founder of modern philosophy because he stands out among the early philosophers who brought the deep intellectual troubles in the developing modern consciousness to the surface for reflective thought in a way that began the great modern philosophical controversies. His solution to the categorial conflicts between the humanistic and the scientific perspectives was the division of the world. He would let the humanistic perspective define the world of mental substances and the new scientific perspective define the world of physical objects. But with this dualism, no unified world-view was possible and the human involvement in both realms was totally unintelligible. Kant claimed that scientific language and theoretical knowledge were restricted to the realm of phenomenal objects and that humanistic discourse had application, with the possibility of generating belief but not theoretical knowledge, to the realm of things in themselves. Various forms of idealism have attempted to resolve the conflict by translating scientific discourse into humanistic language; while various forms of materialism and naturalism have tried to reduce the categories of humanistic thought to those of the scientific conceptual system or otherwise show that humanistic discourse has no ontological import over and above that of scientific language. And various forms of skepticism, subjectivism, constructivism, and relativism have given up on the possibility of resolving the problem in a way that would make possible an integrated culture and a unified world-view.

At this date, it may seem foolhardy for anyone to take on these big questions again. Four centuries of exploration and debate on these issues by some of the best intellects of the modern age have produced neither proof of the coherence and validity of the intellectual foundations of the culture as it has historically evolved nor agreement among philosophers on a coherent alternative that is fully responsible to all our human powers and to all sectors of the culture, to say nothing of reconstruction of the culture itself in a philosophically trouble-free way. Nevertheless, these problems are too important for us individually and for the future of our civilization, even for the future of humankind, to let go of them. We have to keep trying.

Furthermore, it is not true that the modern philosophical debates have accomplished nothing. Although a prominent school of philosophy is still committed to the validation of the philosophical assumptions of our materialistic culture and another school denies the need for validation and thus rejects the role of philosophy in cultural criticism and reconstruction, it is increasingly clear to many that there are deep troubles in the foundations of modern Western civilization and that our culture is pathologically distorted and in need of reconstruction from its foundations up. It is important to try to locate the difficulties and to explore ways of correcting them. This can be done only by proposing and developing theories about the problems and possible solutions, even if they are found to involve difficulties. Indeed, it is an important part of the task of philosophers to expose the difficulties in proposed philosophical theories. But all too often philosophers become so engaged in this part of their enterprise that they forget about the problems within the culture itself, which should be the focus of the whole philosophical enterprise. Such theories, even though they may not in the end stand up under critical examination, may deepen our understanding and enlarge our vision. No theory in any field has immunity to trouble. But some are more adequate than others. We have to keep trying for a more adequate theory.

Of course a philosopher cannot simply propose a theory, show that it is more adequate than the philosophical assumptions embedded in the culture and more adequate than other theories proposed by philosophers, and have it dislodge and replace the cultural assumptions and thereby reconstruct the culture. Even the task of convincing other philosophers of the merits of a proposed theory is far more difficult than the task of a scientist in convincing fellow scientists of the merits of a new theory. Philosophers themselves are deeply immersed in the culture and are usually already committed to some explicit philosophical theories. Both the assumptions they share with the culture and their commitment to articulated philosophical views color their way of looking at problems and possible solutions as well as their way of weighing considerations in support of a theory. So a reasoned consensus in philosophy is most difficult to achieve. It is always easier to obtain recognition for philosophical theories that, if true, would validate the dominant assumptions of the existing culture or those of some powerful institution. This is why philosophy has been, for the most part, the handmaiden of science in the modern age, just as it was the handmaiden of theology in medieval Europe. A philosophical theory that challenges the dominant assumptions of a culture has a difficult time gaining recognition. But this does not count against a philosophical theory in the same way a lack of agreement counts against a scientific theory, for often there are explanations for the lack of agreement other than lack of evidence or supporting reasons.

None of these considerations argues against the possibility of truth

and objectivity in philosophy. They only show how difficult the philosophical enterprise is. Philosophy is the highest level of the reflective
and critical consciousness of the culture. It is an important way of
bringing critical intelligence into the cultural evolutionary process. It
plays a conspicuous role only in times of cultural revolution, but it has a
continuing role in more stable periods. And of course it plays a similar
role in the various disciplines and subcultures in their development and
in the lives of individuals. We cannot let go of philosophical problems
because they are difficult or because we cannot hope to achieve a ready
consensus.

Like so many others, being a child of this culture, I have had to
wrestle with these problems deep within the modern Western mind in
trying to find some coherence in my own thought and life; I hope that
my struggle can, in some small way, contribute to the struggle of our
culture for coherence and truth in its foundations by making a contribution to other individuals in their struggle for understanding and coherence in their thought and lives. It is only through individual understanding and transformation that philosophy can affect the culture.

This work is an effort to develop a view of persons and the social
world and a world-view that will be philosophically sound and defensible and also supportive of our efforts toward human and social well-
being. Indeed, a way of conceptualizing reality that is not supportive of
the human enterprise in this manner is philosophically suspect, just as a
way of conceptualizing things in science that does not, in principle, support the technological enterprise is regarded as suspect.

CHAPTER 2

The Humanities and
Cultural Criticism

The problem of self and world in our modern culture is not one that lends itself to the methods of scientific investigation nor to a practical problem-solving approach under the guidance of scientific knowledge. It calls for the kind of understanding and critical judgment that is relevant to inner development and inner direction of individuals, institutions, and societies. It calls for refined and highly developed humanistic methods of cultural analysis and criticism that will lead to personal, cultural, and social reorientation and reorganization from within.

Unfortunately, the problem is so deep and pervasive in the culture that it puts into question the legitimacy of the very methods that must be employed in trying to solve it. In this chapter, after a brief discussion of the present plight of the humanities, we shall explore the viability of the humanities, especially philosophy, as ways of cultural criticism and reconstruction.

The Humanities

It is commonplace to say that the humanities bake no bread, that they do not have practical value, that they are cherished for their own sake or for personal enrichment of those who study and engage in them. A congressman once asked how we could justify the expenditure of the taxpayer's money to support the humanities, for, he said, they, unlike the natural and the social sciences, have no social utility value. A colleague in philosophy says that the justification for teaching the humanities, especially philosophy, is that they, like games, open up for the students new sources of pleasure. Many humanists are frightened by, and want to reject, talk about the usefulness of the humanities. They take pride, or at least pretend to, in the alleged fact that the humanities are valued only for themselves. The sciences of course have intrinsic worth, too. To understand things, to resolve perplexities, and to achieve an ordered world in our understanding of things are not only necessary conditions of sanity and of living a life; they are also inherently satisfying and worthwhile. So the humanities are not alone in having inherent worth. If they stand alone, it is in having only inherent worth.

The humanities, however, have their utility value as do the sciences, even though much of their potential in this regard is unrealized. Where the sciences have their utility value in providing knowledge that guides our efforts to gain manipulatory mastery of the conditions of our existence, the humanities have their utility value in terms of their contribution to the overall healthy development of the culture, including science, and the development, nurture, and support of persons, institutions, and the social order in which people live and have their being.

The humanities, as intimated in the first chapter, are abstract, discursive, intellectual disciplines that deal with subject matters that have not only factual structures but structures of meaning. Consider persons, institutions, and societies and their states and acts; languages, symbol systems, texts, records, myths, legends, oral and written histories; literary, artistic, religious, scientific, theological, and philosophical works; and even nature and the world itself insofar as they are taken to have an inherent structure of meaning as in some theologies. Furthermore, the humanities take their subject matter to have an inherent normative and value structure. They assume that there is a way for the subject matter to be and that it is ordered according to reasons for being one way rather than another. Accordingly they treat their subject matter as subject to evaluation and appraisal in terms of its own nature and context. They employ the categories of fact, meaning, and value in describing and explaining their subject matter as well as in their evaluation and appraisal of it. In fact, the distinction between description and explanation on one hand and evaluation and appraisal on the other cannot be sharply drawn in the humanities. The multidimensional humanistic framework of thought is grounded in the full range of human experience, including somatic and sensory experience, affective and conative experience, self-knowledge, intersubjective experience and reflection, perceptual understanding of others, expression perception, and perception of grammatical and logical structures and relationships within semantic states and acts.

The humanities, then, are ways of studying humanity—persons and their cultural and social world—from within a framework of thought grounded in the full range of human experience, for the purpose of achieving knowledge and understanding that has both inherent worth and utility value. The utility value lies in its contributions to the overall healthy development, conservation, and correction of the culture and to the development, nurture, health, and empowerment of persons, institutions, and the social order as a whole. Insofar as the basic categories of this framework of thought are given a theoretical employment in our effort to understand the wider world in a way that would render things and events intelligible and provide support for humanity and the human world, the humanities have an integrating intellectual framework, one that could come to define our intellectual life and to guide and to support the human enterprise.

But insofar as we, in our theoretical efforts to comprehend the wider world, think only in terms of rendering intelligible and gaining manipulatory control over the realities available to us through sensory experience under scientific refinement and thought grounded therein, we will employ only the factual categories of the empirical sciences. From within this naturalistic view of knowledge and the world, the humanities not only lack a unifying, integrating theoretical dimension, they have to accommodate themselves to an alien intellectual framework. Both their subject matter and their framework of thought have to be reinterpreted and explained in a way that fits them into the naturalistic perspective.

The failure of all the contorted theories philosophers have developed to give a satisfactory naturalistic interpretation of the language of the humanities indicates that something must be wrong with the enterprise. The fundamental error of naturalism, or so this work argues, lies in our modern preoccupation with the kind of human needs that can be satisfied by manipulatory action and the kind of knowledge that will increase our power to satisfy them. These preoccupations and our successes with them gave rise to the restricted naturalistic view of the semantic and knowledge-yielding powers of the human mind. But there are human needs beyond the reach of manipulatory power—humanistic needs, the needs of selfhood and community. These include the need for an identity—for a social place in a normative structure; the need for intersubjectivity—for a shared culture and for shared experiences, attitudes, thoughts, and actions; the need for self-respect and the respect of others; the need for something worthy of devotion and commitment; the need for meaningful relationships, meaningful experiences and activities, and meaningful work; the need for a meaningful and worthwhile life; the need for a well-ordered society with room and support systems for each to live a human life worthy of one's humanity and individuality; the need for a frame of interpretation and explanation that would make sense of, and provide support for, human existence, the social world, and the experiences and realities that empower and sustain individuals and societies from within.

Whether there are semantic and knowledge-yielding powers of the human mind that underwrite the epistemic authority of the dimensions of the culture that feed these humanistic needs is a most important question. When we transcend our naturalistic assumptions and predispositions, a good case can be made, as Chapter 5 will show, for the thesis that affective and conative experience, perceptual understanding of others (including expression perception), and reflective awareness, as well as sensory experience, are capable of providing us with knowledge-yielding encounters with reality. If this is so, then these powers are capable of funding the language and symbols of morality, politics, religion, and the arts and the language of the humanities with meaning, and of providing data for a larger house of knowledge than modern naturalists think possible. We must overcome the widespread (but false and perverting) assumption that the epistemic authority of the culture is grounded solely in sensory perception and the canons of scientific thought. But we must not follow the lead of some contemporary skeptics and give up on the idea of the epistemic authority of the culture and join those who would "overcome epistemology." What we need is not abandonment of our efforts toward an epistemological validation of the culture but a more adequate epistemology that will do justice to the whole spectrum of the semantic and knowledge-yielding powers of the human mind and to all sectors and dimensions of the culture.

It is up to humanists, even if the humanities are presently debilitated and in disarray, to explore the present state of the humanities and the general health of the culture. If they should conclude that in fact the humanities and the culture generally have been perverted and disordered under the prevailing epistemological and metaphysical assumptions and patterns of intellectual respectability, they have the responsibility to develop the authentic humanistic perspective and its framework of thought and to pursue vigorously the rightful role of the humanities in the criticism and development of the culture and the social order. Only when the humanities have established their own authentic identity and legitimacy will they earn the respect and support of society. Only then will they be able to play their proper critical, reconstructive, and integrative role in the overall culture; only then will they be able to help in the development of the intellectual vision, the ideals, the standards of excellence, and the wisdom necessary for an advanced civilization under modern conditions.

Some humanists fear that the utility value of the humanities will be misconceived and that emphasis on it will lead inevitably to the misuse and perversion of the humanities. There is a real danger here. The use of the humanities in a propagandistic or partisan way to gain power and control over the subjectivity of others is not only a violation of people; it is also a corruption and perversion of the humanities, for it turns them away from their proper ends and methods.

Unlike the sciences, the humanities have their practical application and utility only through education, for they pertain to the inner development and direction of persons, institutions, and societies. While we have to have specialists in the humanities to advance the disciplines and the culture in general and to serve as educators and advisers, everyone has to be a humanist; each one has to do his or her own humanistic thinking. This is why humanistic education has to be so pervasive, extensive, and continuous throughout the society.

With this preamble in mind, let us turn to the matter of how the humanities can help with our cultural problems.

The Social Character of a Culture

We need to distinguish between what Raymond Williams calls the *social character* and the *structure of feeling* of a culture[1] and what I have called the *cultural mind*.[2] The social character of a culture is its valued system of attitudes and behavior—its approved and preferred forms of life and society. A culture's social character is most clearly manifested in its gods (or conceptions of God) and heroes, its villains and outcasts, and its entire status system, both in its living history and in its art and literature. Here we are concerned with not simply the kinds of persons, institutions, and behaviors the culture in fact generates, but also the kinds that it strives to generate and takes pride in and the kinds it merely tolerates or condemns and would like to eliminate. Obvious distinctions come to mind. Is a culture aristocratic, bourgeois, or socialist? Is it individualistic and egalitarian or organismic and statist? Is it racist or sexist? What are the dominant institutions of the society? What is the occupational hierarchy according to income, prestige, and respect? Who and what are glorified in celebrations, rituals, and awards? What are the recognized forms of human and social perfection and corruption? Most of the distinctions involved in such questions are based on, and presuppose, ideals of what it is to be a human being as well as ideal forms of life and society.

The social sciences and the humanities may work together in exposing and analyzing the social character of a culture, but the social sciences, left to their own methodological resources, do not engage in critical analysis and assessment of the social character of a culture and the persons, institutions, and social order it generates. They can help only in getting at what the social character of a culture is, how it has evolved, and the factual conditions under which it changes. They leave the normative and evaluative dimension to the humanities and to religion, art, politics, concerned citizens, opinion makers, and institutional and societal leaders. The humanities, however, are the primary disciplinary resource of the culture for this function. And they may be seriously hampered to the extent they are influenced by the social and behavioral scientist's way of conceptualizing and explaining their subject matter. If humanists are to be able to perform their evaluative and critical functions, they must describe and explain their subject matter in their own categories.

The Structure of Feeling of a Culture

In assessing the social character of a culture, humanists have to deal with the culture's "structure of feeling" and its "cultural mind" as well. The structure of feeling is constituted by the lived experience of the people. Here we are concerned with what human life is like as actually lived within the personal and social forms the culture generates. Those who live within a culture have an understanding of this that is difficult for the outsider to gain. But anyone within a culture lives a particular personal life-form and may be blind to what it is to live some of the other life-forms of the society. How many corporate executives in our society know what it is like to be a fifty-year-old laborer whose factory has closed down? How many men in our society know what it is like to live the life of a woman? How many women know what it is like to live the life of a man? How many white people in the United States know what it is like to live the life of a black person in our society? How many heterosexuals know what it is like to be a homosexual? And so forth. We all tend to be foreigners to life-forms other than our own. And how many of us really know what it is to live our own life-form? How can we know without also knowing other possibilities? How much self-understanding do most of us have? How much are we capable of without understanding others?

The arts, especially the literary arts (poetry, drama, the short story, and the novel) present to us the feeling of life as lived within certain identities and forms and under certain circumstances. Great artists have to have a profound imagination together with understanding, grounded in rich lived experience, and a talent for expression that enable them to know in some expressible form the realities of lived experience under the constraints of given personal characters, social forms, and circumstances. D. H. Lawrence said that the novelist is superior to the scientist, the theologian, and the philosopher, for only the novelist gets at life whole. Without the works of artists, neither we nor the artists themselves would understand very deeply our experiences and what they reveal about our forms of self and society.

Artists push the social character of a culture against reality in lived experience in a way that makes an implicit judgment on it. They also explore and test other human possibilities. A noted literary historian and critic said that the study of literature should be a requirement in a college curriculum because literature shows the possibilities of life. That is certainly an important part of the rationale for such a requirement; but an equally important part is the implicit judgment that lived experience as presented in literary works makes on the possibilities of life they portray. All too often we concentrate on the aesthetic qualities of works of art, which have more to do with form than substance, but there is an important sense in which the form and substance are integral to each other. No work without aesthetic qualities can successfully express what it is a work of art tries to express. An aesthetically marred work fails with regard to its substance to the extent that it is marred, for the aesthetic appropriateness of the form of a work of art to what it expresses is essential to its success as an expression.

Works of art not only add to the sum of human experience the aesthetic experiences of the works of art; they also reveal to us how we and others are constituted, how we and others live our lives and experience the world, and what it would be like for human beings to constitute themselves and society and to live and experience the world in novel ways. Furthermore, works of art reveal the structures of factuality, meaning, normativity, possibility, and necessity as they are encountered and manifested in lived experience. It is by pressing forms of life and society against these structures of reality (especially the structures of possibility, necessity, and normativity) that works of art make implicit judgments on them. The works of art of a culture constitute a great expressive, revelatory, and critical resource; they provide us with our primary access to the structure of feeling of the culture in which we live as well as with some understanding of what the structure of feeling of alternative cultures would be. But without instruction in how to understand the arts and without the history, interpretation, and criticism provided by critics and humanities scholars, works of art would remain largely an untapped, opaque resource.

Structures of feeling are inherently judgmental, for lived experience comes in positive, indifferent, or negative modes; and an indifferent experience is just as much a value experience as one with a positive or a negative tone. In total cultural criticism, what we are primarily concerned with in the structure of feeling are the value tones of the deep and pervasive feelings and attitudes of those who share a somewhat common identity and form of life. Do they feel good about themselves or not? Do they live with high life morale or with anxiety and life despair? Do they live with a zest for life or is life something to be put up with and endured? How do they relate emotionally and attitudinally to others, to family, to society? How do they relate to their own mortality and that of others who matter to them? What really matters to them? What are their priorities in life? What is the character of their gods and heroes? Of their devils and villains? What do they count as the significant experiences in their lives and in the history of their people? And so forth.

From knowledge of such experiences, especially as they are expressed in the art of the culture, we gain some understanding of how the people's own lived experience judges their identity and forms of life and society. This is a judgment based on the reality encountered in lived experience over time; it is a judgment that we must take seriously in cultural criticism. It is an overall experiential judgment that can provide some measure of confirmation for the general orientation of the culture or it can indicate that something fundamental in the culture is wrong. The tone of life structured by a culture reveals whether the culture makes for human flourishing or whether it chokes or perverts human beings and thwarts human living. It provides an experiential judgment on the social character of the culture, or at least on some of the forms of life the culture and its social order generate. When the spirit of life as lived within a culturally constituted form of life reveals that something is wrong in the culture, it may not be able to show what is wrong. If not, other methods of cultural criticism are called for.

Philosophy and the Cultural Mind

Certain kinds of problems in the foundations of a culture show themselves in philosophical perplexities. These are logical difficulties that challenge the culture more deeply than ordinary logical inconsistencies that only challenge the truth of some belief or taking. These deep-rooted problems challenge the internal structure of beliefs or takings; they challenge the language or grammar of certain types of sentences, or the concepts or apparent logical form of some kind of statement or other illocutionary act. The challenge may extend to the form and meaningfulness of various kinds of symbols. Whole universes of discourse may be put in jeopardy. Indeed, our ability to mean or to know anything at all may be called into question. But limited skepticism that calls into question only an area of the culture is the most common variety.

Philosophical doubt is not doubt about an ordinary matter. It calls into question a component of the cultural mind: a belief or assumption about the meaning or logical form of a type of discourse or whole area of the culture; not just any belief or assumption about the meaning of a word or the grammar of an expression, but a belief or assumption about the semantic or knowledge-yielding powers of the human mind and correlatively a belief or assumption about the categorial structure of some subject matter or even of the whole world. (Let it suffice for now to say that by "categorial structure" of something we mean a very basic structure that is so tied up with our ways of experiencing it and talking about it that, with all things considered, we cannot consistently experience it or think about it as significantly different.)

Philosophical problems, then, call into question whether it is possible for us to mean something that we seem to mean or to know something that we think we know. Correlatively, philosophical perplexities call into question whether it is possible for something to be categorially what we take it to be or to have the categorial features we take it to have, or even whether the world has the categorial structure we take it to have. Hence, broadly speaking, philosophy breaks down into epistemology, metaphysics, and philosophy of culture, with the philosophy of culture being the study of the epistemological and metaphysical issues in different sectors of the culture (such as science, mathematics, history, morality, art, religion) and in the culture as a whole.

With the rise of professionalism in philosophy, philosophers tend to abstract philosophical problems from the cultural contexts that generated them. Indeed, in trying to solve philosophical problems in the culture, philosophers often generate further perplexities entirely of their own making. Other philosophers concentrate on these philosopher-generated problems and lose sight of the culture-based problems that were being addressed in the first place. Consider, for example, the philosophical effort that has been spent on the problems created by Descartes, Hume, and Kant. G. E. Moore once said that if he had never read philosophers, he would never have become aware of any philosophical problems. Wittgenstein at times seemed to suggest that philosophical problems were generated only by the misunderstanding of language by philosophers. The history of philosophy is often presented as though the philosophers of the past constituted a closed set who addressed problems of concern only to one another and that philosophy has been a closed discipline from the beginning. Students and our colleagues in other fields often think of philosophy as a well-developed, highly technical field, but one that has nothing to offer other disciplines and without any application in lived experience. All too many, both in and out of the profession, think of philosophy as engaged with problems that happen to interest a few intellectuals but may be safely ignored by all others.

As indicated in Chapter 1 (and earlier in *Philosophy and the Modern Mind³*), the most important problems that engage philosophers emerge out of their culture. The work of philosophers is essential for enlightened cultural development. But philosophers cannot keep their work in professional isolation and have it be effective. For their work to count for something, they must provide leadership in culturewide explorations and debates on philosophical problems in the culture.

In recent decades, philosophers have moved into the discussion of many problems that are being debated in the society: health care, mental illness, biomedical ethics, abortion, death and dying, discrimination and inequality, affirmative action, crime and punishment, technology and economic growth, and various issues of public policy. Traditionally philosophers have engaged in public controversies over freedom and the authority of the state, individualism and statism, socialism and economic freedom, authoritarianism and cultural freedom, science and religion, and so forth. The public issues that philosophers tend to be drawn into are those in which the culture is unsettled in its response, not because of ordinary conflicts of interests or incomplete factual knowledge, but because of philosophical uncertainties and conflicts deeper in the culture. In other words, they are issues in which some of the considerations that bear upon them are philosophical and there are different views or assumptions in the society about these philosophical matters.

Just as deep philosophical problems and differences in the general culture are reflected in our thought about public issues of the day, philosophical problems and differences in the foundations of a particular discipline show themselves in the way the discipline responds to particular issues in its own development. Nearly all disciplines have their schools of thought that will not be dissolved into a disciplinary consensus simply by further investigation of the subject matter, for schools of thought usually are grounded in philosophical differences in ways of defining and approaching the subject matter. Any intelligent debate between them must bring into review the frameworks of description and explanation and the methodology from within which they identify and study their subject matter. And here philosophical sophistication is needed. Professional philosophers who have an understanding of the discipline in question can be helpful in this endeavor.

What is more, the framework (or frameworks) within which specialists in a discipline approach their subject matter cannot be held for long in isolation in reflective thought. The languages of the several disciplines are specialized forms and extensions of ordinary language.

And their subject matters, along with that of common-sense experience and thought, make up, in some fundamental sense, one world. Questions inevitably arise for the thinking person about how all these frames of description and explanation of the several disciplines fit together into a coherent perspective on the world, for they often appear to be in conflict. So the battle of the schools within disciplines is magnified in the conflicts among disciplines and between specialized disciplines and common-sense experience together with the traditions of thought in morality, politics, and religion. Such conflicts, as we have already indicated, are especially acute in our modern culture between the sciences and the humanities.

While the structure of feeling of a people may implicitly judge the social character of a culture and indicate that something fundamental is wrong, philosophical conflicts in our ways of thinking point to specific problems in the foundations of the culture; they call into question the cultural mind, our operating assumptions about the constitutional principles and powers of the human mind and of the basic structure of the world. These problems in a culture define the agenda of philosophy.

Philosophical Skepticism

Unfortunately, the operating assumptions in our culture generate serious questions about the credentials of philosophy as a responsible discipline for dealing with these problems. Indeed, skepticism about philosophy, which arises from cultural assumptions about the nature of knowledge and the knowledge-yielding powers of the human mind, leads to doubts about the legitimacy and meaningfulness of the problems we are trying to address.

Wittgenstein in his later work waged a relentless attack on Cartesian types of philosophical skepticism about ordinary and scientific discourse by fostering skepticism about philosophy. The problems of philosophy were attacked as unreal. They were said not to be genuine problems in the culture, for it makes no sense to say that language in its primary uses is problematic. Philosophical problems, he contends, are the product of misunderstandings on the part of philosophers of how language functions in the different sectors of the culture. If there were no philosophers, there would be no philosophical problems. "When we do philosophy," Wittgenstein says, "we are like savages, primitive people, who hear the expressions of civilized men, put a false interpretation on them, and then draw the queerest conclusions."[4] "Philosophy," he says, "is a battle against the bewitchment of our intelligence by means of language. . . . [It] may in no way interfere with the actual use of language; it can in the end only describe."[5]

Gilbert Ryle characterizes the task of philosophers as similar to that of lawyers.[6] Their role, he says, is to help settle interdisciplinary conflicts. He thinks of typical philosophical problems as those in which different disciplines or universes of discourse appear to give conflicting answers to the same questions. He asks us to consider the apparent conflicts between the ways of thought of religion and science, ethics and psychoanalysis, and Everyman's rational appraisal of behavior and behavioristic psychology. He thinks that the apparent conflicts are not real, for, he claims, there are no common questions. It is a confusion, he says, to think of two disciplines or areas of discourse as giving alternative and contrary answers to the same questions. Each discipline, he contends, addresses its own questions; and when these questions are properly understood, they are seen to have their meaning in terms of the framework of the discipline in which they arise. The role of the philosopher, in his view, is to help settle interdisciplinary controversies by clarifying the questions of each discipline and showing their uniqueness so that the several disciplines can get on with their internal affairs, free from foreign entanglements.

Such radical pluralism takes no account of the apparent truth that there is one language for which the several universes of discourse are specialized forms and extensions and that there is one world to which the subject matters of the several disciplines belong. If this were not so, how could we gain entry into the several disciplines or move back and forth between them? How could they be taught to beginners? How could communication take place between them? How could the results in the special disciplines bear upon the problems of one another and the problems of common-sense experience and ordinary life? If there is one language in which the languages of the special disciplines meet, is there not a framework of thought that is presupposed by all disciplines and all universes of discourse, regardless of how it is interpreted and explained in the end? And must not the basic structure of this framework of thought, that which makes understanding possible across disciplines, cultures, and times, define the basic structure of a unified world?

Furthermore, when a discipline describes and explains its subject matter, does it not place that subject matter in the world? And in doing so, does it not operate with commitments about the basic structure of the world? Does a discipline not have and show categorial presuppositions about the world? Is it not in what different disciplines presuppose or show about the world, rather than in what they say explicitly about their subject matter, that they come into conflict? While they may not offer conflicting answers to common questions about their specific subject matters, do they not sometimes presuppose conflicting answers to common philosophical questions about the structure of the world?

Nelson Goodman, in *Ways of World-Making* (1978), acknowledges that a language, a universe of discourse, or a symbol system of any kind, whether verbal, pictorial, or whatever, defines a world in describing or depicting its subject matter. But he argues against the thesis that all universes of discourse presuppose or can be integrated into a common language, and he denies that a unified world-view is possible. He contends that there are as many worlds as there are conceptual or symbol systems. Furthermore, he argues that there is no conflict between conceptual systems and the worlds they generate, for there is no such thing as the real world. A world is a construction and human beings can and do construct multiple worlds.

If we accept Goodman's view of multiple languages and worlds with no common language and no shared world, how do we communicate across languages and understand diverse symbol systems? How can we move from one world to another? What are the connecting links and passageways? His answer seems to be in terms of how worlds are made and what they are made of. "The many stuffs—matter, energy, waves, phenomena—that worlds are made of," he says, "are made along with the worlds. But made from what? Not from nothing, after all, but *from other worlds*. Worldmaking as we know it always starts from worlds already on hand; the making is a remaking."[7] So worlds are connected through the worlds out of which they are made. It seems that those who occupy different worlds can understand each other only to the extent they can move into a common ancestor world and learn from there how to enter the other's world by following the way in which it was constructed from materials in the common world. Different conceptual systems and worlds are connected through conceptual history, not through their relationship to the "real" world.

Goodman acknowledges that there are constraints on us in constructing a world, although we cannot test a world-version or frame of reference by comparing it with a world undescribed, undepicted, or unperceived. Only a *right* world-version constructs a world: "A willingness to welcome all worlds builds none."[8] Goodman goes on to say, "For a categorial system, what needs to be shown is not that it is true but what it can do. Put crassly, what is called for in such cases is less like arguing than selling."[9] In proposing a categorial system, Goodman says, one is not "so much stating a belief or advancing a thesis or a doctrine as proposing a categorization or scheme of organization, calling attention to a way of setting our nets to capture what may be significant likenesses and differences."[10] Insofar as a world version is verbal and makes statements, it may be true; but "truth cannot be defined or tested by agreement with 'the world'; for not only do truths differ for different worlds but the nature of agreement between a version and a world apart from it is notoriously nebulous. Rather . . . a version is taken to be true when it offends no unyielding beliefs and none of its own precepts."[11] "But the line between beliefs and precepts is neither sharp nor stable," Goodman says. "Beliefs are framed in concepts informed by precepts."[12]

Fundamental to Goodman's position is the claim that there are conflicting true world versions. Obviously they cannot be true in the same world; so he holds that there must be many worlds.[13] And he regards them as irreducibly many; they cannot be unified into one world just as his many conceptual systems cannot be integrated into one language.

With his pragmatism and pluralism, Goodman is in the mainstream of classical American philosophy. According to John McDermott, the main theme of American culture and philosophy is that of Promethean man, creator of both himself and the world, continually remaking both, with almost unlimited possibilities.[14] For William James, this task was viewed largely from the perspective of the individual; for John Dewey, it was more a collective enterprise, with greater appreciation of the limitations imposed by traditions and institutions.

Primordial reality for James is somewhat like the chaos that God brought to form in the Genesis creation story. It is, as McDermott says, "ultimately unintelligible, fraught with chance and novelty," but "subject to the constitutive role of human life."[15] For James, the theory of the constituting presence of the human spirit led to several radical theses, which McDermott summarizes: "First, the world as we know it is inseparable from how we know it. Second, shifts in the human version of the world result in nothing less than shifts in the world itself. Third, . . . the history of human life is a history of reality, for without human life, the source of intelligence so far as we now know, the blunt existential reality of the physical world, would have no meaning whatsoever."[16] Furthermore, the human self "is on its own for its own creation within the flow of experience."[17]

McDermott thinks that James's view of the Promethean self was corrected by the emphasis on community and society in Royce, Dewey, and Mead. The self, McDermott concludes, is a social construct, but James was right in that it is "the personally idiosyncratic seeker of relations who puts a distinctive cast on the world."[18]

The picture McDermott gives us is that of a culture gone wild, cut loose from epistemic accountability to the real world. It is just such a theory of culture that Richard Rorty has made popular in many intellectual circles. He rejects the concept of world, whether one or many. He accepts discourse without the constraints of epistemic responsibility; he rejects the notion of a common framework of thought grounded in the constitutional principles of the mind and confrontations with reality. With these restraints abandoned, epistemological and metaphysical problems evaporate, and philosophy, as it has been historically conceived, has no cultural function. The only role left for the philosopher as distinct from specialists in other disciplines is that of "the informed dilettante, the polypragmatic, Socratic intermediary between various discourses" who may charm "hermetic thinkers . . . out of their self-enclosed practices."[19] In the ongoing conversation, disagreements between disciplines and universes of discourse may be compromised or transcended. But culture is simply the ongoing conversation and it develops where it will. No universe of discourse requires validation other than its survivability in the continuing conversation.

But there are startling inconsistencies in Rorty's position. While rejecting both the need for, and the possibility of, philosophical validation of other sectors of discourse, he holds that philosophical discourse, as it has been practiced for centuries and as it continues, does require validation and he wants to shut it down for lack of it. Yet he attempts to validate what amounts to a materialistic metaphysics and to discredit traditional humanistic and religious discourse with contrary presuppositions.

Much of the skepticism about philosophy, and even about knowledge of reality in other areas of the culture, has its source in the inability of philosophy in the modern age to solve the problem of self and world—the problem of the integration (or reconciliation) of the languages of the humanities and the sciences and the achievement of a unified world-view. Ever since the great cultural fracture in the early modern period, the divorce of our descriptive/explanatory language from our humanistic conceptual system, philosophers have not been able to put the culture and the world back together again. It is not surprising that there are those who call for the abandonment of the task, saying that it never was a problem anyway. If we sacrifice belief in a real world and give up the notion of epistemic restraints on the culture, then these so-called philosophical problems do vanish; they are seen as illusory products of the primitive but beguiling beliefs in reality and the possibility of knowledge.

It is true that philosophical problems are usually the result of false assumptions or beliefs about the constitutional principles and powers of the human mind and about the basic constitution of the world. And in trying to solve philosophical problems, sometimes we do have to dig deep into the structure of our belief system to locate and dislodge the culprits. But do we have to go so deep and sacrifice such basic beliefs as these: that there are constitutional principles and knowledge-yielding powers of the mind, that there is a world, and that the principles and powers of the mind and the structure of the world impose constraints on the culture we generate? Is only such a radical solution possible?

In the days when universities still insisted on "moral" regulations of student life in women's residence halls and had housemothers to live with and to chaperon the students, housemothers were often in tension and conflict with their charges as they tried to carry out their responsibilities. After such regulations were abandoned in the 1960s and housemothers lived on in the residence halls as friendly counselors to the students, one counselor who had previously had a particuarly difficult time reported: "Everything is fine now; nothing is wrong anymore." Rorty's way of solving our philosophical problems is like that. He would solve our so-called philosophical problems by giving up the belief that anything is philosophically wrong (or right) in the culture, except in philosophy as a misguided cultural discipline.

Those who are prepared to give up belief in a real world and epistemic restraints and requirements on the culture as a way of getting rid of "philosophical problems" probably thought all along that how we dealt with these problems was not humanly and culturally important; that these issues were "problems" only for a few intellectuals and that they had little, if any, bearing on the development of the culture and the life of the people. With such a view, they could accept the judgment that the work philosophers historically have done could be abandoned with little or no consequences, except for philosophers. The abandonment of philosophy would be something like the abandonment of contract bridge or chess. The players would miss it, but other activities and goods of the society would be unaffected.

On the contrary, the cultural mind of a historical community is vitally important, for it consists of the organizing and governing ideas of the culture and it shapes the development of the culture and the way it functions; and philosophical perplexities in the culture indicate trouble in the cultural mind that could affect the whole culture, the lives of the people, and the social order. Although such problems might be worked out in time by the inner dynamics of the culture and the historical forces that influence it, philosophical analysis and criticism is the only way to diagnose such problems and to bring them under the corrective influence of reflective thought. This is important for the ongoing healthy development of the culture. Furthermore, for individuals and the culture in general, not to gain a critical understanding of the cultural mind is to be blindly enslaved to it. To rest content in such cultural provincialism is to fall short of our human potential. Philosophical understanding of one's cultural mind is part of what it is to be fully human; it is an important part of the truth that makes us free.

We cannot rest content with Goodman's multiple worlds. A critical mind requires a unitary consciousness, and a unified consciousness requires a unified world-view. This is so because a critical mind is sensitive to logical conflicts within *its* semantic states and acts, especially to those it can bring under reflective review. It is not possible for a self to have conscious semantic states and acts so disconnected that one could not feel their logical connections and, therefore, could not bring them under reflective review and criticism. What would it be for the self to have such states or to perform such acts? What would make them one's own? This is what Kant meant by the claim that, in principle, one can prefix "I think that" to every sentence that expresses a belief or thought that one has. Isolated sets of semantic states and acts that define different worlds cannot belong to the same self, for they define different selves as well. Multiple worlds, in Goodman's sense, would mean multiple selves. Whatever threatens the unity of one's world or the integrity of one's culture threatens the unity and integrity of one's self. Selfhood requires an integrated culture and a unified world. This is what is behind our low level of tolerance for the unintelligible and behind the human quest for the intelligibility of all that we experience. We find ourselves under the felt imperative, grounded in our constitution as an epistemic self, to place what we experience in the world in a way that preserves the unity of the world. Whatever we have to count as real but cannot place in the world as we understand it is disturbing because it threatens our world-view and the unity of our consciousness. We preserve our sanity, the integrity of our mind, either by reconstructing our view of the world so that the recalcitrant reality can be placed in it, or by discrediting the apparent reality so that it need not be placed in the world.

Goodman agrees that without restraints on truth-claims no world-view would be generated. A world-version is taken to be true, he says, if it offends no unyielding beliefs and does not violate any of its own precepts. But he does not acknowledge that there are necessary constitutional principles of the human mind and categorial concepts and principles grounded in them that give us a priori knowledge about the basic structure of any world of which we could have knowledge and in which we could act and live our lives. Nor does he recognize that there may be unyielding beliefs based on epistemic encounters with the world. His pluralism and constructivism follow from his rejection of these two kinds of constraints on us in what he calls "world-making."

Even on Goodman's pragmatic account of how we choose the precepts that bind us in world-construction, why couldn't we choose precepts that would require an integrated culture and one world? If we did, world-versions that could not be true in one world simply could not be true at all. They would have to be revised in some manner under the constraints of truth. Then what would be the argument for one or multiple worlds? Presumably the test he would apply would be

whether the conceptual nets that defined one's world or those that defined multiple worlds would catch the largest and most *significant* set of
similarities and differences. But what would be the measure of significance?

It seems clear that Goodman is assimilating all concepts to the paradigm of empirical concepts and all theories of the world to the scientific
model. It makes sense to talk about multiple scientific theories that no
one knows how to unify; and it may be more fruitful to work with a set
of such theories than to insist on an impoverished unified theory. But
the framework within which the scientist operates in formulating and
testing theories is broader than the conceptual system internal to any of
the theories; and it is presupposed by all the theories the scientist constructs. Furthermore, there is always an intellectual thrust within us for
a unified theory. We can never be satisfied with anything less. We
count the fragmentariness of our theories as a defect and as a mark of
their provisional character; we count unity and wholeness as virtues
and as goals toward which we strive in our theorizing. We would count
a unified theory superior to a set of conflicting or unrelated theories,
provided it had comparable scope and explanatory power. We feel it
imperative to continue the search for a unified theory.

Categorial Analysis

Contrary to Goodman, the position taken here is that philosophy is
fundamentally different from empirical science or any other first-order
universe of discourse. It is not concerned with constructing a conceptual system for catching similarities and differences within the range of
experience. Rather philosophy is seen as addressing philosophical perplexities that arise in conceptual systems already in use. Its method is
categorial analysis.

Categories, as the term is understood in this work, are the most
basic concepts in human discourse. Philosophers through the ages have
attempted to identify, to analyze, and to develop theories about categorial concepts and the principles they presuppose or entail. Some have
thought of the categories as inherent in human experience, thought,
and life; other philosophers have thought of themselves as proposing a
new or reconstructed categorial system as more adequate than the one
in use. The approach of the former may be regarded as analytical and
critical, cutting through appearances to what the inherent categories of
the human mind really are; the method of the latter is often said to be
revisionary or speculative. But categorial analysis, in one form or another, has been accepted through the centuries as the business of philosophy.

The so-called revisionists, from our perspective, are only revising some accepted account of the categories, not the categorial structure of the human mind itself. The position taken here is that categorial analysis is analytical and critical. It attempts to expose and to achieve a clear understanding of the categories inherent in human experience, thought, and action. No empiricist or constructivist theory of concept formation can account for our categorial concepts, for these concepts provide the framework for, and are presupposed by, all empirical inquiry and theory construction. Consider Hume's *Treatise*. Certain ideas command his special attention, for they are rendered problematic, if not bogus, by his empiricist theory of ideas. The list includes space, time, existence, meaning, external world, material substance, self, mental substance, cause and effect, good and evil, truth and falsity, knowledge, probability, and the like.

In knowing and in seeking to render intelligible what we know, we are under the constraint of some precepts that are not subject to choice but that make choice and other human acts possible. Such precepts are "constitutional" principles of the mind. In knowing and seeking to render intelligible what we know, we have to operate with some conceptual delineations for which we have no alternatives, conceptual delineations that make knowledge and action possible. We call such conceptual delineations "categorial," for they indicate basic forms and structures we presuppose in making other conceptual distinctions.

Categorial concepts are a priori. This does not mean, however, that categorial terms are clearly defined and fixed throughout human history. They are a priori in that they are grounded in the constitutional principles and powers, and thus in the basic normative structure, of the human mind. A reflective being with the power to take something to be at a certain place, to be of a certain kind, to be in a certain state or condition, and to be subject to or to undergo change also has the power to make such categorial discriminations as existence, space, time, individual, property, fact, and causation. A reflective being who has the power to be interested in, or afraid of, something and has the power to act in pursuit, or in avoidance, of it also has the power to make such categorial delineations as value, freedom, and action. Whoever is capable of inquiry and self-criticism is capable of such categorial delineations as self, subjectivity, meaning, reasons, validity, objectivity, truth, knowledge, action, right, wrong, and the like. In short, the ability to make categorial discriminations is inherent in the kind of activities that make human knowledge and action possible. There could be neither human knowledge of, nor human action in, a world that was not subject to these categorial discriminations. And a "world" without these would not be a world in any meaningful sense.

Of course being able to make categorial discriminations does not require the ability to think and to talk about them; indeed, it does not even require categorial terms, not at the most elementary level anyway. The acquisition of categorial terms and the development of their meaning come later, both in human history and in the life of the individual. But even if one has well-developed categorial terms and the power to talk about categorial delineations, one may not have a clear understanding of what is involved. Achieving such an understanding is the most important task of philosophy.

Furthermore, there are some unyielding beliefs that are grounded in these constitutional principles of the mind and the categorial delineations they require. One unyielding belief we have already considered is that there is one world and that everything we count as real must fit into it. This is an a priori belief grounded in the necessary precepts (the constitutional principles) of a knowing human agent, or, what amounts to the same thing, in the normative structure of the human mind that makes knowledge and action possible. The reflective criticism that makes human knowledge and action possible requires the unity of the self and the unity of the self requires that what one knows and acts on be located in a unified world. Put simply, if where I am now has no determinate relationship to places I have been before, then it was not *I* who was in the other places; if the world I now know has no structure in common with the world I once knew, then it was not *I* who knew the other world. I can know who I am only by connecting what I now know with what I have known before. A self cannot know and act in radically different worlds. And selves that had knowledge of, and lived in, radically different worlds could not have an intersubjective relationship; they could not interact and communicate. Indeed, we cannot even make sense of there being selves knowing and acting in radically different worlds, for if such worlds contained knowing and acting selves, they would have in common all that makes selfhood, knowledge, and action possible.

We know categorial truths to be necessarily so, for we cannot make sense of their denials. They are grounded in the constitutional principles of the human mind, and any effort to deny them would run afoul of the presuppositions of human knowledge and action, including the act of denial itself. Philosophical dialectic, all the way from Socrates to Henry Johnstone[20] and Alan Gewirth,[21] has been an *ad hominem* form of argument that appeals to what everyone must accept on pain of inconsistency by virtue of what he or she is committed to as a thinking, knowing agent. Transcendental arguments in philosophy are similar to dialectical arguments; they appeal to what one must acknowledge to be the case if one is to consider knowledge in general or some special kind of knowledge possible. It is what one is committed to in the constitutional principles of the mind that makes possible a priori categorial knowledge of the world.

Unlike simple logical inconsistency that calls into question only the veridicality of some experience or the truth of some belief, philosophical problems, as previously observed, consist of logical difficulties in our ways of experiencing and thinking that put in jeopardy the assumed semantic and knowledge-yielding powers of some mode of experience, the apparent form or meaning of some mode of discourse or symbolism, the taken-for-granted categorial nature of some subject matter or even a whole world-view. Critical examination of problems of this kind involve or lead to (1) an assessment of the semantic and epistemic powers of human beings, (2) an analysis of the form and meaning of the language and symbolism of the several sectors of the culture (science, mathematics, religion, art, normative discourse, philosophy, etc.), and (3) reasoned conclusions about the categorial structure of various subject matters and the world itself.

These three dimensions of philosophy (epistemology, philosophy of culture, and metaphysics) are not separate areas of study that can be carried out independently. There is an epistemological, a cultural, and a metaphysical dimension to every philosophical problem. Although we may focus attention on one dimension of a problem, we cannot do full justice to it without taking into account the other two dimensions as well. Epistemological views must be tested not only by an analysis of our epistemic team of concepts and what it makes sense to say about our several modes of experience and thought, but also by an exploration of the power of the views in question to account for the meaning and knowledge developed in the culture. Philosophy of culture must be worked out dialectically with epistemological and metaphysical views and assumptions. And metaphysical views have to be developed and tested by an analysis of the form and meaning of the language and symbolism of the culture in light of defensible epistemological views and assumptions. The ideal toward which philosophy strives, and philosophy's ultimate test, is the formulation of a comprehensive categorial system in terms of which all areas of the culture can be interpreted and understood without leaving or generating any insolvable philosophical perplexities, and on behalf of which valid dialectical arguments can be addressed to everyone by virtue of commitments inherent in the constitutional principles and powers of the human mind.

A fundamental point where this view is at odds with Goodman and other constructivists is on the nature of the basic precepts involved in the human enterprise. It holds that they are not a matter of choice but constitute the inherent normative structure of the human mind and are presupposed by all human activities, including experience, thought, and choice. Goodman's voluntaristic theory of knowledge is a consequence of his voluntaristic theory of value language. Value subjectivism, if thought through, leads to a total subjectivism; for if the ethics of thought is subjective, all knowledge-claims must be subjective.

Also contrary to Goodman and other anti-foundationalists, the position taken here is that confrontations with reality impose restraints and requirements on knowledge-claims, even on our empirical conceptual system as well as on empirical beliefs and judgments. It is true that we cannot compare our experience of objects and our descriptions of them with unconceptualized objects. Criticism of the notion of the given has been well taken. Nevertheless, there are stubborn non-categorial conceptual delineations in experience that are not subject to elimination or serious modification by theory construction. Both I and my dog experience some of the same identifiable, movable objects in our environment; otherwise we could not play frisbee together. The dog's visual discrimination of objects is hardly theory-laden in any significant sense. Neither are my visual discriminations of objects that I share with her. The fact that human beings can interact in a coordinated way with languageless, nonrational animals and with other human beings of whatever culture indicates that we share with them common ways of experientially delineating objects and that at a basic level we share with them a somewhat common semantic environment. This indicates that we have conceptual delineations that are relatively culture-free and that our theories must accommodate. These experiential discriminations must be a function of how things are, even if this must include how we are biologically and psychologically constituted in the order of being. If our biological and psychological constitutions are constant, the variations that occur at this level in the discriminated objects of experience must be attributed to what we experience. And there are beliefs and takings involving these discriminations that are imposed upon us; reality will not let us reject them without forcing us to suffer severe penalties. An important mark of the real is that it objects; it imposes a strict discipline on our cultural ways. There are constraints on our culture both at the level of concepts and categories and at the level of beliefs and precepts. These restraints emanate from both the constitutional principles of the human mind and from the nature of things as manifested in our experiential encounters with reality.

Anti-foundationalists, unhappy with past theories of the foundations of culture, give up the search for an adequate theory and proclaim that there are no foundations. In this respect, they are in the company of those who, unhappy with past epistemological theories, want to overcome epistemology; those who, unhappy with past metaphysical theories, reject metaphysics as based on a set of pseudoquestions; those who, unhappy with past ethical theories, reject moral philosophy as based on a mistake; and those who, unhappy with all past philosophy, reject philosophy itself as based on unreal problems. It is too obvious to say that all such rejections are based on a philosophical theory about what is a real problem and what is not.

The culture must be held accountable to both the constitutional principles of the human mind and to reality as manifested in our knowledge-yielding experiences. Cut loose from these restraints and requirements, the culture grows wild; guidance by false beliefs about what these constraints require or allow systematically distorts the culture and undermines its ordinary self-corrective processes. The search for the foundations of the culture is a difficult but vitally important enterprise. It is essential for the kind of cultural criticism that can lead to the diagnosis and correction of a deranged cultural mind and make for the integration and healthy development of the culture.

Categorial Analysis Illustrated

We have been reflecting on philosophical problems and categorial analysis in the abstract. It may be helpful to consider a little history of philosophical thought on a particular problem.

A philosophical problem, as previously indicated, is a perplexity generated by misleading or conflicting ways of looking at or thinking about something that challenges some of our categorial beliefs or assumptions. For example, suppose we think of value predicates in the way in which we think of ordinary physical-object predicates. We are then likely to try to locate what they mean in the way in which we locate what physical-object predicates connote. If so, we are likely to place values in the spectrum of primary and secondary qualities. Classical utilitarians tended to do this. Arguing in a similar way to some modern philosophers who said that the colors of objects consisted of the primary qualities in the objects by virtue of which they gave rise to color sensations, classical utilitarians claimed that the goodness of objects consisted of their primary qualities and relations that gave rise to sensations of pleasure. But then it was noticed that pleasure is as relative to the condition of the subject as colors are to the light in the physical medium. So we get either a tertiary quality or an interest theory of value. The tertiary quality theory held that values were even more subjective than colors and other so-called secondary qualities. Interest theories held that for something to have value was for it to be the object of an interest; that for it to be good was for it to be the object of a positive interest and for it to be bad was for it to be the object of a negative interest.[22] On any of these accounts, scientists were fully justified in eliminating value concepts from their descriptive/explanatory language.

G. E. Moore noticed that predicative value sentences were peculiar in that they did not ascribe properties in a way that described their objects in any ordinary way, but he did not call into question that value predicates semantically locate properties or that predicative value sentences make truth-claims.[23] He posited non-natural properties for value predicates to locate—properties that are not constitutive of the objects that possess them. However, he gave no account of how we could fund value predicates with meaning—how we could establish semantic ties between value predicates and these peculiar properties.

In light of the logical positivists' empirical verifiability theory of meaningful discourse, value predicates were taken to have only emotive meaning, not semantic or cognitive meaning. This was an alternative way of accounting for the meaningfulness of value language. Even G. E. Moore said at one time that this may have been what he was getting at.[24] But this account involved no non-natural (non-empirical) properties, only non-semantic meaning of words and sentences—their capacity, by virtue of their associations or the history of their use, to show or to arouse feelings and attitudes. From this development emerged the so-called use theory of meaning. "Ask not for the meaning but for the use of a word or sentence" became something of a motto for the Wittgensteinian school of philosophy.

With the development of modern logic, increased attention was given to syntax. In truth-functional logic, attention was focused on the form of basic statements. They were all taken to be of the "*Fx*" or "*F(x,y)*" form with an appropriate quantifier. Everett W. Hall took seriously Moore's insight that predicative value sentences were peculiar, but he did not accept the idea of non-natural properties.[25] He concluded that to say something was good was to say that it had the properties it ought to have. So he took the "ought" sentence to be the basic form of value discourse. Just as Wittgenstein, in the *Tractatus*, held that "*Fx*" or "*F(x,y)*" showed the form of facts (the exemplification of a property by a particular or the exemplification of a relation by a set of particulars), Hall held that "*X* ought to be *F*" or "*X* ought to be *F* to *Y*" showed, in a parallel way, the form of values. In other words, values were not non-natural properties but non-natural "facts," or at least they were parallel with facts, not properties. He preferred to say that values were not facts at all, for he conceived of facts in terms of the exemplification of properties by individuals and of relations by sets of individuals. "Ought," like the predicative "is," was taken to show a way in which properties and relations can be "in" individuals, and thus indicated a way in which things can be constituted.

In several critical discussions of Hall's position, I contended that "X ought to be F" cannot be the basic form of value sentences for two reasons.[26] First, the sentence "There ought to be an x that would be F" is just as basic as "X ought to be F." In other words, there is an "ought" that is parallel with the existential "is," just as there is the "ought" that is parallel with the predicative "is." Second, "X ought to be F" is not complete in the way in which "X is F" is complete; and "There ought to be an x that would be F" is not as complete as "There is an x that is F." "Why?" asked of such claims asks for something quite different from what it asks for with regard to "X is F" and its kind. It asks for what it takes to complete the sentence in a way that one could know its truth-conditions. In other words, it asks for the completion of the sentence. A sentence with the form "X is F" can be a complete sentence; whereas a sentence with the form "X ought to be F" is never complete as it stands.

Drawing on the way C. I. Lewis[27] and others had interpreted contrary-to-fact conditionals, I maintained that the basic value sentence has the form "If X is F, then Y ought to be G" or "If X is F, then there ought to be a y that would be G," where the "ought" in each case goes with the "if/then" connective rather than with the consequent. On this view, the central issue in value theory becomes how to interpret the "If . . . , then . . . ought . . ." in such sentences. It may be understood as the conditional of what I called a natural practical argument, in which the conditional clause contains the factual premises and the "ought" clause contains what is enjoined in the imperative conclusion.[28] Good-reasons ethicists hold that the facts asserted by the premises in an acceptable argument of this kind constitute *reasons* for the imperative conclusion. Therefore, according to these philosophers, the sentence "X ought to be F" simply says that there are reasons for X to be F without giving the reasons; and the question "Why?" when applied to this sentence asks what the reasons are for X to be F.

However, this does not tell us what turns facts into reasons. What is it for the facts asserted by the premises to be reasons for the imperative conclusion? Emotivists say it is simply that comprehension of the facts asserted by the premises will move or incline most people to accept the imperative conclusion or to favor that which it prescribes. Stephen Toulmin appeals to ethical rules of inference comparable with logical rules of inference to license the drawing of the imperative conclusion from the factual premises.[29] Kurt Baier talks about underlying consideration-making beliefs that provide the connection between premises

and conclusion.[30] Alan Gewirth claims that underlying all ethical reasoning is an analytic normative truth.[31] Others talk about desires, preferences, commitments, choices, or social conventions that function as
suppressed imperative premises so that the validity of such practical
arguments turn out to be based in a logical relation after all.[32]

In both *Ethical Naturalism and the Modern World-View* and *Philosophy
and the Modern Mind*,[33] I argued that not all good practical arguments
are logically valid; that the conditional of some such arguments, somewhat like the contrary-to-fact conditional, indicates a real connection
that has to be known through experience. Basic "If . . . , then . . . ought
. . ." sentences, accordingly, locate normative requiredness as part of
the structure of the real world. This requiredness is unique and categorial in a way parallel with existence, exemplification, and causation.
"Ought" talk is of and about such requirements. To say of something
that it is good is to say that it is more or less the way it ought to be; to
say that it is bad is to say that it is not the way it ought to be. If there is
nothing that something ought to be, then whatever it is or whatever
condition it is in, it is neither good nor bad. Normativity is what is basic
in the value realm. Hume noticed that the basic contrast between value
and fact was the contrast between "ought" and "is," not the contrast
between "good" and "red," "heavy," or any other natural property.

The Importance of Epistemology

So in philosophy we have to get the grammar and the logic of our
expressions right in order to get our categories right. But this is not
enough; we have to get the semantics of our language right as well. In
fact, we cannot get the grammar and the logic right without getting the
semantics right and vice versa. And we cannot get our semantics right
without getting our epistemology right. In fact, in some instances we
cannot get the logical form of our expressions right without determining whether they mean what they seem to mean; and we cannot determine whether it is possible for them to mean what they seem to mean
without getting our epistemology right. This is so because our assumptions or theories about the semantic and knowledge-yielding powers of
the human mind determine for us how language can be funded with
meaning and thus what our options are in the analysis of both the form
and the meaning of words and sentences.

Without a correct epistemology of sensory perception, for example,
we cannot get the semantics of physical-object language right. It is now
rather widely accepted that phenomenalistic analyses of the meaning of
physical-object language was based on a mistaken epistemology of sensory perception. In the modern age most of the problems in the philos-

ophy of the humanities and the philosophy of the a priori disciplines stem from empiricist epistemological assumptions or theories that render suspect the apparent meaning and truth claims in these universes of discourse. This is especially true in value theory and ethics. Opposition to first-order modal logic is largely epistemologically motivated. Extensional logic seems to be dictated by empiricism.

In trying to get our epistemology straight, we have to explore the semantic and knowledge-yielding powers of the human mind. For instance, does sensory experience have a semantic dimension through which physical objects are *present to us* so that we can establish semantic ties between language on one hand and items and features of an external physical world on the other and verify or falsify truth claims about physical objects? Or are only subjective, private appearances (phenomenal objects) *present to us* in sensory experience so that it is not possible for us to have semantic and epistemic outreach to alleged external physical objects? It is widely recognized that value language (including predicative value sentences, imperative sentences, and "ought" sentences) is tied in with our affective and conative experiences (pro and con feelings, attitudes, and desires of all kinds) just as physical-object language is tied in with sensory experiences. How we understand the categorial nature of this domain of experience determines for us how we can interpret the meaning of value language. Do affective and conative experiences have a semantic dimension and an empistemic power by virtue of which value language has a semantic tie to structures in the world? Or is the categorial nature of value experience such that we have to understand the relationship of value language to it and to the world in some other way? In other words, do value experiences provide us with epistemic encounters with reality? And if so, do we encounter a dimension of reality through value experience that is not available to us through other modes of knowledge-yielding experience? How we answer these questions determines for us how we can philosophically interpret the semantics of value language and the normative dimension of the culture.

In the epistemological analysis of sensory experience, value experience, or any other mode of experience, we have to get at the categorial nature of the experience in question. How do we do this? It is not a matter for empirical psychology, which can tell us about only the contingent features and structures of its subject matter. We explore the categorial nature of a mode of experience, or any other subject matter, by clarifying the logical grammar of the language we use to report and to describe it and by exploring what it is meaningful to say and what it is not meaningful to say about it. For example, sensory experiences have objects; they are *of* things; they have to be identified, individuated, and described in terms of their objects. These objects are, in a peculiar sense, *present in* the experiences; they are *semantic* contents of the experiences, as distinct from existential elements of them, but they are nonetheless constitutive of the experiences. It makes sense to talk about *expressing* one's sensory experiences as distinct from describing them; that is, it makes sense to talk about putting what was *in* the experience *in* language or *in* a painting. It makes sense to talk about a sensory experience as illusory or veridical and as consistent or inconsistent with other experiences or beliefs. It makes sense to talk about a sensory experience as the ground for believing or disbelieving a truth-claim. Considerations of these kinds bear upon our question about the categorial nature of the mode of experience. And the conclusions we come to about the categorial nature of a mode of experience determine how language can be grounded in (or related to) it and whether (and how and of what) it can be a source of knowledge.

Epistemological analysis of all modes of experience and reflection is vital for our philosophical analysis of both the syntax and semantics of the various universes of discourse in the culture. If we operate with false assumptions about the semantic and knowledge-yielding powers of the human mind, we will inevitably misconstrue the syntax and semantics of some areas of discourse and form false beliefs about the categorial nature of their subject matter. Thus errors in epistemology generate errors in philosophy of culture and in metaphysics. Indeed, errors in any area of philosophy generate errors in other areas, for philosophy is systematic.

How Metaphysics Is Possible

There are, as previously remarked, restraints and requirements on the culture both from the constitutional principles of the human mind and from epistemic encounters with reality. Philosophical criticism of the culture has a special responsibility to the constitutional restraints of the human mind. In this regard, philosophers may be thought of as constitutional lawyers for the culture before the jury of the people. Scientists, moralists, political theorists, artists, historians, religious teachers, and all others bear responsibility for the restraints and requirements of reality on the development of the culture through epistemic encounters.

If philosophy is cultural criticism in terms of the constitutional principles of the human mind, in what sense is metaphysics (philosophical knowledge of the world) possible? If categorial concepts such as *physical object, property, fact, normativity, causation,* and the like are grounded in the constitutional principles and powers of the human mind, in what sense, if any, do they apply to that which our experience and thought are of or about? It seems clear that these concepts apply necessarily to the world as it is present to us in experience and thought. This is similar to the way we can know things about the formal structure of the sentences formed in a language through our knowledge of the grammatical rules of the language or the way we can know something about the formal structure of a government and its acts from knowledge of its constitutional laws. On this basis we are entitled to at least an "internal realism" about the categorial structure of the world. But is categorial knowledge of the world of or about the subject matter of experience and thought *in its independent existence*? Or is such knowledge of or about the objects of experience and thought only *in their presence to the human mind*?

Contrary to what Kant says, there are good reasons for a strong realistic interpretation of the categories, even though the categories are grounded in the constitutional principles and powers of the human mind rather than in empirically discovered delineations and structures of the passing panorama. (1) In discovering what the constitutional principles and the semantic and knowledge-yielding powers of the human mind are, we have to determine (or at least have faith that we can) what the categorial structure of our several modes of experience and thought is in their existence and not merely what it is in our knowledge of or thought about them; otherwise the whole epistemological effort would be futile. And there are good reasons against epistemological nihilism, the arguments of some contemporary philosophers notwithstanding. (2) Unless the categorial structure of the objects of experience and thought pertains to them in their independent existence and not merely in their semantic presence to us, action in which we, in our existence, alter things in their existence under the guidance of knowledge and thought would be unintelligible. Internal realism with respect to metaphysical categories, along with rejection of a stronger realism, is plausible only from within a spectator view of knowledge. (3) From within the perspective of a strong categorial realism that includes value realism, it is reasonable to believe that the human mind has a functional structure (that is, the human mind exists and has the normative structure it has in order to make it possible for human beings to know the items, features, and structures of the world and to relate to, and to act on, them under the guidance of knowledge and critical judgment) and that, when one's mind functions well according to its own inherent constitutional principles, one does know items, features, and structures of the world, at least in part, as they are in their independent existence. In other words, the strong realist theory of the categories renders intel-

ligible some important matters, whereas internal realism or the subjectivist theory generates philosophical perplexities and absurdities.

Even with a strong realistic theory of the categories, there is a problem about whether the a priori character of categorial truths reflects, or
indicates, a necessity in the world. The certainty of categorial truths (we
argue for a categorial truth claim by trying to show that it must be so;
we argue against such a claim by trying to show that it could not be
true) lies in the fact that they cannot be denied without doing violence
to our basic framework of thought and thus to the constitutional principles of the human mind. Any framework of thought that is not
grounded in, and required by, the constitutional principles of the human mind is not basic and may be consistently denied. But every denial
of components of the basic framework of thought is inconsistent with
its own presuppositions. Therefore categorial truths hold for all possible worlds. But since a *possible* world is one that is consistently thinkable, this does not help us with the problem about whether the epistemic necessity of categorial truths translates into a metaphysical
necessity in the structure of the world in the world's independent existence. If categorial realism is correct, we may assume that if the basic
structure of the world had been different, the constitutional principles
of the human mind would have been different to make knowledge and
action possible. But where can we stand either to affirm or to deny that
such an alternative world and such an alternative constitution of the
human mind are real possibilities? All we are warranted in saying is
that our categorial claims, when we get them right, are true of reality in
its independent existence and would be true of any possible world; but
we cannot say that the world *necessarily* (in a non-epistemic sense) has
this structure, even though we cannot conceive of a positive alternative.
This is to acknowledge that we are categoriocentric beings and that any
beings with semantic and epistemic powers would be likewise. There is
no reason, however, to regard this as a predicament. It is enough to be
able to know that the categorial claims we cannot consistently deny are
not only necessarily true of the world in its presence to us but true of
the world in itself.

This is not to deny, however, that there may be dimensions or structures of the world in itself that are totally inaccessible to our semantic
and epistemic powers. We could never rule out that possibility. The
extent to which the realities we do know defy being rendered intelligible within the categories of the human mind suggests that we do not
have access to the whole picture. There seem to be inherent limitations
on what we can know and understand. There are transcendental mysteries, intimations of intellectual problems that transcend the powers of

the human mind, which we formulate in ill-formed questions that perplex us but for which the basic framework of human thought makes possible no responsible answers.

Conclusion

In our effort to formulate the unyielding beliefs grounded in the constitutional principles of the human mind about the categorial structure of the world, it will not do for us to develop our epistemological and metaphysical views with our focus on modern science and then allow these conclusions to shape our philosophical understanding of the humanities. We must take the humanities and their common-sense counterpart seriously. In our humanistic talk about persons and cultural and social phenomena, we are concerned with the common language of all human activities and with the primary realities we all know. This work contends that the humanistic conceptual system, properly understood, is both epistemologically and metaphysically valid. Furthermore, it argues that our overall intellectual framework that defines the world and makes sense of our experiences and the realities we know, including ourselves and our cultural and social environment, must incorporate our humanistic conceptual system rather than reduce it to another system or explain it away in an effort to sustain the scientifically determined intellectual vision of the world. The sciences must be understood philosophically in a way that accommodates the humanistic perspective, for the humanistic perspective is the most basic and inclusive that we have. Everyone can be shown dialectically to be committed to it and necessarily so. Both the philosopher and the scientist must acknowledge, on pain of inconsistency, the validity of the humanistic perspective, for philosophical and scientific thought are activities from within (and presuppose) the humanistic perspective. So we must have a humanistic view of the culture and of the world, one that accommodates science, rather than a naturalistic view of the world based on the scientific conceptual system that tries, however heroically, to make sense of the humanities and their conceptual system. Only a humanistic view can do full justice to the semantic and knowledge-yielding powers of the human mind, avoid insolvable philosophical perplexities in the interpretation of the culture, and provide an integrated culture and an intellectual vision of humanity and the world that will empower and sustain persons and the social order.

The task of these introductory chapters has been to orient us toward the problems we shall address and in the approach we shall take. This should be helpful in understanding and coming to terms with what is to follow. But it is also true that what has been said here needs what is to follow in order to be fully intelligible. The whole has to be understood in order to understand the parts and vice versa.

In the following chapters, we shall consider the basic humanistic categories, a humanistic theory of knowledge, a humanistic view of persons and the social world, and the significance of humanity and the humanities for our world-view and beliefs about ultimate reality.

CHAPTER 3

Meaning and Subjectivity

Persons have an environment and they interact with it. This is an innocent enough statement. It would be true of anything we could mention. Yet there are profound problems about persons and their environment, both with regard to what their environment is and how they are related to it. We know of no other creatures with a similar environment and with a similar involvement with their world. There are, of course, other beings who share part of the picture, but not the part that is most important to us as human beings.

For a beginning, let us say that persons have both an existential and a semantic environment. At the lowest level, people are bodily in the world and share an existential environment with everything in their space-time frame. At the present time, for example, I share the same existential environment with my computer, the chair in which I am sitting, the dog lying at my feet, and the other things around me. There is a whole array of things that are existentially present with me in the room. Up to a point, I interact with the other physical occupants of my space and time in much the same way as they do with one another. But my dog and I share an environment that is excluded from the mere things around us, for some of these things are *present to* us as well as existentially *present with* us. Here we are introduced to what may be called our "semantic" environment—that which is present to us in some mode of experience, memory, imagination, or thought; or, to put it another way, that which is the intentional object or the semantic content of some mental state or act.

Any being with a semantic environment has an "interior" or subjective domain. In fact, these are simply alternative ways of describing the same reality. My dog, of course, shares only a small portion of my se-

49

mantic environment. Hers is restricted, I assume, to what is available to her through somatic sensations, sensory perceptions, simple wants and emotions, and rudimentary rememberings and imaginings (rerun and feigned perceptions). A human being's semantic environment, however, may encompass the whole world and more, including the past, the distant present, the future, the possible, even the impossible, what might have been, what ought to be, what ought to have been—whatever one can experience, remember, expect, imagine, symbolize, or think or feel in any way. Our human interactions with our existential environment are in terms of its semantic presence to us, not just its existential presence with us.

Our human actions in these interactions have their own semantic (subjective) dimension—the intentions that structure them and in terms of which they are describable, plus the whole web of beliefs, attitudes, expectations, and other plans of which the intentions are a part. Furthermore, the semantic dimension enriches the existential realm as well, for semantic states and acts and their logical structures and relationships, along with persons, social structures, and cultural objects of all kinds, are all part of the existential environment. This, however, is a claim that needs defense in our present intellectual climate. Attention will be given to it later.

Although my dog has limited semantic powers, she can *take in* much of what is going on around her; in fact, in many ways she can do it better than I can. She is aware of another dog walking through the yard that I would never discern; she hears my wife drive up before I know of her arrival. But if we mean by "consciousness" reflexive awareness (self-aware awareness), there is little reason to think that my dog is capable of much consciousness. There are, however, indications of some. Pain is, as Chapter 5 will argue, reflexive awareness of a bad condition in one's body. And my dog certainly seems to be capable of pain. Furthermore, she seems capable of anticipating that something she expects to happen will hurt. She must have a rudimentary self-image, for she has a sense of territory, a feeling of belonging, and she shows jealousy and feelings of shame. But there is not, or so it seems, a sufficient level of consciousness (reflexive awareness) to make possible self-criticism. The feeling of shame that she shows sometimes is perhaps only an awareness (or at most, a reflexive awareness) of my critical attitude toward her, not a rudimentary self-criticism. There would have to be a more highly organized consciousness for that than the dog appears to have.

Persons have semantic powers of a higher level and of a different order. They have powers for semantically appropriating their existential environment in much of its complexity, including its categorial dimensions, contingent aspects, interconnections, and dependencies; for semantically entertaining possibilities and even impossibilities; for semantically grasping needs and normative requirements and for forming intentions and plans; for acting and interacting in their existential environment to reconstruct it and to control its future; for creating imaginary worlds; and for critical assessment and development of oneself and others, one's culture, and one's social order. Semantic powers of these proportions require highly developed and skillful use of semantic tools (language and symbol systems), the accumulative culture of a historical community, a complex social system, critical and creative powers, a self unified under some normative self-concept, and a world unified under a frame of description and explanation.

If one born of human parents should biologically mature without a human sociocultural environment from the time of birth (a large assumption, of course), he or she could not function as a person; nor would a group of such beings fare much better, not for many generations anyway. If one should survive in such an impoverished environment, one would have rudimentary somatic sensations, sensory perceptions, desires, emotions, intentions, memory, and imagination, and one would be able to act in a limited way. But all these abilities would be more like their counterparts in a dog or a chimpanzee than their counterparts in normal, mature human beings as we know them, for these abilities would be unaffected by the higher powers made possible by language and symbol systems and would not be informed by the accumulative learning made possible by intersubjectivity in a historical community. In fact, such beings might be less capable semantically than other higher animals, for these human powers, which are so susceptible to cultural development, may be less determined genetically than their counterparts in other animals. Certainly the perceptual and behavioral powers of other animals mature more rapidly, with less dependence on teaching and learning. We don't know much about the maturation of basic human powers outside of a social and cultural environment, but we have reason to think that under such conditions even our most elementary experiences would be greatly impoverished.

Yet at some point in the evolutionary process, our ancestors had only culturally undeveloped semantic powers, much like those of other higher animals; and with these powers, perhaps only slightly more advanced than those of their near-kin, they, as a "community," developed semantic tools (language and symbol systems) and thereby greatly extended their semantic powers, their subjectivity and their intersubjectivity, their actions and their interactions, their selfhood and their community, and their world. This was a tremendous leap and a great transformation. There had to be physiological developments that made the cultural and social evolution possible, but once cultural and social factors appeared, even in rudimentary form, they, no doubt, became important factors in biological evolution itself. The important point, for our purposes, is that our ancestors somehow developed semantic tools and thereby generated new and extended semantic and critical powers, and thus transformed themselves from animals who were largely driven by genetically based instincts, biological desires, and environmentally conditioned responses into human beings with all that that entails.

A Realistic Theory of Meaning and Subjectivity

This story of human development is based on a semantic theory of the mental. But first a word about the semantic. We ordinarily think of the semantic as the meaning dimension of language. Semantics is usually understood as the study of the meaning of words and sentences. In some contexts it is contrasted with phonetics, in others with grammar, and in still others with the study of reference. Here we are speaking of the semantic, in a generalized sense, as the realm of meaning, including reference.

We talk about the meaning of a variety of things: natural and historical events, signs and signals, words and sentences, symbols, linguistic acts, nonverbal behavior, literary and other artistic works, dreams, life, history, and so forth. Among these we may distinguish between those things that have an inherent meaning and those that do not. When a natural event, for example, functions as a sign of something with which it is connected, as in the case of smoke and fire, there is no inherent meaning in the sign. Although the event or condition may move the thought of a perceiver to that with which it is naturally related, there is no semantic connection between the two to be grasped or understood by the perceiver. The natural sign is not an *expression*; what the natural sign is a sign of is not semantically in the sign. Also, words and sentences, although standard ways in which people of the language community mean certain things, have no inherent meaning except in the linguistic acts of persons. They have linguistic uses but no inherent meaning until put to use in semantic acts. They mean only when used by someone to mean something. Although words and sentences have standardized uses, they mean in a given situation what the speaker or writer meant in using them, even though he or she may have misused the language.

A book is a set of the author's linguistic acts. A reader, in understanding the book, understands the author. The semantic dimension of the book is part of the semantic dimension of the author. What is semantically *in* the book was in the mind of the author and comes to be *in* the mind of the understanding reader. This is communication.

There are those who say that in understanding a text the reader is unconcerned with what the author meant; that the text means what it says to the reader, which is what it is read as meaning. The understanding of a text, it is said, has its own historicity. The way a text is understood in one age may be quite different from the way it is understood in another. So the meaning of a text is said to be dynamic; it changes from age to age, if not from reader to reader. It is true that a word has its meaning in a sentence, the sentence in terms of the paragraph of which it is a part, the paragraph in terms of the chapter or book of which it is a part, and the book in terms of a wider culture in which it is embedded. And with the passage of time, the wider culture of which a text is a part develops and changes. By virtue of this developing cultural context, the meaning of the book, which is nothing but the set of linguistic acts of the author, may develop also. But this does not mean that there is no meaning in the text to which a reading of it is accountable and with respect to which the reading is correct or incorrect.

The view that there is no inherent meaning in the text, what the author meant in his or her linguistic acts, results from trying to assimilate language to natural signs where there is no inherent meaning. Smoke means fire to a perceiver, but fire is not a semantic content of smoke as such. To understand smoke at a given place and time is to know its cause, not to grasp its meaning, its semantic content. When we want to know about natural signs and what they mean, we have to investigate only what people take them to mean; and what people take them to mean may vary from time to time and from culture to culture. We might even talk about what natural events signify or say to people and acknowledge that this is a function of both the natural order of things and the people's receptivity, which is a matter of their belief system or cultural condition. A change in their belief system might result in a change in their perception of the meaning of a particular natural phenomenon. With this model in mind, it is not surprising that one would conclude that a text means what readers, in their time and under their cultural conditions, take it to mean; that, in other words, a text means whatever it means to a reader, or, at best, that it means whatever it means in common to some set of elite readers in a given age. On this view, it seems to follow that what the author meant in using the words and sentences is irrelevant.

Of course, in some situations, others may be a better authority on what a text means than the author. But what they are a better authority on is what the author meant in writing the work; that is, the meaning of the linguistic acts of the author in their cultural context, for his or her linguistic acts constitute the text. Configurated ink marks on paper do not make a text. To take them to be words and sentences is to take them as the embodiments of semantic acts. If not the acts of the author, then whose? There are no free, unpossessed linguistic acts. If readers perform their own linguistic acts upon perceiving the ink marks, they are not reading but composing the text. No one who has had one's writing interpreted and criticized by others can doubt that reading and composing often become confused and run together, for misreading is a kind of composing. But regardless of how much the distinction is blurred in practice, the distinction has to be preserved if we are to make any sense of communication and intersubjectivity.

It may be that the best test of what a text means is what it is read in common to mean by well-qualified readers. The issue, however, is whether the consensus among qualified readers of the text constitutes confirmation of the correctness of the reading of the inherent meaning of the text, or whether the consensus endows the text with a meaning that it otherwise would not have. This issue is not unlike whether agreement among witnesses about what one did on a given occasion constitutes confirmation of their report on one's action or constitutes what one did. The assumption here is that a correct description of an action must include the intention that was embodied in the act. A further assumption is that physical movements of a body do not constitute an action unless they embody an intention of the agent. No attribution of an intention by observers, regardless of how much agreement, can convert physical motions into actions or one action into another. So how can the attribution of meaning by readers to physical marks constitute them into statements, questions, and the like?

The approach here is wrong. Texts are not like natural signs. Where natural signs have meaning primarily to observers, language in use has inherent meaning; it is used to mean something by the speaker or writer, and the linguistic act embodies that meaning. A reader, in understanding the linguistic act, grasps the meaning inherent in the act.

Perhaps the best way to locate inherent meaning is, as intimated in Chapter 2, through certain prepositions that have a semantic use in contrast with an existential use. We may talk about what is *in* a book in the sense in which what is mentioned or reported in the book may be said to be *in* the book; and we may talk about what is *in* the book in the sense in which a bookmark may be *in* the book. The former is the semantic sense of "in," and the latter is the existential sense. Talk about words and sentences, statements and questions, and the like being in the book is also the existential sense of "in"; but here the mode of existence is quite different from that of the bookmark, for what is said to be existentially in the book is of a different category of being. Indeed, the book itself has to be conceived under a different category.

The book must be thought of not as a physical thing but as something that can have multiple physical embodiments. This is not the usual type/token distinction. The point is is not that the pattern of ink marks can have multiple instantiations but that the meaning and logical structure of the linguistic acts of the author can have multiple embodiments by virtue of the multiple instantiations of the pattern of ink marks. But not even multiple instantiations of the pattern of ink marks are required for multiple embodiments. Handwritten sentences may be replicated in various forms of print; statements made in one language may be expressed in different sentences of the same language or sentences of other languages. Embodiment is not the instantiation of a type. There is an interior, an inner realm, to an embodiment that is lacking in an instantiation; there is something to be grasped or understood through reading. To interpret an instantiation is to know the form or type instantiated; to interpret an embodiment is to read it, to grasp what is semantically in the body in question.

Parallel with "in," there are semantic and existential uses of "on," "of," and "about." We can talk about what is *on* one's mind and what is *on* one's head; what is *on* the agenda and what is *on* the chair; what a concept or a picture is *of* or what a fragment or a part is *of*; and what a sentence or a book is *about* and what is *about* the place.

The semantic use of these prepositions (the use in which a semantic "relation" is designated) is by no means restricted to talk about language. We talk as readily about what is *in* one's mind (*in* one's experience, memory, dream, fantasy, thought, expectation, and so forth) as we do about what is *in* the newspaper or *in* a book. In like manner, we talk just as freely about what one's experiences and thoughts are *of* as we do about what names and descriptions are *of*; and just as freely about what thoughts and beliefs are *on* or *about* as what statements or books are *on* or *about*. Therefore, we feel justified in applying the concept of the semantic beyond the realm of language and discourse to whatever is semantically *of, about,* or *on* something and to whatever has something semantically *in* it—to whatever has a semantic object or a semantic content.

Our discussion of the semantic dimension of books and persons introduces us to what is known in the literature as *intentionality*. We must not confuse intentionality in this sense with the intentions on which people act. Of course intentions related to actions have the feature of intentionality, but this is true, or so this work claims, of all mental states and acts. Most of the discussion of intentionality has concentrated on propositional attitudes. Two features of belief-statements have received special attention, namely, the failure of existential inferences and of inferences based on extensional identity within intentional contexts. Consider the following statements:

1. George believed that his grandmother was his grandfather's second wife.
2. Sarah Graham was the second wife of George's grandfather.

We cannot validly infer from (1) that someone was the second wife of George's grandfather. Thus the failure of existential inference from within the belief context. Nor can we validly infer from (1) and (2) that George believed that Sarah Graham was his grandmother. Thus the failure of inference based on extensional identity within the belief context.

Although beliefs are paradigms of intentionality, it would be a mistake to define intentionality in terms of these two features of belief-statements, for such a definition would not bring together all the categorially relevant subject matter. It would exclude, for example, identifying references such as the one reported in the sentence "George mentioned Sarah." We could validly infer from this statement that there is someone who was mentioned by George. If we should discover that the apparent act of mentioning Sarah failed to locate or to refer to someone, we would conclude that the apparent act of *mentioning* was apparent only; for an act of mentioning requires an independent object. Nevertheless, the object is *internal* to the act as well. A proper description of the act, as in the case of a thought, must include its object as internal to, and constitutive of, the act. Knowledge of the act itself, whether self-knowledge on the part of the speaker or perceptual understanding of the act on the part of a hearer, includes knowledge of its object as an *inexistential* constituent of the act itself. Sarah is *taken up* semantically, so to speak, in her concrete individuality, not under some abstract conceptualization, into George's act of mentioning her. It would be meaningful to clarify his reference by saying that the Sarah he had *in mind* was his grandmother. Because acts of non-descriptive identifying reference *take up* their whole object *into themselves inexistentially*, substitutions based on extensional identity hold for reports or descriptions of such acts. For example, from the two statements "George mentioned Sarah" and "Sarah is George's grandmother," we can validly infer that George mentioned his grandmother.

The important thing about an intentional state or act is that it contains something *inexistentially* within itself; it has a semantic object or content. The object or content may be of any category of being and may have an existential or some other independent status as well as its internal inexistential status. Indeed, some terms such as "saw," "mentioned," and "know" require, by virtue of their achievement-claim, that the objects of the acts they are used to report actually exist or have some independent standing. The failure of existential inference and of inference based on extensional identity simply points out clear-cut cases in which a wedge can be driven between the inexistential and existential status of the objects concerned and thereby establishes the internal inexistential status of the object. But mental states and acts for which the existential status of their objects is required also contain their objects inexistentially.

In an effort to formulate a definition of intentionality that would do justice to the full range of categorially related subject matter, I proposed, in an earlier work, that "a state or act is intentional if and only if a proper (philosophically clarified) report or description of it must be in terms of a *conceptual delineation of or reference to something else as part of the structure of the state or act in question.*"[1] This formulation, however, was not explicit about whether the *conceptual delineation of or reference to something else* had to be part of the structure of the state or act in question, or merely that a proper report or description of the state or act would have to involve a conceptual delineation of or reference to *something else* as part of its structure. On the latter reading, normative requirements (for example, *X*'s being *F* in situation *S* normatively requires that *Y* be *G*), as well as mental states and acts, would be intentional. It does seem that such requirements, if there are such, have inexistential contents; and so the categorially related subject matter may be more extensive than we thought. With this in mind, I kept the broad concept of intentionality and spoke of *semantic* intentionality as a special mode of it. A state or act is semantically intentional, I said, "if and only if a proper report or description of it must be in terms of a semantic act (an act of reference or conceptual delineation in some mode) and its object as inexistentially present in the structure of the act itself: in the case of [non-descriptive] reference, the object's being inexistentially present in person, so to speak; in the case of conceptual delineation, the object's being inexistentially present just as conceptually delineated and in no other way."[2]

It needs to be pointed out that the same words may be used in one sentence to make an identifying reference and in another to make only a conceptual delineation: for example, "The president is in California" and "George believes that the president is in California." In the first sentence, "the President" is used to make a descriptive identifying reference; in the second, it occurs as a conceptually delineating expression, without making an identifying reference.

This leaves us with the semantic undefined. We may use the concept of intentionality to characterize and to illuminate semantic states and acts, but there is more to such states and acts than intentionality: what we locate and present by such terms as "the semantic," "the mental," "meaning," and "subjectivity." We may differentiate semantic intentionality from normative intentionality, for example, by the fact that whatever has a semantic dimension may be spoken of as an *expression* or as in principle expressible, as being not merely observable but "understandable" (in the sense in which we speak of *understanding* what someone says or does), as having a logical form or structure and the like. In other words, there is the language of meaning, a team of concepts, that applies to what we refer to as the semantic and the mental; and there seems to be no way in which we can talk about this subject matter without involving this team of concepts. It seems that we cannot define semantic words in terms of non-semantic words, that we cannot say what we say in the language of meaning in any other mode of discourse. If this is so, semantic terms are categorial terms and meaning seems to be a categorial structure in reality.[3]

Representationalism: The Naturalistic Challenge

The account of meaning and subjectivity given above seems unexceptionable when we look at the relevant subject matter in terms of our ordinary ways of talking about it. But states, acts, and expressions with an inherent structure of meaning are an embarrassment to modern naturalism, for they cannot be accredited within scientific empiricism or placed in the world as naturalistically defined. So from the naturalist point of view, meaning cannot be what it appears to be. So-called mentalistic semantics is rejected not because it can be shown to be false with respect to its own subject matter, but because the account is not framed in terms of the prevailing canonical conceptual system, which has been developed independently of the phenomena of meaning and subjectivity.[4] A choice has to be made. If we accept the categorial account of meaning given above, the naturalistic world-view would have to be rejected. If we insist on the naturalistic world-view, then meaning has to be shown not to be what it appears to be; the language of meaning and subjectivity has to be shown not to be categorial in its own right but reducible to, or explainable in terms of, the language of existence and factuality. Various efforts have been made throughout the modern period to square the language of meaning and subjectivity with modern naturalistic scruples.

The representative theory of meaning has been one of the major efforts to accommodate the language of meaning within the existential and factual framework of scientific thought. It has assumed a variety of forms, but all of them have taken an observational approach. Meaning must be identified with, or accounted for in terms of, encounterable objects and their factual and causal features and relations. One *thing* is taken to mean another. The inquiry about meaning is guided by the question: What kind of a "relationship" holds between two entities when one means the other? And prior restraints are imposed on the kinds of relationship that can be acknowledged. They have to have a respectable empirical pedigree.

The Classical Empiricist Theory of Representations

The representative theory of meaning was worked out in detail by early modern empiricists in their theory of sense impressions and ideas. We shall reconstruct their theory in a way that will reveal its difficulties and help us understand the representative theory of meaning in general.

The representative theory of perception was an effort toward the naturalization of sensory experience and the whole realm of epistemology. We have sensory experiences *of* things. And, for empiricists, all knowledge of the world is based on, or is developed out of, such experiences. But how are we to understand *sensory experiences of objects*? What is the meaning of the preposition "of" in this context?

We talk about *ideas of things, images of things, experiences of things, pictures of things, copies of things, impressions of things,* and various kinds of *likenesses of things*. All of these were taken to be akin. Likenesses are the simplest: *A* is a physical likeness of *B* if it closely resembles *B* in its physical surface properties. An impression is slightly more complex: *A* is a physical impression of *B* if and only if it is a likeness of *B* and if the resembling form of *A* is an effect of the corresponding form of *B*. A stock example of a physical impression is a foot print in the sand. Copies are still more complex. Even physical copies are not simply physical impressions. There is an activity associated with a copy. A copy is a product of copying. Even if a copy of *B* is a physical impression of it, it has to be produced as an impression of *B* in order to be a copy of *B*. In the expression "*A* is a physical impression *of B*," the preposition "of" indicates a complex physical relation that involves causality. But in the expression "*A* is a copy *of B*," "of" indicates not only a more complex relation but one that involves a different kind of causality. To describe something as a copy is to attribute to it an intentionalistic etiology. In a purely physical world, there could be physical impressions but no copies.

Pictures and visual images are not simply visual copies. Even a photo impression as such is not a graph or a picture. It is just a certain type of an impression. But it may be also either a copy or a picture. In the sentences "*A* is a picture of *B*" and "*A* is an image of *B*," unlike in "*A* is a copy of *B*," "of" indicates a semantic relation. It is not simply that *A* has a certain likeness to *B* and that it was caused or produced in a certain way or for a certain purpose; *B* is presented as the *semantic object* of *A*, or, what amounts to the same thing, *B* is presented as the *semantic content* of *A*. Pictures and images, like words and sentences, have a semantic dimension.

Vocal sounds produced by parrots, regardless of the fact that they may be audibly indistinguishable from spoken words and regardless of the fact that someone or some group of people may take them to be words, are not words. They are not given a semantic dimension by physical similitude to spoken words. Nor can the "talk" of a parrot be given a semantic dimension by being taken to be a set of linguistic acts. In like manner, weather etchings on a stone or configurations in the clouds, regardless of how physically similar they may be to written words or drawings of objects and regardless of what they are taken to be by observers, are not words or pictures. They do not have the appropriate etiology and they have no inherent semantic content or object. They are simply physical objects that resemble certain other things. For observers, they may call to mind the things they resemble. In this regard, they may function as natural signs by virtue of the physical resemblance, but they have no semantic content about which one could be right or wrong. If people take *A* to be a sign of *B* by virtue of some nonsemantic relation that holds, or is believed to hold, between *A* and *B*, *A* is a sign of *B*. But words, pictures, and images are not that way. They have a semantic content to be understood.

Words and pictures also have an essential connection with their production. Causally, images are closer to impressions. They need not have an intentionalistic etiology. But unlike impressions, they can be identified and described only in terms of their objects. Consider mirror images, for example. If one takes an image to have an independent existence and to be identifiable and describable in terms of its own inherent properties, one does not take it as an image but either as the object of which it is an image or as an impression. Of course there are uses of the terms in which the distinction we are drawing between images and impressions is blurred. But the distinction is there in ordinary usage and it is important for our purposes.

The above account of natural signs is a functionalistic theory. According to it, "*A* is a sign of *B*" attributes a function to *A* that may involve or be based on a natural relation to *B*, but it does not attribute a semantic relation to *A* and *B* to be discovered in the objective, independent world. The function attributed to *A* is that of directing the thought or action of an observer or agent to *B*, or simply causing the thought of, or an action in relation to, *B*.

Some who have thought of sense experiences as impressions may have interpreted the semantic language about sense experience in terms of the purely factual language of impressions. For those who do, the "of" in the expression "*A* is a sense experience of *B*" is taken to indicate the same relation as the "of" in "*A* is an impression of *B*." This relation, as we previously observed, consists of resemblance and a causal relation. So a sense experience of an object, on this theory, is understood as an existent that resembles or shares the form of its external cause, with nothing more to the semantic dimension of the experience than that.

If this is what the sensory experience of an object amounts to, how can it yield knowledge of its object? What is it for the object to be *in* the experience, to be a *content* of it? What is it for the sensory experience to be a source of *information* about its object? Can it be that the form (the properties) of the object is existentially replicated in the sense impression? If so, what is it for the sensory experience to be illusory or veridical? Is this just a matter of the closeness of the resemblance? Impressions of objects may vary in degrees of clearness and distinctness; but the objects also may vary in this manner. We may assume that the object of a clear and distinct impression is itself clear and distinct in a corresponding way, but we cannot assume that an unclear and indistinct impression of an object does not resemble its object just as closely. And what kind of an existent is a sensory experience of an object? Is it another entity in the same space-time continuum as its object? What kind of properties does it exemplify? Are they the same kind of properties as those of its object? If so, a sensory experience would be just another physical object with physical properties; a sensory perception of a car would be another car, or at least a physical object with the surface qualities of a car.

In order to save the theory from such absurdities, its advocates said that a sense impression is an existent with its own properties, but it is not a physical existent with physical properties in the space of its object; rather the impression is said to be a mental entity with the kind of properties mental entities have. A sense experience, on this view, is an impression in a mind, but it is of a physical object. A mind, it was said, is not itself an occupant of the space of the objects of its impressions but rather a "subjective" replica of space, perhaps an impression of space. Even though sense impressions are said to resemble their objects and to be describable with the same predicates, the words cannot mean the same thing when applied to a sense impression as they do when applied to its object. As the space of an impression is a subjective replica of the space of its object, all the properties of a sense impression are subjective properties. Some of them may be replicas of their corresponding properties in the object, but some of them may not resemble the properties in the object that produced them. This is the difference marked by the classical distinction between primary and secondary qualities.

So the effort to reduce the semantic dimension of sensory experience to the existent and the factual gives rise to a distinction between two realms of existence and factuality, namely, the physical and the mental. But even so, regardless of how closely a sense impression replicates or resembles its object, in what sense is it *veridical* (or regardless of how much a sense impression is unlike its object, in what sense is it illusory), unless it somehow *claims* or is *taken* to be like or to manifest its object in these respects? It seems that in spite of all the effort to reduce the semantic to the existent and the factual in talk about sensory experiences of objects, the semantic refuses to disappear.

What is it for a sense impression to *claim* (or to be *taken*) to be like (or to manifest) its object? At this point, a theory of ideas has to be introduced. In this school of thought, an elementary idea was said to be a copy or reproduction of a sense impression, only fainter and less distinct but otherwise like its original. In other words, an idea was conceived as a mental existent with its own inherent properties that resembled the sense impression of which it was a copy. But it is said to be an image, not an impression. For some, particularly John Locke, the mind was conceived as more than a subjective replica of space; it was conceived as a substance with powers of its own. The mind was regarded as passive with regard to impressions but as active in relation to ideas. Simple ideas were reproductions or copies of simple sense impressions. Complex ideas might be copies of complex impressions, or they might be combinations of ideas in ways for which there never were corresponding impressions. Although ideas were thought of as *of* (in the sense of "copy of" or "reproduction of" or "projection of") their corresponding impressions, they were also said to be *of* the objects of these impressions. For example, according to the theory, my idea of an apple is a copy of a complex impression of an apple (or a composite of copies of such impressions), but it also is an idea *of* an apple, not an idea of an impression of an apple. This "of" seems to indicate a genuine semantic relation. The idea of X seems to take the impression of X to signify or to manifest X and its properties. It treats the impression as if it were a natural sign of its nonsemantic object. And only at this level is talk about veridical or illusory sense experience possible.

This is a functionalistic theory of the meaning of sense experiences. It holds that an elementary sense experience is an impression in and of itself. As such, it is said to have an object but not a semantic object. Its object, according to the theory, is, as with the foot print, that which it resembles and of which it is an effect. It is not that the "of" in "sense experience of X" is taken to mean the same as the "of" in "sense impression of X." Rather it is that the sense impression is taken to *represent*, or to stand for, its nonsemantic object. In other words, semantic discourse about sense experience pertains to sense impressions, not as descriptions of their inherent properties and natural relations, but with respect to their function as natural signs or representations based on their resemblance and causal relation to their nonsemantic objects.

The picture is now greatly complicated. The effort to account for the semantics of sense experience in terms of the categories of existence and factuality has divided the world into physical and mental realms of existence and factuality with resemblance and causal relations holding between them. The semantic aspect of sense experience is accounted for not as an inherent dimension of sense experience but as a function or role sense impressions have. Two problems stand out. Can sense impressions, understood in terms of this classical empiricist account of them, serve the representative function attributed to them? Furthermore, the representative function of sense impressions presupposes a semantic dimension of ideas. Can the semantics of ideas be explained without acknowledging meaning as a basic category?

How are we to understand this functionalistic way of thinking about sense impressions? This theory was based on the assumption that our epistemic access to sense impressions was unproblematic. Indeed, the distinction between the *existence of* a sense impression and its *presence to* a sensory being was collapsed. Berkeley collapsed its existence into its *presence to one*. Thus his famous dictum: "To be is to be perceived." Hume, on the other hand, collapsed a sense impression's presence to one into its existence. If any meaning is preserved for the phrase "X is present to Y" (where X is a sense impression) over and above the simple existence of X (except in terms of its presence as the object of an idea), it is that of X's membership in the set of sense impressions and ideas that, according to Hume, constitute one's self. However, talk about the existence of a sense impression apart from such membership would not make sense on Hume's account.

In any case, Hume rejected the representative theory of sense experience on the grounds that we could not make sense of the claim that sense impressions functioned as signs of external objects, for we could not make sense of talk about (could not have ideas of) such external causes and the resemblance of sense impressions to them. So he concluded that sense impressions are original existences without any representative quality. They cannot function as representations of their nonsemantic objects, for we cannot talk meaningfully about such objects. Sense impressions are not really *impressions*; they are not *of* anything. They have been misnamed by a misleading analogy. The "of" in "sense impression of *X*" is the "of" of apposition; the expression is the same as "the sense impression, *X*." So for Hume, discourse about external physical objects is not meaningful, for it is impossible for us to have *ideas* of natural relationships between sense impressions and such objects by virtue of which sense impressions or anything else could function as natural signs or representations of them.

Hume, then, gave up on the representative theory of sense experience by concluding that basic sense experiences do not have a semantic relationship to external objects, whether inherent or functionalistic. But he subscribed to a representative theory of ideas. He regarded ideas as images and, as such, as "copies" of sense impressions or as composites of "copies" of sense impressions. Apparently an idea of a given sense impression was a "copy" or "reproduction" of it for Hume only in the sense that the idea was subsequent to the impression and like it but less vivid. Ideas of memory were distinguished from ideas of the imagination in that the former were more vivid than the latter and tended to follow the order of their antecedent impressions, whereas the ideas of the imagination were weaker and much freer in their associations, for they had no order of antecedent impressions to which they were related.

Wherein lies the representative quality of ideas, as Hume would call it? Does it consist of the "copy" relationship between the image and its object? If so, there is no more inherent meaning in the image than in the sense impression, but it does have the potentiality of being, in some sense, a representation of its nonsemantic object.

On the representative account, in what sense does the image represent its correlative sense impression? In our ordinary way of thinking about natural signs, *A* is a sign of *B* if, on the belief that a natural relationship obtains between *A* and *B*, the presence of *A* to one calls to mind *B*. Is this how, in Hume's language, an image *represents* the sense impression of which it is a "copy"? Images and sense impressions seem to be at too deep a level for such an account to make sense. The framework in terms of which we talk about natural signs does not pertain here. No distinction can be drawn between the existence of the image and its presence to one. And there is no distinction between the occurrence of the image of the sense impression and the sense impression's being called to mind. The image is just how the sense impression is called to mind, whether in memory or imagination. But in what sense is the sense impression present to someone? Perhaps Hume would say that it is present to the person who is constituted by the set of sense impressions and images of which the image in question is a member. Then does Hume reduce the semantic relationship of the image to the sense impression to the "copy" relationship, which consists of resemblance, comparative weakness, and being subsequent in time? That is a possible interpretation, but a functionalistic interpretation is nearer the mark.

In memory, imagination, and discourse, according to Hume, an image represents (or stands for) the sense impression of which it is a "copy." We must remember that Hume is a phenomenalist. Accordingly, he interprets our ordinary language about physical things as about actual and possible sense impressions. In memory, images are combined and connected in ways that represent combinations and connections of their antecedent sense impressions. In imagination, images are combined and connected in ways that represent possible combinations and connections among sense impressions, including the sense impressions that would occur and the way they would be combined and connected under certain conditions. And in discourse or writing, or simply in verbal thinking, words (which are complex impressions with functions in thought and discours) occur; and as they do they cause (or have associated with them) images that represent or stand for their correlative impressions. Thus through the representative function of images, things (complexes of actual and possible sense impressions) are thought and talked about.

In this account of imagining and thinking-in-words, what is it for an image to *represent* or *stand for* the sense impression of which it is a "copy"? The most obvious thing to say is that the image "calls to mind" or "presents to one" the original of which it is a "copy." But this is just what we are trying to explicate. If the *calling to mind* or *presenting* of the image's original is simply the occurrence of the image, then the semantic aspect of the image would seem to be either something unique and irreducible and inherent, or identifiable with its "copy" relationship to its original. In the former case, the impression would be inexistentially present in the existence of the image. The semantic would not be explicated in non-semantic terms. It would have to be acknowledged as a basic, irreducible category. On the other hand, if the semantic aspect of the image were identified with the "copy" relationship, the impression would not be *present* in any sense; only the image, a copy of the sense impression, would be present and it would be existentially present.

As it is conceived in this tradition, the "copy" relationship of the image to an impression does not require the presence of the impression. In Hume's view, "A is a copy of B" is not a truth about A that can be discovered by inspecting A *alone*. It is only by comparing A and B that the "copy" relationship could be discerned. Thus for the occurrence of A to *mean* B (for A to be *of* B in the semantic sense) it is not enough for A to occur; and it is not enough for A in fact to be a copy of B. It has to be known, or taken, to be a copy of B. In other words, A

functions as a natural sign of B; the presence of A "calls to mind" B by virtue of a known or believed non-semantic relation (the "copy" relationship) of A to B. With regard to A, its semantic presence has been collapsed into its existence. For the image A to be present to one is simply for it to exist. But the existential and the semantic presences are driven apart with regard to the impression B. When B is present through its image it is semantically present but not existentially present. Then, are we left with an unreduced and unexplained-away semantic presence?

This is not all. Could the "copy" relationship between an image and an impression be validated on the basis of the Humean account? If the original impression were not inherent somehow in the image, how could one know what impression an image copied? And how could one know that the image was a faithful copy? One can no more compare an image with the existent impression it allegedly copies than one can compare an impression with its alleged external cause. At best one could only compare two or more simultaneous images of the alleged impression. And how could one compare a complex impression with an image that had projected it? There is even a problem about how one could compare two images. Comparison presupposes semantic presence (presence to one) as distinct from existential presence. But, according to the theory, all this talk about making comparisons has to be interpreted in terms of the occurrences of impressions and images.

On the assumption that the theory is true, it seems that if we probe deep enough, ideas and impressions alike collapse into what Hume would call "original existences without any representative quality." And the theory is shown to be absurd, for the comparison of images and impressions on which the theory is based would be impossible if the theory were true.

So even within the framework of image and impression talk, either meaning (semantic presence) is presupposed as distinct from existence and factuality or the whole enterprise collapses into nonsense. Even if we could accept Hume's denial of the semantic dimension of sense impressions, the semantic aspect of images would seem to be basic and irreducible.

It seems to be a mistake in the first place to think of "impressions" and images as existences factually constituted. We do not identify and describe a sense experience or an image in terms of the properties exemplified in it. We individuate and describe it in terms of its object. In other words, we locate and describe an experience or image in terms of what is semantically in it, not in terms of what is existentially in it. To conceive of an experience or an image as an existent constituted by existing parts and exemplified properties is already to collapse the semantic into the existent and the factual. The mischief is already done. No satisfactory theory of meaning can be built on this mistake.

One of the most important tests of a philosophical theory is whether it generates further philosophical perplexities and absurdities. No theory in the history of philosophy has been more fertile in this respect than this classical empiricist theory of the meaning dimension of sense experience and ideas. It was this theory of meaning that generated the major problems in modern epistemology about the possibility of knowledge of an external, independent reality.

It was an easy transition from this theory of the meaning of words and ideas in terms of images and impressions to the pragmatic theory that words and ideas do not represent an independent reality, not even a set of actual and hypothetical sense impressions, but rather are guides or recipes or connections that lead to or produce new experiences; or perhaps that they are instruments for reconstructing or transforming problematic experiences. But there was still the problem about how words and ideas guide, prescribe, direct, or lead to new experiences. All of this is still semantic talk. Even if experience and thought cannot present to us external, independent realities, they must, according to the pragmatist account, present to us past and future experiences, however conceived. Indeed, a present experience is saturated with meaning. No occurrence devoid of inherent meaning is an experience. By its very nature, an experience has semantic content. Indeed, John Dewey regarded an experience as a structure of meaning. And Dewey, even in his most naturalistic moments, did not try to reduce or explain away meaning. In this sense, he remained a humanist, if not an idealist, in his metaphysics. He was not a naturalist in our sense of the term.

The Modern Functionalist Theory of Representations

In spite of all the difficulties it has generated in the past, the representative theory of meaning is still alive in one form or another. It has been built into our vocabulary. Philosophers speak as a matter of course of words, ideas, and experiences as representations; and they speak of what words, ideas, and experiences are of or about as what they represent or stand for. The meaning of a representation is often identified with what it represents. This is natural enough in ordinary contexts where questions arise about what words and symbols mean. But when we ask philosophical questions about meaning, the assumption that meaning consists of the objects of words and experiences can be misleading. What we need to know is what it is for one thing to mean or to represent another. In other words, we need to know what semantic "relations" are. This is more basic than questions about the nature of semantic objects. Students of semantics, approaching the subject from the perspective of an observer of two sets of entities, have sought to account for the relations that hold between them in a way that would not disturb the naturalistic view of the world.

A modernized version of the classical empiricist theory of mental representations is prominent in current philosophy of mind and cognitive psychology. Instead of talking about images and impressions—entities that are supposed to be epistemologically basic—subscribers to the current representational theory of the mental theorize about an "internal language" that is instantiated in the states and processes of the brain. The brain states or events are not taken to be physical impressions or copies of anything; nor are they identified and described in terms of their inherent properties. Whatever they are in themselves, the theory is concerned with them only as physical tokens of representations. We have physical tokens of words and sentences in speech and writing. From the perspective of the speaker or writer, bodily states and processes involved in the production of the patterned sounds or ink marks may be regarded as integral to the tokens of the words and sentences by which speakers or writers mean what they do in their linguistic acts. Indeed, truncated versions of these processes that fall short of producing sounds or ink marks may still mean whatever the completed production of the sounds or ink marks would have meant. We may speak of this as thinking to ourselves in English or whatever our language happens to be. Furthermore, it is said, we have physical tokens of a "natural" language in our psychological states and acts, such as perceptions, feelings, and desires, that are not "in" any ordinary language. This is said to be true even of animals and children before they learn a cultural language. This thesis is compatible with the claim that a cultural language will infiltrate into the most elemental operations of the mind.

The "mental representations" of which brain states and processes are tokens, whether connected with a cultural language or not, are thought of in much the same way as words and sentences of a cultural language. They are patterns of internal physical states and events with syntactic and semantic functions. In fact, when we think in a cultural language, whether out loud or to ourselves, the brain states and events indirectly token words and sentences of the language. They token patterns of brain states and events that are involved in, or associated with, the production of tokens of words and sentences. Where the classical theory spoke of words and sentences of the spoken or written language as having ideas (images) as their internal or mental counterparts, the present theory posits only brain states and events. And just as the classical theory thought of images and impressions as more basic than words and sentences of a conventional language and as capable of representing things and states of affairs to a limited extent without being associated with words and sentences of such a language, the present theory thinks of brain states and events in a similar way. According to the theory, brain states and events token natural representations that are not connected with a conventional language. These representations are thought of as "words" and "sentences" nonetheless, but as natural rather than cultural words and sentences, for they are the products of biological evolution and of the functioning of the individual organism in its environment.

The tokens of representations, whether in a natural or a cultural language, are concrete physical states or events. They are instances of a physical form or pattern. Any instance of such a form or pattern, unless significantly modified by its context, has a common or similar representational function as any other instance of it. This does not mean, of course, that the representational function cannot be borne by different typed brain states and processes. Certainly in cultural languages the same linguistic functions may be carried by alternative types of physical tokens. The important questions arise about the representational function. Those with naturalistic scruples are, as the Humeans were before them, committed to finding an account within the categories of existence and factuality. But this is their most challenging test.

Having shown how mental activity is, as Wilfrid Sellars would say, "languaging,"[5] it follows that philosophy of mind is philosophy of language. Our concepts pertaining to the intentionality of the mental are syntactical and semantical concepts pertaining to language. But how can these be analyzed in acceptable naturalistic categories?

Behaviorism was for a time the hope of naturalists, but it is now widely accepted that behavioristic analyses are inadequate. It takes account of only causal relationships between observable inputs and behavioral outputs. Cognitive psychologists recognize the need to fill in between such inputs and outputs with "mental" (or intentionalistic) states of the organism that are causally related to one another as well as to inputs and outputs. But how can such mental states be dealt with scientifically?

Sellars says that behavioristic theories of semantics were based on a false presupposition. It was assumed, he says, that sentences like "'E' (in *L*) means *Y*" are relational and that the relation in question can be defined in behavioral terms. But he says that the sentence only appears to be relational; that "means" is really a specialized form of the copula "is." For example, he says "'und' (in *G*) means *and*" may be perspicuously rendered "'und's (in *G*) are ·and·s," where "·and·" means not "and" but the function "and" has in English. Similarly, he says that "stands for" merely seems to stand for a relation. Instead of saying that "'Triangularity' stands for or names the property triangularity," he would say "'Triangularity' is a ·triangular·"[6]

Sellars extends this analysis of the semantics of language to our talk about brain states and processes as constituting intentional systems. He would paraphrase the sentence "*P*-states mean *this is triangular*" (where "*P*-states" denotes certain brain states) as "*P*-states are ·this is triangular·s." He concludes: "Our primary concepts pertaining to intentionality can be shown not to concern unique modes of relationship between mental events and reality, but rather to provide a technique for classifying mental events by reference to paradigms in our background language."[7]

This of course simply shifts the burden to the explication of the function of the paradigms in the background language. Even if "means" in such expressions as "'E' (in language L) means *Y*" could be shown to be a specialized form of the copula such that "'E's (in L) mean *Y*" translates into "'E's (in L) are ·*Y*·s," we must still say what ·*Y*·s are. Can we do this without reinvoking semantic concepts?

A variety of complicated accounts of such functions have been given.[8] For present purposes, the gist of the matter is something like this. The function of an item in a representational system is its causal role. According to the standard version of functionalism, as formulated by Jerry Fodor, functional states are "type-individuated by reference to their (actual and potential) causal relations; you know everything that is essential about a functional state when you know which causal generalizations subsume it." In the psychological case, "the generalizations that count for type individuation are the ones that relate mental states to one another." So the mental states of an organism constitute "a network of causal interrelations." Given this, "we can assume," Fodor says, "that each mental state can be identified with a node in such a network: for each mental state there is a corresponding causal role and for each causal role there is a corresponding node"; or, what amounts to the same thing, "each mental state can be associated with a formula . . . which uniquely determines its location in the network by specifying its potentialities for causal interaction with each of the other mental states."[9]

Even if mental representations are individuated by their causal roles, what gives them their propositional content? They have inferential relations as well as causal ones. Some contemporary philosophers are willing to tolerate propositions as objects of propositional attitudes to account for the inferential patterns. Fodor says: "If physicists have numbers to play with, why shouldn't psychologists have propositions?"[10] Some think that propositions can be handled by formal semantics without leaving any ontological danglers to disturb the naturalistic vision of the world.[11] Some are willing to settle for a partial isomorphism between the causal and inferential networks. The basic point, according to this theory, is that "the causal role of a propositional attitude mirrors the semantic role of the proposition that is its object."[12] Others try to reduce the inferential relations to causal relations. Sellars says "inference is, at bottom, the sort of thing Hume had in mind when he speaks of the association of ideas."[13] The inference patterns involved in an organism's strategies for finding objects of given kinds, according to Sellars, are "uniformities in the occurrence of representational states. Certain kinds of representational states tend to be followed (or to be followed by the absence of) certain other kinds of representational states."[14]

Mental states of an organism, however, are not only in causal interaction with one another; they have causal relations with things in the environment. As Sellars says, "a suitably trained RS [representational system] can come to be in a 'This is a triangle' state by virtue of being irradiated by a triangular object."[15] Also mental states may cause the organism to act in certain ways. According to Sellars, for an organism to be in the mental state that is a representation of itself as jumping will, under certain conditions, trigger a jumping. "In such cases," he says, "the representation of itself as jumping becomes a primitive form of 'choosing to jump.'"[16]

So what is it for a symbol to represent an object and what is it for it to represent the object as F? "The root of the idea that symbol S represents O," Sellars says, "is the idea that S belongs to a RS in which it is so connected with other features of the system (including *actions*) as to be the focal point of a strategy for finding O." And for a representational state P to represent an object as F is for P to consist of a symbol S that has a property F' and for the organism in that state to have a strategy for finding F-objects.[17]

Criticism of Modern Functionalism

There are other versions of the representational theory of the mental and of the naturalistic theory of representations. But the sketch we have given shows something of the form any representational theory of the mental must take under the governing objective and constraints of naturalism. The various theories currently being explored differ largely with respect to details in response to internal criticisms. They are all versions of the broad doctrine of functionalism, which Ned Block and Jerry Fodor characterize as the general doctrine that "the type-identity conditions of psychological states refer only to their

[causal] relations to inputs, outputs, and one another," where the inputs are sensory stimulations and the outputs are behaviors.[18] Our concern is whether any theory within these constraints of naturalism can
be adequate to the relevant subject matter.

First of all, what is the relevant subject matter? Talk concerning
what a word or sentence in a language means does not capture fully
our talk about meaning. There is a point to the claim that words and
sentences have uses or functions but do not mean anything except
when they are used by a speaker or writer to mean something. What is
primary, as Paul Grice contends, is not word or sentence meaning
(which is a matter of the use or function of a word or a sentence) but
utterer's occasion meaning.[19] One may use a word or sentence to mean
according to a standard use of it, or one may use it to mean in an
extended or nonstandard way. But it is the speaker or writer who
means something in using the word or sentence, not the word or sentence as an item in the language. Nor would a shift to tokens of language items suffice. There are many tokens of words and sentences of
a language that are not components of linguistic acts. Meaning, in this
area, seems to reside in the linguistic acts of speakers and writers, not
in language items or their tokens as such.

Perhaps it would be said that utterer's occasion meaning could be
captured by talk about tokens of words and sentences that are causally
connected with brain states of the speaker, which in turn have causal
connections with his or her other representational brain states.

But when a speaker means something, it is not that his or her linguistic act *means* something in the way in which a dictionary maker says
that a word or symbol means this or that; it is that the linguistic act is a
structure of meaning or has a meaning dimension. Meaning seems to
be inherent in linguistic acts in a way in which it is not in situations in
which some natural phenomenon is said to mean something else by
virtue of a natural relation, such as smoke means fire or certain natural
phenomena mean that a bear is in the area. In such situations, there is
no meaning inherent in the situation, only the natural relationships
that signify to an observer with the requisite background knowledge
that to which the observed phenomena are related. To be able to know
what the phenomena mean, no powers are required of the observer
other than the power to perceive the facts, the power to have the relevant background factual and causal knowledge, and the power to make
the appropriate inferences. But these powers alone seem inadequate
for understanding what someone says or does.

The inherent meaning in a linguistic act seems to be akin to the
meaning inherent in acts of all kinds. We cannot individuate and identify an act on the basis of physical structures and causal relationships.

We have to describe it in terms of what the agent is doing—in terms of the intention that is embodied in or informs the act. Of course in a linguistic act the primary thing one is doing is saying or meaning something, whereas in a non-linguistic act the primary thing one is doing is replacing a light bulb, going to town, or performing some other act. But an act, whether linguistic or not, has its identity and unity in terms of something other than its physical constitution, physical causes and effects, or other factual relationships. The components of the act are integrated by its intent or plan. The act is something that can succeed or fail, be completed or left incomplete, be right or wrong, justified or unjustified, intelligent or stupid, and so forth. For another to "perceive" what one is saying or doing involves grasping or understanding that which gives it unity and identity. And this seems to be a structure of meaning about which others can be correct or mistaken. Indeed, the speaker or agent may not know fully what one is saying or doing. Sometimes others may know better than we do what we are saying or doing. We often make discoveries about such matters as we go along, often from the interpretation of others.

Furthermore, we talk about the meaning of experiences, memories, stories, works of art, human lives, history, and so forth. All of these phenomena, along with linguistic acts and acts in general, have to be grouped together categorially because they have, or at least seem to have, a unity and identity in terms of an inherent structure of meaning. They all are subject to being talked about in terms of a team of concepts that we may call the language of meaning.

Can this unifying and defining structure of meaning be explicated in terms of causal relationships of physical states and occurrences or the causal roles of types of physical states and occurrences? When we focus our attention on the relevant physical dimension (the physical states and occurrences and their causal interrelationships) of an entity such as an act, an experience, a life, or a story and take these to be the reality of the entity, we cannot but feel that the meaning, the unity, and the identity have been lost. We have to ask, Where is the meaning? Where is the unity and the identity? Where is the act, the experience, the life, or the story? These kinds of entities seem to have evaporated.

Functional Theory of Sense Experience

Perhaps some naturalists would explain the apparent structure of meaning of such entities in the way in which philosophers traditionally have explained the colors of a painting and the complex organization of sounds in the performance of a sonata. It has been widely accepted for a long time that colors and sounds are not what they seem to be;

that they are appearances, not physical properties. Although we take some things to be unified and to have their identity in terms of an organization of colors and sounds, colors and sounds as such, according to the traditional theory, belong to the realm of appearance, not reality; or, in another voice, we might say that colors and sounds are really the complex of primary qualities of physical things by virtue of which they appear to us color- and sound-wise.

Regardless of what we make of this philosophical theory of secondary qualities, a similar move is not available with regard to meaning. The secondary-quality theory of colors and sounds has the realm of appearances and phenomenal qualities with which to work. But if the naturalistic reduction of meaning works, there is no phenomenal realm, for phenomena in this sense are simply contents of the mind—things *as they are present to us*. But this is just what is being explained away. So we have no realm to which we can assign what seems to be lost when we reduce the realm of meaning to complex physical states and their causal roles in a physical system. Furthermore, if the naturalistic reduction of meaning and the mental were accepted, we could no longer accept the classical theory of secondary qualities and "raw feels" of somatic sensations, for, as remarked above, we would have to reject the subjective realm of sensory appearances and phenomenal qualities in terms of which it is constructed. In fact, it is not at all clear how such a linguistic theory of the mental and such a theory of the meaning of language could give any plausible account of what people have taken to be the subjective, phenomenal dimension of experience, dream, imagination, thought, and action. Perhaps the language in terms of which we talk about such things would be assigned to folk psychology to be replaced by the language of a scientific psychology. But even if one were to accept such a position, one would still have the responsibility to explain how the language of folk psychology was possible in the first place and to show how it could be replaced without leaving residues of subjective qualia.

Some have spoken of phenomenal qualities as properties of mental representations. Sellars says, for example, "I agree with the classical view that there is a domain of 'inner episodes,' properly referred to as 'thoughts,' which are . . . *analogous* in important respects, syntactic and semantic, to linguistic structures, and are functionally connected with linguistic behavior. These episodes have properties of the kind which are articulated by a sound phenomenology of mental events."[20] He would say, if our reading of him is correct, that a certain representational state of one's brain may be "red" (in the phenomenal sense) and by virtue of being "red" represent an object as red (in the physical property sense). Sydney Shoemaker speaks of mental states with a "phenomenological" character as "qualitative states." One has introspective awareness of such a qualitative state of one's own, according to Shoemaker, when it gives rise to a "qualitative belief," that is, a belief that one is in this particular qualitative state. Such qualitative beliefs are said to have connections with our perceptual beliefs about the world and, through these beliefs, with actions. "While it may be of the essence of qualitative states that they are 'ineffable' in the sense that one cannot say in general terms, or at any rate in general terms that do not include names of qualitative states, what it is for a person to be in a particular qualitative state, this does not prevent us," Shoemaker contends, "from giving a functional account of what it is for a state to be a qualitative state, and of what the identity conditions for qualitative states are."[21] On this view of phenomenal qualities, they are not "mental" in any significant sense. For both Sellars and Shoemaker, they are qualities of brain states or events. They are private in the sense that they give rise to "introspective awareness," or what Shoemaker calls qualitative beliefs, which cannot be shared. Others cannot have this kind of "awareness" of the phenomenal qualities of one's own brain states, for one's brain states cannot occasion qualitative beliefs in another in this manner. If another person were to perceive the brain states involved in my somatic sensations and sensory perceptions, this person would have his or her own phenomenal qualities in doing so but would not perceive the phenomenal qualities involved in my bodily sensations and sensory perceptions. Nor would I recognize them if I were to gain visual or other sensory access to my own brain states. Nevertheless, Shoemaker hopes that his account does not commit him "to anything which a clear headed opponent of 'private objects,' or of 'private language,' should find objectionable."[22] He also thinks that although we cannot eliminate names of such qualities, we can give an account of their identity conditions and of what they are without using any "mental" concepts. This sounds as if he would identify the so-called phenomenal qualities with properties that would be acknowledged in a scientific account of the brain. However, this would be a theoretical identification, not one based on perceptual recognition.

So perhaps the contention is that the phenomenal qualities have been considered mental because they are the causal ground of what Shoemaker calls "qualitative beliefs" (which are beliefs to the effect that one is in a certain qualitative state) or because they are "internal" representations or pertain to brain states that are representations. That is, according to the functionalist theory, they are "mental" only in that they have a certain causal role. Being mental in this sense is not an ontological status. Whatever the reason for calling these qualities "mental," both Shoemaker and Sellars want to show that there is nothing mental that cannot be accounted for in physicalistic language.

In any case, phenomenal qualities are very peculiar qualities. There is a long standing problem about whether a distinction can be drawn between the *existence* of such qualities or qualitative states and their *presence to one*. Sellars's and Shoemaker's way of talking about them assumes that they are properties exemplified in brain states and events that have certain causal roles. Shoemaker talks about "awareness" of such qualitative states in terms of the qualitative beliefs to which they give rise. Regardless of whether such a qualitative state can exist without giving rise to a corresponding qualitative belief, Shoemaker assumes that a distinction can be drawn between the existence of such a qualitative state and the qualitative belief to which it gives rise. Therefore, he would say that there is a difference between the existence of a qualitative state and its presence to its owner.

This distinction is important to his account of "presence to" or "introspective awareness of" in terms of a qualitative belief that can be analyzed in terms of a causal role of brain states in a complex system. In fact, it seems that any physicalistic functionalist theory of the mental must locate phenomenal qualities in the brain or some bodily state or process. The fact that such a theory has no other options is one of the weakest and most vulnerable points of physicalistic functionalism.

For a surface to appear yellow to a person is not a qualitative belief, for it is not a belief at all. It is not even a "taking." It is something more primitive. Yellow is visually present to one whether one believes or takes anything to be yellow or even takes anything to appear to be yellow. Perhaps Shoemaker's qualitative belief is just the belief that a yellow expanse is visually present. If so, what does one believe when one believes that a yellow expanse is visually present? If there is the belief "A yellow expanse is now visually present to me," is it not possible for a yellow expanse to be visually present to me? And is not a yellow expanse's being visually present to me different from its existence? Indeed, may not a yellow expanse be visually present to me without existing at all? Something is wrong when we analyze the sentence "A yellow expanse is visually present to me" as "Something is a yellow expanse and it is visually present to me." We can refer to things with semantic presence as well as to existent things. If this were not so, we could not refer to fictional characters, events, and places.

The absurdity of assigning the so-called phenomenal qualities an existential status in brain states of the perceiver is greater than the absurdity of creating the realm of sense impressions and images as existing entities to exemplify them. It seems far more plausible to hold that some physical objects are yellow in their visual presence to us than to assign the quality yellow to our brain states, even if this should force us to acknowledge that yellow and other such qualities were exemplified in perceived physical objects in their existence.

It seems that every effort to reduce the category of semantic presence in sensory experience to the factual categories of existence and exemplification results in absurdities. This is a compelling argument against such reductive theories. The category of semantic presence seems indispensable for the intelligibility of sense experience.

If we must acknowledge an inherent structure of meaning in sense experience, then the major reason has been removed for denying structures of meaning in other kinds of experience and in thoughts, acts, lives, stories, works of art, or expressions of any kind, for the admission of meaning as irreducible to existence and factuality at any point shatters the naturalistic world-view.

Functional Theory of Propositional Attitudes

Some who admit that there may be a stubborn problem about phenomenal qualities seem convinced that a satisfactory functionalist theory of propositional attitudes as "internal" representations is possible and that in time we may find a more satisfactory way of accounting for qualia. But how satisfactory is the functionalist theory of representations and the representational theory of propositional attitudes?

According to the representational theory of language, tokens of certain types of sounds and ink marks represent items and features of the world. But what is it for such sounds or ink marks to *represent* items and features of the world? The obvious thing to say seems to be that they call to the listener's or reader's mind the items and features in question; that is, perception of tokens of certain types of sounds and ink marks present to the perceiver (in a uniform way) items and features other than the linguistic tokens and their features. Thus the tokens of linguistic types, in their perceptual presence to one, are said to stand for or to represent certain perceptually absent items and features that may or may not obtain in the world. On this approach, philosophy of language has to include philosophy of mind.

The representational theory of propositional attitudes, however, tries to understand the mental after the model of the representational theory of language. There is obviously a problem here. If the representational theory of language presupposes the mental in the form of things being immediately *present to* or mediately (representationally) *present to* people, would not a representational theory of the mental in terms of an "internal" language presuppose the mental at a still more basic level? The fundamental challenge to any naturalistic theory of language and meaning is to show how this regress can be blocked.

Those who believe that meaning is solely a matter of synonymy of linguistic expressions, denotation of words, and truth conditions of sen-

tences and that these matters can be explicated indepedently of mentalistic language will try to explicate our mental talk about things being
immediately and mediately present to people in terms of the semantics
of an "internal" language—a natural language the tokens of which are
brain states and episodes. But if these brain states and episodes are
typed according to their semantic and inferential roles, can their semantic and inferential roles be reduced to, or explicated in terms of,
their causal roles in a physical system consisting of sensory inputs, tokens of other "internal representations," and behavioral output?

Fodor accepts an irreducible distinction between the semantic/infer-
ential and causal roles of internal representations and settles for a partial isomorphism between the two. Some but not all of the inferential
patterns of internal representations, he says, are matched in their
causal patterns. In his account of propositional attitudes,[23] Fodor accepts propositions and their logical relations. But he seems to think that
the causality of the mind is restricted to the factual structure of the
organism. He regards the parallels between the mind and the electronic computer and between psychology and artificial intelligence as
nearly complete.

Those who accept this position have a problem, as Fodor recognizes,
about how a state of the organism is connected to a proposition to form
a particular propositional attitude and how the proposition is related to
that which it is about. It does not make sense to talk about the organism's grasping the proposition in an epistemic sense as some have
talked about a mind's apprehending a proposition; nor is it easy to
make sense of how the proprosition represents a fact or a state of affairs. If we acknowledged *semantic presence to* one or *semantic presence in*
psychological states and acts, we could regard a proposition as a fact or
state of affairs semantically present in a psychological state or act of
someone. On this view, a propositional attitude would be just such a
psychological state or act with a fact or state of affairs (not a proposition) as its semantic content.

So, if we admit propositional attitudes (conceived in this manner)
and facts or states of affairs in our ontology, there is no need to admit
propositions also. We can abstract the semantic contents of psychological states and acts, and talk about them as concepts and propositions—
that is, as properties and facts in their semantic rather than existential
status. But this does not warrant existence claims for concepts and
propositions, which would be to take concepts and propositions as independent objects of conceptual and propositional attitudes rather than
as internal, constitutive aspects of the attitudes themselves.

But what about such conceptual and propositional attitudes with
their inherent structures of meaning? Can they be analyzed and ex-

plained in terms of the existential and factual constitution of organisms and their causal interactions with their existential environment? This is the program of materialistic functionalists in the philosophy of mind.

Sellars, as previously recounted, contends that for a symbol or representational state to represent an object *O* is for the symbol or representational state to be part of a representational system of an organism in which it is connected with other features of the system (including actions) in such a way that it is "the focal point of a strategy for finding *O*."[24] The purpose of such an analysis is to show, for ontological purposes, that intentionalistic concepts can be eliminated in favor of purely existential and factual concepts. But "focal point," "strategy," and "finding" are intentionalistic concepts. How can they be analyzed out? Sellars does not tell us. Until they are, his program is left incomplete; and the incompleteness suggests that intentionalistic concepts are likely to be smuggled in at some point in every effort to naturalize meaning and the mental.

Functional Language

Even the concepts of causal *role* and *functional* system are suspect for a materialistic ontology. The important question for our purposes is whether functional language in philosophy of mind can be philosophically explicated without imputing something ontologically significant to the constitution of the individuals involved. Materialistic functionalists hold, as we have observed, that psychological concepts are used to delineate functional roles of some physical states or episodes (or types and patterns of such) in a causal structure. The functional roles, they contend, consist of a network of interconnected causal relationships, which can be instantiated in only a physical structure.

Contrary to the traditional view that a material substance is such by virtue of having only physical properties, the position taken here is that a material substance is an organization of energy or causal power in a purely existential and factual way; that is, it is an organization of energy into an existent that has only exemplified properties and relations; and, if it contains any elements or parts, they too are existents that only exemplify properties and relations.

It should be kept in mind that exemplification is a mode of existence; it is the way properties and relations exist. In the logical schema, "There is_1 an x such that x is_2 F," "is_1" indicates existence, and "is_2" indicates exemplification. This is the basic sentence form for reporting and describing material substances. The forms "Fx" and "$F(x,y)$" indicate factual structures, that is, the exemplification of a property by an existent and the exemplification of a relation by a set of existents, respectively. So material substances, categorially speaking, have only existential and factual structures. Energy transfers and transformations within and between material substances alter only their existential and factual constitutions.

There is, of course, a limitation on the kind of properties material substances can have. They cannot have any properties that would involve or generate internal relations or any form of interiority that would be incompatible with extensionalism. If we exclude natural necessity (as the strict empiricist is wont to do), objective essences, causation, and natural laws (in any full-blooded sense) are excluded also. One may well ask whether there are any material substances in this strict sense. Liberal materialists, however, would make room for natural kinds, materialistic causation, and natural laws, but they would tolerate no other mode of constitution other than existential, factual, and causal (in the materialistic sense).

Hilary Putnam at one time construed functionalism as neutral with regard to the materialist/nonmaterialist controversy.[25] Psychological concepts, according to him, delineate simply functional roles in a causal structure without regard to the ontological nature of the bearers of the roles. Just as a computer might be made of different kinds of material, so a psychological being might be made of material stuff and be a material thing or be made of soul-stuff and be a soul. It would make no difference to us as human beings which was the case, he insists, as long as the functional organization described in psychological theory (and presumably in sociological theory) remained the same.

It is no doubt true that it does not matter what kind of material a computer is made of as long as it makes possible and sustains the relevant functional structure as well as any of the alternatives. But surely there is a category mistake in pushing the analogy to the level of material stuff and soul-stuff. What could the terms "soul" and "soul-stuff" mean if psychological language were logically independent of such concepts? If the autonomy of the mental could be established in the sense Putnam has in mind, these terms would be emptied of all their meaning. There would be no candidates for the bearers of the roles in the functional structure described in psychological language but physical entities, states, and processes (or types and patterns of these). Thus his position collapses into materialism after all.

Let us take a look at materialistic functionalism in general. The crux of the matter is whether the functional organization that is reported and described in biological, psychological, and personalistic language can be shown to involve nothing ontological other than existential, factual, and materialistic causal structures (causal structures that engage only existential and factual dimensions of things).

To call something an engine or a carburetor is to attribute to it a functional organization. No one is likely to question the claim that such functional talk shows nothing about the real structure of the thing in question but what could be stated in a set of causal statements about material entities, states, and processes (or types and patterns of these). But even here an explanatory account of the functional structure, with its underlying materialistic causal relationships, would raise questions about the involvement of other categories in the wider context required for its intelligibility.

To call something a computer or word processor is far more difficult for the materialist. Even reports and descriptions of the functional structure, without getting into an explanatory account of why it is as it is, involve categories that are problematic for the materialist. The functional organization itself requires relationships between a conceptual, logical structure and a physical, causal structure. With just the physical entities, states, and processes, there would be no *computing* or *word processing*.

Psychological and personalistic reports and descriptions present yet another magnitude of difficulty for the materialistic functionalist. Here the conceptual, logical, and other apparently non-materialistic structures seem to be engaged directly in the causal processes within the individuals being described.

Materialistic functionalists must not only show that psychological and personalistic talk is functionalistic; they must show that the functionalistic talk itself has no special ontological significance. On the face of it, functionalistic talk is a form of value discourse. Whatever has a functional organization may be spoken of as well formed or malformed, as well functioning or malfunctioning. A carburetor may have a good or a faulty design; it may be in good condition or defective; it may work well, poorly, or not at all. The heart is a pump. To think of it as such is to think of it in terms of its function. The function provides us with the ground for talking about it as well formed or deformed, as functioning well or poorly, and so forth. An office is defined in terms of its function—the duties of the office. We may talk about whether the office is well organized for the fulfillment of its function, or whether it has a structural problem. We may speak of the office holder as well suited for the office and doing well in it, or as ill suited for it and performing poorly in it. Functional concepts in general locate their objects, not in terms of the properties or parts that exist in them, but in terms of what the objects exist and are structured to do. This is what the materialistic functionalist speaks of as the objects' roles.

Functions and roles are formulated in imperative sentences; they are things to be, to become, or to do. Artifacts are typically thought of under functional concepts. We think of them in terms of what they were designed and made to do. The carburetor was made to regulate the injection of fuel into the internal combustion engine. This was something the engine "needed," for otherwise the engine could not perform its function. The function of the engine is to provide the power to run something else—a lawn mower, a sawmill, a car, and so forth. And these have their functions in terms of human activities and values.

All of this is value discourse. It will be helpful to summarize the salient points of the realistic theory of value indicated in Chapter 2 and developed in the earlier books of this trilogy.[26] "*X is good*" can be analyzed into an "ought" judgment and a predicative statement in this manner: "*X* is good" means that for some property (or complex of properties) F, X ought to be F and X is F.[27] In other words, "*X* is good" means X is more or less the way it ought to be. If there is no way X ought to be, then whatever way it is (whatever properties it exemplifies), it is neither good nor bad. In other words, value "properties" are not first-order properties that can be exemplified by something. We talk about the good-making properties of things. We say of something that it would be good if it had certain properties; or that it is good in that it has certain features. We think of value "properties" as supervenient on factual properties, or value truths as supervenient on factual truths. All of these considerations support the claim that what we assert with a predicative value sentence is a combination of what we report with an "ought" sentence and a factual or existential statement. So the "ought" sentence is more basic than the predicative value sentence. Failure to recognize this fact sets philosophers off on hopeless searches for the meaning of value predicates. And failure in these searches usually results in some form of value nominalism or psychologism.

The "ought" judgment cannot be forced into an existential or predicative form. The basic "ought" forms are taken to be (1) If X is F, then X (or Y) ought to be G, and (2) If X is F, then there ought to be a y that would be G. In both (1) and (2) "ought" goes with the "If . . . then . . ." connective, not with the consequent. The "If . . . then . . . ought . . .," like the "If . . . then . . ." of contrary-to-fact conditionals, are understood to indicate a real connection, a normative requirement, which holds between the fact indicated by the antecedent and the fact enjoined in the consequent. The presence of one property (or complex of properties) in an individual may normatively require the presence of some other property (or complex of properties) in that individual or others; the existence of an individual or a set of individuals in a context, or the organization of a set of individuals, may normatively require the existence of other individuals.

In other words, normativity, what we locate by the word "ought," seems to be a basic structural feature of the world somewhat in the manner of existence, factuality, and natural necessity. It has to do with the constitution of things—with the way in which properties, things, and facts are connected; but it is none of these. Even G. E. Moore, who recognized the uniqueness of the concept of good, tried to force value into the property category, but as a peculiar property that is not exemplified by a particular in a way that constitutes a fact. Nonetheless he disturbed the view that value is a property and opened the way for it to be considered something just as basic but different from property, exemplification, existence, or fact.

The imperative sentence also has a close kinship with the "ought" sentence. Admittedly it has a more restricted use and a different force in communication, but the logical ties between the two forms are clear. An imperative premise in an argument can be replaced with an "ought" sentence without affecting the conclusion; and vice versa. The question "Why?" asked of an imperative admits of the same kind of an answer as it does when asked of an "ought" judgment. In many contexts, an "ought" judgment entails an imperative. In spite of the limitations of the grammatical forms of the imperative sentence, we may express a philosophical truth by saying that an "ought" sentence is an enriched imperative sentence; it reports the imperative (the requirement) that the imperative sentence gives and says of it, without giving them, that there are objective grounds or reasons for what is enjoined in the imperative. In other words, the "ought" judgment says that there is a context (facts, values, essences, necessities, or whatever) that normatively requires that which is enjoined in the judgment. The corresponding imperative sentence simply gives the imperativeness of that which is enjoined without claiming that there are objective grounds or reasons for it. What is semantically presented in imperative sentences, along with the claim of an objective ground, can be presented in corresponding "ought" sentences. To be sure, the full force of the imperative sentence would not be preserved in many cases. But this is not what we are concerned with at this point.

Without some acceptable account of how we have epistemic access to inherent normative structures, we would have to reject the reality of such a dimension of things, for in the end we could not make sense of our talk about these structures in a way that would support their reality as distinct from the existential and factual constitution of things. Fortunately we are not in such a predicament. There are compelling rea-

sons, as we shall see in Chapter 5, for believing that affective and conative experiences, which provide experiential grounding for value
language (including value predicates and deontic concepts), have a semantic and logical structure and are knowledge-yielding under critical
assessment.

Function concepts, then, are value concepts. To attribute a functional organization to something is to attribute a normative structure to
it. The normative structure we attribute to artifacts in function discourse about them is regarded as not embedded in their internal causal
dynamics. We typically regard only the existential and factual structures of the things to be so involved. In the computer, human beings
have preestablished a harmony between the logical processes and the
materialistic causal processes of the hardware. So it seems acceptable to
say that nothing happens internally within the computer but by materialistic causation. But the situation is different in biology. The functional organization of the organism seems to be directly involved in its
internal causal dynamics. The natural causal processes that produced
the organism also generated and work to sustain its functional organization.

As long as we think of these causal processes in materialistic terms
(as engaging only existential and factual structures) as does Darwinian
evolutionary theory, we are compelled to try to work out a way of understanding the alleged functional organization that will be compatible
with our assumptions. And the conclusion, for anyone in the grip of
these assumptions, is likely to be that the alleged functional organization is only the complex pattern of interconnected materialistic causal
relationships in the organism and its environment that can be discovered scientifically. In other words, from within the materialistic perspective, one has to hold that the "functional organization" of the organism really is not a normative structure after all; that our functional
discourse, with its value implications, is simply a manner of speech
from a practical perspective, with no ontological significance.

Darwin's theory of evolution was not simply an empirical hypothesis
subject to confirmation or refutation by scientific data. It was an effort
to bring biology within the materialistic metaphysics of modern science.
Specifically, it was an effort to eliminate value concepts from the conceptual system in terms of which biological structure was described and
explained. The bias of modern science, and of modern thought in general, against a descriptive/explanatory use of value concepts is a long
story; but, as indicated in Chapter 1, the heart of the matter is the
governing interest in knowing and understanding things in a way that
would, in principle, give us manipulatory power over them. This gen-

erated a dependency in science on sensory perception and thought grounded in sensory experience; and in time this was developed into an empiricist theory of knowledge and a materialistic metaphysics. The descriptive use of language came to be restricted, by definition, to existential and factual concepts. But to the extent we take functional talk seriously, to the extent we take it to be genuinely descriptive (not just ascriptive), we have to take the normative structure of the organism seriously. And if value realism of the kind indicated above is true, there is no reason not to take functional concepts seriously as part of our descriptive, explanatory language. Perhaps it is time for modern science, especially in the biological, behavioral, and social areas, to liberate itself from the epistemic and conceptual restraints of its constitutive interest in gaining mastery over nature. Certainly it is time for philosophy to challenge this cultural bias of modern science.

So genuine, or non-reductive, functionalism in biology is anti-materialistic, for, ontologically speaking, functionalism means that an organism has a normative structure. An organism is not only existentially and factually constituted; there are components, properties, and structure it ought to have and there are processes that ought to be going on in it. In addition to its existential content, it has an inexistential, normative content. This would be so even if it were existentially and factually the way it ought to be. Furthermore, if we admit the reality of the normative interiority of the organism, there is no longer any reason for rejecting teleological causality within its inner dynamics. The causal processes within the organism work to realize and to sustain its normative structures and functions. Why not accept that the normative requirements themselves, together with the existential and factual constitution of the organism, are engaged in the causal processes? That is what teleological causality involves.[28] All of this indicates that a biological organism is not a material substance—that it is not fully describable in the categories of existence and factuality.

The Irreducibility of the Language of Meaning

If this analysis of functionalism in biology is correct, then functionalism in psychology will not achieve the intended naturalistic reduction of the mental. Even if functionalists were successful in their reductive analysis of meaning and the mental, functionalism would leave us with the category of normativity and its dependent value "properties" as well as the categories of existence and factuality. But even with a basic language that includes value concepts as well as those of existence and factuality (that is, one that allows talk about *functions* in an irreducible sense), the language of meaning and the mental stubbornly resists functionalistic analysis. Indeed, there is a wider conviction in the philosophical community that naturalistic reduction of the language of meaning and the mental is even more problematic, if anything, than the naturalistic reduction of the language of normativity and value. But if the category of normativity has to be acknowledged, the compelling reason for the reductive analysis of meaning and the mental is lost.

Functions, as contended previously, are normative in structure. "X has the function F" does not mean that F is something that X does. It is not the case that, if you know the causal laws (in the scientific sense) under which a functional state is subsumed, you know everything there is to know about its function. "X has the function F" means that F is something *for X to do*. When X has the function F, X may do F well, poorly, or not at all. But what we are interested in at this point is this: When a brain state or episode has a function in a representational system, what is its function? What is it *to do*?

Functionalists of the Sellars school would say that the function of a brain state in a representational system is to cause certain other brain states or behaviors of the organism that have functions of their own in a strategy of the organism for finding a particular object or objects of a certain kind. But, as previously indicated, "strategy" and "finding" are intentionalistic concepts. A strategy is not a causal system that produces a certain result. If we say that a plant has a strategy for exposing its leaves to the sun or for finding water and nutrients, we know that we are speaking metaphorically. If we say that the human eye has a strategy for keeping whatever we are looking at in focus, that too is metaphorical. No term can have only a metaphorical use, for a metaphor is built on and presupposes a literal use of the term. A strategy is a plan for accomplishing some goal. To have a strategy, in the literal sense, is to have both an end and a way of attaining it *in mind*. And when the end in mind is *to find* a certain object, the finding involves *recognizing* the object as the one being sought. We may speak about the plant's finding the sun light by growing tall and turning toward the sun and about its finding water and nutrients by extending its roots in the direction of the more moist and richer soil, but this, too, is metaphorical. However complex and layered and interlocked such causal structures may become, so long as they engage only existential and factual states, it seems that talk about them in terms of "strategies," "ends," "finding," and the like will remain metaphorical.

Regardless of how detailed and complete we may be in describing a human activity in terms of naturalistically conceived sensory inputs, brain states, behavioral outputs, and their causal structure, it would always be meaningful to ask: But does he or she have an end and a way of achieving it *in mind?* And regardless of how successful we might be in giving such a naturalistic description of one engaged in looking for and finding an object, let us say a screwdriver, it would always be meaningful to ask: But was he or she literally *looking for a screwdriver?* And did this person literally *recognize* the object he or she picked up *as a screwdriver?* We ask these questions of the behavior of a programmed robot. And we would have to ask them with the same force of human behavior as conceived and described in naturalistic terms by the materialistic functionalist. The meaningfulness of these recurring questions indicates that there is no logical contradiction in accepting any such naturalistic description of an organism and denying that "it" was literally *looking for a screwdriver* and that "it" literally *recognized* the object "it" picked up *as a screwdriver*.

We talk not only about human beings doing such things as looking for and finding screwdrivers, but about their looking for the truth, searching for knowledge, constructing theories, writing books, creating art works, defining and living lives for themselves, building institutions and nations, engaging in extensive cooperative endeavors across generations, and so on. It boggles the mind to think of what a materialistic functionalist reduction of all our talk about the human scene would be like. It would certainly put a heavy burden on the physical constitution and the naturalistic causal laws of the universe. However difficult it would be to conceive of such a universe, we would have to ask of it whether there was *literally* any meaning, any knowledge, or any mistakes in it; whether there were *literally* any functions, any value, any purpose, any intelligence, any freedom in such a world; whether human beings literally engaged in undertakings, performed actions, and lived lives with more or less integrity; whether human beings were *literally* under rational and moral imperatives; and whether some human beings were *literally* rational, some irrational, some moral, and some evil; and so forth.

Materialistic functionalism in philosophy of mind tries to replace our literal meaning of our basic semantic and mental terms with metaphorical uses of them. This is highly suspect in and of itself. It makes the metaphorical uses of these terms problematic. If materialistic functionalism is correct, all animals, including human beings, are complex, natural robots. Nothing is literally *present to* them; they have nothing literally *in mind*. It makes sense to ask of some things whether they are literally psychological beings or robots. And it makes the same sense to ask of anything conceived and described in the canonical language of materialistic functionalism whether it is literally a psychological being.

With the literal meaning of our psychological language replaced with the metaphorical meaning of the materialistic functionalist, our higher level talk about psychological states and acts and language becomes highly problematic and suspect. Logical predicates apply only to things with a meaning dimension or to things that are incomplete if they do not have a meaning dimension, such as sentence-forms with space markers for words or component sentences. If our semantic talk about psychological states and acts have only the metaphorical meaning acknowledged by the materialistic functionalist, what would it mean to say that a belief was *self-contradictory* or that a set of beliefs were *logically inconsistent*? What would it mean to say that one belief *presupposed* another or that one thought *logically followed from* another? Would we not have to look for a plausible metaphorical reconstruction of logical language? What would such a reconstruction look like? Would not such reconstructions at each higher level become more contorted and less believable? It does not seem to make sense to talk about a logical inconsistency or necessity in a purely physicalistic universe, however complex its causal structure might be. Could any plausible reconstruction preserve the sense of logical talk in such a world?

Rational appraisal language, including moral discourse, is especially problematic for materialistic functionalists. It generates for them what I have called "the antinomy of the mental."[29] The appraisal of human behavior as rational or irrational, moral or immoral, correct or mistaken, right or wrong, justified or unjustified, or the like seems to be inappropriate when behavior is described and explained in scientific factual and causal terms. Each of these ways of talking seems to crowd out the other. As people come to understand and to think about the happenings in nature in scientific terms, they stop looking for justifications as they did when they thought of such events as *acts* of God. It seems totally unacceptable to most people in our scientific culture to think of a drought, an earthquake, or an epidemic of AIDS among homosexuals as punishment, for the punishment thesis explains in terms of justifying reasons, which are relevant only to acts—to events with an identity and unity constituted by an intention, an inherent structure of meaning. And the same process seems to be at work as we think about and try to understand human behavior in scientific categories.

Some claim that the logical tension between the two teams of concepts is apparent only; that the two ways of talking about human behavior are really compatible and can be shown to be when properly understood. Yet it seems that even in the last analysis rational appraisal language and the descriptive/explanatory language of science cannot be applied consistently to the same subject matter, for they presuppose

different and conflicting answers to questions about the categorial nature of the subject matter, especially about the nature of the causality
involved.[30] This is the old problem of freedom versus determinism. It is
not an argument about whether human acts are caused or uncaused; it
is a dispute about the nature of the causality involved. It is not a dispute about whether causality in human behavior involves only the existential and factual domain or normative requirements as well. That is
an important issue, but the central question here is whether facts and
normative requirements in their *semantic presence* have a part in the
causal dynamics of human behavior. Defenders of the freedom thesis
believe that human behavior is not determined by the existential and
factual conditions alone; not even by the existential and factual and the
normative, but primarily by the facts, values, and embodied structures
of meaning that are semantically present to one in experiences,
thoughts, and intentions that are subject to correction by critical review.
Reduction of the language of meaning and the mental to the categories
of existence and factuality seems to leave rational appraisal language
without any appropriate subject matter; but if this is so, the scientific
enterprise itself is impossible. In other words, the extension of the de-
scriptive/explanatory conceptual system of science to human thought
and behavior leaves no room for scientific inquiry. This is the antinomy. If the two teams of concepts—scientific and rational appraisal
languages—do presuppose different kinds of causal structures so that
they cannot be consistently applied to the same subject matter, then
there is no possible solution to the antinomy that will save naturalism.
Any reductionistic analysis of rational appraisal language that would
make it applicable to a subject matter with only existential and factual
structures would be shown by this fact to be mistaken.

And what sense can materialistic functionalists make of our talk
about what a story means as distinct from what its words and sentences
mean? What sense can they make of discourse about meaningful and
meaningless experiences and activities? The complaint of the person in
depression that nothing is meaningful any more? Questions about the
meaning of life, art, and history? Discussions about the meaning of our
humanly created environment? Or even religious claims about the
meaning of the natural world? They are likely to dismiss all of this as
having nothing to do with semantics and thus as irrelevant to their
concerns. But a theory that integrates the whole realm of the language
meaning and explains the connectedness may be superior to one that
divides it into unrelated parts connected only by ambiguous language.

Materialistic functionalists in the philosophy of mind and language
have proven to be much more sophisticated than the classical empiri-

cists with their sense impressions and images. But meaning seems to elude them in much the same way as it eluded the earlier representationalists. Perhaps the trouble lies in representationalism itself.

Conclusion

Representationalism, as we observed early in this discussion, is grounded in an observational approach to language and meaning as items and features located in the world of objects. Something perceived is taken to mean something else. According to the theory of perception one holds, the objects are taken to be phenomenalistic or physicalistic. To Hume, what was perceived was a sense impression or an image; to materialists, it is something physical. The perceived object is said to represent or to stand for something else. From within this approach, there is no alternative; we must try to locate meaning in the realm of the objects of sensory awareness and their relationships. And not being able to find it there, we conclude that meaning cannot be what it seems to be; and so we construct an account of it in terms of what can be found there, even if, in our reconstruction, we can give the language of meaning only a metaphorical meaning that collapses into meaninglessness.

The persistent way in which meaning eludes the reconstructions of the naturalist (whether in the phenomenalistic or physicalistic mode), as indicated by the recurring meaning question and the troubles generated for logical, rational appraisal, and moral language, should be sufficient reason in itself to abandon the project. But the faith of the naturalist, so deeply rooted in our modern culture, dies hard.

From within the humanistic approach, we do not try to locate meaning among the objects of sensory awareness, for we are constituted by and live within a sea of meaning. We are in touch with meaning through our existence, our living, and our social relationships— through our self-knowledge and person and expression perception. We take some states, acts, subjects, and objects to have their unity and identity in terms of an inherent structure of meaning. It is not that one thing with a factual unity and identity of its own represents or has some complex causal relationship to something else. Such states, acts, subjects, and objects have an "interior" structure constituted by semantic intentionality. Experiences, memories, thoughts, acts, expressions, persons, lives, stories, theories, institutions, societies, and so forth cannot be analyzed into factually constituted elements and their external relations as the representative theory of meaning purports to do. Meaning is an essential and irreducible dimension of such entities. It is as basic as existence, factuality, and causality. It is categorial.

The fact that from within the humanistic approach we can make so much better sense of our language of meaning, value, personhood, and the social and cultural world should be sufficient grounds to validate the humanistic perspective. Furthermore, as we will see later, there are appropriate epistemological foundations for the humanistic approach; and, therefore, the supposed epistemological necessity for a naturalistic reconstruction of the language of meaning is unfounded.

CHAPTER 4

Knowledge and Objectivity

We have characterized psychological states and acts as discrete, with their identity and unity constituted by an inherent structure of meaning. They are defined by a semantic content and a grammatical or logical form. Whether a psychological state or act is a belief, a perplexity, a desire, an intention, or whatever, is a matter of logical form. Such a structure of meaning requires embodiment, but its particular body (its specific physical dimension) is not essential to its identity. We do not have to include a description of the physical dimension of a thought or a statement in order to identify it. We do have to report or describe its semantic content and logical form. These are not independent of each other. In language, the grammar of an expression enters into the determination of its meaning. Consider a declarative sentence and its correlative interrogative: "It is snowing." and "Is it snowing?" Or consider the two ways one may read the headline "THE DEMOCRATS ARE REVOLTING," according to whether one takes "revolting" to be part of the verb or an adjective. The same is true with regard to psychological states and acts. Form and content are locked together; both are essential to the unity and identity of the state or act.

Behavioral Knowledge

The problem for this chapter is how psychological states and acts yield (or constitute) knowledge. It seems clear that even if some such states or occurrences could "come up" alone in a categorially alien environment, which seems impossible, no isolated psychological state or occurrence could constitute knowledge. Indeed, no such isolated state or occurrence could constitute a truth-claim; it could not take what was semantically present in itself to be, to ought to be, to be possible, or to be anything. The isolated state or occurrence could not have the logical form of an assertion in any modality. In other words, taking, thinking, or believing—the making of a truth-claim in any form or mode—requires an integrated semantic system. All such states or acts are systemic; the whole system is implicated in each.

Perhaps, in simple psychological systems, all instances of semantic presence are instances of taking what is semantically present to be (perception) or taking it as something to be or to be done (desire). But even such takings do not stand alone; they are functions of a system of semantic states and acts. Indeed, nothing is a semantic *act* if it just happens as an effect of "blind" causes; a semantic act is generated in and by a semantic system. If a simple physical occurrence such as an artificially induced passage of an electric current through a segment of brain tissue should occasion a psychological occurrence, it would be because it involved the physical base of a psychological system and activated that system. Even if such an occurrence had a semantic content and the logical form of taking X to exist or to be F, it would not have the requisite etiology to be a truth-claim. Truth-claims don't just occur; they are made. They are acts; and only an integrated psychological system can act in the appropriate way.

Simple psychological systems that can generate an act that takes something to be, or that takes something to be of a certain kind (or takes something as something to be or to be done), may not be capable of any critical assessment of such takings. It takes a more sophisticated system to make the distinction between what seems to be and what is. Psychologically, we do not progress, at the most basic level, from appearings to takings or assertings, but rather from takings and assertings to appearings and seemings. The distinction requires reflective critical powers. But simple takings and assertings do not occur singly; they have to be integrated with other takings or beliefs. Integration at lower levels, however, is not the product of reflection and criticism; it is the direct result of the inner dynamics of the normative teleological structure of the system.

If the most basic psychological states or acts are in the form of perception or desire (or some prototype of such), they must be systemic; that is, they must occur within some form of a semantic system. And if this is so, their identity and unity as individual perceptions or desires are not as self-contained atoms; they partake of the system in which they occur. It would seem, then, that atomistic anlysis and extensionality (atomic elements with only external relations) have a very limited place in psychology. Even protoperceptions, protodesires, protofeelings, protoemotions, and protoactions are holistic in that they are not the sum of their elements or parts and they do not stand only in extensional relations to other psychological states and acts. They are, both in their identity and existence, system-bound.

Regardless of what may be true about the internality and systemic character of psychological states and episodes, certainly only holistic psychological systems can be knowledge-yielding. No single psychological state or occurrence as such could be an instance of knowledge. In their most primitive form, psychological states and occurrences do not seem to differentiate explicitly between simple semantic presence and existential presence. A psychological occurrence may give rise to a response to its content as *existent*. A newly hatched chicken "sees" feed at its feet and pecks at it. A dog "picks up" the scent of a rabbit and begins the chase; the rabbit "hears" the bark of the dog and flees. Although most such "takings" are correct, they do not constitute *knowledge* in the human sense. They are, however, a forerunner of knowledge. We may speak of them as proto- or behavioral knowledge.

"Stimulus/response" psychology has its greatest plausibility at this level. It thinks of the causality involved in purely naturalistic terms. The physiology of the protoperception is thought of as a "mechanical" switch that turns on the motor reaction. The process is taken to be of the same order as many other physiological responses to neural impulses in the body. The semantic intentionality of the protoperception is regarded as entirely superfluous, if present at all, as far as the causal account is concerned. This, of course, assumes that there is no semantic intentionality involved in the physiological *responses to* neural "signals" in the autonomic nervous system. But even talk about "signals" and "switches" presupposes semantic intentionality. A signal is a bearer of *information*. And a switch is not simply a link in a naturalistic causal chain; it is a link that "redirects" a causal chain for a *purpose*. Where there are no *ends*, there are no switches.

The important question here, for our purpose, is whether normativity can provide the ends without semantic intentionality. (Of course stimulus/response psychologists are not likely to acknowledge normative structures in organisms in this sense.) Normative states, by their constitution, involve ends (something that ought to be or the way something ought to be), but could the inherent ends of normative states be causally operative without "information," a semantic factor? And even if they could, would it be possible for purely factual changes to redirect a teleological process without a semantic factor?

Perhaps a change in the factual situation would be reflected in what was normatively required. Suppose that a situation S_1, in which X was required to be F, changed into situation S_2; and that in S_2, X was required to be G rather than F. If so, would "information," in a semantic sense, be required to redirect the teleological process to the new end? Must events and facts that give rise to changes in a process that keep it moving toward its normative end be considered as "signals" and thus as "information"-bearing? We talk this way in genetics about biological systems and in engineering about automated physical systems. Is this simply a manner of speaking? Assuming that our semantic talk about "signals" and "information" with regard to automated physical systems is only metaphorical, is it likewise metaphorical with regard to genetics? In terms of the inner dynamics of an airconditioning system, the thermometer, speaking literally, provides no *signals* or *information* to the system. Changes in the thermometer are only "mechanical" causal factors, for there is no inherent normative structure that defines the process. But the situation seems to be different with an organism, modern science and naturalistic philosophy not withstanding. There seem to be inherent normative teleological processes involved in the development and ongoing functioning of organisms. Is "information"-talk only a manner of speaking here also?

Even if we hold that "information"-talk is uneliminable for the subject matter of biology, we still have the problem about whether it has a literal or only an analogical meaning. (We may assume that if "information"-talk in biology were metaphorical, it would be eliminable.) Perhaps there is something that is to purely normative teleological processes what information and "reasons" are to semantic teleological processes, but, not having developed a distinctive vocabulary for it, we extend our "information"- and "reasons"-talk from the psychological realm to biological organisms and even to contrived physical systems. If this is so, perhaps our "signals" and "information" language is *analogical* with regard to organisms but only *metaphorical* with regard to mechanical systems.[1]

Regardless of the position we take on these issues about normative teleological processes, a semantic teleological process involves a semantic outreach that extends the teleological process beyond, and distinguishes it from, the simpler normative teleological process.

In any case, talk about "switches" makes sense only in the realm of artifacts where "mechanistic" causal chains are redirected to externally imposed ends. In situations where "ends," whether conceived in terms of semantic intentionality or only in terms of normativity, are internal to a causal process, there is no logical room for "switches" in the literal sense, for the normative requirement is internally effective in moving the so-called "switch." It is no longer a "mechanical" process and so, strictly speaking, there is no switch.

If there were no implicit distinction made in behavior between what was semantically present and what existed, there would be no taking and no mistaking; because taking, and thus mistaking, presuppose the distinction. In situations where a physical impact of an object on an organism, whether by touch, sound waves, refracted light waves, or however, causes a "behavior" on the part of the organism with no intervening semantic presence of the object to the "agent," there is no literal *behavioral* response. This is what we take to be the case with the computerized robot that possesses touch, sound, and light "sensors." It is what Descartes took to be true of nonrational animals. However, a fourfold distinction needs to be made: *physical causality*, which engages only existential and factual structures; *normative teleological causality*, which engages normative as well as factual structures and may involve such semantic factors as "signals" and "information" in some form; *psychological causality*, which engages semantic factors in a more full-blooded sense as well as factual and normative structures; and *rational causality*, which is a more complex psychological causality that involves consciousness as well as semantic, logical, factual, and normative structures.

Whenever we ascribe *psychological behavior* to organisms and intend this not just as an ascription but as a description, we are imputing to them a semantic-presence factor in their behavioral response. The semantic-presence episode is not just a peculiar, isolatable link in a naturalistic causal chain; it is embedded in a semantic teleological process, which is more complex than a purely normative teleological process. It involves not only a process or action with an inherent end, but one with a *purpose*, an end in "view," an end that is semantically as well as normatively in the process. Furthermore, it is a process in which events or facts become causal factors or *explanatory reasons* through their semantic presence.

The semantic presence of an object in an elementary behavioral process involves, or so this work claims, the taking of what is semantically present as existent. This is a behavioral taking; it may be correct or mistaken. When it is correct by virtue of its causal conditions, as distinct from its being correct by happenstance, we may call this proto- or *behavioral* knowledge as distinct from *rational* knowledge. Strictly speaking, the distinction between semantic and existential presence is not drawn at the purely behavioral level even though we may talk about the correction of mistakes at this level. A dog hits the trail of a rabbit and begins the chase. Suppose that in a short time she reverses her course. We are likely to say that she *took* the rabbit to have been headed in one direction but soon discovered that she had made a *mistake*. The behavior we attribute to the dog presupposes a distinction between the semantic and existential presence of the direction of the rabbit, but we need not attribute to her any recognition of her mistake as such. All we are warranted in saying is that there was a causal condition for the initial taking and there was a causal condition for the second taking, which was in fact the reverse of the first.

The causal conditions, however, are peculiar. They are different from the causal conditions of physical happenings. There is a semantic and normative structure involved. It makes sense to say literally that the dog made a mistake or that she got it right in a way in which it would not make literal sense to say the same thing about a robot. The causal process is more akin to that of human action where the causes are clearly double-aspect *reasons*, reasons that both justify and explain. This is a distinction that can be made internally in human behavior but only externally for the dog.

Where does the double-aspect reasons talk (talk about reasons as both explanatory and justificatory) become appropriate? About normative teleological processes or only about semantic teleological processes? It is sometimes said that for something to be a reason that justifies, it has to be known, believed, or taken to be the case in the action or process in which it has a justificatory status. In other words, something can be a reason of this kind only in a semantic teleological process. But consider the way it seems appropriate to talk about reasons in normative teleological processes. Why, for example, does blood coagulate when it is exposed to air, as in the puncture of one's body? Suppose we accepted as an answer the statement: Coagulation of blood under these conditions seals the puncture. Would one with a teleological view of nature accept this fact as only an explanatory reason? Or would it be accepted as both an explanatory and a justificatory reason? The fact that coagulation of the blood under these conditions seals the puncture might be taken to bear as a reason both in an explanatory and a justificatory way on the fact that the blood leaking from a punctured body coagulated.

To admit that it makes sense to talk about justificatory reasons in normative teleological processes is not to deny that justificatory reasons function differently in semantic teleological processes, especially in rational teleological processes. In our dominant culture, we recognize justificatory reasons only in rational action. But in a more general sense, a justificatory reason may be regarded as one that answers the question why something is *good* or why something is *right* or why something *ought to be* or why something *ought to be a certain way*. An explanatory reason is one that answers the question why something *is* or why something *is the way it is*, including why there is a particular normative requirement in a situation. In any genuine teleological system, one in which an inherent normative structure is causally operative, whether with or without a semantic or a rational dimension, the answers to the existential and factual "Why?" and the answers to the normative and value "Why?" tend to be one and the same. So we have reasons that are both explanatory and justificatory.

It seems that we can speak meaningfully about signals, information, and justificatory reasons with regard to any normative teleological process. This may indicate a semantic dimension, even if very low grade at some levels, in all normative teleological processes. If so, behavioral knowledge seems to require an enriched semantic dimension; things and structures have to be semantically present, not only *in* a process, but *to* some organized whole with an inherent teleological structure such as an organism. If there is a semantic dimension to any genuinely teleological process, perhaps only elements and states of the teleological system are caught up in the semantic dimension. At the recognizable psychological (or behavioral) level, things and states of affairs not internal to the teleological structure may be caught up in its semantic dimension and thereby become involved in the teleological causality of the organized whole. We may think of this as the external outreach of the semantics of a teleological process. In this way, the teleological system can draw upon, and incorporate into its own teleological processes, elements from its external environment; that is, things not caught up in the internal teleological processes of the organism by normative requirements alone may be brought into the inner dynamics of the system by semantic appropriation. Here is where teleological systems become behavioral.

An organism does not simply affect its environment and it is not simply affected by its environment. It acts on its environment. It appropriates something from, or alters something in, its environment to fulfill an inner need or requirement of its own. In order to do this, the organism has to be an internally organized teleological system to which some effects of external causes on it are signals. When the whole organism moves to meet a need in response to a signal, we have behavior. Responses to signals that do not engage the organism as a whole are not behavioral. This is the case with many reflexes and internal processes of the organism.

What this amounts to is that behavior requires a certain kind of categorially complex organization of a system that acts as a whole on, or in relation to, its environment in response to information-bearing signals to meet needs of the organism. We speak of an *organism* here because the internal organization of a system that makes behavior possible is precisely the kind in terms of which we define an organism.

In short, behavior involves behavioral knowledge. It requires an internally organized self-maintaining and self-correcting system that involves factual, normative, and semantic structures in its inner dynamics and overt behavior. This is why robots do not replicate the behavior of organisms; they only simulate it. They do not have the requisite internal categorial structure.

Rational Knowledge

There is an important distinction between behavioral and rational knowledge. The former is a behavioral taking that could be either correct or incorrect but is in fact correct. Behavioral mistakes can be corrected in behavior. The dog corrects her mistake about the direction of the rabbit she is tracking. We make behavioral corrections all the time in such commonplace things as keeping our balance in walking or riding a bicycle, in maintaining our course in driving a car, and the like.

There seem to be counterparts to behavioral corrections in the internal operations of an organism, but we are less confident about the attribution of a psychological dimension to them. There are some internal processes that seem to be on automatic control most of the time but can be put under mind control and even become intentional acts—breathing, for example. So there are, or seem to be, autonomic physiological processes in the human organism that are or can be psychological activities part of the time. The line between the biological and the psychological is not very sharp and distinct at some points, at least. Nevertheless, biological organisms seem to be able to operate as normative teleological systems without any obvious psychological dimension.[2] But even with regard to what appears to be purely normative teleological processes, it makes some kind of sense, as previously observed, to talk about signals (even false signals), information, mistakes, and self-correcting processes. This kind of talk seems to have a stronger, non-metaphorical meaning when it is about biological systems than when it is about mechanical or electronic artifacts.

Rational knowledge is possible only where a *reflective* distinction, not simply a behavioral distinction, can be drawn between the semantic presence and the existence of an object; for rational knowledge is not just behaviorally taking something semantically present to have an independent status, and being correct in doing so by virtue of the causes of the behavior in question. Such knowledge involves having *reasons* that cause the taking in question by justifying it—reasons that justify the taking and provide an explanation of both why one took whatever it was to be the case and why one got it right. In the behavioral case, the reasons are directly causal: They do not cause by justifying; there is no reasoning, no planning, no review, just the causal process. But the reasons do, nonetheless, provide an explanation for why one got it right.

A Naturalistic Theory of Rational Knowledge

Rational knowledge is an especially troublesome nest of problems for naturalists. There are two aspects of any justified true-belief theory of knowledge that are especially problematic for them, namely, the value and semantic concepts such a theory must employ. Alvin Goldman makes a heroic effort on their behalf.[3] He goes to great length to deal with the value concepts in his theory but makes only suggestions about the semantic concepts.

Goldman's analysis of "*S* knows that *P*" may be briefly summarized in this manner:

1. *S* believes that *P*;
2. *P* is true;
3. *S*'s belief in *P* is a result of a reliable belief-forming process, which was itself acquired (or is sustained) by a reliable second-order process;
4. *S*'s belief in *P* is justified; that is, (a) *S*'s believing that *P* is permitted by a right system of justificational rules (J-rules) and (b) this permission is not undermined by *S*'s cognitive state at the time;
5. A J-rule system is right if and only if it permits certain (basic) psychological processes, and the instantiation of these processes would result in beliefs with a truth ratio that meets some specified high threshold (greater than .50).

With regard to semantic concepts, Goldman admits that his theory draws on the language of folk psychology in speaking of beliefs with semantic contents and semantic properties such as being true or false. He makes no serious effort to square this with his commitment to a scientific psychology. He regards it as a problem in the philosophy of mind, which he says he need not go into very far for the purposes of epistemology. But he does give some indications of how he would deal with the problem.

In speaking of the general utility of proposition concepts with regard to doxastic attitudes (believing, being certain, thinking it likely, doubting, suspending judgment, and so forth), Goldman says "I shall avail myself of this talk, but only as a *façon de parler*." He regards propositions "as a temporary theoretical posit from which we should ultimately ascend to a better theory."[4] So he speaks of the contents of beliefs as propositions. And he regards propositions, not beliefs, as the primary bearers of truth-values. He accepts the realistic position that it is the world that makes propositions either true or false. But all of this is simply an indulgence or a way to make do for now while we wait for a *better* theory, presumably one that will be cast in more scientifically respectable terms.

The divorce of propositions (and concepts) from the mental helps clean up the mental and prepare it for a scientific psychology; and it makes room for semantics and logic, freed from messy, embarrassing psychological realities. But this unnatural division generates two sets of problems: (1) how psychological states and acts are related to concepts and propositions and (2) what concepts and propositions are and whether, and if so, how, they are in the world.

Goldman, as previously observed, sets aside the second set of problems. With regard to the belief construct, he says there are at least four approaches open to cognitive science: (1) reduction—that is, belief being identified with, or explained in terms of, scientifically respectable elements; (2) replacement—not being "scientifically tenable posits," beliefs "will ultimately be discredited and abandoned like phlogiston"; (3) neutrality—although cognitive science may not now be able to assign semantic content or account for how it can be done, this does not imply the overthrow or illegitimacy of beliefs, for it may allow that a good "psychosemantics" could do so. (Note that Goldman sees the problem as the *assignment* of semantic content, not how psychology can deal with a subject matter *with an inherent semantic content*; apparently, for him, semantic talk about psychological states and acts is a matter of attribution, not description); and (4) refinement—an approach that is not an alternative to the others, for it does not address the problem of content, but only discriminates a "richer array of distinct content-bearing states" and thus makes the conceptual resources of cognitive science and epistemology more realistic.[5]

Goldman adopts a combination of (3) and (4). In short, he proposes to make do in his present epistemological work with the language of folk psychology (and, we might say, the language of "folk semantics" as well), but with some refinements. He will allow himself to talk about beliefs-with-contents, propositions, and truth-values. Nevertheless, he seems to regard this as a temporary expedient. Like so many others, Goldman is skeptical about the language of "folk psychology" and "folk semantics" because of his abandonment of humanism in favor of a theory of knowledge based on modern science as the paradigm of knowledge. He has the modern naturalist's faith that all of this mentalistic and semantic talk can, and no doubt will, be made scientifically respectable. But he leaves it to others in cognitive science or philosophy of mind (or perhaps to himself in the future) to work this out.

Value concepts, as well as semantic concepts, are indispensable to any justified true-belief theory of knowledge (or for any theory of knowledge, for that matter). Goldman, in his theory of what it is for someone to know that *P*, talks about *reliable* belief-forming processes, *justified* beliefs, and a *right* system of *justificational rules*. He tries to cash these value terms into what he regards as acceptable coinage.

A *reliable* belief-forming process, he says, is one with a propensity to yield a high ratio of true beliefs, "higher—perhaps appreciably higher —than .50."[6] "A second-order process," he says, "might be considered metareliable if, among the methods (or first-order processes) it puts out, the ratio of those that are reliable meets some specified level, presumably greater than .50." If, for example, a threshold of .80 is set for both reliability and metareliability, then "a second-order process is metareliable if and only if at least 80 percent of the processes (or methods) it produces are at least 80 percent reliable."[7]

It should be clear that Goldman has not reduced or explained away the value dimension of reliability. He gives us factual (non-value) *criteria* of reliability, not a non-value theory of reliability. His criteria are truth-linked because his whole epistemology assumes that beliefs *ought to be* true and that our belief-producing processes or methods *ought* to generate beliefs that are the way beliefs *ought to be*. So the value concepts remain. They are simply hidden in assumptions.

What about *justified* beliefs? This is another value dimension of beliefs and belief-forming processes. Goldman tells us that justified beliefs are those *permitted* by a *right* system of *justificational rules* when this permission is not *undermined* by the believer's cognitive state at the time. Value words in the definition are indicated by italics to show how difficult it is to eliminate them. Permission presupposes a value test; being permitted presupposes that what is permitted meets or has passed the relevant value test, for otherwise the permission itself would be at fault. In other words, being permitted presupposes that what is permitted is the way it *ought to be* in the relevant respect. A permission can be *undermined* only by some relevant condition's not being the way it *ought to be*.

What about *justificational rules*? Rules are recognized general imperatives. Some rules, the rules of a game, for example, are constitutive of what ought to be or what ought to be done. They can be changed by agreement of the rule-makers. But even in such cases the rules are not purely arbitrary. They have to make sense; and they may or may not make a good game. Some rules, however, are formulations of general imperatives binding in a situation independently of rule-makers: the rules of fair play, for example. And the laws enacted for the governance of a society, for the most part, are corrigible with respect to an antecedent and independent normative structure. In most cases, the agents and activities governed have identities and are subject to normative requirements with respect to which they may be appraised independently of the promulgated laws. The same seems to be true for the justificational rules for beliefs. Rule-making in such areas has the character of discovery, not the character of constitutivity. Legislation of this kind does not *constitute* what is normatively required; it formulates and declares an officially recognized version of what ought to be or ought to be done (or, negatively, what ought not to be or ought not to be done).

Goldman acknowledges that the system of justificational rules with respect to which a belief may be permitted is subject to being appraised as *right*. In explicating what this means, he says that a system of justificational rules is right if and only if it permits the kinds of psychological processes that would result in "a truth ratio of beliefs that meets some specified high threshold (greater than .50)."[8] We arrive at a criterion of rightness, he says, by considering a list of possible candidates and asking of each what rule system would be generated by it. We then "reflect on implications of these rule systems for particular judgments of justifiedness and unjustifiedness" and "see whether these judgments accord with our pretheoretic intuitions. . . . But our initial intuitions are not final. They can be pruned and adjusted by reflection on candidate rule systems."[9] The test is, following John Rawls's test for principles of justice, "considered judgments in reflective equilibrium."[10] A criterion may be tested also by its completeness: Does it generate a complete rule system, one that, in Goldman's words, "would imply justifiedness or unjustifiedness for all cases of belief and all doxastic attitudes?"[11]

This appears to be an attempt to assimilate the rightness of epistemological justificational rules to the rightness of the rules of a game; that is, rules that are constructed, not discovered, but rules that would be acceptable to all participants regardless of their particular abilities and circumstances because everyone could expect to benefit from them. We might say, for example, that the rules of a competitive two-team ball game were right (would be accepted by all participants who considered them without regard to their particular abilities and circumstances) if and only if they permitted activities that would result in some specified ratio of successes for each of two comparable teams but with the winner uncertain until late in most games. The effort is clearly to get away from any antecedent and independent normative structure with respect to which the rules would be corrigible. The rules made by rule-makers for games are presumed to constitute the whole normative structure involved. All that is involved, it is assumed, is a *desired* end and the factual, causal structure of things.

For some games there are known inventors, official rule-makers and rule books. Other games, however, are folk games; they have developed and taken shape over generations, with no known rule-makers. Nevertheless we assume that the ground of their rules is not different from invented games with identifiable rule-makers. Furthermore, we assume that the rules of both invented and folk games are binding on players by virtue of a tacit contract among them.

Rawls seems to assume that the principles of justice have the same kind of status as the rules of a folk game; and that a philosopher formulates the principles of justice much as one would go about discovering and formulating the rules of such a game. The codifier of the rules of a folk game would try for an explicit and complete set of rules that would involve the minimum modification of the way the game was customarily played and refereed. This is what "considered judgments in reflective equilibrium" amount to. And Goldman takes the same approach to the justificational rules for beliefs. The assumption for Rawls is that there is no justice apart from an accepted set of principles of justice; and the assumption for Goldman seems to be that there are no justified beliefs without accepted justificational rules for beliefs. Goldman's second-order set of right procedures that generate justificational rules for beliefs seem to have for him the status that the hypothetical principles-making, ignorance-veiled convention has for Rawls.

But does not the nature of a game as such, a game in general, involve a normative structure? We may invent a particular game—football, for example—but does anyone invent *the* game (or games in general)? Do any rule-makers make the rules for games in general? If not, what is the source of the normative structure involved in the idea of a game in general? What is the relationship of games to play? And is play *the fulfillment of a need* of beings with human powers? In other words, does the normative structure of human beings require play? And does human play require games for its development and perfection? And are games as such constituted by a normative structure? Is this normative structure presupposed by the rules of a particular game? If this is so, the rule-makers of particular games do not make or constitute the normative structure of games in general. Rather, it is a normative structure to which the rule-makers of a particular game are responsible. It is not enough to say that in creating or modifying a game, rule-makers are governed by a concern for what people will enjoy playing or watching; for one's enjoyment of playing or watching a game seems to be either an experience of the satisfaction of a *need* of one's self, a self-based normative requirement, or sheer appreciation of the perfection of the game or of the skill involved in playing it. Of course enjoyments can be deceptive; they can occur without the satisfaction of a genuine need or the perfection of either the game or of the playing of it. And the satisfaction of one need may be frustrating to others and the realization of one value may involve the sacrifice of others. The point is that games have, and are tailored to, normative structures that are not constituted by rule-makers. Games are good or bad; they are subject to being improved, even perfected.

If even the rule-makers for games are responsible to some given or presupposed normative structure, surely any system of justificational rules for knowledge-claims is responsible to an independent normative structure within which beliefs are formed. Beliefs are formed and criticized within this normative structure quite independently of the formulation of any system of rules. Epistemic and logical criticism of beliefs does not depend on the work of rule-makers, whether they be individuals or historical communities.

Goldman talks as though a system of justificational rules had to be generated by a set of metaprocedures and that both the justificational rules and the metaprocedures had to meet a test in terms of some set of desired truth-linked consequences. This suggests that we would have to have a set of *meta*-metaprocedures for generating and testing metaprocedures, and so on. It seems that the only way to escape the infinite regress involved in such an account of the criticism of beliefs is to give up the naturalistic assumptions that the theory is designed to protect, and to recognize that the context of belief involves an inherent normative structure. It is this normative structure to which human beings in all societies are sensitive in their criticism of belief. Folk logic and folk epistemology are common-sense knowledge of this semantic and normative structure. Insofar as logicians and epistemologists formulate rules for the criticism of beliefs, they are both articulating what has been tacitly recognized in folk logic and folk epistemology, and correcting and developing folk logic and folk epistemology by examining the inherent semantic and normative structure of belief and its context. At best, the truth-linked consequences of following such rules constitute a criterion or test of their correctness; they do not constitute their rightness.

There is no way of escaping either the semantic or the normative dimension of belief. There is no way of reducing either of these to something else more respectable in naturalistic circles; neither is there any way of explaining them away.

We must take seriously the language of humanistic psychology. This suggests a semantic theory of the mental and a realistic theory of meaning. We have argued for inherent meaning as a basic, irreducible, categorial structure of experience, thought, belief, intention, and action; indeed, anything behavioral, mental, cultural, or social. The rejection of this conclusion seems to lead inevitably into unsolvable philosophical perplexities.

Concepts and propositions are abstractions that we can isolate and talk about. As abstract entities, they are independent of our talk and beliefs about them; we may be correct or mistaken about them. But their mode of existence, their mode of being in the world, is as an aspect or dimension of a psychological (or some other semantic) state or act. Concepts and propositions are *instantiated* in semantic states and acts, the most obvious of which are psychological. They are part of the *existential* structure of a psychological state or act. This is not a matter of being the intentional objects of such states and acts. Of course concepts and propositions, as anything else, may be the intentional object of (or an inexistential element in) a psychological state or act; but that is not what we are talking about here. Different people can share the same concept or proposition by each person's having a psychological state or act that instantiates the same abstract semantic structure, just as two physical things can share the same abstract geometrical figure by instantiating it.

Formal semantics deals with abstract semantic structures in much the same sense as geometry deals with certain abstract spatial structures. Formal logic deals with the logical aspects of these abstract semantic structures. Only something with a semantic dimension can exemplify or instantiate a logical form.[12] We can abstract a semantic structure from its psychological instantiations; and we can further abstract the logical forms exemplified in semantic structures and consider them in abstraction, not only from their existence in psychological states and acts, but also in abstraction from the abstract semantic structures in which they are exemplified—in abstraction from concepts and propositions. But this whole array of logical forms and semantic structures find their instantiations in psychological states and acts. They are in the world both as existential aspects or structures of psychological states and acts and as inexistential elements (semantic contents) of other psychological states and acts that take them as their objects.

Abstract entities contrast with fictional characters, places, and events in this respect: Fictional entities are in the world only as inexistential elements of psychological states and acts; abstract entities may be in the world existentially by instantiation and as inexistential elements of psychological states and acts.

Perhaps it needs to be said that, on this view, linguistic states and acts are kinds of psychological states and acts. Linguistic and other symbolic states and acts in some enduring physical form, such as writing, drawings, sculpture, and so forth, are "frozen" psychological states and acts; they mean what the author or creator meant by or expressed in them or what they have come to mean in the developing context of the thought and life of the culture.

A scientific psychology that does not take account of such realities as inherent structures of meaning with their logical forms generates a limited and restricted science, regardless of how useful it may be. An epistemology that does not show how knowledge of such realities is possible will be doomed to antinomy and incoherence. Philosophy of mind and philosophy of culture that do not acknowledge such realities cannot be consistently thought through; what such a philosophy asserts will be inconsistent with its own presuppositions.

A Humanistic Theory of Rational Knowledge

I have argued elsewhere for a modified version of the justified true belief theory of rational knowledge.[13] According to this account, for *S* to know that *P* (where *P* is a fact, a value, a normative requirement, a possibility, a necessity, or whatever may be asserted in a truth-claim or taken to be the case in any form) is (1) for *S* to take *P* to obtain in the world; (2) for *S* to be correct in taking *P* to obtain in the world (that is, for *P* actually to obtain in the world); (3) for *S* to have good reasons or grounds for taking *P* to obtain in the world (that is, reasons or grounds with sufficient justificatory power to justify *S*, under the circumstances, in taking *P* to obtain in the world); and (4) for the reasons or grounds *S* has for taking *P* to obtain in the world to be responsible for *S*'s getting it right (that is, for *S*'s reasons or grounds for taking *P* to obtain in the world to be such that they would provide an adequate explanation of why *S* was correct in taking *P* to obtain in the world).

In (1) we speak of "taking *P* to obtain in the world" rather than "believing that *P*." In earlier works, I spoke of "thinking that *P*," with this phrase understood as an act or commitment that could be performed or made in any of a variety of forms—in abstract thought, overt statement, perception, memory, expectation, assumption, presupposition, or whatever. But "taking *P* to obtain in the world" is a phrase with less baggage from past philosophical controversies than either "believing that" or "thinking that." It has the virtue of being a very general term. Taking some semantic content to be real comes in all the forms that epistemic mistakes do. It remains an open question whether there are any forms of taking something to obtain in the world that do not admit to mistakes. But whatever is involved in knowing that *P*, claiming that one knows that *P* involves claiming that one takes *P* to be the case (to obtain in the world in some sense) and that the taking is not a mistake. Some have claimed (notably C. I. Lewis and Wittgenstein) that if there were a form of taking *P* to obtain in the world that was not subject to error, it would not be a form of knowing that *P*, for the claim that one knows that *P* contains the implicit denial that one is mistaken, which would not make sense unless there was the possibility of a mistake. What is important in the knowing claim is the simple denial that the taking is a mistake. The denial of the possibility of a mistake for the kind of taking involved is a stronger claim that entails the simpler denial. Indeed, some (notably Plato, Descartes, and H. A. Prichard) have claimed that this stronger denial is involved in a knowing claim. This issue is the basis of Norman Malcolm's distinction between what he calls the strong and the weak senses of "know."[14] Our formulation captures only the weaker sense, but the stronger claim is not excluded. To claim that one knows that *P* is not to claim that one's grounds or reasons are so good that one could not be mistaken; it is to claim only that they are good enough and that one is right on the basis of them. If one's grounds or reasons for taking *P* to obtain in the world should be so good that one could not be mistaken, so much the better. The account would cover such a case.

Some might object to the phrase "taking *P* to obtain in the world" rather than "taking *P* to be true" or "taking *P* to be the case." Actually there is a shift in the meaning of "*P*" in the phrases "taking *P* to be true" and "taking *P* to be the case" or "taking *P* to obtain in the world." In the former phrase, *P* is an assertion, a statement, or a taking in some form; in the two latter phrases, *P* is simply a semantic content with a certain form; in the simplest case, as in "that *X* is *F*" or "*X*'s being *F*," *P* is a fact in its semantic presence, without any projection of it into the world. There are some advantages and fewer liabilities to this way of putting the matter.

The world is the place we assign contents of subjective states and acts in their stubborn independence. Even a character in a novel is independent of the way he or she is present to the reader. A reader can be mistaken about such a character in as full-blooded a sense as one can be mistaken about a person in history. Fictional characters are inhabitants of the real world, but as fictional characters. In ordinary fiction, only characters, places, facts, situations, and events are fictitious; scientific laws, possibilities, necessities, normative requirements, and values are the same as in history. There are certainly limits on the possibilities of fiction, but it seems clear that the possibilities extend beyond the existential and the factual. We could have radical fiction in which, to some extent, normative requirements, scientific laws, possibilities, and necessities (as well as individuals, particular facts, situations, and events) were fictitious.

Some of the entities we talk about may reside only in some universe of discourse such as mathematics, scientific theory, or religious myth. They too have an independence of our particular thoughts and beliefs about them, but they are like neither fictional characters and events in a novel nor existential subject matter. If such entities are not in the world, they are logically tied to, and under constraints from, our concepts and beliefs about what is in the world existentially in a way in which fictional characters and events are not. Entities of this kind are in the world in their own unique way as the semantic content of theory or myth, even when the question is still open as to whether they are existentially in the world as well.

We must conceive the world in a broad enough way for it to contain whatever we can have knowledge of—whatever we can justifiably and correctly take to have a status that is independent of its semantic presence to us. So the real world *seems* to contain concrete space-time individuals, events, properties, facts, normative requirements, values, structures of meaning, contingencies, necessities, possibilities, fictional characters and happenings, theoretical or mythical entities, and so forth. Of course it is important for us to analyze and to clarify how things that are independent of their semantic presence to us are in the world, including how we and our semantic states and acts with their contents and how our cultural objects (stories, reports, histories, theories, art objects, and so forth) with their semantic contents are in the world. This task involves trying to get a clear understanding of the knowledge-yielding powers of the human mind (our ways of establishing some independent status for the semantic contents of our semantic states and acts) and trying to get an equally clear understanding of the basic structure of the world by virtue of which it can accommodate such a variety of kinds of things. If we have a restricted view of our knowledge-yielding powers and a narrow view of the basic structure of the world and the ways in which things are in the world, we will either reject an independent status for many of the semantic contents of our minds and of our cultural objects or try to identify them with something that will fit into the basic structure of the world as we understand it.

For these reasons, in the anlaysis of "*S* knows that *P*," "*S* takes *P* to obtain in the world (in the manner appropriate for *P*)" makes clearer what is involved than either of the expressions "*S* believes that *P*" or "*S* thinks that *P*." But some would say that it achieves the greater clarity by taking on greater philosophical liabilities, for it, in effect, commits us to a theory of believing that *P* (or of thinking that *P*) and even to a theory of truth. Such commitments at this point in the analysis, however, can be a virtue. For one thing, they preclude the early acceptance of some pragmatic, coherence, or other subjectivist theory of knowledge and truth. Such theories are last-resort measures; they should be turned to only when all versions of a realistic theory have been found to be unacceptable. Realism is the starting point. It is the way things appear to be. We should not abandon it before we are forced to do so. A realistic epistemology is less problematic from within a general humanistic outlook than from within our prevailing naturalistic assumptions. Without humanism, a full-blooded realism is not tenable. Indeed, knowledge in any form is threatened.

So, in our analysis of what it is for S to know that P, "S takes P to obtain in the world" means that S takes P, the fact (P of course could be a normative requirement, a causal law, or whatever; but, for simplicity, let us assume it is a fact) that is the semantic content of S's psychological act, to be existent (to be in the world) in the manner appropriate for the kind of fact it is. In like manner, "P is true" means the fact that is inexistentially in the abstract semantic structure P (in the proposition P) obtains in the world. In most instances no harm is done if we do not differentiate between a semantic structure, whether concrete or abstract, and its semantic content. But for present purposes, this difference makes a difference. It is the semantic content of a structure of meaning, whether a psychological act or a proposition, that is taken to be in the world. The way a fact is in the world is quite different from the way a proposition is in the world. That it is raining in Chapel Hill at t_1 is a fact that is in the world as a slice of what Chapel Hill is at that time; the proposition *It is raining in Chapel Hill at t_1* is in the world by being instantiated in at least one psychological state or act.

As we have seen, we must also take normative and value talk seriously; we must acknowledge normative structures as a dimension of the world. This is particularly evident with regard to distinctively humanistic subject matter—all behavioral, mental, cultural, personal, and social realities. No where is the normative more undeniable and indispensable than in the realm of knowledge. Thinking, believing, intending, and reconstructing beliefs and intentions under criticism are as natural for human beings as eating and digesting food. Inherent structures of meaning and normativity are as essential to such psychological states and acts as physical and chemical structures are to eating and digesting food. All efforts to show that inherent structures of meaning and normativity are not what they appear to be seem to violate what they really are and to render unintelligible how they accomplish what we must acknowledge that they do. The elaborate theories that we develop to make good our naturalistic predilections often hide these unpalatable truths from us by overloading our attention with technical details.

The human mind must have its own inherent, causally operative normative structure by virtue of which it forms and corrects beliefs and knows various kinds of things. It does not have to "follow rules" in doing so. The inherent normative structure is dynamic and at work in the formation and correction of beliefs or takings in various forms.

In the analysis of what it is for S to know that P, the sentence "S is correct in taking *P* to obtain in the world" not only means that the taking was correct in that the fact *P* obtains in the world, but it presupposes that the act was *an effort to be correct* about the matter. Furthermore, the statement presupposes that *S*'s taking *P* to obtain in the world has a certain kind of etiology—that the act has grounds or reasons that are both explanatory and justificatory. Only something with an inherent structure of meaning and normativity and that is produced in a context with inherent structures of meaning and normativity involved in its causation can be said to be correct or incorrect. Nothing that has either a purely existential and factual constitution or purely existential and factual causal conditions is subject to any form of rational appraisal. Any analysis of what it is to know something that does not recognize this must be wrong, for to call something an instance of knowing that *P* entails that it is subject to rational appraisal as correct and as justified; and such rational appraisals presuppose that the state or act is subject to *description and explanation* in semantic, logical, and normative language. Modern scientific descriptive/explanatory accounts of natural events such as earthquakes, tornadoes, thunder storms, diseases, and the like logically crowd out questions about their rightness and their justifiedness. People who still insist on biblical ways of talking about such happenings as punishment for, or warnings about, the wickedness of the people also insist on talking about them as *acts* of God; that is, they insist on describing and explaining them in semantic and normative terms. The two teams of concepts go together. Rational appraisals of a subject matter cannot be divorced from a semantic and normative descriptive/explanatory account of it.[15]

What is it, then, in *S*'s knowing that *P*, for *S* to have good reasons or grounds for taking *P* to obtain in the world? The most obvious thing we can say is that *S* has beliefs, assumptions, and/or experiences that justify the act under the circumstances; that in the total relevant context, as it is present to *S*, there are positive grounds or reasons, not nullified or cancelled by other considerations, that normatively require the act and make it worthy of being performed by *S*.

In other words, in the case of *S*'s knowing that *P*, the justification for *S*'s thinking that *P* is not so much a matter of the act's being *permitted* under some set of rules as it is a matter of its being normatively required in the semantic, normative, and factual context in which it takes place. Rules would be applicable only in so far as they captured the real normative structure inherent in the situation. Following a set of rules often results in absurd behavior in concrete situations precisely because the rules do not capture the normative structure of the real situation. This is what is fundamentally wrong with a bureaucracy that tries to operate by rules rather than the judgment of competent people in concrete situations. It is what is wrong with "mechanical" or rule-book decision procedures in most life situations.

The last condition specified in our analysis of knowing is that the grounds or reasons that *S* has for taking *P* to obtain in the world must provide an adequate explanation not only of the occurrence of the act, but especially of its success—of *S*'s getting it right. The grounds or reasons that can justify one's thinking that *P* and explain why one got it right in this manner have to be in the form of one's assumptions, beliefs, attitudes, or experiences. Although such assumptions, beliefs, attitudes, and experiences, without being true or veridical, can justify (or at least excuse) and explain one's taking *P* to obtain in the world, they cannot adequately explain why one was correct in doing so without themselves being both true or veridical[16] and complete or comprehensive enough with respect to the relevant objective situation. Whenever luck, guesses, or multiple errors that cancel themselves out are part of the explanation of why one got the matter right, the taking in question is not an instance of knowing that *P*.

Behavioral and Rational Knowledge Contrasted

We have spoken of behavioral and rational knowledge. What is the difference? Regardless of whether a semantic dimension is involved in teleological processes below the psychological level, we may say roughly that we have behavior whenever a complex individual moves, changes, or acts as a whole for some end on the basis of the semantic presence of the end or some condition of it. An end may be only normatively present in something. This seems to be the case in the development, growth, and maturation of an organism. In many instances, the conditions for the realization of such ends seem to be brought about and to work their effects under normative requirements. If we posit a semantic dimension for such ends and means, it will be for theoretical reasons. The subject matter does not wear a semantic dimension on its face. But semantic concepts are necessary for our primary descriptions of behavior, for in behavior ends and means are present to the agent in desires and intentions and relevant circumstances are present in sensory awareness, however rudimentary and primitive the desires, intentions, and sensory perceptions may be.

Behavioral knowledge, as previously observed, involves correct takings, without the benefit of a critical process, about what ought to be or about what is factually the case. There is no operative distinction between what seems to be and what is. So no reasons are needed to move from what seems to be normatively required to what is taken to be normatively required; no reasons are needed to move from what seems to be good to what is taken to be good; no reasons are needed to move from what seems to be factually the case to what is taken to be factually the case. In other words, in behavioral knowledge, perceptual takings (including desires and feelings) are generated by the unconscious workings of the inner dynamics of individuals in conjunction with their physical interactions with the environment; and these sensory perceptions, desires, and feelings produce or generate their actions. When mistakes are made, changes in the signals from the environment may occasion new sensory perceptions and feelings that replace the earlier mistaken ones and thus bring about a "correction" in the action. Sensory perceptions, desires, feelings, and intentions, even at the most unreflective and primitive level, involve takings, which may be correct or mistaken; and, if they are correct, they may give rise to unproblematic, successful action.

According to our understanding of these matters, a primitive sensory perception involves the semantic presence (in a sensory mode) to one (the complex biological and psychological being one is, which need not be a person) of something as it is in some factual respect; a primitive desire consists (in part) of the semantic presence (in an experiential mode) to one of a normative requirement grounded in one's own being; a primitive feeling includes the semantic presence (in an experiential mode) to one of something as being or not being the way it ought to be; and a primitive intention involves the semantic presence (in the form of a controlling desire) to one of something as something for one to do or to bring about. In all of these cases, what is semantically present—whether a fact, a normative requirement, a value (something's being the way it ought to be), or an imperative, a requirement for action under the circumstances (something for one to do)—is taken to obtain in the world. This is indicated by the way all of these relate to, and bear on, the actions of individuals in relation to their environment. They all presuppose reasons that validate them. None are acceptable as arbitrary. Actions generated by these psychological states and acts may or may not be successful and, even if successful in the short run, they may not be fully successful in the long run. If the actions are not successful in the short run, they are likely to be changed by new perceptions, feelings, and desires arising from the ongoing interactions with the environment. We speak of such actions as involving mistakes and corrections. But such primitive agents have no truck with either mistakes or corrections *as such*; they are totally absorbed in the ongoing generation of perceptions, feelings, desires, intentions, and actions by the inner dynamics of their own being in interaction with their environment. To be sure, new dispositions can be developed and old dispositions eliminated. In this sense, there is learning. But there is no self-monitoring, no self-review, no self-criticism, and no long-term planning. These require higher-level semantic powers, which make self-criticism possible and inevitable. And with higher-level semantic and critical powers, there is a significant transformation of lower-level psychological states and acts.

This does not mean that the causation of non-personal psychological states and acts lies solely within the organism's physiological dimension and its bodily interactions with its physical environment. Rather the claim is that there is an important teleological process operating within the biological organism and among its psychological states and acts as such. In a biological organism with a significant psychological dimension, some psychological states and acts normatively require others and bring them about, while some normatively reject and eliminate others. In normal psychological beings of this kind, the physiological dimensions of their psychological states and acts are integral parts of the psychological states and acts and are caught up in their causal dynamics. Nevertheless, the acts of such a being are not personal acts. They are not rationally caused; that is, they are not caused by awareness of their justifying reasons. They do not have the kind of freedom that we attribute to rational acts. They do not have as their subject a psychological being that is unified under a transcending, unifying, critical center—an *I*.

Rational knowledge involves higher-level semantic and critical powers. Reflective awareness takes lower-level psychological states and acts and their logical and normative relationships as its content. Being *conscious* of X is being aware of one's awareness of X. This is essential for relating X to other things in one's thought and experience. Isolated states or acts of consciousness are not possible. Any conscious state or act that is individuated by a particular content—a perception of a particular thing or event, for example—is necessarily part of a larger consciousness; that is, every conscious state or act is a state or act of some self, a unitary consciousness with a transcending center, which (in its more developed form) is expressible as *I*. This unitary and unifying transcending center provides a perspective on lower-level semantic states and acts and their logical and normative relationships and it facilitates the melding of them into a dynamic, coherent whole. No single, isolated conscious state or act of a psychological being would have the requisite subject pole.

The causal dynamics of the psychological states and acts of a conscious being is much more complex than for a psychological being with only first-order psychological states and acts. Through the higher level of awareness, a wider range of psychological states and acts and the logical and normative structures they form enter into the ongoing generation and cancellation of psychological states and acts of all kinds, including intentions and the performance of overt acts. Just as first-order desires, feelings, and sensory perceptions bring factual conditions into the teleological processes of the organism that would not otherwise be so engaged, higher-level, reflective awareness brings a wider range of factors into the teleological dynamics of the psychological system. And, just as even minimal psychological beings have a freedom in relation to their environment that plants do not have, psychological beings with reflective awareness have a level of freedom in their psychological states and acts and overt behavior that mere psychological beings do not enjoy.

We speak of compulsive behavior in human beings. What we mean is that some desires and emotions are directly causal in the generation of behavior, with their causal power unaffected by the higher-level awareness that brings a wider range of considerations to bear. Memories of past experiences, expectations for the future, other desires, commitments, feelings, and judgments seem to make no difference. The rogue desires and emotions proceed as though the others did not exist or did not matter. In such cases, we speak of the weakness of will or the lack of willpower. The will of a person is simply the resolution of the whole self under reflective supervision. Psychological beings without consciousness have no will, even though they are usually causally unified and put forth all their effort on behalf of one desire at the time. As long as there is unresolved division within a conscious being about a matter, there is no will. We sometimes say that we have "two minds" about what to do, meaning part of one's self is united for one action and part is united for a contrary action. But such a person is in a state of indecision. One may, at the conscious level, resolve the differences and achieve what looks like a unified mind on the matter, only to find that subversive forces are at work at the unconscious level, or even that some desires and feelings out in the open field of consciousness refuse to be denied. We talk about "losing control," not being able "to help oneself," "being beside oneself," "being out of one's mind," "not being oneself," and the like.

The inherent normative structure of psychological states and acts, which is partly supervenient on the logical relationships of the psychological states and acts in question, is to a large extent directly causally operative; that is, the normative requirements holding among psychological states and acts are effective without being caught up in a higher-level awareness. People, for example, may find themselves, instantly and without reflection, totally unable to accept a given statement. Something within them resists and repels it; however much they may want to accept the statement, they cannot. What seems to be going on in such situations is that the existing system of psychological states and acts of these people has no logical room for what would be the new belief. They have beliefs or assumptions logically inconsistent with the statement. Even though such people may not be aware of these objecting beliefs or assumptions, these beliefs and assumptions have the power to block the acceptance of the statement in question. If they should come to have experiences and beliefs that compelled acceptance of the statement, the resisting beliefs or assumptions would have to be canceled or modified to make logical room for the new belief. This is a dynamic process that can go on without the benefit of reflective, critical thought. Indeed, without a primary level of mental causality of this kind, reflective, critical thought would not be possible. But a psychological system that is limited to this level of normative teleological processes is greatly restricted, just as a biological system that is limited to normative teleological processes without the benefit of psychological states and acts is greatly restricted. Reflective awareness not only brings together a far wider range of psychological states and acts into the normative teleological process of the mind; it increases the level of correctness and reliability of psychological states and acts. Furthermore, through the semantic contents of this wider and more reliable range of psychological states and acts, a far wider range of external factors are brought into the behavioral process.

What we have called behavioral knowledge is the correct but non-reflective takings of a psychological system that produces successful actions. Rational knowledge, however, consists of correct takings that were generated in a reflective, critical process, that stand justified under rational criticism, and for which the reasons that justify them are also explanatory reasons for their correctness.

Objectivity

The correctness of the takings involved in psychological states and acts presupposes objectivity, both in behavioral and rational knowledge. Indeed, the takings themselves are simply acts that project their semantic contents into some objective status; they loosen their semantic contents from themselves and posit them in the world. What is an inexistential element in a subjective state or act is taken to be independent of that subjective state or act. In simple behavioral knowledge the organic self relates behaviorally to, or has a disposition to relate behaviorally to, what is semantically in one of its subjective states or acts as independent of it. This requires the unity and integration of the behaving organism so that it is capable of successful coordinated behavior in its environment by virtue of the semantic presence of items and features of the environment to the organism. Reflective takings, genuine judgments, require a higher-level unity and integration of the semantic dimension of the organism; they require a genuine mental self, a mind—an organized, self-functioning, self-regulating subjective domain with a transcending center, an *I*; and they require a world—an ordered, dynamic realm of independent objects.

Objectivity, then, concerns the status of subjective content. We have subjective and objective attitudes toward our own mental states and acts and toward those of others. If one drinks orange juice immediately after brushing one's teeth with a certain brand of toothpaste and concludes that the orange juice has gone bad, one takes the experience to be objective; but if one faults the experience as unreliable because of the chemical effect of the toothpaste on one's taste buds, one takes the experience to be subjective. If one has a visual or auditory experience of a dead relative, as Hamlet did of his father, and concludes that one has encountered a ghost, one takes the experience to be objective; if one regards the experience as a dream or a hallucination, one takes the experience to be subjective.

We need to be sensitive to the ambiguity of the terms "subjective" and "objective." We may talk about a subjective state and mean simply a state with a semantic content—an experience, a dream, a thought, or whatever. Here we are placing the state categorially. No evaluation is made. We may also say that a given experience or thought is subjective. Here the issue is not categorial placement; calling the subject of discussion an "experience" or a "thought" has done that. The point is epistemic appraisal. In this sense, a subjective experience or thought is one for which we cannot claim veridicality or truth because of its etiology; it is one that was produced or influenced too much by the conditions of the subject, whether physical or mental. It is an experience or thought for which the conditions of its occurrence invalidates or casts suspicion on its objective claims.

The same ambiguity pertains to the term "objective." When we talk about the *objective* situation, we may mean the situation as it is quite apart from what it is taken to be by partisans in a dispute about it. But when we say that one is objective about the situation, we mean that the conditions under which one experiences and thinks about the situation do not invalidate or raise doubts about one's experiences, beliefs, and judgments about it; that one's ways of experiencing and thinking about the situation are reliable and may be right; that if one's beliefs are to be challenged, they must be challenged on the basis of evidence about the objective situation, not by pointing to the conditions of the subject that may have distorted one's experiences and beliefs or rendered them unreliable in some way.

Epistemic appraisals turn on the subjective/objective distinction. Trusting, uncritical minds take nearly all of their experiences and beliefs and what they hear and read to be objective. As we become more critical, we become more objective. A case can be made for the claim that humankind has become progressively more critical and objective, especially in recent centuries. This is the point of Hume's remark that it is amazing how much more orderly the world becomes as we turn the pages of history from antiquity toward modern times. It is not easy to find an order in the world when we cast into it the semantic contents of most of our mental states and acts. We can, of course, err in the opposite way. We may be too critical and label too many of our mental states and acts as subjective, with the result that we have a highly orderly but greatly impoverished world. Excessive epistemological puritanism has been the chief intellectual sin of the modern mind.

Levels of Subjective and Objective Appraisals

There are a number of levels of *subjective/objective* appraisals of experiences, beliefs, and judgments. The first and most superficial level concerns the simple veridicality of experiences or the truth (or validity) of beliefs and judgments. Here the charge of subjectivism may take the form of the claim that the personal bias, prejudice, or special interest of some people makes suspect the simple *truth* of their perceptions, memories, or beliefs about a situation. This is a typical way of challenging the testimony of a witness or the objectivity of a prospective juror or judge in a court of law. We demand objectivity in our search for truth because subjectivism makes our truth-claims suspect. But we may be misled by the ambiguity of the words "subjective" and "subjectivity." Skeptics may conclude that all truth-claims are subjective and therefore suspect because a truth-claim is by its very nature a subjective act. It is true that a truth-claim is a *subjective* act in the purely categorizing sense; but it does not follow that every truth-claim is subjective in the epistemic appraisal sense. If it is, this is something that has to be shown. But the very claim is suspect; for if it were true, its truth would make the claim itself suspect along with all other truth-claims.

If every truth-claim is subjective in the appraisal sense, it is because all truth-claims are made from within a distorting or misleading point of view. Every point of view is subjective in the categorizing sense; but is every point of view subjective in the epistemic appraisal sense? Must an objective point of view be a point of view from nowhere?[17] That is, must an objective point of view be no point of view at all? Or is an objective point of view one that is reliable, or at least one that is not an obstruction, in the search for truth? Before we can answer these questions, we must explore deeper levels of subjectivity in the appraisal sense.

The Objectivity of Secondary Qualities

We may have doubts about the objectivity of our language as well as the objectivity of our truth-claims. Some think that our perspective on, and our ways of experiencing, things can affect how they appear to us in general and thus even affect the meaning of our words so that we attribute to things features and properties that are dependent on, and products of, our ways of experiencing them. In other words, things may have features and properties in their presence to us in experience that they do not have in their existence. Since the seventeenth century it has been widely held that this is the case with so-called secondary qualities. Colors, sounds, odors, tastes, felt thermal qualities, and so forth are taken to exist only in sensory experiences, not in the physical objects to which we ordinarily attribute them. It is said that for something to be red, for example, is for it to have the requisite primary qualities for it to be experienced as red by normal human viewers under some standard set of environmental conditions. This theory is so solidly entrenched in our modern scientific view of the world that hardly anyone would dare to question it.

The relegation of secondary qualities to sensory experience is taken to be a major landmark in the achievement of an objective view of the world. The world becomes more orderly and manageable if we can exclude from it not only the contents of our dreams, hallucinations, and other experiences that do not hang together in a mutually supporting way with our mainstream experiences, but also if we can exclude much of the content of our coherent and mutually supporting experiences such as the colors, odors, and tastes of things. Of course we have to be able to explain what is excluded on the basis of what is admitted. In this case, secondary qualities are explained as effects in experience of objects constituted by primary qualities.

Four arguments may be given for the subjectivity of secondary qualities: (1) the variability of secondary qualities with the physical and psychological conditions of perception; (2) the indefinability of secondary qualities except in terms of their relation to sensory experience; (3) the apparent lack of involvement of secondary qualities in the causal structure of physical objects; and (4), which is based on (3), their expendability, as found by modern physical scientists, for the purposes of scientific theory of the physical world.

The major objection to the subjectivist interpretation of secondary qualities is the problems it creates for a theory of experience. This interpretation leaves us with phenomenal secondary qualities and the problem of how they are in the world. In what are phenomenal secondary qualities instantiated? Phenomenal objects with their own subjective space-time continuum? This is the phenomenalist solution. Or are secondary qualities adverbial qualities of acts of sensing? And what are acts of sensing if they can exemplify such qualities? If we deny that secondary qualities are exemplified by physical objects, we seem to be forced to acknowledge physical objects and their properties, phenomenal secondary qualities and something subjective in which they are instantiated, and semantic states and acts with their logical properties and relations. This seems to leave us with three levels: the physical, experience, and the purely mental (semantic states and acts), with experience being either something nonphysical but purely existential and factual in its constitution or a peculiar nonlogical factual structure of certain semantic acts.

If experience is conceived as nonmental and nonphysical, problems arise about how experience is in the world and how thought and knowledge can be about anything other than experience. Nothing has created more problems for epistemologists and metaphysicians than this semantically opaque barrier between thought and the so-called external world. Reductionistic phenomenalists deny the reality of physical objects and their properties.[18] Non-reductive phenomenalists, notably G. E. Moore and C. I. Lewis, have tried to hold on to both physical realism and a phenomenalistic view of experience.[19] John Dewey tried to blend thought with experience and experience with nature. He regarded experience as a dimension of nature, a product of interactions in nature. But experience, unlike deeper levels of nature, according to Dewey, could be troubled and problem-ridden. Thought, also a higher-level process in nature, was regarded as a response to, and a way of reconstructing, experience to rid it of its troubles. This was an effort to embed experience and thought in the dynamics of nature by reconstructing the language of science in terms of humanistic categories and by reconstructing humanistic language in terms of the language of science.

If secondary qualities are conceived as nonlogical properties of semantic acts of sensing physical objects, it is difficult to make sense of how the properties are *in* the acts. It will not do to have them semantically in the acts, for that would make them adjectival properties, not adverbial, and place them existentially in the objects of the acts—these objects being conceived either as physical or phenomenal. If secondary qualities are truly adverbial properties of acts of sensing objects, they must be instantiated in the acts. Yet it does not make sense to say that a semantic act has such a property. A visual experience of a physical object is not colored.

It seems that we must conclude that secondary qualities are properties of physical objects in their semantic presence to us in sensory experience and that they appear to be and are commonly taken to be properties of physical objects in their existence. An important question for those who would deny that secondary qualities are properties of physical objects in their existence is whether it makes sense to say that a physical object appears to have sensory qualities that no physical object could have. Does it make sense to say that something appears to be *F* if it makes no sense to say of anything that it really is *F*?[20] We know what it is for an object to appear to have a property that some object might have but that the one in question does not. We know what it is for something to have a property in a certain medium or under certain conditions but not to have it in other situations. Perhaps colors are properties physical objects have in the medium of light, with the color of a physical object changing with the composition of the medium. In like manner, perhaps tastes are qualities substances have in solution, smells are qualities substances have in the air (or some suitable medium), sounds are qualities that certain activities or processes have in an appropriate medium. There are, however, secondary qualities that do not seem to be relative to a medium: for example, the many felt qualities of things, such as felt softness, hardness, smoothness, various thermal qualities, and the like.

There are other qualities we attribute to things. We may experience a room as gay or gloomy; we may speak of a place as exciting or dreary; and so on. Some have referred to these as tertiary qualities. These, unlike secondary qualities, are primarily psychological qualities. People are cheerful and gay or sad and gloomy, excited or bored, and so on. These are kinds of psychological states and moods or dispositions. When we say, for example, "The house is cheerful and gay," we may mean that the house is an *expression* of cheerfulness and gaiety— that it expresses the cheerful and gay spirit of its designer; or perhaps that it was designed as an expression of cheerfulness and gaiety, even though the designer may not have had these traits. Sometimes we may mean by the sentence that the room, quite apart from whether it expresses, or was designed to express, cheerfulness and gaiety, contributes to and supports a cheerful and gay mood on the part of its occupants—that it is the kind of room that one experiences with positive emotions, which in turn incline one toward a positive outlook on other things.

There seems to be no problem about the instantiation of "tertiary"

qualities in psychological states and acts. To be cheerful or sad, excited
or bored, or anything of the kind is to be in a certain *kind* of psychological state. So it makes sense to talk about the attribution of tertiary
qualities to physical objects as a *projection*. But it does not make the
same kind of sense to talk about the attribution of secondary qualities
to physical things as a projection. The attribution of secondary qualities
to physical objects is primary; indeed, it does not make sense at all to
attribute (in the instantiation sense) secondary qualities to psychological
states and acts. If we treat secondary qualities as primarily semantic
contents (inexistential elements) of acts of sensing and regard the attribution of them to physical objects as only a projection, then they have
no existence or instantiation anywhere. It is highly problematic for basic qualities to have this kind of primary status, that is, inexistential
presence, in the world.

Phenomenalism, whether reductionistic or coupled with physical realism, took its departure from the view that sensations were private
existences, not psychological states or occurrences with semantic contents. Once we reject this existential and factual view of sensations, the
traditional view of secondary qualities is no longer tenable. Some have
concluded that sensations are bodily states or occurrences, mainly occasioned by external causes. We may be tempted, as Bertrand Russell was
at one time, to attribute secondary qualities to these bodily states and
processes as their primary locus.[21] Or we may conclude, as Wilfrid
Sellars does, that some bodily effects of external objects trigger in us a
conceptualization of them as analogous to their external cause;[22] thus,
for example, when a red triangular object affects our eyes in a normal
way we say that we have an "impression of a red triangle," meaning
that we are in that nonintentional state normally caused by our eyes
being affected by a red triangular object. In other words, when one has
a sense experience of a red object one is affected red-object-wise. This
would mean that "red" applies primarily to objects and only secondarily
as an adverb.

But what do secondary-quality words mean when they are applied to
the objects of experience, the external causes of our sense impressions?
Apparently Sellars takes common-sense objects of sensory perception
to be red in a straightforward way just as they are solid, triangular, or
whatever; but he takes the whole common-sense object of perception,
with both its primary and secondary qualities, to be something like a
Kantian object of experience, except that, for him, the things-in-themselves—as distinct from how they manifest themselves to us in experience and from what they are taken to be in common-sense thought and
perennial philosophy—are not beyond the ultimate reach of scientific
theory. Only such individuals and properties as ultimate scientific the-

ory will need are regarded as embedded in the ontological structure of the world.

Each of these reconstructions of the classical subjectivist theory of secondary qualities has its problems. Secondary qualities of brain states have all the problems of secondary qualities of other external objects. Russell only moved the problem from an external object to a bodily effect. The central problems remained; indeed, they were complicated. What kind of an account can we give of "seeing" our own nerve endings? What role can secondary qualities play in the account? Or how can we make sense of the claim that what we really do when we think that we see external physical objects is to see the inside of our own bodies? It forces us to the conclusion that what we know in a primary way are our own internal bodily states and processes (not the private, subjective states and events of the phenomenalist) and that our account of other physical things in causal interaction with our bodies is a theoretical construction to explain our internal bodily states and events. But then the problem about how we have perceptions of ordinary external physical objects is replaced with the problem of how we have perceptions of states and processes inside our own skin, these states and processes being equally external from an epistemological point of view. At least we are familiar enough with seeing ordinary external objects with their primary and secondary qualities. When we see nerve endings, in any recognizable sense of the term, they, too, are seen as having primary and secondary qualities; we see them in the same way as we see any other external things. One can come to the conclusion that ordinary perception is really perception of our own bodily states and processes only if one's philosophical assumptions and physiological theory of perception make it impossible to accept the common-sense view that we see ordinary physical objects with both primary and secondary qualities. But this conclusion denies the facts to be explained and to which philosophical and scientific theories of perception are responsible and in terms of which they are to be tested.

Sellars's claim that visual sense impressions are physical effects in our bodies of external physical objects and that they "have intrinsic properties which have a logical space formally similar to the logical space of the colours of physical things" and that "in the scientific picture of the world the counterparts of the colours of the physical object framework will turn out to be aspects, in some sense, of the percipient organism"[23] is only a more sophisticated version of Russell's position. Both are physicalizations of the phenomenalist theory of sense experience and physical-object language. They are attempts to show that the psychological, the semantic, the logical, and the normative aspects of perception and other aspects of human existence can be accounted for ultimately in terms of the existential and factual categories of scientific thought.

It is time to reconsider the reasons for the subjectivist theory of secondary qualities, although nothing seems more firmly established in the modern mind. The first reason listed above was the variability of experienced secondary qualities with the conditions of perception. This is not a telling argument against objectivity, for experienced primary qualities also vary with the conditions of perception and this fact does not convince us of their subjectivity. The way in which the size, shape, and motion of things appear vary according to the position and perspective of the observer. And, as previously indicated, much of the variability of perceived secondary qualities of objects may be attributed to the medium in which the object exists. The color of an object, for example, may vary with the light just as the size, shape, and solidity of an object may vary with the temperature. So why should such variableness count for subjectivity of secondary qualities but not for primary qualities?

The second argument for the subjectivity of secondary qualities was the indefinability of secondary qualities except in relation to our experience of them. To be a red object, it is said, is to be the kind of object that would be experienced as red under some standard set of conditions. From this, it is thought to follow, as Thomas Nagel says, that "[t]he red appearance of red things . . . cannot be noncircularly explained in terms of their redness, because the latter is analyzed in terms of the former."[24] But this is not an argument only against secondary qualities; it is an argument against any simple quality or any complex quality (consider purple, for example) that is analyzable in terms of an internal structure or complexity of simple qualities. What is being demanded is definability in terms of a certain kind of component or relationship, the kind in terms of which we analyze primary qualities such as squareness, solidity, motion, and so forth.

The primary arguments against the objectivity of secondary qualities are that, in the modern view of things, they are not part of the causal structure of the physical world and, therefore, they are not needed in the theory of the physical sciences. Once value concepts were eliminated from the descriptive/explanatory conceptual system of the sciences, with the consequential elimination of the concepts of teleological change and causality, the objectivity of secondary qualities was doomed. But in a world in which there were objective values and teleological change and causality, secondary qualities might have a causal role. It is clear that colors, sounds, odors, tastes and felt secondary qualities play a significant teleological role in the behavior of sentient beings; but they play this role through their semantic presence to behaving organisms. If the forces of nature worked for the realization of beauty and of identities constituted in part by secondary qualities, then secondary qualities would play a significant role in the teleological dynamics of nature below the psychological level. (Does it make sense to say that the form of the human body expresses human selfhood? And if so, does it make sense to say that this fact has something to do with why the form of the human body is what it is?) Indeed, if behaving organisms and their powers were products of teleological processes of nature, then, to the extent secondary qualities and the identities and beauty grounded in them featured teleologically in the behavior of sentient organisms, secondary qualities would play a teleologically causal role, even if somewhat indirectly, in the non-behavioral processes of nature. So from within a humanistic descriptive/explanatory conceptual system, there are no compelling reasons against, while there are strong reasons for, the objectivity of secondary qualities.

The Spread of Subjectivism

Once subjectivism became accepted as a solution to the philosophical problems raised by the modern reformation in science, it seemed to know no limits. It spread through the culture like wildfire until it had engulfed everything, including science itself. Indeed, idealists used the technique against the scientific party (the materialists) by concluding that the only place to drop a secure anchor from within our free-floating subjectivity was into, not out of, subjectivity itself. But selfhood, divorced from an independent and objective world, became highly problematic and tended to collapse in upon itself; it tended to disintegrate into a set of free-floating subjective states and events. This is close to the position at which Hume arrived. Kant tried to save the unity of the self and the public world by interpreting unitary space and time as forms of sensibility, the basic organizing categories and principles of the public world of science as grounded in the forms of judgment, the basic principles of morality as grounded in the form of a rational will, the unity of the self in terms of the form of reflective thought, and the ideas of soul, world, and God as grounded in the forms of reason (of arguments). Kant thought that, by restricting the possibility of knowledge to objects as they are or might be present to us in categorially structured and conceptually organized sensory experience with its forms of space and time, he had made room for belief in, but not knowledge of, an independent realm of things-in-themselves. But others concluded that Kant's limits on the possibility of knowledge were limits on the thinkable and that belief itself was limited by the limits of the thinkable. So even the concept of things-in-themselves was discredited. The idea of objectivity collapsed into the idea of publicity or intersubjectivity. But the necessary and universal forms of subjectivity that, according to Kant, made public objects, intersubjectivity, and rational will possible became relativized and historicized by post-Kantians. Subjectivism, historicism, relativism, and pluralism are the primary themes of modern interpretations of culture. The ultimate in subjectivism has been the loss of the framework within which the distinction between subjectivism and objectivism makes sense. Some have embraced this as a triumph in which the subjective/objective distinction and all the problems associated with it have been transcended and overcome. This is like those who would overcome moral problems by discrediting and rejecting the distinction between right and wrong.

The subjectivist march in modern thought began, as we observed in the beginning, with the elimination of humanistic concepts, basically value and meaning concepts, from a descriptive/explanatory role in modern science. This reconstruction of the conceptual framework in terms of which we seek intelligibility was made necessary by the restriction of scientific method to sensory observation and thought grounded in sensory experience in our search for the kind of knowledge that would make it possible for us to predict, to control, and to remake our physical environment and thereby better serve our materialistic needs. Philosophy, in the modern period, has concentrated on trying to validate this reformation of science and to help people to come to terms with this intellectual revolution by working out interpretations of all sectors of the culture that would be consistent with it. The result has been an uncheckable drive toward subjectivism. From within this perspective, we have not been able to secure a single beachhead in objective reality, not even in science.

Conclusion

Any serious intellectual challenge to modern subjectivism and relativism must address their source, namely, the elimination of the humanistic concepts of value and meaning from our conceptual framework in terms of which we seek intelligibility and define the world. This necessitated some naturalistic theory (whether subjectivist, reductionist, or whatever) of the language of value and meaning. The primary thesis of this work is that the only genuine antidote to modern subjectivism and its subversion in all sectors of the culture is a realist theory of value and meaning. The claim is that without a realist theory of both value and meaning we cannot give a defensible account of the semantic and knowledge-yielding powers of the human mind that would make possible an objectivist (realist) interpretation of any sector of the culture; but that, with the right kind of realist theories of value and meaning, an account of the semantic and epistemic powers of the human mind that will support a broad objectivist theory of the culture is possible. In the following chapter, we shall explore just such a theory of our semantic and knowledge-yielding powers.

CHAPTER 5

Semantic and Epistemic Powers
of the Human Mind

As we indicated in Chapter 2, there are restraints and requirements on the culture from both the constitutional principles of the human mind (its inherent normative structure) and from our epistemic encounters with reality, which provide us with both our basic data and semantic ties with items and features of the world. These restraints and requirements apply to both our language and symbol systems (to what we mean) and to the truth and justification of our truth-claims (to what we know). Limits on our knowledge-yielding powers are limits on our semantic powers and vice versa. Although linguistic puritanism of the kind represented by the positivist's *empirical* verifiability theory of meaningfulness has long since been abandoned by most philosophers, what was at fault was the positivist's narrow theory of verification. There are good reasons for maintaining a broad verifiability criterion of meaningful truth-claims. Whoever makes an apparent truth-claim for which there is no comprehension of what would count for or against it, does not make a genuine statement. Whoever understands a statement (whoever knows, even in part, what it states), knows something about how its truth would bear on one's belief system and thus on the world.

Grounds of the Culture

In the philosophical analysis of the culture, we have to assess what we apparently mean and what we claim to know in the different sectors of the culture against what it is possible for us to mean and to know in light of our philosophical assumptions and theories about the semantic and epistemic powers of the human mind. And, of course, we have to check our assumptions and theories about our semantic and epistemic powers against what we mean and know in the different sectors of the culture. Any assumption or theory about our semantic and knowledge-yielding powers that renders suspect some important sector of the culture and forces us to accept some theory of the sector of the culture in question that does violence to it, or generates unresolvable philosophical perplexities, thereby casts doubt on itself. Failure to recognize an error in our account of, or assumptions about, the semantic and knowledge-yielding powers of the mind could lead to systematic error in our philosophy of culture and even to systematic distortion in the development of the culture. This is what seems to have happened in modern Western civilization.

How we philosophically analyze the meaning or explain the use of a particular mode of discourse or kind of expression turns on our philosophical assumptions or views about the categorial nature of the mode of experience or subjective activity in which the discourse or expression is grounded. The important question to explore about the mode of subjectivity in which a type of discourse or expression is grounded (or in terms of which its use is explained) is this: Does the mode of subjectivity in question have the categorial nature to fund the language or expression with meaning in a way that establishes semantic ties between the language or symbol in question and items, features, or structures of the world? In other words, does the kind of psychological state or act to which a mode of discourse or symbol is basically connected have its own semantic outreach that makes possible a semantic tie between the language or symbol and a semantic content of the psychological state or act? If we conclude that the mode of experience or psychological activity does not have the requisite categorial nature to fund the mode of discourse or symbol with meaning, then we must either discredit the mode of discourse (or symbol) or look for the best theory that would explain its use.

We saw, in Chapter 3, how the classical British empiricists analyzed the categorial nature of sense experience in such a way that they concluded that it was not possible for physical-object language, which everyone will agree is connected basically with sensory experience, to mean what it seems to mean, that is, to have semantic ties to external physical objects and their properties. This led them to deny the metaphysical reality of physical objects and to construct a phenomenalist theory of the meaning of physical-object language. It is widely agreed that value language is basically connected with affective and conative experience. And so our assumptions or views about the categorial nature of affective and conative experience will determine for us the options to consider in our philosophical analysis of the meaning of value language (or in our explanation of the use value language has). Similar issues have to be explored for each of the major subdivisions of the culture and its language and symbol systems. According to Kant, our a priori concepts are grounded in the forms of the human mind in such a way that they do not have a semantic connection with items, features, or structures of the world in a manner that makes possible an epistemic application of them to the world in its independent existence; rather some of them apply epistemically only to objects as they are present to the human mind through the senses and others have only a regulative function in the activities of the mind. It seems clear that we have to know how language is related to the human mind and know the nature of the area of the mental to which it has its primary connection in order to determine how it relates to the world.

One of the fundamental theses of this work is that we, as human beings, have certain natural semantic powers with which we can semantically appropriate and hold present to us items, features, and structures of our environment, and that by developing language and symbol systems as semantic tools, we develop and greatly extend these natural semantic powers. Yet regardless of how highly developed and extended our language and symbol systems may become and how they may develop and transform our natural semantic powers, they remain grounded in, and restricted by, our natural semantic powers. So our philosophical analysis of, and theories about, our complex language and symbol systems and how they relate to the world are dependent on our views and assumptions about our basic psychological powers by means of which language and symbols are funded with semantic content, that is, given semantic connections with items, features, and structures of the world.

So how can we ground language and symbol systems to the world? There are those who say that we construct a language and that in doing so we construct the world to which the language applies. There is some truth in this, but not as much as constructivists think. Strictly speaking, we do not *construct* a language; in the process of our own growth and development, we, not as individuals but as a people, *develop* a language. The constructivists fail to take into account the kinds of restraints and requirements that are involved in the process. Alternatives and options are limited by both the nature of our semantic and knowledge-yielding powers and by the nature of the world. There are grounds that must be respected. The anti-foundationalists in epistemology reject a particular theory of what the grounds are, but, instead of looking for a more adequate theory, they reject the very idea of foundations. The only restraint they acknowledge on the culture is internal coherence, with nothing permanently fixed. It is a thesis of this work, as we indicated in

Chapter 2, that the constitutional principles of the human mind and the modes of epistemic encounter with reality provide foundations for the culture, both with regard to meaning and knowledge. What these foundations provide over and above the requirement of internal coherence, which is itself one of the constitutional principles of the human mind, are certain more-or-less unyielding points in the culture around which coherence must be achieved. All elements and claims in the culture are not equally negotiable in the search for internal coherence. The demand for coherence is itself unyielding. Concepts grounded in the constitutional principles of the human mind (categories) are not subject to renegotiation in the manner of empirical concepts. This is not to say that our understanding and formulation of such concepts are incorrigible but that there is a different kind of ground or basis for them. In an important sense, they do not have to be learned or understood in order to be had; they are conditions of, and make possible, understanding and learning. And the takings (or truth-claims) in epistemic encounters, even though they may be corrigible, have a self-warrant and justified stubbornness that other truth-claims do not enjoy.

There are two topics on the agenda for this chapter: the nature of epistemic encounters and the epistemic-encounter capabilities of the human mind. These matters were addressed in *Philosophy and the Modern Mind*. The results are summarized here and some important points are further developed. These are difficult matters, and the position advocated goes against the prevailing orthodoxies. Every effort, even repeated efforts, have to be made to make the position convincing to those with deeply ingrained contrary assumptions or theories.

Epistemic Encounters

Epistemic encounters[1] are, first of all, instances of knowing. Although "know" is a dispositional, achievement term, there are episodic epistemic terms, such as "see," "hear," "recognize," and so forth. So the general analysis in Chapter 4 of what it is to know can be adapted to epistemic encounters. An epistemic encounter involves these factors: (1) Some subject, S, takes P (let us say some fact, but it could be a normative requirement, a necessity, a structure of meaning, or whatever) to obtain in the world; (2) S is correct in taking P to obtain in the world; (3) S is justified in taking P to obtain in the world; and (4) the justifying reasons that S has for taking P to obtain in the world are responsible for the correctness of the taking, that is, they provide an adequate explanation for S's getting the matter right. But we are not talking about S's simply knowing that P; we are talking about an *encounter*, an encounter with what is known. So what more must be added? Two conditions: (5) *S*'s taking *P* to obtain in the world is partially self-warranting, that is, the taking itself, the fact that it occurred, is a validating reason for itself—the fact that the taking occurred is evidence for its correctness; and (6) *S*'s taking *P* to obtain in the world is dependent on *P* as a fact in the world, that is, *P* as a fact in the world is essential to the explanation of why *S* took *P* to obtain in the world.

Conditions (5) and (6) need further elaboration. An instance of thinking that *P*—an instance of taking *P* to obtain in the world—is at least partially self-warranting if its etiology includes factors that not only cause but justificationally support the thought or taking. When a knowledgeable and experienced mechanic, for example, has trouble starting a car and has a hunch that the trouble lies in the distributor, the fact that this thought occurs to the mechanic is evidence that it is the distributor, whereas such a hunch on the part of a layperson may have no evidential value at all. The difference lies in the fact that the causes of the two hunches are quite different. The complex causal conditions of the mechanic's hunch include detailed knowledge of how an automobile engine is constructed, how it works, what can go wrong with it, effects of specific conditions in the engine on how it will or will not work, long experience with engines and their troubles, as well as the present discriminating experience of the difficulty in starting the engine. With these causal conditions, the hunch of the mechanic has credibility. That the hunch occurred makes it worth pursuing. But who knows what caused the hunch of the layperson? Perhaps a report saying that someone who had had trouble starting a car had corrected the problem by replacing the distributor. In such a case, there would be little reason to take the hunch seriously.

The hunch of the mechanic, however, is not an epistemic encounter, even though, let us assume, it meets the first five conditions specified. Although the hunch is correct and its causal conditions contain justifying conditions for the hunch, the truth-conditions of the hunch are not among its causal or explanatory conditions. The mechanic might have had the same hunch with the same credibility on the basis of a written or oral report on the repeated troubles others had had in starting the car, without ever confronting experientially the car and the difficulty in starting it. Here the truth-conditions of the hunch would not be among its causal conditions. This is why thought experiments do not work on matters of contingent factual connections. They may provide factual hypotheses for experiential testing; they may even eliminate some factual hypotheses; but they do not endow the taking of any factual hypothesis to be the case with epistemic-encounter status.

Condition (6) specifies that the central *truth-condition* (as distinct from the justificational conditions) of a thought or taking (the fact, normative requirement, structure of meaning, or whatever, that is asserted or taken to obtain in the world) must be among the causal conditions of the thought or taking in order for it to be an epistemic encounter; that is, the state of affairs thought or taken to obtain in the world must be a central factor in an adequate explanation of why the thought or taking occurred. For example, at this moment I visually take my computer video to be immediately in front of me. And we may safely say that the correct explanation of my visually taking the video to be there in front of me is the truth that the video is, in fact, there immediately before me. Only if one had reason to doubt that the video was really there would one have occasion to look for any other explanation.

The paradigmatic epistemic encounter is a sensory perception of a familiar middle-sized physical object in easy range of one's sensory powers, such as my visual perception of the video directly in front of me, only two feet from my eyes. All the six conditions seem to be readily satisfied. But we should not take the way in which the central veridical condition of a sensory perception is causally related to the sensory perception as definitive of the kind of causal dependence an epistemic encounter must have on what is known in an epistemic encounter. Although many modern philosophers, in effect, have done just this, there are overwhelming reasons for concluding that such a position is far too restricted; it generates too many unsolvable problems in our effort to interpret and to explain the apparent meaning and knowledge we find in the culture. Indeed, such a restricted view of the causal dependence of an epistemic encounter would give us such a limited view of the epistemic-encounter capabilities of the human mind that it would give rise to skeptical questions about even sensory perception itself as a mode of epistemic encounter; for we cannot have knowledge of physical objects through sensory perception without also having knowledge of sensory perceptions—that is, knowledge of their inherent meaning structures, their logical and normative relationships with other perceptions and beliefs, and so forth. In other words, unless we were capable of epistemic encounters other than sensory perception of physical objects, we could not have epistemic encounters with physical objects through sensory perception.

In *Philosophy and the Modern Mind*, I adopted, as a criterion of whether instances of a mode of experience were typically causally dependent on that of which they were experiences, the mode of experience being the source of new ideas, whether empirical or categorial. The assumption was that no mode of experience could be a source of original ideas without a causal relationship between what the ideas applied to (what they were of or about) and at least some instances of the mode of experience in question. This is a big assumption that was not unpacked or justified in *Philosophy and the Modern Mind*. Nevertheless, it seems plausible that the human mind cannot, on its own, generate original ideas (ideas that are not analyzable or definable in terms of other ideas) that have application to the world or to items and features in the world; in other words, the ultimate source of such ideas must be that to which the ideas apply and the explanation of why we have these original ideas must be in terms of that to which they apply.

Those for whom this is not convincing must hold that experience does not have an inherent structure of meaning, or, if it does, this does not make it categorially unique. Philosophers who take Humean sense impressions to be original existences with no semantic dimension, or who adhere to the Kantian manifold of sensation or Lewisonian sense data (as in C. I. Lewis' *Mind and World Order*) need a constructivist mind to account for concepts and an ordered world. It was from within these assumptions that the Kantian "Copernican revolution" occurred. Philosophers who regard the natural effects of environmental conditions on human beings as only bodily states and processes have to tell a complex evolutionary story about the development of linguistic behavior and how language has application to the world; and such philosophers have to account for all that we talk about as mental in terms of their evolutionary story about language. A modified version of the Kantian Copernican revolution in the theory of concepts is carried forward in this evolutionary theory of language and the mental.

However, from within our semantic theory of the mental and realistic theory of the semantic, it seems quite plausible to hold that veridical instances of a mode of experience in which original ideas are grounded—or from which such ideas could be derived—have a causal dependence on that which they are of or about; for, in principle, those original ideas could be grounded in, or derived from, just those particular instances of the mode of experience in question. This is not to deny that a great deal of history and culture lies behind our mature experiences of even simple and elementary things. In primitive experiences of things (experiences relatively unshaped by a cultural history), there are, we may assume, discriminations that are relatively culture-free. Objects are semantically present in the experiences through selected aspects or features. Behavior in relation to objects is guided by certain of their features rather than others. Objects are behaviorally "recognized" in terms of selected features. We attribute such experiential and behavioral discriminations to animals. Such discriminations are, however, locked in the experiences in which they occur. Reproduction of them requires reproduction of the experiences in memory or imagination. They do not have the logical status of full-fledged concepts, but they are protoconcepts; things are semantically held in the experiences and behaviors in terms of the semantic presence of some of their features and structures. It seems absurd to hold that the conceptual and categorial schemes and structures of our culturally mature semantic states and acts were developed without a causal dependency on the nature and structure of that to which we apply our concepts and categories. And it seems equally absurd that culturally developed concepts and grammatical structures could emerge or be developed without a base in discriminations and structures in "natural" (uncultured) semantic states and acts causally dependent on what they were of or about. In other words, the best explanation of why the human mind has the structure that it has and why we have the categorial and empirical concepts that we have is their dependency on the way the world is constituted in its existence.

If our semantic theory of the mental is correct, no other theory about the ground of our conceptual system would make sense of the properties and structures that objects of experience have in their semantic presence to us. The only exceptions would be those features or properties for which the theory of projection would make sense, that is, features and properties that have their *existence*, as distinct from their inexistential presence, in the psychological states and acts as such (for example, the so-called tertiary qualities). But it seems that the structure of basic statements or takings, for example, must be what it is because of the structure of facts (necessities, values, and so forth), not the other way around, even though we are locked in, and cannot operate at all outside of, the basic logical grammar of our semantic states and acts. While, in an important sense, we may project the form of basic statements onto the world, in a more fundamental sense, intelligibility is furthered by thinking of the form of basic statements as dependent on the structure of the world; for how else could we make sense of the capacity for knowledge of the world on the part of beings in, generated in, active in, and sustained in the world? A thorough-going constructivism generates more philosophical perplexities than it solves. Furthermore, it is unnecessary.

So it does seem that, if a mode of experience is a source of original ideas, veridical instances of it must have a causal dependence on that which the experience is of or about. Thus we seem justified in employing the question of whether a mode of experience is the source of original ideas as a criterion or test of whether it makes possible epistemic encounters with reality. But the answer to this question does not tell us what constitutes a particular experience in that mode as an epistemic encounter. This is accomplished by our present analysis, which includes, as the sixth condition, that the central veridical or truth condition of the experience (of the taking that is inherent in the experience) must be among the explanatory conditions for the occurrence of the experiential taking.

Modes of Epistemic Encounters

With this analysis of epistemic encounters, let us now consider what the epistemic-encounter capabilities of the human mind are. This is a most important but much neglected question in modern philosophy. But without a thorough exploration of it, philosophy of culture, or philosophy of any sector of the culture, proceeds on the basis of blind assumptions.

In *Philosophy and the Modern Mind*, the primary candidates for the modes of epistemic-encounter capabilities of the human mind were taken to be "somatic sensations, sensory perceptions, affective and conative experiences, self-awareness, perceptual understanding of structures of meaning (including people and their behavior), and rational insight or intuition" (pp. 71–72). This is obviously a rough grouping that needs clarification and refinement. Somatic sensations, certain modes of affective and conative experience (for example, bodily pains and pleasures, bodily hunger and thirst), and perceptual understanding (which is sometimes called "expression perception") are all sensory or at least have an important sensory dimension. What I meant to include under sensory perceptions were those of the so-called external senses, including the usual sight, touch, hearing, smell, and taste. Self-awareness and reflective awareness are related to perceptual understanding in a way that is parallel with the way somatic sensations are related to external sensory perceptions; and rational intuition (or insight) is closely tied up with self-awareness, perceptual understanding, and reflective awareness. Nevertheless, it is useful to classify the candidates for epistemic-encounter powers as somatic sensations (internal sensory perceptions of bodily states and processes), external sensory perceptions, affective and conative (or what may be called "non-indifferent" or "value"[2]) experiences, self-awareness (consciousness), memory, reflective awareness (including rational intuition), and perceptual understanding (including expression perception).

Somatic Sensations

Somatic sensations (for example, tickles, itches, aches, pains, soreness, dizziness; being hungry, thirsty; sensory hedonic experiences such as the enjoyment or suffering of certain bodily states, processes, or activities; simply feeling good or bad bodily; feeling tired or rested; felt scratches, pricks, burns, cuts; felt stiffness, fullness, internal pressure;

and felt heartbeats, breathing, bodily movements, positions of the body) are, we contend, semantic states and acts in which their semantic contents are typically taken to exist. They are primarily modes of awareness, not contents of awareness, even though they may be reflexive and thus turn back on themselves, so to speak. This is more obviously so for those somatic sensations for which we do not have a special name and have to identity by mentioning their content as in "felt scratches," "felt stiffness," "felt heartbeats," and so forth. Where we have a name, as in the case of tickles, itches, pains, we are likely to be misled into thinking that what is named is the object of an awareness, not the state or act of awareness itself. And so we are likely to think that we have a peculiar set of objects, for they do not seem to be states and properties of the body. They are commonly called "sensations," meaning not acts of sensing but the objects of such acts that have no existence independently of the acts; that is, it is commonly held that for the objects of sensing to exist is for them to be sensed. Here we have the origin of the sense-datum theory. Classical British empiricists went on to assimilate all sensory experiences to this model. But the theory is now widely and rightly regarded as based on an error.

Sensations, we suggest, are "internal" perceptions of bodily states and occurrences. We say "internal" to differentiate such perceptions from perceptions of our own bodily states and occurrences by means of our ordinary external senses such as sight and touch. This seems to be true for those sensations for which we have special names. A physical tickle, for example, is an awareness of something lightly touching and moving on the surface of one's body. Although tickling one may make one laugh, the tickle sensation has a negative tone; it is an awareness of the lightly touching movement as a disturbance that one wants discontinued. The laughter that being tickled may produce is peculiar in that it is not an experience of the situation as comical; it is more like a physical reflex. Yet we speak, perhaps metaphorically, of being "tickled" by an incident or a story, meaning that it makes us laugh. We also speak of being "tickled pink" by something, meaning simply that we are highly pleased by it. So tickles seem to have both positive and negative hedonic tones; they are seldom, if ever, indifferent sensations. An itch is a somatic awareness, definitely in a negative mode, of a skin irritation. We have a strong compulsion to scratch the area of the skin semantically in the itch. The desire to rub or to scratch the area of the skin in the itch is so closely interwoven with the itch sensation that we may think of the itch sensation, after the pattern of hunger and thirst, as both affective and conative. But there is this difference: in hunger and thirst, the conative factor seems to be dominant, with the awareness of the lack or deficiency subsidiary; in the case of an itch, the affective aspect seems to be dominant and the conative factor second-ary.

One may speak of having a pain in one's lower back, of feeling a pain in one's lower back, and of one's lower back being in pain. We can bring coherence to these different ways of talking by thinking of so-matic pains, in the primary sense, not as a peculiar qualitative state of a region of one's body, but as sensations of some disorder in a region of one's body; that is, as instances of simple inner-sensory awareness of a local bodily disorder—the bodily disorder being semantically in the in-ner-sensory state or occurrence. One may feel the sensation of the dis-order; that is, one may have self-knowledge of the somatic awareness of the disorder—the sensation may become a fully conscious awareness (a centered, focused awareness) of the disorder. Thus one has a pain sen-sation in one's lower back; one feels a pain in one's lower back; and one's lower back is in pain.

It is often said that it does not make sense to talk about an unfelt pain. It is true that one cannot have self-knowledge of one's own unfelt pains. But, as we just observed, it seems to make sense to say that when one feels a pain, one feels or is aware of a pain sensation. This suggests that a pain sensation might exist without being felt. One may feel an intense pain in one's back at t_1 but at t_2, immediately following, become so focused on, and engaged by, some external happening or so en-gaged in concentrated thought on some subject, that one did not feel the pain in one's back at all; and yet at t_3, a little later, one might feel the pain in one's lower back. Was the pain one felt at t_3 the same pain as the one one felt at t_1? And did it exist unfelt at t_2? Does it make sense to say that a lower animal to whom we do not attribute a centered consciousness has pains? There are different kinds of pain-diminishing drugs. Scopolamine is a memory suppressing drug sometimes used in childbirth. It narrows the present of one's consciousness so that one does not have the experience of enduring pain; and later one has little, if any, memory of the pain. Memory is an essential dimension of con-sciousness. It is the capacity to integrate mental states and acts into a unified whole. Without memory we cannot have experiences or do things that require a span of time. Without any memory, we have no consciousness; as one loses one's capacity for memory one loses other mental powers. With a reduced range of memory, one lives in a very narrow present of the moment and when the moment is gone, it is gone forever. Remembering is a matter of making past states and acts of consciousness part of one's present unified consciousness. But in the primary sense, memory integrates and holds together one's present unified consciousness over an extended present. Anesthesiologists say that sodium pentothal, given in the arm, will put one to sleep (obliterate consciousness) immediately, but that the drug will not, within a safe range, obliterate pain sensations. What are they saying? Apparently not simply that the drug fails to paralyze the reflexes, for at least some distinguish between putting one to sleep, obliteration of pain sensations, relaxation of the muscles, and paralysis of the reflexes. So it seems to make sense to talk about unfelt pains, unless we choose to restrict pain-talk to fully conscious states—to reflexive, self-aware pains that are integrated into one's present consciousness. If we should restrict pain-talk this way, we could not say that we feel a pain, but only that we have a pain. Ordinary discourse, however, seems to distinguish between pains as conscious states (states of integrated reflexive awareness) and as simple states of awareness. It is the latter kind of pain that may exist without one's having self-knowledge of it.

Dizziness is another sensation for which we have a name. The word names, not a felt nonphysical quality in one's head, but rather the reflexive awareness of a condition or state in one's head; for example, dizziness is a mode of being conscious of a physical disorder in one's head. As with simple pains and aches, the specific factual condition in the head is not present in an experience of being dizzy; what is present in being dizzy is some disorder in the factual conditions in the head that disturbs mental functions. It is only through scientific research that we can find out just what the factual conditions are that constitute the disorder—perhaps insufficient blood supply to the brain and thus insufficient oxygen in the cells of the brain. We also speak, perhaps in a secondary or metaphorical sense, of being made dizzy by a complicated theory or set of facts. Here we may have a breakdown of semantic functions from overload rather than from a physical disorder.

Being hungry and being thirsty are somatic sensations that may involve awareness of some factual conditions of the body such as contractions of stomach muscles in the case of hunger or dryness of throat and mouth in the case of thirst, but what is essential in both cases is awareness of a bodily lack (a deficiency) and an awareness of what is required, such as, food in the case of being hungry and liquids in the case of being thirsty. In other words, hunger and thirst are somatic sensations of value conditions and normative requirements of the body. Each is both affective and conative. One can have these bodily deficiencies and needs without being aware of them; that is, one can have the bodily lacks and needs without being hungry or thirsty in the psychological sense. And, as in the case of pain, perhaps there is room to talk about simple awareness of such bodily lacks and deficiencies, even though we usually reserve the terms "hunger" and "thirst" for forms of consciousness, not forms of simple awareness.

The same analysis can be given for those somatic sensations that we speak of as *felt* bodily states and processes, for example, felt cuts, scratches, and heartbeats. In such cases, the content of the awareness or consciousness seems to be more purely factual. But the same analysis holds whether the content is factual or normative or both. In simply feeling good or bad physically, the semantic content is more purely normative; what is present in the feeling is the systemic normative condition of the body. But in many somatic sensations, both factual and normative conditions are present in a prominent way, as in itches, soreness, and tiredness.

So, in the strong sense of somatic-sensation terms, one cannot be dizzy without knowing it, one cannot be in pain without knowing it, and one cannot itch or be physically tickled without knowing it for the same kind of reason that one cannot take a walk without walking; for being dizzy, being in pain, itching, and the like, in the strong sense of these terms, are all modes of consciousness—just as taking a walk is a form of walking. This leaves open, however, the possibility that, in the weaker sense of these terms, there may be somatic sensations or simple awareness of both normative and factual bodily conditions that are not a mode of consciousness; that is, both normative and factual bodily conditions may be semantically present in events and processes in the body and may be taken behaviorally by the organism to obtain existentially, without being integrated into a centered consciousness.

If the above analysis is correct, we must conclude that somatic sensations (at least in the strong sense of sensation terms) are epistemic encounters with the factual, normative, and semantic states and conditions of our own bodies. Semantic conditions are included because, in fully conscious modes of somatic sensations, one has self-knowledge of one's somatic sensations, which, as we shall argue later, may be the subject matter of reflective awareness.

Somatic sensations, then, are states or occurrences with a semantic content; their semantic content may be taken (either purely mentally or behaviorally) by the system of which it is a part to obtain existentially in the body. It makes sense to talk about somatic sensations as illusory or hallucinatory. One with an amputated foot, for example, may take one's foot, which no longer exists, to be in an itch or to be in a pain; and one may have an area of one's body in a pain and take something to be wrong in that area when the real disorder is located elsewhere. One may have hunger sensations—be hungry, without a bodily lack or need for food. So both the factual and the normative contents of somatic sensations may be taken falsely to obtain in the body, even though this may seldom happen. But it does not make sense to talk about one's consciously having a somatic sensation one does not have. One cannot, for example, *feel* a pain one does not have. The pain one feels may be illusory or hallucinatory, but the *feeling* of the pain, the pain's being consciously had, cannot be illusory or hallucinatory. Even dream pains seem to be real. When one has a pain in a dream one still has it upon awakening. This is not so with other dream sensory experiences. Perhaps we do not have dream pains, only real pains embedded in a dream. In any case, it seems that for a state of consciousness, a state of self-aware awareness, to contain within its content a simple sensation, the sensation must exist. Some have taken this to mean that for a sensation to exist is for it to be felt. Others take it to mean that self-awareness in this kind of case is infallible. These conclusions are drawn when consciousness is thought of as meta-awareness, or introspection, of states and acts of awareness.

Perhaps meta-awareness is the wrong model of consciousness. It may be that a conscious experience of X, as distinct from a simple awareness of X, is not so much a matter of a higher-level awareness of an awareness of X, but rather a matter of how one's awareness of X is integrated into one's unified system of semantic states and acts. Perhaps a conscious awareness of something is a focal or centered awareness, not a meta-awareness. Perhaps the focal point of a system of semantic states and acts is the dynamic area or the cutting edge of the system; and perhaps a simple awareness is more peripheral or relatively removed from the dynamic area of the integrated system where adjustments and changes are being worked out. So we might speak of relatively active and passive states and acts of awareness, with the more active ones being the more focal. This may involve some measure of reflectiveness, or perhaps simply reflexiveness, for the interconnectedness of the semantic states and acts in the focal area is involved. The term "meta-awareness" suggests that the primary awareness is a passive object. The point is that, in conscious states and acts, the zero level of awareness is primary. It is where the mental activity is going on. It is like performing some overt act that requires minding in the process of doing it. This is why "reflexive awareness" is preferable to "reflective awareness." In introspection, the paradigm of meta-awareness, the primary mental activity is at the metalevel.

A pain sensation may move back and forth from being focal to becoming peripheral; indeed, it may become so peripheral that it ceases to make much of a difference, if any, among the semantic states and acts of the subject. If the best way to think about fully conscious semantic states and acts is in terms of reflexive focal awareness, which seems to be the case, then of course one cannot have a conscious pain without having a pain, one cannot have a fully conscious thought that X is F without having the thought that X is F, one cannot have a fully conscious intention to do X without having the intention to do X, and so forth; but one can have pains, thoughts, intentions, and the like that are not fully conscious. We have self-knowledge of our fully conscious states and acts in the sense that we cannot be in doubt or in error about whether we are in such states, for to be in doubt or in error about whether one oneself is in such a state, or whether one is performing such an act, is for the state or act in question to be less than a fully conscious one. Furthermore, conscious states and acts are readily open to reflective review. They are out in the open, so to speak, not hidden under or behind other semantic states and acts. In reflective review, we do not have to hunt them down or search them out; they provide a starting point in the search for reflective self-knowledge.

We should not confuse simple self-knowledge of one's own subjective states and acts with reflective awareness. The former is a matter of a semantic state or act being so integrated in one's selfhood that one can avow or recall it; the latter is a matter of how a semantic state or act is generated—it is mindfully generated or sustained by conscious interaction of a set of semantic states and acts. Not all conscious states and acts involve reflective awareness, but they are all subject to it in a fully developed and normal human being. In fact, reflective awareness itself is a conscious state or act; if it were such by virtue of a still higher level reflective awareness, we would be caught in an infinite regress in our conception of reflective awareness. States and acts of reflective awareness are conscious in that they are states and acts of focal awareness, not in that they are the content of a higher awareness.

Somatic sensations, then, are constituted by a semantic structure and have a semantic content, either factual or normative or both; the semantic content is taken to obtain in one's body; and somatic sensations may be illusory, hallucinatory, or veridical. Furthermore, of all perceptions, somatic sensations are, perhaps, the most self-warranting; their occurrence is, perhaps, the most dependent on their veridical conditions. Thus they seem to qualify fully as a kind of epistemic-encounter power. And through this mode of epistemic-encounter capability, we acquire knowledge of existential/factual and normative/value states and structures of our own bodily selves. We have to employ existential, factual, normative, and value language in formulating and reporting their semantic contents. Furthermore, in having fully conscious somatic sensations, we have simple self-knowledge of them, which is sufficient to be able to remember them and to report them, provided we have the appropriate language; and these sensations are subject to reflective review or introspection on the part of those with sufficiently developed powers. So in having conscious somatic sensations, we have knowledge also of semantic states and structures. Even if we could reduce the semantic content of external sensory perceptions to existential and factual structures, we could not reduce the semantic content of somatic sensations in this manner, nor the semantic structure of the somatic sensations themselves. If this is so, our bodies cannot be purely physical substances, that is, substances constituted by purely existential and factual structures, for, as known through and by somatic sensations, they are constituted normatively and semantically as well.

In this whole discussion of somatic sensations, especially of conscious somatic sensations, it should not be assumed that an organism could have such developed somatic sensations in isolation from other semantic powers. Somatic sensations develop in interrelationship with external sensory experiences (henceforth referred to simply as sensory experiences) that, in their knowledge-yielding power, reach beyond the boundaries of one's own body.

Sensory Experience

As previously remarked, sensory experience is the most widely acknowledged mode of epistemic encounter. In fact, it is often regarded as the source of all of our knowledge. In somatic sensations, affective and conative experiences seem to be just as basic and elementary as perception of factual conditions; they also seem capable of occurring independently of perception of the facts. Indeed, among somatic sensations, affective and conative experiences are the more prominent. We know a great deal about the normative conditions of our bodies through somatic sensations, but very little about their factual conditions. But in sensory experience, perception of factual conditions seems to be primary. To be sure, sensory experiences come interwoven with affective and conative experiences and with expression perception or perceptual understanding in general; but perception of facts seems to be basic, with the other modes of experience somehow supervenient or dependent on it. We take it for granted that for something to be pleasing or repulsive, desired or despised, it has to be present to us in some factual constitution. There are, however, some apparent exceptions. A person may sense hostility or trouble in a situation or have a foreboding of disaster without any apparent factual clues. However, our conviction that affective and conative experiences of external situations are dependent on comprehension of the facts is so strong that we explain these apparently exceptional cases by attributing to the person subsidiary or subliminal perception of factual clues. And we widely assume that perception of other people's feelings, intentions, and thoughts must involve sensory perception of the factual structures of their bodies, bodily behavior, or some physical effects of their bodily actions. However this may be, sensory experience is a very important foundation for human knowledge.

We can study scientifically the factual conditions of both somatic sensations of bodily conditions and sensory experiences of environmental circumstances. We know that there are nerve impulses that somehow turn into, or are connected with, somatic sensations of bodily conditions in the one case and sensory experiences of external objects in the other. We can study how physical and chemical conditions in the body affect the nerve fibers and the physical and chemical processes in the nerves and the brain; how things in the physical environment impinge on the body and affect the nerves and the brain; and how processes in the nerves and brain affect the muscular structure of the body and move the body or parts of it. But in such a scientific study we do not discover any somatic sensations or sensory experiences as terminal states or connecting links in the processes. For these reasons, some deny their reality altogether. Some attribute the concepts of somatic sensations and sensory experiences, along with all concepts of subjectivity, to folk psychology and regard them as destined to be replaced by genuine scientific concepts; others regard all subjective phenomena as epiphenomenal, without any causal role; others identify subjective states and processes with the states and processes identified and studied by neurophysiologists; still others identify psychological states and acts with the functions or causal roles of the states and processes identified and studied by neurophysiologists; and so on. We saw some of the difficulties with these naturalistic maneuvers in Chapter 3 and I have argued against them elsewhere.[3] We cannot escape the acknowledgement of somatic sensations and sensory experiences for what they are: bodily states and occurrences with a semantic dimension. They have a semantic content and a logical structure and a web of logical and normative relationships with other semantic states and acts. The semantic content is subject to being taken by the system within which it is embedded to be existent; and, if so, the whole state or occurrence, with all its categorial dimensions, is subject to epistemic and logical appraisal. Neurophysiology is condemned by its methodology to miss the semantic, logical, and normative dimensions of somatic sensations and sensory experiences and of all other psychological states and acts as well. So we cannot have a strictly scientific explanation of how neurophysiological states and processes occasion somatic sensations and sensory experiences, for somatic sensations and sensory experiences are not effects, in any acceptable scientific sense, of their neurophysiological conditions. All efforts to conceive psychological realities in a way that would make them amenable to such an account do violence to the subject matter.

Epistemologically speaking, sensory experiences with semantic contents that are taken to have an independent existence are a starting point. Yet, insofar as we take a sensory experience to be an epistemic encounter, we regard the semantic presence of an object as dependent on the existence of the object. This must not be confused with the view that the object of the sensory experience, with the characteristics it has in its semantic presence, is a peculiar existent (in other words, a mentalistic sense impression) that is both an effect of an external cause and a representation of its cause. To conceive the matter in the sense-impression way is to try to reduce an inherent structure of meaning to an association of two existents based on a natural relation between them. We argued against such a position in Chapter 3. The object that is semantically in the sensory experience may or may not exist; if it does exist, it is the object semantically in the sensory experience that exists in the external world. The same object may be semantically in the experience and existentially in the world. The objects in my visual experience at the moment of this writing, for example, are among the objects in my study. The same words are used to report and to describe both sets of objects; and the words are used with the same meaning in both cases. An object may have properties in its semantic presence that it does not have in its existence; that is, the sensory perception of an existent object may be false in that the existent object may be taken to have properties that it does not have. And certainly the existent object always has features and properties other than those it is experienced as having. But unless the sensory experience is either hallucinatory, a certain kind of an illusion, or part of a dream, an existent object is semantically in the experience in person, so to speak. It is not some representation of the object that is in the experience.

Some might say that to identify the object semantically in a veridical sensory experience with an existent object is an enigma wrapped in a mystery. We cannot explain what it is for something to be semantically in an experience or thought any more than we can explain what it is for something to exist; nor can we explain what it is for something to be semantically present *with certain properties* any more than we can explain what it is for something to exist with certain properties. These are categorial matters. They provide the framework within which explanations can be given, but there is no framework in terms of which they themselves can be explained. The representative theory of meaning tries to explain semantic presence in terms of existence, but we saw in Chapter 3 and elsewhere both the futility of the effort and the intellectual troubles it generates. We have to accept, I have concluded, that in the interactions between our bodies and our environments, objects with some of their properties become semantically present to us in sensory experiences, and that we can correctly take some of these to obtain existentially in the world. We can discover something about the factual conditions under which this occurs, but we cannot account for how these conditions bring about the semantic dimension of the sensory experience.

Our exploration of the physical effects of external objects on our bodies and how these effects reverberate in our nervous and muscular systems takes us only so far. In this way, we discover something about the bodily conditions under which semantic occurrences and activities take place in the body; but none of this explains how bodily states and processes become experiences. We can explain, for example, how the eyes and ears, as transducers, convert energy in the form of light waves and sound waves into neural impulses in somewhat the same way as we can explain how the telephone converts sound waves into electrical impulses, and vice versa, and how the television camera and the television receiver convert light waves into electronic waves and back to light waves for the eyes of the viewers. But we have no locatable transducers that we understand for converting cerebral impulses into semantic states and acts. The transformation of a cerebral state or process into a sensory experience with a semantic content that is reportable and describable in language applicable to external physical objects is not anything like the other transformations mentioned. While we can make transducers that perform similar transformations as the eye and the ear, we do not know how to make transducers that will perform the transformations that somehow take place in the brain (and perhaps in deeper recesses of organisms and other forms of organized energy).

Perhaps the closest analogy we have with the relationship between physiological states and processes and psychological states and acts in general is the transformation of ink marks or sounds into linguistic acts and thus into statements, questions, commands, and the like. Sentences and statements are not effects of ink marks or sounds, however dependent the former may be on the latter. It is entirely a different kind of relationship. Those who pursue the causes and effects of ink marks and sounds within a methodology restricted to purified sensory observation for data-gathering will never come upon, in either their observations or theory constructions, any linguistic acts. Such things fall outside the world available from within such a methodology. In like manner, sensory experiences and all psychological states and acts fall outside the world available to modern scientific methodology as it is widely understood and practiced. Yet nothing is more open and available to human beings or more essential, even for the scientific enterprise itself.

We have to acknowledge structures within ourselves and within our world that are constituted existentially, factually, and semantically (and logically and normatively). How and why these categorial dimensions are melded together in our experiences and psychological states and acts of all kinds do not lend themselves to a scientific explanation; nor do we have any other kind of explanatory framework in terms of which an explanation could be given. We cannot even appeal to a divine creator as an explanatory hypothesis, for the God-hypothesis presupposes what is to be explained; it simply attributes the categorial structures of human reality to ultimate reality.

Just as some factual and normative conditions of one's own body are semantically present in somatic sensations and are taken to obtain in one's body, some existential and factual conditions of one's environment are semantically present in sensory experiences and are taken to obtain in the world. Simple experiences of these kinds must occur in the normal functioning of complex organisms. We may speak of proto-concepts, protopropositions, and protoimperatives at this elementary level. A protoconcept is the semantic presence of a feature or property, a protoproposition is the semantic presence of a fact, and a protoimperative is the semantic presence of something for one to do or to have. Here we have to assume that some neurophysiological processes function semantically; that is, they have a semantic dimension and, by virtue of the nature of the complex processes involved and the conditions of their occurrence, items, features, and structures of the world are semantically appropriated: They are taken up semantically into the experiences, and, in turn, what is semantically present may be taken by the complex organism to be existent.

We are more accustomed to thinking of concepts as features and properties semantically tied to words or symbols, and propositions as facts semantically tied to "that" clauses or declarative sentences. But words, symbols, and sentences are semantic tools. We could never develop or learn to use them without prelinguistic semantic powers. Without protoconcepts, protopropositions, and protoimperatives, we could never semantically tie features and properties to words or symbols, nor semantically tie facts and normative requirements to sentences. And even when we use words and sentences in semantically appropriating and presenting properties and facts, the physical tokens of the words and sentences we use have to be semantically present to us in a more primary way.

Once we develop more sophisticated linguistic ways of forming and using concepts and propositions and acquire mastery of a language and an extended conceptual system, no doubt our sensory, and even our somatic, experiences are transformed, for the sophisticated conceptual system infiltrates and structures, to some extent, even our most elementary experiences. Infants, for example, cannot literally have stomachaches; although what is in fact one's stomach can be in an ache, one's stomach *as one's stomach* cannot be in the ache, for infants do not have the concept of a stomach or of themselves. But there is no reason for denying that there are, and have to be, primary experiences with their own inherent protoconceptual and logical structures at a prelinguistic level and that these make the development and learning of language possible.

Those who ask how we can know that it is the existent object that is semantically present to us in a veridical sensory experience are led to such a question by the way they think about experience. They think of the semantic presence of an object as a peculiar mode of existence. And so whether it is identical with an externally existent object seems like a genuine question, but such a question presupposes the representational theory of the semantic dimension of sensory experience. If our view of the semantic dimension of sensory experience is correct, the question is not meaningful, for the semantic contents of veridical sensory experiences are the objects perceived. The question about the veridicality of a sensory experience is the question about whether the semantic object of the experience exists and whether it has the properties in its existence that it has in its semantic presence.

Sensory perception of physical objects with their perceptible physical properties is, as is somatic sensation of bodily conditions, a mode of epistemic encounter; for sensory perceptions take a semantic content to be existent, they are subject to being appraised as correct or incorrect, one may have justifying reasons for taking the semantic content in the sensory experience to be existent, and the justifying reasons may explain their correctness. Furthermore, sensory perceptions are partially self-warranting in that the occurrence of the perception is evidence of its correctness, and also the existence of the perceived object is an explanatory reason for the occurrence of the perception.

Affective and Conative Experience

In considering somatic sensations, we discussed somatic affective and conative experiences and concluded that bodily pains and pleasures, itches, dizziness, hunger and thirst, feeling good and feeling bad, and the like are, or can be, epistemic encounters. Contrary to widely accepted doctrine, we contend that all of these kinds of experience have a semantic dimension; that they have a value or normative content and may have an existential and factual content as well; that they have a logical form, either that of an existential or predicative taking—as in the case of a pain, for example—or that of an imperative or normative taking as in the case of a desire; that such experiences, for beings with a language, are subject to being expressed in language as well as being reported and described; that predicative value sentences are necessary for linguistic expression of affective somatic sensations, and imperative or normative sentences are necessary for linguistic expression of conative somatic experiences. Furthermore, affective and conative somatic sensations are subject to such epistemic appraisals as veridical or valid, illusory or hallucinatory. These ways of talking about somatic sensations make sense, even if we do not ordinarily think about them theoretically in these terms. Furthermore, we do have ordinary idioms and habits of speech that suggest this way of conceptualizing affective and conative somatic sensations; and this way of placing them categorially fits in with a general semantic theory of the mental. If they were not conceived this way, they would remain an anomaly, fitting in neither with purely bodily nor mental states and processes.

It is not only in somatic sensations that value and normative conditions can be immediately present semantically—semantically present independently of the semantic presence of the factual conditions. The same is true with regard to some of the value and normative conditions of our own selfhood. We can be anxious, worried, sad, depressed, happy, cheerful, and hopeful and we can feel good or bad without comprehension of the factual conditions on which the normative conditions are dependent. The semantic content of such psychological states may be purely normative. We also have desires and longings that are primary. We do not always first see or think of something and then want it; often we first think of something in wanting it. And there are ill-defined wants and longings that have no specific or general factual content.

Our affective and conative experiences, however, reach far beyond our own bodily and personal conditions as they are available to us in some form of self-knowledge. A wide range of value experiences are emotive responses to otherwise comprehended or envisioned factual conditions or states of affairs. They may be of or about anything whatsoever, actual or possible, that can be semantically present to us in any mode. Some philosophers seem to recognize only affective and conative experiences that are responses to otherwise comprehended facts or states of affairs, but this is obviously too restricted a view. In many ways, as we have observed, our affective and conative experiences are primary. Indeed, the affective and conative dimension of experience affects and governs our comprehension of facts just as much as (or more than) our comprehension of facts affects or governs our affective and conative experiences.

Our present concern is with our affective and conative experiences of otherwise comprehended things and facts (or beings and states of affairs that involve any or all kinds of categorial structures). These include our affective and conative experiences of our own comprehended or envisioned mental states and acts and those of other beings; comprehended or envisioned biological beings, persons, and cultural and social entities and situations involving them; as well as things and facts and states of affairs comprehended more purely through sensory experience and thought grounded therein. For the sake of simplicity, let us speak of our emotive experiences of comprehended facts, with the understanding that *facts* are conceived, in this context, in the categorially rich sense just indicated. My analysis of this kind of nonindifferent experience is a much told story,[4] but perhaps we can gain some new understanding of the subject and make a more convincing case for the epistemic character of emotive responses to comprehended facts.

We have a broad spectrum of affective and conative responses to comprehended facts. We enjoy them and are attracted to them; we are grieved and pained and repelled in comprehending them; we favor or disfavor them in all the ways in which we are capable of favoring and disfavoring; we desire them and we abhor them; we experience them as normatively requiring or precluding some fact or state of affairs, or as compelling or as forbidding a certain action on our part or on the part of others; and so forth. Such experiences are identified and differentiated, not by features and properties exemplified in them as inner states and occurrences or as dispositions toward overt behavior, but by their inherent and constitutive structure of meaning—by their semantic dimension (including content) and logical form.

Suppose that, in choosing a carpet for a living room, one is asked, "How do you feel about the peach-colored carpet?" One might reply, "I feel that it just doesn't go with the other colors in the room." Here one's feeling is identified and reported, not by describing the feeling in terms of its own properties, but in terms of its semantic content, in terms of what one feels. And what is it that one feels? What is it for the peach carpet not to "go with" the other colors in the room? We might say that the colors "clash," but what kind of a clash is it? We might say that the combination is not pleasing to the eye, that it is disturbing. But what is it for the combination of colors to be disturbing to the perceiver? Further efforts to describe the emotive response to the perceived combination of colors lead us back to talking about the carpet and the room. And no set of pure facts about the carpet and the room will suffice. The color of the carpet simply does not "fit in" with the color scheme of the room. What kind of a *fit* are we talking about? Certainly not in the sense in which the carpet might be too large or the wrong shape to fit the room in a physical sense. It is a normative matter. To feel that the peach carpet does not fit in with the color scheme of the room is to feel that the color scheme of the room imposes normative limits on the color of a carpet and that the peach carpet violates those limits. This is the clash that is felt. We cannot fully identify the feeling, the emotive response to the visually comprehended peach-carpet-in-the-room, by simply describing it in terms of its own properties or in terms of its purely factual semantic content. We have to include the normative clash as the most important part of the semantic content of the feeling. The feeling could be *expressed* (as distinct from being described or reported) by simply saying "The colors don't go together" or "The colors clash." In other words, value language is necessary for identifying, reporting, and expressing the feeling. In fact, it is also necessary for a full description of it, if we will allow description to encompass all that is (or could be) true about something rather than just a factual account of it.

The logical form of the feeling is shown by the logical form of the sentence that most adequately expresses the feeling, just as the logical form of a thought is shown by the logical form of the sentence that most adequately expresses it. Of course there can be equivalent sentences, or even more or less synonymous sentences, with different logical forms. Consider, for example, "The color of the carpet clashes with the other colors of the room" and "The color of the carpet does not fit in the color scheme of the room." What is the logical form of the feeling for which either one of these sentences would be a more or less adequate expression? The first sentence is affirmative; the second seems to be negative. Yet to say that the color of the carpet *clashes* with the other colors of the room is to say that the color of the carpet does not fit in the color scheme of the room. The two expressions, "clashes" and "does not fit in," may be taken more or less as synonymous in this context. If so, the negative factor is present in the predicate of both sentences. What they say may be expressed by "The color of the carpet is *incompatible* with the other colors of the room." So the second sentence was not a true negative. Yet the sentence "The color of the carpet is incompatible with the other colors of the room" seems to be closely synonymous with "It is not the case that the color of the carpet is compatible with the other colors of the room." But not quite. Compatibility and incompatibility admit of degrees; the negation of a sentence does not. The negative predicate seems more appropriate than the negative sentence for expression of the feeling. We should have no more trouble finding the true logical form of a feeling than we do in finding the true logical form of a thought or a statement.

An important consideration for the semantic and logical structure of emotive responses to comprehended facts is the way in which they can be transported by inference. If, for example, one has a favorable attitude toward preserving endangered species and comes to believe that the cockroach is an endangered species, one will then either change one's mind (change one's attitude toward preserving endangered species *per se*) or come to have a favorable attitude (or at least an ambivalent attitude) toward preserving the cockroach. The causal theory of emotive responses to comprehended facts does not seem adequate here; for, on the causal theory, it would not make sense to talk about changing one's mind in such a situation (that is, it would not make sense to talk about changing one's prior emotive response to the comprehended facts). We don't change cause and effect relationships; we can change the effects only by changing the causal conditions. But it seems that the person who previously was favorably disposed toward efforts to preserve a species simply because it was endangered but does not at all favor trying to preserve the endangered cockroach has modified his or her emotive response to the preservation of endangered species. Although some story could be told about this situation on the basis of the causal theory, it seems more plausible to say that one came to realize that human beings should not try to preserve all endangered species; but, indeed, they should try to exterminate some, particularly the cockroach.

Attitudes are engendered by inferences from attitudes much as beliefs are engendered by inferences from beliefs. The favorable attitude toward preserving endangered species may be expressed by the sentence "It is good to preserve endangered species." Given this premise and the factual claim "The bluebird is an endangered species," we infer "It would be good to preserve the bluebird." Just as the premise "It is good to preserve endangered species" expresses one's favorable attitude toward preserving endangered species, the acceptance of the conclusion "It would be good to preserve the bluebird" forms a favorable attitude toward preserving the bluebird. Just as one may not be able to believe certain factual truth-claims because of other beliefs one already has, one may not be able to have a positive attitude toward something because of other attitudes one already has; that is, one may not have any logical room for the positive attitude without canceling or altering some prior attitudes.

Even if emotive responses to comprehended facts have a semantic and logical structure and stand in logical relationships as do beliefs, we may still ask whether emotive responses to comprehended facts are knowledge-yielding. First of all, do they have truth-values? Even if we grant that emotive responses that may be expressed by value judgments such as "X is good" or "X ought to be F" may be spoken of as true or false or as veridical or not, what about conative responses to comprehended facts? What about wants, for example? They seem to have a structure more like that of an imperative sentence. One can form a want or a desire, for instance, by accepting what one is told to be or to become in the same way one can form a belief by accepting what one is told is the case. Although we do not assign truth-values to imperative sentences, desires can be formed by logical inferences from desires in the same way emotive states that are expressible in predicative value judgments can be formed by logical inferences from emotive states. We talk about the validity of arguments with imperative premises and an imperative conclusion. Furthermore, we talk about the validity of imperatives themselves, meaning that there are reasons that validate them. Do imperatives have only validity-conditions and have nothing comparable to truth-conditions?

Imperative sentences, insofar as their semantics is concerned (but not with respect to their social force in some of their uses), can be replaced by "ought" sentences. As far as their semantics is concerned, imperative sentences may be regarded as stripped down or incomplete "ought" sentences; they, in effect, say that what they enjoin ought to be. The "ought" sentence says that there are grounds or reasons for such and such to be, that the grounds or reasons in question normatively require that such and such be the case. While the imperative sentence does not say that there are grounds or reasons for that which is enjoined to be the case, it does presuppose that there are such grounds or reasons. We may always ask of an imperative "Why?" with the same force as if it were asked of a corresponding "ought" sentence. So we may say that an imperative sentence captures the requiredness of what is required without reference to the grounds of the requirement; whereas the corresponding "ought" sentence says, without specifying what the supporting reasons are, that the requiredness is not arbitrary or free-floating but is objectively grounded. So although an imperative sentence is not, strictly speaking, true or false, when its full meaning, including what it presupposes, is formulated in an appropriate "ought" sentence, the "ought" sentence has a truth-value. And the validity-condition for an imperative sentence is part of the truth-condition of its corresponding "ought" sentence. Much the same thing can be said about wants and desires, just as what can be said about the truth-value of belief-expressing sentences can also be said about the beliefs themselves.

Emotive states formed by logical inference from other emotive states, like emotive states formed by the acceptance of value judgments offered by others, seem to be more like beliefs than perceptions. It seems that there could be no factual beliefs if there were no perceptions of facts, for without factual perceptions the semantic content and the grounds or evidence for such beliefs would be quite problematic. Indeed, it is not at all clear how they would be possible. For similar reasons, given that value sentences cannot be paraphrased in non-value language, if there were no emotive perceptions and value discourse expressed only value beliefs (emotive belieflike states), the semantic content and the grounds or reasons for the value beliefs would be highly problematic to say the least. In fact, it seems that along with the emotivists we would have to conclude, appearances and consequences not withstanding, that such emotive states have no value semantic content and that value sentences do not have truth-values. This would be disastrous, not only for ethics, but for every area of the culture, for emotive responses and value judgments are involved essentially in all knowledge-claims. So, if value judgments do not make truth-claims and cannot be validated, it would seem that knowledge would not be possible in any area. Value skepticism would generate total skepticism; value subjectivism would generate total subjectivism.

We have already found that there are primary perceptual emotive experiences of our own bodily and personal normative conditions that are unmediated by comprehension of the facts involved. Could these be our only perceptual emotive experiences? Could all of our emotive responses to comprehended facts be emotive beliefs? Perhaps our primary perceptual emotive experiences of the normative conditions of our own selves would suffice to give semantic content to our emotive responses to, and our linguistic value judgments about, comprehended facts. Such perceptual emotive experiences might even provide evidential support for our emotive responses to comprehended facts about our own bodily and personal conditions; but it is doubtful whether they could provide evidential support for our emotive responses to, and value judgments about, comprehended facts other than those of our own condition. We would have a problem about the evidential base of such truth-claims similar to the classical problem about knowledge of other minds. This problem was based on the assumption that we have self-knowledge of our own mental states but no perceptual access to the mental states of others. It was thought that the language of subjectivity was funded with meaning by our self-knowledge of our own subjective states and acts and that it could have the same meaning when we applied it to other persons; nevertheless it was thought that self-knowledge could provide no evidential support for the truth-claims we make about the subjectivity of others. For all we can know about others, it was said, they might be biological "robots," without any subjective dimension.

The problem about knowledge of other minds is a typical Wittgenstenian "fly-bottle" situation. There seems to be no solution to the problem without challenging some of the assumptions that generated it. We shall shortly argue for the claim that we have perceptual experiences of the subjectivity of others—perceptual understanding of their expressions and actions, which is a unique perceptual power that is distinct from, even though it involves, sensory perception of the bodily states and movements of others. In a similar way, there are compelling reasons for believing that not all of our emotive responses to comprehended facts are belieflike; that is, some emotive responses to comprehended facts, and not just our primary unmediated emotive experiences of the normative conditions of our own bodily and personal selves, must be epistemic encounters.

An epistemic encounter, as previously explained, is not only an epistemic taking (that is, a taking that is correct and justified, and for which the justifying reasons are responsible for its being correct) but a taking that is also partially self-warranting and one for which what is taken to obtain in the world is an explanatory reason for the occurrence of the taking. How, then, can an emotive response to comprehended facts be an epistemic encounter? How can it be a perception of the normative dimension of the factual situation comprehended or entertained in thought? How can the normative structure of a factual situation entertained in this manner be a causal condition of one's emotive response to it? Remember the comprehended factual situation may not obtain in the world. It may be entertained in false as well as in true beliefs; it may be entertained as a hypothesis, as a possibility to be realized, or as a fictional situation. The intensity of one's emotive response may vary according to how the facts are present to one, but the response will be favorable, unfavorable, ambivalent, or indifferent in whatever mode the facts are entertained. It is widely assumed that a causal condition of anything must be existent. For this reason, many would say that it was the *thought* of the facts that caused the emotive response, for it seems to be the only relevant occurrent to explain the emotive response.

Suppose normative structures were supervenient on facts. Remember that the most perspicuous form of the "ought" sentence is "If . . . , then . . . ought . . . ," where the "ought" belongs to the connective, not the consequent. This fits in with the supervenient thesis. Certain facts or complexes of facts may normatively require other facts. Thus, if those facts obtained in the world, there would be certain normative requirements grounded in, or emanating from, them; that is, the normative structure would be tied to, and present in, the factual complex. The issue is whether such requirements could be perceived (as distinct from being inferred) when the facts on which they were supervenient were entertained in thought, regardless of the mode in which they were entertained. In other words, the problem is whether the requirement supervening on the comprehended (or semantically entertained) facts could be a causal condition or explanatory reason for the occurrence of the emotive response. It seems clear that if a normative requirement that was supervenient on a set of facts could be discerned at all, it would be discerned when the relevant facts were present in thought or imagination just as readily as if the facts were present in sensory perception.

Everyone will admit that there are emotive responses to facts comprehended in any and all modes. The important question concerns the nature of such responses. Are they simply effects of the comprehension of the facts? Or are they perceptions of the supervening normative requirements? The identification and characterization of emotive responses in terms of their internal semantic and logical structures do not fit well with the view that they are simple effects of the comprehension of the facts. By virtue of their unique semantic and logical structure, emotive experiences are, or so we have argued, the source of original ideas, namely, the ideas of value and normativity. On the purely causal view, the peculiar structure of emotive experiences and the normative dimension of the culture grounded in, and arising from, them would be inexplicable. These matters become more intelligible on the theory that the normative requirement inherent in a complex of comprehended facts, and not simply the thought of the facts, is part of the causal condition of the emotive response. But even if this were so, since there are other causal factors in the occurrence of emotive responses, an emotive response to comprehended facts would not always be a reliable guide to the requirements inherent in the situation. As in the case of sensory experiences, emotive responses to comprehended facts would be subject to criticism. Raw emotive responses would give us only appearances; only critically assessed and corroborated emotive responses would give us knowledge of the normative requirements and the normative conditions of the comprehended facts. This seems to be the point in the practice of considering the facts carefully, taking them to heart, so to speak; thinking about them over some time, if we can; testing our emotive responses to a set of facts against (or with) the emotive responses of others to their comprehension of the same facts. So the epistemic-encounter view of emotive responses to comprehended facts makes sense; there is nothing unintelligible about it; and it makes intelligible our ways of talking about emotive responses to comprehended facts and value judgments related to them. Thus we are warranted, it seems, in concluding that emotive responses to "comprehended" facts, regardless of how they are semantically entertained, are perceptual in nature; they meet the conditions for being epistemic encounters with normative structures and conditions inherent in comprehended factual situations; and so, under critical assessment, they may yield value knowledge about such normative structures.

If we are right in the foregoing epistemological analysis of affective and conative experience and in the claim that value language is categorially unique and irreducible to any other categorial idiom, then there are objective normative requirements and conditions in the world, and we have epistemic access to them in two ways: (1) through primary affective and conative experiences (those unmediated by comprehension of the factual conditions, as in aches and pains, hunger and thirst, feeling good or bad, loneliness, depression, happiness, and so forth) of our own bodily and personal normative conditions; and (2) emotive responses to comprehended facts. If correct, this is a conclusion of momentous importance. The systematic working out of its implications and ramifications would involve a major reconstruction of our modern intellectual culture and have a significant impact on our whole culture and way of life.

Self-awareness

We are aware of much more than we are conscious of. In walking down a flight of steps in deep thought or in conversation, we might show awareness of being at the bottom by not attempting to step down yet another step while totally unmindful of the fact that we had reached the floor. Sometimes we even drive through traffic, stop at stoplights, make turns, and get to our destination without, as we say, having our mind on what we are doing. We may suddenly find ourselves at our destination without out having been conscious of the moves we made in route or of the time it took to get there. We may not be able to recall things we saw or did on the way. So we need to distinguish between being aware of things and being conscious of them.

It is commonly said that being conscious of something is being aware of being aware of it, or, in other words, that consciousness is meta-awareness. Those who subscribe to a representational theory of meaning and a semantic theory of the mental are likely to say that to be conscious of X is to have a brain state (or occurrence) that is a representation of a brain state (or occurrence) as a representation of X. They are likely to say that for one to be aware of items or features of one's environment is for one to have brain states (or occurrences) that, by virtue of their causal history, represent their external causes; and that for one to be conscious of items and features of one's environment is for one to have states that are representations of the representations of items and features of the environment. In other words, to be a conscious being is to be able to scan one's own representations by means of higher-level representations. This is what medieval philosophers called "second intentions," intentions whose objects are intentions.

We challenged the representational theory of meaning and awareness in Chapter 3; the challenge in the following pages is to the meta-awareness theory of consciousness. Apparently there are times when we are aware of being aware of *X* in the meta-awareness sense, but, when we are, the primary mental activity is at the metalevel and it tends to interfere with, or even to paralyze, the zero-level activity. We cannot divide our momentary attention this way without dividing ourselves. When we are aware of being aware of *X* (in the meta-awareness sense), the primary awareness of *X* ceases to be an attending to *X*.

We need at least four distinctions: simple semantic presence of *X* in a state or occurrence, awareness of *X*, consciousness of *X*, and being meta-aware of being aware of *X*. Simple semantic presence of *X* in *Y* (a state of something or an occurrence) need not involve an organized subject to which *X* is present, but awareness of *X* requires a responsive subject to which *X* is present. Being conscious of *X*, as previously suggested, is a matter of how one is aware of *X*: It is to be focally aware of *X*; that is, being conscious of *X* is for one's awareness of *X* to be an integral part of one's system of semantic states and acts in such a way that the system is focused on *X* and is a factor in shaping one's awareness of *X*. Conscious acts of awareness are just that, namely, *acts*. The subject, as an integrated complex system of semantic states and acts, participates in its conscious acts of awareness. These acts are not simply effects of a physical process; they do not simply happen. There is less participation of a subject in a simple awareness of an *x* and perhaps even less, if any, in the simple semantic presence of an item in an occurrence. In a simple awareness of an *x*, there is a systemic response to the semantic presence of the *X*, but the semantic system is not activated in such a way that the whole system focuses on, and is oriented toward, the *X*. On the other hand, in the case of a conscious awareness of an *x*, the whole system of semantic states and acts is focused on the *X*. Simple semantic presences need not require a psychological subject; states and acts of simple awareness of items and features of one's environment do require a psychological subject but it need not be highly organized; conscious states and acts require a highly organized and integrated psychological subject; but only conscious states and acts that are subject to reflective criticism and reconstruction require the level of organization of the subject that we identify with personhood.

Conscious states and acts are dynamic. The complex psychological system of which they are the focus is active in them; they are states and acts of the system in that they are, in part at least, products of the system, not simply items in it. The system participates in their generation. While psychological subjects below the level of persons may be conscious beings (they may be consciously aware of things), we need not attribute to them full-fledged self-knowledge of their conscious states and acts—if by "self-knowledge" we mean the capacity to recall, to reflect on, to criticize, and to correct one's semantic states and acts.

But there may be a kind of self-knowledge, what we may call "proto-self-knowledge," that is the capacity to "hold together" or to "keep in mind" over some period of time what one is experiencing or doing in a way that gives the temporally extended experience or action an identity and unity in terms of an internal structure of meaning. But this will not quite do. We can unconsciously integrate actions, if not experiences, this way. We often do things that take time to do without knowing that we are doing them and without being able to remember having done them after the deed. It would seem odd to say that one has self-knowledge of such acts. We therefore need to qualify our characterization of proto-self-knowledge. Let us say that it is the capacity to "hold together" consciously or to "keep in mind" consciously over some period of time what one is experiencing or doing in a way that gives the temporally extended experience or action an identity and unity in terms of an internal structure of meaning. Perhaps subpersonal psychological subjects have this kind of self-knowledge. We may say of such beings that they "know" what they are going through or doing.

Proto-self-knowledge of this kind may be identified with the kind of memory that is involved in, and makes possible, the integration of a temporally extended experience or action. Consider the kind of memory the loss of which, as in the case of Alzheimer's disease, destroys one's capacity to experience a happening that takes more than a brief moment or to perform an action that takes some time. One may reach the point in the progressive loss of memory where one cannot even hear the utterance of a complex sentence, for one cannot "keep in mind" the first part of the utterance long enough to integrate it with the last part. In a similar manner, one may lose one's capacity to utter a whole sentence by not being able to remember (to keep in mind) what one was saying long enough to get it said.

Persons have full-fledged self-knowledge of their conscious states and acts but may not have self-knowledge of their states and acts of simple awareness or of their "unminded" acts. This kind of self-knowledge of a psychological state or act involves the ability to recall it, to report it, to reflect on it, to criticize it, and to reconstruct it under critical judgment. With recall powers and with expressive and critical powers, we have self-knowledge of our conscious states and acts simply in virtue of being in those states or performing those acts. Then how can we say that there may be beings with conscious states and acts who do not have self-knowledge of them? The suggestion is that they lack the power to reflect on and to criticize them and to report them even though they do integrate experiences over some period of time into a unity as the focal point of their complex psychological system. They may be able even to rerun past experiences that are not continuous with present ones and to feign (or imagine) possible experiences. They have a subjectivity with its own inner dynamics. They are not tied to stimulus/response causal laws. But no doubt the consciousness of beings with higher expressive, reflective, and critical powers is remarkably different from this kind of low-grade consciousness. Beings with only the low-grade kind of consciousness are not capable of the larger integrated unities that are characteristic of conscious beings with reflective, critical powers—such unities as complex experiences, actions, projects, lives, persons, societies, histories, world, and so forth. These are all unities that are either presupposed or generated by reflective, critical consciousness. But the unities of prereflective and precritical consciousness are necessary conditions for reflective, critical consciousness.

Self-knowledge, then, is not reflection on, or introspection of, conscious states and acts, but it is a precondition of reflection. We have self-knowledge of whatever subjective states or acts (or whatever overt states and acts that have a subjective dimension) we can recall, report, or reflect on. While sensory experience of external physical things is the basis of our knowledge of such things, reflection is not the basis of our self-knowledge of our conscious states and acts, but rather self-knowledge of such states and acts is the basis of our reflection on them. There is, of course, a kind of knowledge of our subjective states and acts that is dependent on, and derived from, reflection, but it is a higher kind of knowledge than basic self-knowledge that makes subjective states and acts available for reflection. Self-knowledge of the kind we are talking about is simply the way in which subjective states and acts are integrated into, or are members of, the complex subjective structure that constitutes the psychological subject.

Basic self-knowledge differs from proto-self-knowledge only in the fact that the psychological subject that has the former is a more complex subject with higher powers; and, therefore, the subjective states and acts of which the subject has self-knowledge are positioned differently in the complex; they are subject to being recalled, reflected on, expressed, avowed, and reported. They are highly accessible. We do not have self-knowledge of our subjective states and acts that are not positioned in the structure of our subjectivity in such a way that they are accessible to these higher powers. Particular subjective states and acts that are accessible to these higher powers at one time may not be at another; so we have self-knowledge of them at one time but not at another. We may lose self-knowledge of a subjective state or act of which we once had self-knowledge by a change in its position in our subjective structure without the total loss of it to our selfhood. And perhaps much of what we once had self-knowledge is totally lost as we go along in life so that it no longer survives in our subjectivity. We can also gain self-knowledge of subjective states and acts of which we never had self-knowledge before. Some experience that may not have been even a conscious awareness when it occurred and may never before have been accessible to our higher powers may be brought to consciousness and to future accessibility by certain techniques such as hypnosis or psychoanalytic methods. And we may unearth and bring to consciousness assumptions and commitments that have been operative for years below the level of consciousness by philosophical analysis of what we say and do. We all make discoveries of this kind about ourselves to the extent that we are reflective and self-critical.

Although conscious perceptions are epistemic encounters, neither consciousness as such nor self-knowledge qualifies as an epistemic-encounter power. They have to do with how a subjective state or act is positioned in the complex structure of a subject: Consciousness has to do with how a subjective state or act is integrated into the system of which it is a part so that it is at the focal point of the dynamics of the system; and self-knowledge has to do with the position of a subjective state or act in the system of which it is a part so that it is available for avowal, recall memory, and reflection.

Memory

We have already considered the kind of memory that is involved in our ongoing experiences and acts. We may call this "constitutive" memory, for it is constitutive of all of our experiences and actions. It is a matter of integrating successive states of an awareness into a unified experience or action; it is the power to make temporal parts "members" of a larger whole or simply to constitute a unitary experience or act with temporal duration. However, we should not assume that the temporal parts of an experience are independent elements, for they have their identity as parts of the whole.

Constitutive memory is not a form of meta-awareness. It is in no sense an encounter. It does not have objects. It is a necessary condition for the awareness of objects. It is the way in which temporal parts of an experience or an action are bound together by a structure of meaning that runs through them and constitutes them as a temporal unity.

We might be tempted to say that memory in this form is the source of the idea of time; but it is the source of the idea of time only in that it makes possible a unitary awareness of an object with a temporal dimension. It is the awareness of the temporally spread object that is the original source of the idea of time. This does not mean that *time* is an empirical concept. The discrimination of the temporal spread of an object is inherent in, and a necessary condition of, the experience of an enduring object. Nevertheless, the temporality of the object is not a feature of the object discovered through experience, but, as Kant pointed out, the form of the sensory experience of any object. Yet an awareness has its own temporality, for one can be aware of an event all the time it is happening, only part of the time, or intermittently. The temporal dimension of the awareness itself may be semantically present in recall memory or reflection. So both the awareness of temporally spread objects and the recall memory of, and reflection on, temporally spread experiences may be the source of the idea of time, but constitutive memory as such is not a source of it. So constitutive memory is not a mode of epistemic encounter. It has none of the qualifying conditions.

We speak also of memory as our power to recall previously known facts or practices as when we speak of remembering (or not remembering) someone's name or birth date or how to do something. In such cases, there is no reliving of a past experience, thought, or activity with the remembered fact or way of doing something as its content; there is simply access to what was previously the content of some mental state or act. The ability for this kind of recovery of previous contents of one's mind could in no way be considered as a candidate for an epistemic-encounter power. Acts of recovery of this kind are not encounters; they are not the source of new ideas.

The only form of recall memory that is worthy of consideration as a possible epistemic-encounter capacity is the memory of past experiences and activities. But past experiences and their objects are not lying there in their own time frame to be encountered by a memory experience situated in its own time frame. Rather a past experience, as part of the temporally spread web of one's subjectivity, is brought to the fore; or perhaps we should say that the focal point of the self shifts in such a way as to embrace within itself the past experience.

In recapturing a past experience in the focus of one's consciousness, the past experience is likely to be reconstituted in virtue of subsequent developments of the self; it may take on a meaning through its connections with later developments that could not have been apparent in its original form. Indeed, the meaning inherent in an original experience is always incomplete, for its context is incomplete and its full meaning, like that of a sentence, is context-dependent. In the telling of an experience, one makes it part of one's life story. Experiences untold, especially unrecalled, seem impoverished in meaning. When two people tell a shared experience, it is likely to appear differently in the two accounts, for each tells it as an episode in his or her life story; the integration of the experiences into their respective life stories makes the experiences different. Indeed, the experience may come out differently as recalled by the one at different times in one's own life, not just from the failure of memory or fabrication, but because one's life story changes and the significance of the experience may undergo change.

Recall memory of this kind is a mode of consciousness, and consciousness, as we have observed, is focal awareness—the dynamic point through which one's complex semantic system is active. When we recall an experience, we rerun it, so to speak; that is, it becomes not the object of our conscious awareness but our conscious awareness itself. We are internal to, and the subject of, the remembered experience as we were with the original experience; but the remembered experience has the character of being rerun because we, as subject, participate in the time of the experience while remaining anchored in present time and we are consciously aware of what we experienced in the original experience as in its own time. Our self-knowledge of the remembered experience is of it as the *reliving* of a past experience, not the encountering of a past experience as an object. The content of the remembered or relived experience is the content of the original experience. We believe what we clearly remember in the same way as we believed what we clearly experienced at the time. So recall remembering of this kind is attending to, or focusing on, the content of a past experience in the same way present conscious awareness of an object is attending to, or focusing on, the content of a present awareness. But remembering an experience, unlike an experience of an object, is not an encounter of an object; it is not an encounter with the object of the remembered experience, nor is it an encounter with the experience itself. Therefore, recall memory is not a mode of epistemic encounter.

Reflective Awareness and Rational Intuition

Reflective awareness is not to be identified with self-knowledge; it presupposes self-knowledge. We can reflect on a psychological state or act of our own only if we have self-knowledge of it or if it is present to us in an act of recall memory; and of course we have self-knowledge of acts of recall memory.

Some have claimed that we can reflect on our own psychological states and acts only in so far as they are present to us in memory. Those who subscribe to such a position apparently do not distinguish between constitutive memory and recall memory. It seems clear that we can reflect on our ongoing experiences and activities in the extended present. We discern a misspeaking of our intent as we speak, a grammatical mistake or the inappropriateness of a remark as we make it, the grace or awkwardness of an action as we do it, and the like. Furthermore, we discern something of the logical structure and the logical connections of our experiences and thoughts as we have them, something of the logical character of our inferences as we make them, and something of the character of our actions as we perform them—how they fit in our projects and in the lives we are living, how they bear on others, and how others are reacting to them.

Often reflection on an experience or activity seems to interfere with it. When we reflect on an ongoing experience or activity, the focus of our mental activity, our consciousness, tends to shift back and forth between the experience or act to the reflection, with the result that our consciousness is divided and we may become confused. We all have had the experience of being too "self-conscious" in doing something, even in experiencing something. Certainly reflection could not affect its object unless it were contemporaneous with it. Constitutive memory is involved in all experiences and activities, but experiences and activities do not have to be present to us in recall memory for us to reflect on them.

Reflective awareness of either our present or recalled experiences, thoughts, and actions is a good candidate for a mode of epistemic encounter. Instances of reflective awareness of such states and acts seem to be perceptual. They have experiences, thoughts, and acts semantically present in them. As one reflects on an experience in progress, the experience is immediately present in the reflective act just as, for example, when one sees an automobile collision occur, it is the collision that is present in one's visual experience, not some representation of it. And when one reflects on a remembered visual experience of an automobile accident, the visual experience of the accident is immediately present in the act of reflective awareness.

Reflection on a remembered visual experience may be searching, inquiring, without commitment, or it may be judgmental, that is, it may take the visual experience to have had a clear and detailed content or to have been only a horrifying blur with an accompanying auditory experience. Reflective judgments on one's own experiences, thoughts, and actions, as they are going on or as remembered, may be correct or incorrect. One may reflectively take X to have been in one's visual experience of an accident as the driver of the car that ran the red light, only to realize later that one did not discover X to be the driver of the car until after the accident. We all make mistakes of this kind.

We may of course argue about whether the mistake was in the visual experience as recalled or in our reflection on the recalled visual experience. We can distinguish between the straightforward articulation or expression of the recalled experience and the articulation of our reflection on the recalled experience. When we simply tell how something happened as one usually does on the witness stand in a court of law, we are simply articulating the remembered experience. But when one says such things as "My memory is perfectly clear; I saw X, with that odd-looking cap on his head, with those big-rimmed glasses, and with a cigar in his mouth, sitting behind the steering wheel, just as he entered the intersection," one is articulating one's reflection on the remembered experience. With such a distinction in mind, how could one tell where the mistake occurred when one mistakenly reported having seen X driving the car? Was the error in one's remembered visual experience or in one's reflection on it? It would be possible for one to rerun his or her visual experience of the accident over and over again, with the experience subject to reflection each time. Careful reflection on such reruns might reveal to the witness that the driver of the car that ran the stop light did not have a personal identity in the reruns of the visual experience. This would provide support for the conclusion that the driver did not have an identity in the first act of remembering the visual experience and that the error was in the reflective judgment—that one indepedently knew that X was the driver and mistakenly reported it as an articulation of the recalled visual experience of the accident. Of course it remains possible that the belief that X was the driver infiltrated and distorted the recall of the visual experience. Yet it remains possible for the witness to strip away assumptions and beliefs read into the remembered experience and more or less recapture the original.

What about reflection on an ongoing experience? Could a person make a mistake here? And, if one did, how could he or she discover it? One may reflectively think as one speaks, for example, that one's voice is too emotional and that one is speaking too fast. Such reflective judgments can be checked against the judgments of others or one's own later reflective judgments as one recalls the situation or listens to a replay of a tape recording of it.

Judgmental acts of reflection on one's own subjective states and acts and overt behavior are partially self-warranting, but they may be further supported or disconfirmed by other instances of reflective awareness or by other experiences (as in the case of how one is speaking or performing some act). The justifying reasons for a reflective judgment may be explanatory reasons for its correctness. In many instances, of course, one may have no justifying reasons for a reflective judgment other than its own occurrence, just as one often has no justifying reason for a visual perception other than its occurrence; but in either case the self-warrant of the judgment can be sufficient and the occurrence of the judgment can be an explanatory reason for its correctness. The fact that one formed the reflective judgment under certain conditions of reflection may explain why the reflective judgment was correct.

However, as we have already indicated, reflective judgments on our own states and acts are not solely self-confirming; in some cases, at least, they can be further corroborated or refuted by other experiences and reflective acts of one's own and of others, as in the case of whether one's speech was too emotional.

Reflective awareness of our own subjective and overt states and acts is a source of new ideas. It is one of the sources of our categorial concept of meaning. Also our ideas of experience, memory, imagination, thought, action—indeed, the whole array of our mental, semantic, and logical concepts—are grounded (or at least co-grounded) in our reflective awareness of our own subjective states and acts. Furthermore, the experience, thought, or action that is the object of a reflective judgment may be an explanatory reason for the occurrence of the reflective judgment. At least in most cases, one would not have the reflective judgment that one has about an experience or action unless one had the experience or performed the action; but one could have the experience or perform the action without the reflective judgment.

From all these considerations, we may conclude that reflective awareness, the power for reflective judgments, is a mode of epistemic encounter with regard to one's own subjective states and acts (and one's overt states and acts that have a subjective dimension) of which one has self-knowledge.

It is widely recognized that reflection is perceptual, not only with regard to the internal structure of meaning of one's own conscious and remembered semantic states and acts, but also with regard to the identity and constitution of the intentional objects of one's own conscious and remembered semantic states and acts. This is the basis of our phenomenological description of objects. In such descriptions, we describe objects and situations as they are present to us without making any truth-claims about the objects and situations themselves in their independent being. This is what Husserl meant by bracketing the natural attitude, for the primary judgments in the natural attitude are about objects in their independent existence.

We can reflect on, and have reflective judgments about, not only what is present to us in perceptual experiences, but whatever is present to us in any conscious mode. We can reflect on what someone did yesterday, on Hitler's invasion of Poland in 1939, on Godel's theorem, on quantum indeterminacy, on Eugene O'Neill's *Mourning Becomes Electra*, and so forth. The issue to explore is the power of reflection to yield knowledge beyond the de facto constitution of our semantic states and acts of which we have self-knowledge and beyond the de facto constitution of their intentional objects.

Some claim that we can know by reflection, not only how our conscious and remembered semantic states and acts and their semantic contents are (or were) in fact constituted, but something of how they are (or were) constituted *necessarily*. This is the distinction that phenomenologists draw between ordinary psychological phenomenological descriptions and philosophical phenomenological descriptions. Apparently Husserl considered his eidetic intuitions to be reflective epistemic encounters with essences and necessary structures inherent in semantic states and acts and their phenomenal objects (that is, their contents in their semantic presence). Eidetic intuition, according to this interpretation, would be an epistemic power that would extend knowledge beyond the de facto constitution of the semantic states and acts and their intentional objects, in that it would yield knowledge of an essential and necessary structure of such states and acts and of their objects and thus of all possible instances of the same kind. This would be Aristotelian rationalism in a subjective or phenomenological turn.

Perhaps our most primitive form of reflective awareness is our emotive awareness of the normative and value structures of our subjective states and acts. Having certain experiences and beliefs, we expect something to happen, we are moved to think or to believe some new proposition, we find ourselves resisting some statement or account of a situation, or we are troubled about some belief or plan we already have. Such emotive experiences are not mediated by comprehension of the logical facts, at least not all the relevant ones. In this respect, they are like our somatic affective and conative experiences (aches, pains, hunger, thirst, feeling good, feeling bad, and so forth); they are primary value experiences, more basic than awareness of the structures of logical fact and necessity on which the discerned normative and value structures are supervenient. Nevertheless, the underlying reasons for the normative requirements may be dimly discerned in the emotive experiences themselves. It takes reflective inquiry, however, to excavate the underlying reasons and to bring the logical structure of one's mental states and acts into full reflective view.

In reflecting on our somatic sensations, sensory perceptions, feelings, desires, and the like, we discern not only their semantic contents but the logical (or "grammatical") forms that define and differentiate them as different kinds of subjective states and acts—perceivings, feelings, desires, intentions, and so forth. The forms of these are not unlike the forms of the sentences that are expressions of them, in the same way the semantic content of such experiences is the semantic content of the sentences that articulate or express them. This kind of awareness seems to be required for us even to master the language with which we report our subjective states and acts—such phrases as "I want . . .," "I intend . . .," "I feel compelled . . .," "I feel that . . .," "I see

. . .," "I think . . .," "I guess . . .," "I suppose . . .," "I remember . . .,"
and so on. We also discern logical relationships between or among our
subjective states and acts. We discern their logical inconsistencies, entailments, presuppositions, dependencies, independencies, and the like.
We could not be self-critical and self-correcting in thought and action
without such reflective powers.

   Although we reflect on, and discern some of, the logical forms and
relationships of our subjective states and acts, most of our inquiry into
logical matters is focused on linguistic expressions of our subjective
states and acts. In this way, the semantic dimension, the logical form,
and the logical relationships of our subjective states and acts are made
public and enduring and we can check our own reflective awareness of
their logical form and logical structure be reflecting on them again and
again and by the judgment of others. But whether we focus on our own
subjective states and acts or the linguistic expressions of our own or
those of others, it is by reflective awareness that we discern logical
forms and logical relations. Whether we are examining sentences written on paper or uttered in sounds, they have to be present to us in our
own expression-perception or memory for us to examine their logical
form and logical relationships. Their physical form present to us in
sensory perception or memory would not be sufficient. The purely
physical dimension of a sentence has no logical properties or relations;
only something with a semantic dimension, or something that is incomplete without a semantic dimension, exemplifies logical properties and
relations. We can reflect on and discern logical structures and relations
as such (as distinct from our emotive perception of the normative structure grounded in the logical structures and relations) only insofar as
that which exemplifies them are present to us in some conscious mode
of awareness—either in reflective awareness of our own subjective
states and acts or in perceptual understanding of expressions of our
own semantic states and acts or those of others.

   As presented in Chapter 2, categorial analysis (which has some similarities with philosophical phenomenological analysis but relies more
explicitly on linguistic considerations) yields knowledge of the categorial structure of subjective states and acts in their existence and not
just in their presence to us in reflection on or in discourse about them;
for, if our so-called knowledge-yielding experiences did not have the
categorial structures we attribute to them, they would not, in fact, be
knowledge-yielding, and human knowledge would not be possible.
Therefore, any knowledge of the world presupposes that the categorial
structure of our knowledge-yielding experiences and thought pertains
to them in their existence and not only in their presence to us in our
knowledge of them. But, as we concluded earlier, we are not warranted

in attributing metaphysical necessity to such categorial structures in things as distinct from their transcendental necessity. Whereas transcendental necessity pertains to the structures the world and its contents must have in order for human knowledge and action to be possible, metaphysical necessity of the categorial structures of the world would pertain to them simply as the structures of the world; they would be necessary structures inherent in being as such, quite apart from our knowledge of, and action in, the world.

To say that categorial features and structures have transcendental rather than metaphysical necessity does not rule out that there are necessary structures in the world; it only rules out that the transcendental necessity involved in our a priori knowledge of the categorial structure of a particular subject matter or of the world reflects an independent necessity in the subject matter. But we have reasons to conclude, as we did in Chapter 2, that there are necessary connections in the world—in the causal structure of things, for example. Within any real situation, there are causes and effects. Given the causal conditions and their context, the effects that follow upon them have to happen; that is, the causal events, under existing conditions, necessitate the effects. In other words, there are necessary connections among events. What we are not warranted in concluding is that the transcendental necessity of the causal structure of the world translates into a metaphysically necessary structure. For instance, we are not warranted in saying that it is metaphysically necessary that there be causal connections among events; all that we are warranted in saying is that there is a transcendental necessity that there be necessary connections of this kind among events. We can say something about what the categorial constitution of the world is, even what it transcendentally must be, but we cannot say what it, in the order of being, must be. In order to do so, we would have to be able to appeal to something metaphysically more basic than the categorial structure of the world that necessitated it; and this we cannot do, for the categorial structure itself is transcendentally basic. We have no platform on which to stand to formulate either the question or possible answers about why the categorial structure of the world is as it is, for we cannot consistently think of it as different nor of anything more basic.

Kant, in denying that transcendental necessity translates into, or somehow reflects, a metaphysical necessity inherent in the order of being, concluded that we cannot know any metaphysical necessity. But this is to confuse, for instance, the necessity for a causal structure in the world with the necessity inherent in the causal structure that obtains in the world. The causal necessity between two events in a given context is there in the world to be discovered; it does not hold between the events simply in their semantic presence to the human mind. Nevertheless we do not form the concept of causation by empirically noting connections among events. Our concept of causation is categorial; it is grounded in the constitutional principles of the human mind; it is part of the categorial framework that is presupposed by, and makes possible, empirical knowledge of events and states of affairs. Yet we do not perceive causal connections between events by reflective awareness in thought experiments. Our knowledge of the causal connections among events is empirical, and empirically discovered causal connections pertain to events, not just in their semantic presence to us, but in their existence.

However, we do seem to have knowledge of some nonlogical and noncausal necessary connections by reflective awareness. For instance, we know that a cube must have twelve edges. The claim that this is an analytic truth is an effort to save the empiricist theory of knowledge. Having twelve edges is not an identifying mark for something as a cube; nor is it necessarily the case that "X has twelve edges" can be "logically" derived, according to the analytic theory of logical deduction, from "X is a cube." Of course we may construct our language so that the mathematical truth becomes an analytic truth, but it seems that such a geometrical truth can be known from within a conceptual system in which it is not conceptually analytic.

Perhaps we build our concepts, especially if we are driven by the empiricist theory of knowledge, in such a way that they analytically embrace the necessary connections among properties and facts that we antecedently know by reflection. Some empiricists say, for example, that the concept of a K embraces all that an x must be in order for it to be a K. With this commitment, one is likely to run together and not distinguish between what an x must be in order to be a K according to current linguistic rules or uses and what it must be according to objective necessary connections among properties and facts. Nevertheless, it seems undeniable that we can have knowledge of such necessary connections about some properties and facts from within an impoverished language in which the necessary connections could not be shown to be analytic linguistic connections.

Knowledge of such necessary connections among properties and facts is possible by reflection. Thought experiments work in such cases. When we have X in mind as a cube, we can discover by reflection that it has twelve edges; indeed, we discover that it could not be a solid figure with six sides without having twelve edges. Some properties include or depend on others; for example, being red includes, or depends on, being extended. The relationship is not language-dependent. In knowing it by reflection, we need not reflect on language but only on what is located by the language. There is no way we could have constructed our language so that the connection would have turned out to be contingent. By reflection we also discover that some properties and structures exclude others; we know that many properties and structures of things, quite independently of how we form concepts, are contraries. Nothing can be both red and yellow all over. A tree cannot be evil. A number cannot be blue. There is no way that we could have constructed our language so that what we locate with these words would be compatible. The necessary connection between being a cube and having twelve edges is not obviously one of property-inclusion. Perhaps there are supervenient facts as well as dependent facts—facts that supervene on other facts so that if a particular fact obtains, its supervenient fact (if it has one) must obtain as well. If there were property- or fact-inclusion and exclusion and noncausal property- or fact-dependence and supervenience, such relationships could be discovered by reflection, perhaps only by reflection. A good case can be made for such natural necessities; and, if reflection is an epistemic encounter power, there is no good reason to deny them.

Many have talked about rational intuition as an eye of the mind. What they seem to have in mind is a form of reflective awareness, namely, the power to discern essences and logical and (some kinds of) natural necessities. Reason is our critical power. It is reflective in its conscious mode, but, in much of our thinking, it proceeds by emotive perception of the normative requirements of our beliefs, memories, commitments, and experiences. In confronting a situation, we may be simply moved to think, to expect, or to want or to oppose something. Information available to us in some form, whether from our own experience or from others, may induce us to accept some truth-claim or to consider it worthy of further investigation, without much understanding of the logical relationship between the information and our conclusion.

The reflective person may try to comprehend the logical or other relationships that underlie the normative structure that is emotively perceived; one may even believe that the emotive perceptions are unreliable without such an in-depth understanding. And surely such reflectiveness can make our reasoning more trustworthy. Indeed, careful reflective consideration of the comprehended facts that underlie our emotive responses to, and value judgments about, complex situations make our value judgments more reliable. But we will always reason beyond the limits of our logical enlightenment. In fact, too much concern for logical enlightenment about ordinary matters may convert us into skeptics and leave us in a state of paralysis, unable to come to conclusions or to believe anything or to accept any imperative or plan of action.

The capacity to generate hypotheses worthy of consideration when confronted with a problematic situation is sometimes called the capacity for abductive inference. Here we seem to have reflection on the comprehended problematic situation and emotive perception of what one's belief system, together with the comprehended problematic situation, normatively requires in order to integrate the problematic situation into one's belief system. The worthiness of the hypothesis that occurs to one is a function of the trustworthiness and extensiveness of one's belief system and the adequacy of one's comprehension of the problematic situation. The worthiness of the hypothesis for further investigation consists of the fact that the belief system of an informed and knowledgeable person invests the hypothesis it normatively requires with some probability. The fact that the hypothesis is thought by a knowledgeable person upon comprehending the problematic situation constitutes some evidence that the hypothesis is correct and makes it creditable to that extent. This is a very important power of the mind; it is what makes possible advances in thought and fruitful creativity in general.

Reflective awareness, then, seems to be an epistemic-encounter power with regard to a wide range of subject matter, including one's subjective states and acts, their contingent features and those of their internal objects, their logical and normative structures and relationships, and the larger unities they form—such as one's theories and plans, life episodes, and even the life one is living. Through reflective awareness, we seem to be able to encounter epistemically the grammatical and logical properties, structures, and relationships of linguistic and symbolic expressions that we understand and the features and properties of the larger unities they form. Through reflective awareness, with philosophical methods, we seem to be able to discover transcendental conditions for knowledge and action. Furthermore, through reflective awareness, we seem to discern such objective necessities as inclusion, exclusion, supervenience, and dependence of properties and facts; and what it makes sense to say and what it does not make sense to say both by virtue of the way language has been formed and by virtue of objective compatibilities and incompatibilities of properties and structures of reality.

Reflective awareness yields truths about both contingencies and necessities: truths about contingent properties and structures in our subjective states and acts and their intentional objects; truths about contingent properties and structures of the expressions and symbols we understand and the various unities they form; truths about logical structures and relations of subject matters with inherent structures of meaning; truths about transcendental necessities; and truths about compatibility, incompatibility, dependence, and supervenience of properties and facts. Emotive reflection, both on its own and in response to comprehended facts, yields truths about the normative and value structures of our semantic states and acts.

The major objection to reflection as a mode of epistemic encounter is the problem about how the reflective insight or judgment is dependent on what it is of or about so that the central truth-condition of the judgment is an explanatory reason for the occurrence of the reflective judgment. This is not unlike the problem about how an emotive response to comprehended facts can be an epistemic encounter. The parallel between an emotive judgment and a sensory perceptual judgment is perhaps even more obvious than that between a reflective judgment and a sensory perceptual judgment. Nevertheless, it seems compelling that reflection on subjective states and acts and on comprehended linguistic and symbolic expressions yields some form of knowledge of them that has the character of being perceptual; that is, reflection produces judgments that are somehow dependent on, and are correctable with respect to, their subject matter. But, as with emotive experiences of external situations (situations external to one's body or personal self), the subject matter of reflective judgments has to be present in self-knowledge or comprehended in some mode in order for it to be the subject matter of reflection, with the exception of our primary emotive experiences of the normative structure of our mental system.

Perceptual Understanding

We have the capacity to discern what others are experiencing and doing and to interact with them, to discern what others are saying and to engage in a conversation with them, to understand and to respond to various kinds of expressions and symbols, and to discern and to relate to various social realities. In terms of what semantic and epistemic powers are these things possible?

Those who acknowledge no epistemic-encounter powers other than sensory experience and reflection (or introspection) have trouble in trying to account for these human facts. The classic problem about knowledge of other minds is a product of these commitments. Some have even denied that we have knowledge of other minds on the grounds that it is impossible. Others have tried to construct elaborate theories that would show how such knowledge is grounded in, and derived from, sensory experience and some form of self-knowledge.

We have concluded that meaning is a kind of internality: that experiences, thoughts, rememberings, beliefs, attitudes, plans, and actions have an inherent structure of meaning; that they have an inexistential, semantic content. Furthermore, we have argued that our semantic language cannot be paraphrased or translated into any non-semantic idiom. These claims are null and void unless we have epistemic access to such irreducible internal structures of meaning.

We have already contended that by self-knowledge, recall memory, and reflection we have knowledge of the semantic internality of some of our own psychological states and acts. Could our knowledge of the semantic internality of the psychological states and acts of others be derived from this epistemic base? Perhaps all of our more or less developed experiences and activities are informed by acquired concepts. Could it be that we form our concepts of meaning on the basis of our awareness of our own subjectivity and then infuse them in our sensory observation of the behavior and expressions of others?

According to this account, the formation of our concepts of meaning would be a strictly private affair; yet, language is a social phenomenon. If this were the true account of the formation of our concepts of meaning and subjectivity, a public language of meaning and minds would be highly problematic, if not impossible. Any theory of our concepts of meaning and subjectivity with this burden must be regarded as implausible, if not necessarily false.

Furthermore, at least some non-linguistic and non-reflective animals and prelinguistic and prereflective human beings are aware of others as subjects and agents. Cats and dogs, for example, clearly discriminate between things and sensitive and purposive beings, between living and dead animals, between happenings and actions. They discern and recognize friendly and hostile behaviors of other animals. They even discern a difference between being stepped on or stumbled over and being kicked by a person. Trained dogs, after some transgression, may show shame in the presence of their masters and try to avoid their look. They not only recognize behavior as such; they are sensitive to attitudes and intentions. They acquire some understanding of signs and language.

Children, from the beginning, respond differently to people than they do to things. They are sensitive to differences in feelings, attitudes, and intentions. They recognize the difference between being attended to and being ignored. They are in an interacting relationship with their environment and they quickly learn to distinguish between responses and simple cause and effect relationships. In making this distinction, they are somehow discerning the internality of the responses. Clearly such discernment is not a matter of an experience being informed with concepts generated from self-knowledge and reflection on one's own experiences and actions. Discernment of the responses of others is more basic and primitive than self-knowledge and reflection.

Contrary to the claims of the Lockean tradition, human beings do not form their mental concepts from reflection on their own mental states and activities and then apply them to others on the basis of sensory criteria. Perceptual understanding of others and self-awareness with reflection are co-sources of our concepts of subjectivity and meaning. Furthermore, it seems that perceptual understanding of others matures faster than self-knowledge and forms the first experiential basis of our psychological concepts. Indeed, perceptual understanding of others seems to be just as basic and primitive in human beings and animals as sensory experience of physical objects. In fact, a case can be made for the claim that one's most primitive experience of the environment is an experience of it as responsive to oneself, and that one's most primitive world is an intersubjective world. An alien, unknowing, unresponsive world is a late development in our cultural history.

Children would never learn a cultural language without being in an intersubjective, interacting, and intercommunicating relationship with others at a prelinguistic level. They and those from whom they learn a language must share an environment that is experientially delineated in somewhat common ways by both parties. Children must have some perceptual understanding of how others are experientially delineating their environment and of what they are doing in order to learn their language. This is a strong consideration against the view that all of our categorizing and conceptualizing is language-dependent. Language and language learning are outgrowths of shared experiences, mutual perceptual understanding, and a common environment.

Our interest is in perceptual understanding of others and of their behavior. If some perceptual understanding of others must occur without the benefit of being informed or structured by concepts formed from self-knowledge, and if perceptual understanding delineates its subject matter in terms of its inherent structure of meaning, then perceptual understanding must be an original source of such conceptual delineations. Yet traditional empiricist analysis of sensory experience does not show how this is possible. Meaning is a categorial concept, not an empirical one. Categories are operative in experience, not just in thought. They are operative in experience from its inception; they are not generated by or from experience. The empiricist analysis of sense experience does not account for how we acquire any of our categorial concepts. Causation is a prominent example. So we should not be disturbed when the empiricist's analysis of sensory experience does not account for how we discern the subjectivity, the semantic interiority, of the behavior of others through sensory experience. We do, of course, discover empirically which events are causally connected with each other; and we do discover empirically, but in a different way, which objects have a semantic constitution and which occurrences are actions rather than simply events. Furthermore, we empirically discern the particular subjective structure of the behavior of others; we experientially read what they are doing and saying.

The parallels between the categories of meaning and causality go further. Causality is involved in our experiences as an agent as well as in our experiences as an observer. In acting on, and in resisting, our environment, we feel our acts and the energy exerted in them affecting the environment and we feel the forces of the environment affecting us. In such experiences, we have quite a different perspective on causal relationships than when we observe causal connections among external events. Much the same is true with regard to our experience of inherent structures of meaning. We have self-knowledge of some of our own states and acts of meaning and we experience the meaning of others when we are in an interacting, intercommunicating relationship with them; and we observe the behavior and interactions of others. We could not be simply observers in regard to meaning structures; neither could we be merely observers in regard to causal structures. We could not be an agent in regard to actions without interacting with forces in the environment; neither could we be self-aware and have self-knowledge without interacting and intercommunicating with other selves. Self-awareness and awareness of the subjectivity of others develop together. The categorial delineation of meaning is inherent in both kinds of experience.

Given that we can experientially discover which sensory objects have a semantic constitution, which states and movements of a semantically constituted object have semantic constitutions of their own, and even what the semantic constitution of a particular bodily state or movement is, we check our perceptions of others and of their behavior for internal consistency and mutual support as well as with all our relevant beliefs and with the perceptions and beliefs of others. Indeed, we check our perceptions and beliefs about the subjective constitution of others with their own reports and avowals of their subjectivity. In some respects this critical process has an advantage over our perceptions and beliefs about physical things, for human subjects can reveal themselves to us and object to our errors in unique ways through expressions, avowals, and reports.

Expression-perception is a form of perceptual understanding. Expressions body-forth and make publicly accessible structures of subjectivity. Strictly speaking, expressions are not simply embodiments of meaning, but *intended* embodiments. But we in fact speak of whatever manifests or expresses an "inner" or subjective dimension as an expression. So "perceptual understanding" and "expression-perception" are often interchangeable. Yet "expression-perception" may be reserved for the perceptual understanding of *expressions* in the strict sense of the term. If so, it is only a specific form of perceptual understanding, with no special epistemological significance.

From all that has been said, it seems clear that perceptual understanding is a mode of epistemic encounter. It meets all the qualifying conditions. Acts of perceptual understanding, including expression-perceptions, embody truth-claims that may be correct or incorrect; they may have justifying reasons that explain their correctness when they are correct; they are partially self-warranting; they are the source (or one of the sources) of the categorial concept of meaning and for the whole array of mental, linguistic, and logical concepts; and, when they are correct, their truth-conditions are among the explanatory reasons for their occurrence.

Conclusion

Holding that there are restraints and requirements on the culture both from the constitutional principles of the human mind and from our epistemic encounters with reality, we have, in this chapter, explored the nature of epistemic encounters and the specific epistemic-encounter powers of the human mind.

An epistemic encounter is a knowledge-yielding experience. It involves, according to our account, not only taking something to be the case, being correct in doing so, having good reasons for doing so, and having justifying reasons that are explanatory reasons for the correctness of the taking in question; it also involves the taking being partially self-warranting and the central truth-condition (or correctness condition) of the taking being an explanatory reason for the occurrence of the taking.

In considering somatic sensation, sensory perception, affective/conative experience, self-awareness, recall memory, reflection, and perceptual understanding as candidates for modes of epistemic encounter, we concluded, that all of these, except simple self-awareness and recall memory, qualify as epistemic-encounter powers. Somatic sensation is a mode of epistemic encounter but it does not provide us with any categories distinct from sensory perception and affective/conative experience. In fact, sensory perception and affective/conative experiences simply have a somatic subdivision. So it seems that we have at least four modes of epistemic encounters: sensory perception, affective/conative experience, reflection, and perceptual understanding.

If this epistemological analysis of our semantic and epistemic powers is correct, then our philosophical analysis of the language and symbols of the culture is not under the restraints most modern philosophers have thought, and the problems for which many philosophical theories have been constructed to solve have been undercut. The humanistic conceptual system, in terms of which we constitute ourselves and define and live our lives, is not so problematic after all. Indeed, the world seems to be such, ontologically speaking, that human existence, humanistically conceived, is more or less intelligible in a way that should undermine our modern ontological alienation and help overcome our human identity crisis. But if this is the case, our modern culture, which has been built on our modern assumptions and saturated with our modern theories, may need radical reconstruction.

CHAPTER 6

The Subjective and Normative Structure of Selfhood

The concepts *self* and *person* have close ties. Grammatically the term "self" is more complex and it has a wider extension than "person." But we are interested in the concept *self* only insofar as it is *person*-related. We may talk about "the epistemic self" and "the moral self." And we may say that a person is one who, in a normal, mature state, is both an epistemic self and a moral self. In this sense, we seem to think of a person's selfhood in terms of one's inner constitution that defines one's identity.

Persons

Person is preeminently a humanistic concept. It is to the humanities and to humanistic discourse in general what the concept of a physical object is to the physical sciences and to ordinary talk about physical things.

The assumption is that *physical object* is not an empirical concept. It is not formed by noting similarities and differences among objects of sensory experiences; it is rather a basic concept that is involved in distinguishing between veridical and non-veridical sensory experiences. In other words, *physical object* is an a priori, categorial concept; it is not a product of empirical inquiry, but part of the conceptual framework that makes sensory empirical knowledge possible. This does not mean that how we understand and articulate the concept is fixed and unchangeable. It does mean, however, that what is understood and articulated in a definition of the concept is found by reflection on, and analysis of, the tacit conceptual delineations necessarily involved in knowledge-yielding sensory experience. It means that we must discriminate between sensory experience and existential objects in order to

179

distinguish between veridical and non-veridical sensory experiences. Of course some philosophers have denied that sensory experiences have independent objects and, consequently, have rejected the physical-object category. But the philosophical perplexities that were generated by the resulting idealism or phenomenalism indicate that there was an error in the way in which the semantic dimension of sense experience was understood. After philosophical debate for nearly three centuries, the physical-object category seems to be uneliminable and irreducible in the framework of human thought.

The humanities, as indicated in Chapters 1 and 2, share with ordinary speech a universe of discourse, which, unlike the physicalistic language of the sciences, is grounded in the full spectrum of human experience, including our affective and conative experiences, self-knowledge of our own subjectivity, perceptual understanding of others, and reflective awareness, as well as purely sensory experiences. The language of the humanities involves not only the categories of physical existence and factuality, but also the categories of normativity and value, meaning (semantic intentionality) and logic, and subjectivity and selfhood. The humanities seek to understand and to assess critically human beings and their experiences, activities, expressions, and social structures; and they include efforts in religion and theology to extend humanistic language and ways of thought to the larger world, including ultimate reality.

If the concept of a person is to the humanistic universe of discourse what the concept of a physical object is to ordinary and scientific talk about physical things, this would indicate that, if what we have said about the physical-object category is true, *person* is an a priori, categorial concept also. Indeed, the concept of a person, at least in some rudimentary form, is part of the conceptual framework that makes personal experiences and acts possible. This does not mean that one has to have a formulated concept of a person, or even that one has to be able to define the concept in any explicit way, but rather that one, in one's *personal* experiences and acts (those that qualify as experiences and acts of a person), makes, at least in a rudimentary way, the kind of discriminations (or has the structure of consciousness) that the use of the concept involves. In other words, one has to be present to oneself as a person, at least in a tacit way, but not in the same way in which an object is present to one as a K, in order for one to have the experiences and to perform the acts of a person. So the concept of a person cannot be an "empirical" concept—it is not grounded in the consideration of objects and the selection of features of them as classification criteria. It is an a priori concept inasmuch as it is a necessary condition, not only for empirical knowledge, but also for intellectual and artistic concerns, moral and religious experience, and personal activities of all kinds.

It has been recognized for a long time that reflective criticism, even that which is involved in, and makes possible, perceptual knowledge of physical objects, requires—indeed, presupposes—a unitary conscious-ness with a transcending center. Such a unitary consciousness is a dy-namic semantic system that is present to itself in such a way that the logical integrity of the whole is monitored from the perspective of a unifying center that is a function of the whole system. The unifying center is always the transcending subject of, and thus is presupposed by, each conscious state and act—that is, each semantic state and act that is part of the focal awareness of the system, for there can be no focal awareness of the system without a transcending, unifying center that defines the focus. The integrated system, functioning through the center, is present to itself, and expresses itself, as *I*.

A *knowing* subject, as distinct from a being that may have "percep-tions" of, and correct responses to, the items and features of its envi-ronment by virtue of its biological constitution and causal conditioning, is one that is sensitive to, and moved by, the normative structure grounded in the logical constitution and relationships of one's experi-ences and other psychological states and acts. Such a being has critical powers by virtue of which he or she can be self-corrective and creative. Without these, one would not be capable of knowledge in the human sense (that is, one would not be capable of rational knowledge), for knowing, in this sense, not only involves semantically taking (in contrast with behaviorally taking) something to be the case and being correct in taking it to be so, but also having grounds or reasons for taking it to be so and being open to counter-grounds and counter-reasons. In other words, the *taking* involved has to be a rational act, one grounded in and responsive to reasons. Only a centered act of a unified reflective con-sciousness can be rational in this manner.

Such a centered act has not only an internal object, a semantic con-tent, but also an internal subject. A first person report or avowal of it takes some such form as "I think . . . ," "I see . . . ," "I remember . . . ," "I did . . . ," "I will do . . . ," and so forth. The I is not only the transcend-ing center, the perspective, in which the complex semantic system comes to unity and achieves a focus, it is the whole system, integrated and focused under its transcending center or perspective, that gener-ates and stands behind the centered act in question. The act cannot be divorced from its subject pole anymore than it can be separated from its internal object. But the I, the subject, is not only an element in the formal structure of the act, the defining point of the perspective, but, as the dynamic, self-aware subject of the act, it is both existentially and semantically present in the act. In all personal acts (in all centered acts of a unified reflective consciousness) the person (the productive seman-tic system under the governance of the centered reflective consciousness) is existentially constitutive of the act and present to itself in the act, at least by presupposition and potentially in self-knowledge, if not explicitly.

So the concept of a person, or the delineation that the concept makes, at least in part, is present in, or presupposed by, and is constitutive of, all knowledge-yielding experience and thought, for only integrated and critically assessable experience or thought yields knowledge.

The concept of the self that could be formulated by reflective analysis of the way the self is present in knowledge-yielding experience and thought would not be fully adequate. A human being could not be only a thinker and knower, for one can be such only in the context of the life of an agent. The pragmatists are right in insisting that knowledge is possible only in the context of action. We cannot separate persons as epistemic beings from persons who pursue projects and live a life under the guidance of knowledge and critical judgment. Ideas and truth-claims are tested in living and through action. Knowledge-seeking and knowledge-acquisition presuppose the context of living a life.

Decision-making and action in the pursuit of chosen ends require reflective criticism in much the same way as do knowledge-yielding experience and thought. And such criticism presupposes the transcendental unity of one's life in much the same way as the criticism of knowledge-yielding experience and thought requires the transcendental unity of apperception. The life that one is living is a dynamic, factual, normative, semantic, and logical system that organizes and directs itself through a transcending center and expresses itself as *I*.

The point is that the self (the I) that is present to oneself as the presupposed and necessary subject in knowledge-yielding experience and thought must be identifiable as the self (the I) that is present to oneself as the presupposed and necessary subject of decisions and actions. This seems obvious. Consider the absurdities that would follow from the rejection of it: How could my knowledge, belief, or judgment about a situation be a guide to my action if the self of knowledge were not the self of action? In order to understand a person's action, to know *what* one did, we have to know the intention that informed the action; and, in order to know the intention of an action, we have to know how the agent comprehended the situation, what he or she believed about the situation or took it to be. If the subject (the I) of the intention (and thus of the action) were not identical with the subject (the I) of the beliefs and takings, intentions and actions would be totally unintelligible. It seems clear that we cannot drive any kind of a wedge between the subject of one's experiences, beliefs, and thoughts on one hand and the subject of one's intentions and actions on the other without making selfhood, thought, and action unintelligible.

As an epistemic subject, one finds oneself under the imperatives of rationality; that is, one finds oneself subject to certain principles of criticism in the areas of experience and thought. It is not open to one to be unconcerned about inconsistency and error in one's perceptions and beliefs. Anyone with even minimum epistemic powers is always vulnerable to logical criticism. Commitment to the normative principles of logic is not a matter of choice; it is inherent in being a functioning person, and thus in being capable of choice.

Also as a rational *agent*, one is subject to principles of criticism. One appraises means in relation to ends, immediate ends in relation to longer-term goals, long-term goals in relation to one's life as a whole, and one's life as a whole in terms of its worthiness for one as the kind of being and as the particular individual one is. The last step is not necessarily last in a temporal sense. It is simply where partial reflective criticism of purposive action leads. Criticism short of it is manifestly incomplete. The imperative to live a worthy life of one's own is presupposed in reflective criticism of intention and action just as the imperative to seek truth and to be rationally justified in belief is presupposed in reflective criticism of experience and thought. A person is vulnerable to moral criticism in the way in which one is vulnerable to logical criticism. Commitment to the principles of moral criticism is inherent in personhood in the same manner as commitment to the principles of logical criticism. Moral education, as education in logic, taps into imperatives inherent in one's being as a person.

In insisting that an epistemic self must be a moral self, we do not intend to deny that cats, dogs, chimps, and severely retarded human beings have, in some sense, "perceptual knowledge" without being moral agents; but we do deny that they qualify as *epistemic persons*— beings who critically assess experience and belief and seek to place what they take to be real in the world under some description and explanation that would render it intelligible. In order to seek such an integrated and ordered world, one has to be an integrated self with a transcending center; and being an integrated self (that is, a being for whom integration is a normative requirement that is causally operative in one's inner dynamics) requires that one seek an integrated and ordered world in which what is real is intelligible. Furthermore, one cannot be an integrated self without an integrated life. A rational agent has to place an act in a life much in the same way a knower has to place a known object in the world. But is a unified life enough? Does one have to place an act and the life of which it is a part in a unified world with a dimension of value and meaning? This is a question to be explored later.

The crucial point is that the self that is, by its constitution, under an imperative to know (to critically assess experience and belief) and to understand (to place what is taken to be known in the world as unified under some frame of description and explanation) has to be an agent under an imperative to define and to live a life that would stand justified under reflective criticism. Only a being struggling under an imperative to be an integrated self and to live an integrated, justified life would be under an imperative to seek a reliable, integrated view of the world. If one were simply reacting to what was immediately present in sense experience in terms of immediately felt need or instinct or conditioned response, one would not have a governing concern to be correct in perception and belief and to render intelligible what one experiences. It is an integrated self living an integrated life that requires an integrated world; it is the life of a rational agent that requires one to be a knower.

As a knower-agent, then, one is, through one's tacit self-concept, present to oneself as a person. This self-concept is not simply of oneself as a subject, as a unified self generating centered acts; it is a normative self-concept, for it is of oneself as a subject who is under logical and moral imperatives that impinge on one as categorical responsibilities. Failure to fulfill these imperatives is quite different from failure to satisfy a desire or an instinctual drive; it faults one's integrity as a person and thus jeopardizes one's being.

All of this is very sketchy, but perhaps it will suffice for the fundamental point that one has to be present to oneself as a person, not as the object of one's experiences, thoughts, and intentions, but as the reflective subject of such semantic states and acts. Thus the concept of a person is not an empirical concept; it is not the product of, but a presupposition and constituent of the subject of, critically assessed experience, thought, intention, and action. The self, in performing personal acts, is delineated *as a person* in its presence to itself in its personal acts. Thus the concept of a person is a categorial concept. In this respect it is like the concept of a physical object, but the two concepts are presupposed in knowledge and action in different ways. *Person*, unlike *physical object*, is not grounded in the distinction between veridical and non-veridical sensory experiences, but rather in the conditions that make possible the drawing of such a distinction by a knower-agent.

Not only do we have a tacit categorial concept of a person, but we develop an explicit concept. We do this with all of our categorial concepts, but the concept of a person receives special attention because of its centrality and importance in our personal lives and in education, morality, law, the arts, and religion. There have been special efforts to articulate and to interpret the categorial core concept of a person in general and how it features in our individual normative self-concepts.

To the extent the categorial concept is misinterpreted or denied, one's particular normative self-concept and one's selfhood and the life one lives may be distorted or perverted, for the basic rational and moral imperatives are anchored in the tacit categorial concept of oneself as a person. And of course we learn a great deal "empirically" about human persons in general and about ourselves in particular, just as we do about physical objects and our own bodies. Anyone's categorial normative self-concept will be fleshed out "empirically" in many ways, including what it is to be a *human* person, who one is among other people, what one's strengths and weaknesses are, what one's individual needs and ideals are, what one's special responsibilities and rights are, and so forth.

Our position is in agreement with Kant's fundamental insight that the imperatives of rationality, including morality, are grounded in personhood and that persons do not constitute a natural kind. It is easy, of course, for us to confuse human beings and persons, for in the minds of most of us, the two classes are extensionally equivalent. But it is not a logical truth that all persons are human beings. It may not be even causally necessary for persons to be human beings, or even factually true that all persons are human beings. Any substance that would embody the form and generate and sustain the powers of a person would suffice. For all we know, there may be, or at least could be, nonhuman persons.

But this does not mean that natural-law philosophers who ground rationality and ethics in human nature are wrong, for human beings, humanistically conceived, are persons; that is, they are beings who, by their natural constitution, ought to develop the requisite powers and to define and to live a life under the organizing and governing rational and moral imperatives of personhood.

Human Beings

Human being appears to be an empirical concept of a natural kind. Nevertheless, we seem compelled to acknowledge that human beings are persons. It would seem, then, that to the extent "X is a human being" entails "X is a person" (remember, an immature or impaired person is a person), *human being* is not entirely an empirical concept. But "X is a rock" entails "X is a physical object"; and, as we observed earlier, *physical object* is not an empirical concept. The two cases, however, are not quite parallel. Being a physical object, or at least having a physical dimension, is necessarily true of all "external" objects known or knowable through sensory experience and thought grounded therein. Being a person is not true of a human being for that kind of reason. *Person* is, as we have observed, an a priori concept in quite a different way than *physical object*. If "*X* is a human being" entails "*X* is a person," it is not because of a condition that makes human beings knowable, but because of a peculiar constitution of the beings denoted by the concept that has been taken up into the concept itself. In other words, anything that is a human being has an inherent normative structure that is such that if the individual is not, or does not develop into, a functioning person, something is, or will be, wrong with him or her. This indicates that the concept *person* is an ingredient in the concept of a natural kind even though it is not itself the concept of a natural kind.

It follows that the concept of a human being is not a scientific concept of a natural kind. *Human being*, as a scientific concept of a natural kind (according to the prevailing view of scientific concepts), might be specified by a chromosome number or as a generalized bipedal primate mammal, in contrast with the anthropoid ape defined as a bipedal primate mammal specialized for arboreal conditions. *Human being*, in the sense intended here, is a humanistic concept. It requires normative, semantic, and logical, as well as factual, dimensions of that to which it applies. Furthermore, it involves the a priori humanistic concept *person*. Yet *human being* itself is not an a priori concept for entailing the concept *person* any more so than *rock* is an a priori concept for entailing the concept *physical object*.

But we still have to ask whether human beings, in the humanistic sense, constitute a natural kind. The answer, it seems, must be yes; but, in order to have the metaphysical room for such a position, we must conceive nature, not just persons and human beings, in humanistic categories, or else accept some kind of special creation for humankind. The only alternative would be to reduce, or to explain away, humanistic language in such a way that it would be shown to have no special ontological import. Valiant efforts have been made to do this, but human persons, it seems, cannot be ontologically vanquished. All efforts to make them disappear turn out to be works of magic, producing only verbal illusions.

One who acknowledges humanistically conceived natural kinds recognizes an irreducible and uneliminable distinction between what is existentially in something and what is normatively in it and what is semantically in it. All three of these are recognized as basic, irreducible modes of constitution, with no one explainable in terms of the others.

Whereas the functional concept of an artifact (*engine*, for example) locates its objects in terms of what they have been designed and made (or selected) by an external agent to do, the concept of a normative natural kind, according to the humanistic metaphysics here proposed, semantically appropriates an inherent function of things of that kind with respect to which they are well formed or malformed by their own inner dynamics. In other words, there is an inherent normative structure in such things—that for which they exist and that which they are structured to do; and this normative structure is caught up somehow in the natural causal processes that produce and sustain them. But unlike the case of the artifact, the concept of a normative natural kind (as distinct from the form that is the semantic content of the concept) is not involved in the processes that produce and sustain the things in question. But the form that is semantically present in the concept is normatively present and may be existentially present in varying degrees, in things of a normative natural kind. This form, in its normative presence in such individuals, is involved in the causal dynamics that produce and sustain these individuals. For example, where the idea of a carburetor is involved in and guides the processes that produce carburetors, the *idea* of a heart is not involved in the processes that produce a heart in a developing embryo. Nevertheless, the *form* that is semantically present in the idea of a heart seems to be normatively present in the processes in a developing embryo that produce a heart; and it is with respect to this normative presence of the form of a heart in the embryo that we judge the heart that is produced as well-formed or as malformed. Such a conception of a natural kind is humanistic, for it involves value concepts in a descriptive/explanatory role.

A normative social kind is peculiar in that the *concept* of the kind, not just the structure or function specified by the concept, is internal to, and engaged in, the inner dynamics of the individuals located by the concept. One cannot be a police officer, for example, without the concept of oneself as a police officer; and the concept one has of a police officer will affect how one performs in the position. Thus the individuals of a normative social kind have not only a factual and a normative structure but also a structure of meaning. They have features, properties, and elements existentially, normatively, and semantically in them.

Some normative social kinds are conventional. For example, police officer, judge, professor, and the like are generated by a division of responsibilities in a society. There is something to which the concepts of such kinds are responsible, for the concepts, or the offices they define, may be appraised as well formed or not; but these concepts do not answer to some structure or function inherent in the human beings to whom they apply. Police officers, for example, are trained in terms of, and form themselves by, the concept of the office. They are more true to the concept than the concept is true of them. In this respect, concepts of conventional social kinds are like concepts of artifacts, except that the concept of a conventional social kind is involved in the internal structure and causal dynamics of individuals of that kind.

The question with which we are concerned is whether humankind is a *natural* (in contrast with a *conventional*) normative social kind. The concept of a human being, as in the case of the concept of a conventional normative social kind, is intimately and essentially involved in the being and inner dynamics of human beings. One could no more be a mature, functioning human being without the concept of oneself as a human being than one could be, and function as, the president of the United States without the concept of oneself as the president of the United States. In order to live the life of a human being, one has to be a self unified under, and constituted by, a normative self-concept—the concept of oneself as a human person and as the particular individual one is; and one has to live in a world unified under a frame of description and explanation. One has to have self- and present-transcendence; one has to engage in self-review and self-criticism with a regard for history, the future, and others, and, indeed, the whole context of one's existence. Without a normative self-image of oneself as a human person, a human being would have no distinctively human emotions, aspirations, or problems. There would be no intellectual pursuits, no guilt feelings, no moral motivations, no human pride or self-respect, no political life, no human artistic concerns, no religious consciousness. Without these one would not live the life of a human being.

The form of a human person is normatively in all human beings, regardless of how immature or impaired they may be; but it has to be semantically present to them through their normative self-concept (that is, it has to be semantically in their normative self-concept) for it to be realized existentially in their being. Hence the concept of a human being, unlike the concept of a conventional social kind, is both true of a human being and something to which a human being should be true. It is true of human beings with respect to the form that is normatively in them; it purports to formulate what one, by one's nature, ought to be or ought to become. The concept can be correct or incorrect, for there is an inherent normative structure of a human being to which it is accountable—of which the nonrealization is a mark of immaturity, retardation, impairment, abnormality, or moral defect. Such a concept is not only *of* or *about* one; it is constitutive of one's being. An erroneous concept of oneself as a human person could have a pernicious effect on one's life; indeed, one could be a monster.

So one's normative self-concept as a human being, although it contains the core categorial concept of personhood, is, in part, an "empirical" concept. It is formed from, and tested in, our intersubjective experiences and critical judgments in such a way that it is an a posteriori concept. If our normative self-concept as a human being makes for a flourishing life with ongoing self-esteem and continuing respect and approval of others, if it is shared by others with similar results in their lives, and if the shared concept in a society provides the foundation for, and makes possible, a well-ordered and well-functioning society, we have ample grounds for saying that human beings constitute a natural normative social kind, even if persons as such do not.

Thus, if this analysis of the concepts of personhood and humankind is correct, there is no real conflict between a Kantian-like ethical theory and a natural law theory of ethics. There is an a priori ground for ethics in personhood and there is a ground for ethics in the nature of human beings as a natural normative social kind.

Logic and Selfhood

Earlier we discussed how I and my dog share a somewhat common environment. Part of the existential environment that is semantically present to me is also semantically present to her. Ordinary physical objects, rabbits, squirrels, cats, dogs, and human beings are present in some form to both of us. And so are physical events, signs, and linguistic and other acts. Even some normative conditions and requirements are present to the dog as well as to me. She is sometimes hungry and thirsty; she hurts and feels bad under some conditions, but usually seems to feel good; she is sometimes angry or fearful; sometimes she shows jealousy and sometimes shame; she may show even perplexity or anxiety and an attitude of inquiry in a situation; but usually she seems to be at peace with the world and with herself.

We may even be tempted to say that my dog is aware of some logical relationships, for on many occasions she seems to have some expectation and sometimes seems to be surprised. It is reasonable to interpret such an expectation as a "belief" implicitly "inferred" from a set of "beliefs" and current perceptions; and it is equally reasonable to interpret such a surprise as awareness of an inconsistency between an expectation and a current perception. However, such "inferred" beliefs or takings might be causally (teleologically) generated by the normative requirements involved without the mediation of awareness—without the normative requirement's being felt. In such a case, there would be no awareness of either the normative requirement or the logical relationships in which it was grounded. Perhaps most of our insights, hunches, and creative ideas are generated in this manner. We know not why they occur to us. We may speak of them as "coming to us out of the blue." Some may hesitate to call this process "inference."

Perhaps ideas can be generated by (1) a process of "suggestion" or "association of ideas" in which the occurrence of one simply causes another to occur, (2) causally operative normative requirements that are grounded in the logical structure of our belief/precept system, (3) awareness of the normative requirements of our belief/precept system (by feeling constrained or restrained in thinking this or that), (4) awareness of the normative requirements of our belief/precept system and indirectly by awareness of the logical structure in which the requirements are grounded, or (5) awareness of the logical structure and thus awareness of the normative requirements grounded in this structure. Any of these processes, except (1), might be called "inference," but (2) would have to be regarded as a tacit inference; indeed, the inference in (3) is more tacit than in (4) or (5).

My dog may be capable of tacit inferences of the kind in (2). Inferences of this kind are essential in behavioral knowledge. Inferences in all of these senses are involved in rational knowledge, but there could be no rational knowledge with only tacit inferences of the lowest kind. Knowledge is more rational the more it involves enlightened forms of inference. While my dog is capable of behavioral knowledge, there is no reason to think that she is capable of rational knowledge. Yet in being surprised, as she seems to be in some situations, if the recent analysis of *surprise* is correct, she *feels* the normative clash between her expectation and perception of the situation, even if she is not aware of the logical grounds of the felt normative conflict.

Human beings are rational animals. We not only have psychological states and perform psychological acts that in fact have logical structures that play a significant role in the teleological causality of behavior; we are, in normal, more or less mature states, *sensitive* to the normative requirements grounded in the logical structures and relationships of our psychological states and acts and in their cultural expressions. Furthermore, we are, in varying degrees, aware of the logical structures underlying the normative requirements of our belief/precept systems. In order to be taught logic, one has to be a psychological being in whom the normative requirements grounded in the logical structure of one's psychological states and acts are both directly causally effective and felt. The teaching of logic enlightens one about the logical structures underlying the normative requirements and thus heightens one's sensitivity to logically grounded normative requirements in thought.

The Nature of Logic

There has been a great deal of confusion about logic as a discipline. It is sometimes identified with ethics, sometimes with grammar, sometimes with mathematics, and sometimes even with the empirical sciences (or at least taken to be similar in methodology); but it is widely assumed or claimed that logical truths are uninformative about the world and that logic is without ontology.[1] Much of the disagreement or confusion about the nature of logic is grounded in prevailing assumptions and views about the nature of meaning and value. Those who hold that there are neither inherent structures of meaning nor objective normative structures have a problem about logical discourse and what it is of or about. With a realist theory of meaning and value, we have an easier task in making philosophical sense of logical discourse.

We talk about logical properties, logical relations, logical facts, and logical structures in much the same way as we talk about grammatical properties, grammatical relations, and grammatical structures. However, unlike the way we talk about grammar, we do not talk about English or French logic. It is true, of course, that grammatical terms (for example, "sentence," "noun," "verb," and their counterparts in other languages) apply across languages. But for something to be a sentence, a noun, a verb, or anything of the kind, it must be in a language and it cannot be (except in a qualified sense) in two or more languages. This is not true of a statement, a thought, an assumption, an expectation, a perception, or the like. While one might claim that a statement has to be in some language, the same statement can be in different languages. Its identity is not tied up with any particular language. Grammar emphasizes the form of the body of thought, not its soul; logic pertains to its inner being, an inherent structure of meaning. For something to be a statement, a thought, an assumption, or anything of the kind is for it to be an inherent structure of meaning with a certain logical form. Being conditional, categorical, disjunctive, and the like are logical forms. Entailment, presupposition, consistency, inconsistency, and so forth are logical relations. Some of these have grammatical counterparts, but the logical realm is more basic than the grammatical.

Nothing purely physical has a logical property or structure. In a purely factual world, or even in a purely factual and normative world, there would be no logical properties, relations, or structures. In such a world, there might be physical or normative necessities or incompatibilities and clashes, but there would be no logical entailments or inconsistencies. This is why the strict empiricist and physicalist have a philosophical problem about the nature of logic. Nothing that is fully accessible to us through sensory experience, or even through sensory and emotive experience and thought grounded therein, has a logical property or structure. Whatever is constituted in part by a logical structure or exemplifies a logical property or relation has an inherent, constitutive structure of meaning; or, as is the case with the logician's schematic sentences, it is abstract and incomplete to the extent it does not have a semantic dimension.

Logical form, logical properties, and logical relations are the peculiar form, the peculiar properties, and the peculiar relations of states and acts of meaning (or of their linguistic vehicles or expressions). If philosophers reject the realist theory of meaning, they must reject the realist theory of logic; but when philosophers accept the realist theory of meaning, the realist theory of logic is relatively unproblematic for them. When we place experience, thought, and culture in the world, we also place their logical properties, relations, and structures in the world. Insofar as we acknowledge ontologically states and acts of meaning and complex organizations of them, we acknowledge logical properties, relations, and facts as part of the structure of the world.

It is important to be clear about the realist theory of meaning and logic intended. It is not the classical theory; it is neither Platonic nor Aristotelian. Logicians and philosophers develop abstractions from our semantic states and acts, or more specifically from language and discourse. Terms and sentences as such are taken to mean what they are standardly used to mean by speakers and writers. And so we speak of *the meaning* of words and sentences and come to think of it as some kind of peculiar object to which words and sentences are connected; the objects associated with terms are called "concepts" and those associated with declarative sentences are called "propositions." Platonists take these to be objects of rational apprehension and to exist in their own right; indeed, they regard them as what is ultimately real, for they are said to be changeless, eternal objects. Aristotelians take concepts and propositions to be abstractions from the realm of mutable, temporal substances and their properties. In both cases, meaning is identified with *what is meant* by words and sentences in their standard uses; and logic is regarded as the study of the necessary structures and relations of meanings. The Platonist regards logical structures and relationships as necessary features and relations of eternal objects; the Aristotelian regards them as necessary structures and relationships of abstracted features of the world.

Donald Williams expressed the classical realist theory of logic in these words:

> The new student of the problem is likely to be instructed that logical principles are only "laws of thought" or "laws of language," that they are "empty," "trivial," "tautologous," that being compatible with any possible state of affairs, they say nothing about matters of fact. . . . Persons who explain that logic is mental or verbal continue to distinguish sharply its principles from ordinary psychological generalizations, like Freud's doctrine of the libido, and from workaday rules of language like the direc-

tions for the placing of the verb in dependent clauses in German. They admit, implicitly or explicitly, that logic embodies necessary rules of any possible thought or language which shall discover or delineate the truth about this or any other world. That logical principles are "empty," "trivial," "tautologous," turns out to be just a derogatory restatement of the fact that they are necessary and self-evident. That they are "compatible with any possible state of affairs" and so do not determine "matters of fact" is, so far as it affects our purposes, an invidious way of conceding that, being principles of necessity, they do not determine any contingent or non-necessary facts and that they are incompatible, naturally enough, only with the impossible. These strictures do not depart seriously, therefore, from the traditional account, shared by men as diverse as Plato, Leibniz, Hume and some of the most precisian of contemporary mathematical logicians, that the principles of logic are abstract and analytic truths concerning the necessary traits of the simplest elements of being— quality, relation, instance, negation, number, and so forth.[2]

Our claim is that logic pertains to the features, structures, and relations of meaning as actual or possible semantic states and acts of psychological beings; it pertains to nonpsychological items, features, and structures of the world only insofar as they are inexistential contents of actual or possible semantic states and acts; it pertains to language only in so far as language is involved in actual or possible semantic states and acts. The logician's concepts and propositions are abstract forms (with a semantic dimension) of actual and possible semantic states and acts; they are instantiated, not in that of which they are true, but in the semantic states and acts of a subject.

We have to distinguish between the laws of natural necessity and the laws of logical necessity; the former hold among such things as properties, kinds of things, facts, normative requirements, and values in the realm of actual or possible existence; the latter hold among concepts and propositions—properties, kinds of things, facts, normative requirements, and the like *as meant in a certain way* in some actual or possible semantic state or act. Concepts and propositions may be constructed in such a way that some natural necessities may become logical necessities in a particular language. This may confuse the distinction, but it does not obliterate it. From within most any language, natural necessities may be recognized that are not also logical necessities; and in any language, there will be logical necessities that are not natural necessities. Mathematicians, for the most part, are interested in logical necessities only insofar as they capture or bear upon natural relations. Mathematics applies to items and features of all things in their existence in a way in which logic does not; logic applies to only semantic states and acts in their existence.

Logic and the Mental

Psychologists typically study psychological states and acts, not as instantiations of concepts and propositions and thus not in terms of their logical structures and relations, but as existent states and occurrences and in terms of their causal conditions as understood from within a scientific approach.

It has become customary in modern thought to purify psychological subject matter in order to make it a suitable area for empirical scientific study. Accordingly, the language of meaning and the language of logic have come to be understood as applicable only to language. Semantics is understood as the study of the rules for the application of language to items and features in the world and logic as the study of the formal rules of language, the rules by which items of language may be combined or related to one another. The study of the relation of language to the psychological states and acts of the user is reserved for a separate discipline called "pragmatics." Psychological subject matter, without a semantic and logical dimension, is taken to be purely factual in its constitution and thus within the domain of a purely scientific psychology.

Psychological states and acts, if they are semantic as we have argued, have a logical form; indeed, the logical form of a psychological state or act enters into, and is constitutive of, its very identity. Something is, in part, a perception, a desire, a belief, an intention, or anything of a psychological kind by virtue of its logical form. Furthermore, psychological states and acts are not just related conjunctively, temporally, spatially, and causally in a naturalistic manner; they are related to one another logically. The complexes of which they are a part have a logical structure. They also have a normative structure, but, unlike biological organisms (conceived as normatively and teleologically organized), their normative structure is grounded largely in their semantic and logical structures. The kind of psychology that ignores the semantic, logical, and normative dimensions of its subject matter cannot adequately describe and explain it. It is not simply that there is more to tell in the same way there is more to tell about a business than is told in the accountant's financial statement; it is that the naturalistic psychologist's account of psychological subject matter is false both in description and explanation—it misrepresents what is the case and why it is as it is. But this is not a simple straightforward error. The mistake lies in the naturalistic psychologist's methodology and conceptual system. Neither the relevant subject matter nor the correct account of it is available from within the scientific approach.

In an earlier chapter we observed that psychological states and acts do not stand alone, that they are, by their nature, systemic. They are not only members of a larger whole but involve the larger whole in their identity. Organized psychological states and acts are not atomistic and extensional. In their most primitive form, psychological states and acts are embedded in, and serve, a biological organism. Indeed, this is true of more sophisticated organizations of psychological states and acts as well; but, in the more advanced forms of psychological organization, it is more a matter of the biological being a dimension of the psychological than the psychological being an extension of the biological—that is, the psychological comes to have its own needs and ends. Roles are switched. The psychological is no longer primarily the servant of the body, but rather the body becomes more the instrument of the complex psychological organization. We call such a complex psychological organization a "mind." It has a unity and identity of its own, but there is no reason to think that it could maintain its identity and unity apart from its biological dimension. A mind has to be embodied. This is not simply a contingent, empirical truth: We can make no more sense of talk about a disembodied mind than we can of talk about a disembodied book.

The illusion that the concept of a disembodied self makes sense stems from self-knowledge and reflective awareness of some of our own mental states and acts that presuppose a transcending unity of the self but do not seem to involve awareness of a bodily aspect. Consequently it seems that we can imagine ourselves as disembodied. Some claim that whatever we can imagine is possible.[3] But it is not at all clear that what is imaginable is consistently thinkable. Imagination does not flesh out presuppositions and entailments. Consider M. C. Escher's drawings.[4]

It is questionable whether there are any purified conscious mental states and acts that do not involve awareness of some bodily aspect; but even if there were such, they would be dependent on mental states and acts that involved awareness of one's own body. This is not simply a causal thesis. The language in which we talk about such purified mental states and acts presupposes language about physical things. We cannot make sense of language devoid of a physical dimension. We cannot make sense of meaning, and thus of the mental, apart from something physical. There cannot be a substance the basic constitution of which is semantic or normative, or both; for both semantic intentionality and normativity necessarily involve factuality. The concept of a purely physical substance, one with only a factual constitution, may prove to be incoherent when fully thought through; but, if our analysis of meaning and the mental is correct, the concept of a purely mental substance is manifestly absurd.

A mind, then, is a complex organization of psychological states and acts. It is holistic in terms of both its logical and normative structures. Mental states and occurrences, constituted as they are by inherent structures of meaning, have internal relations with one another so that they do not have independent, atomlike identities and descriptions; they are logically webbed into larger wholes and the larger wholes tend to be logically webbed also. The internal logical relations of mental states and acts do not seem to bear causally on their existence in a direct way. Inconsistent experiences, beliefs, and thoughts are compatible with respect to their existence; they are incompatible only with respect to their veridicality or truth. In like manner, the presuppositions and entailments of experiences and beliefs do not indicate existent semantic states and acts that embody the presupposed and entailed concepts and propositions. The facts that S believes P and that P entails Q do not indicate that S believes Q. This is why logic as a discipline is not concerned with the laws of thought in the sense that psychology is concerned with the laws of psychological states and acts. But the laws of logic do pertain to the structure and relations of semantic states and acts and to the formal conditions for their validity and truth.

Logic and the Ethics of Thought

This brings us to the normative dimension of the logical web of semantic states and acts. Many modern logicians and philosophers think of the connection between truths of formal logic and the ethics of thought as similar to that between the truths of mathematics and science and the ethics of behavior in general. "In spite of a considerable tradition," Donald Williams said, expressing a widely held view,

> logic itself is not a "normative" science but a purely descriptive one. A logical formula does not lay down that a person who believes a certain kind of premise ought to believe a certain kind of conclusion, nor even that a person ought to believe that a certain kind of premise entails a certain kind of conclusion. It only asserts flatly that a certain kind of premise does entail a certain kind of conclusion, take it or leave it, as chemistry asserts that hydrogen and oxygen combine to make water. The obligation to believe logical principles and to infer in accordance with logical principles is derived indirectly, from the fact that logical principles are true and that propositions logically inferrible from true propositions must be true, and that it is *good* that we should believe what is true. It not only is good in a general way, redounding to the greater glory of God or to the greatest happiness of the greatest number, but is so advantageous to each believer singly that every man who knows what is good for him is committed to believing, so far as he can, in accordance with logic.[5]

While no one would deny the utility of thinking logically, there is a more intimate connection between the normative and logical structures of thought than Williams acknowledges. An important part, but not all, of the normative structure of a set of semantic states and acts is grounded directly in their logical dimension. Beliefs, by virtue of what they are in terms of their logical structure (remember that it is their logical structure that makes them a form of taking), ought to be true. An untrue belief (or a false taking in any mode) is a faulty belief (or faulty taking), just as a heart that will not pump a sufficient amount of blood for the body under normal conditions is a defective heart. A belief or a taking has to be self-consistent to be true; and a set of beliefs or takings has to be consistent for all of them to be true. Thus a belief or set of beliefs ought to be consistent. In other words, the logical aspect of semantic states and acts is an important ground of their normative dimension, and logical features and relations are among what is normatively required of semantic states and acts. So there are normative laws of thought basically and essentially connected with the strictly logical laws of thought. Contrary to Williams, the values of thought are, in part, constitutive of "the glory of God" (if this means the general goodness of the universe) and of the greatest good, rather than being derivative from either.

Furthermore, it seems that the logical aspects of semantic states and acts become causally effective both through the direct causal efficacy of normative requirements grounded in the logical structures of the mental and through *felt* normative requirements (whether with or without comprehension of the logical structures in which the normative requirements are grounded). The dynamics of thinking, whether enmeshed in ongoing experience or in abstract thought in language, is teleological, except perhaps in reverie or "free association" of ideas. In serious thinking, thoughts, for the most part, simply occur one after the other. They seem to come from nowhere with the greatest of ease; nevertheless, they are usually connected in a logically appropriate way. If this were not so, we could not give coherent lectures or write coherent papers and books. Of course we do not have thoughts occurring this way on subjects of which we are ignorant. The new thoughts are produced by the normative requirements of the antecedent thoughts in conjunction with one's stored beliefs about the subject. The normative requirements are not usually felt; they are directly causally productive. This is what we have called a purely normative teleological process. At times of course, we review certain of our beliefs and *feel constrained* to accept, or to reject, some other proposition; or we find ourselves resisting some statement, even though we do not know just why. Sometimes

beliefs previously held firmly are loosened or dislodged by such a review. In such cases, we are aware of a normative requirement that is
based on a logical relation. This is a semantic teleological process, for
the normative requirement is causally operative through being felt—by
being semantically present to the thinker.

A mind, like the biological organism that embodies it, is holistic in
that it has its own internal, causally dynamic normative structure in
which the whole complex imposes normative requirements on the particular psychological states and acts of which it is constituted. Although
a mind is an extension of, and is grounded in, a biological organism, its
teleological system transcends the teleology of its biological organism. It
does not exist simply to serve the biological needs of the organism. It
has its own needs and ends that may even take precedent over the
biological.

The semantic states and acts of a particular person stand in logical
and normative relationships with the semantic states and acts of others,
but these logical and normative relationships do not enter into the internal causality of one's mind in the same way as the logical and normative structures of one's own semantic states and acts. Of course consistency or inconsistency obtains between two beliefs (or takings in any
mode) regardless of whose they are; and something is wrong with two
inconsistent beliefs regardless of whose they are. But such relationships
causally make a difference only when they hold among beliefs of the
same subject. Of course, when one becomes aware of another's belief,
one may directly feel its normative clash with a belief (or complex of
beliefs) of one's own, or one may "see" the inconsistency and then feel
the normative conflict. One will feel the normative conflict, however,
only to the extent that one has respect for the other person's beliefs.
Regardless of how clearly we perceive the inconsistency of our own
beliefs with those of others whom we totally discredit, we will not feel a
normative clash between our beliefs and theirs. So the perceived inconsistency will work no change in our own beliefs; but a perceived inconsistency between our own beliefs and those of a respected person may
disturb, or even dislodge, some of our own. The difference here lies in
the fact that we ourselves tend to accept the known beliefs of the persons we respect as reliable believers so that the logical tension between
a belief of our own with a belief of such a person becomes a logical
tension between two beliefs of our own; namely, the particular belief in
question and the belief that the other person's beliefs are trustworthy.
This is why people often try to discredit the trustworthiness of the beliefs of a person who disagrees with them rather than try to disprove
the beliefs themselves. They try to remove the felt sting of the contradiction rather than bother to show the falsity of the contradictory be-

lief, for it is often a much easier task. What all of this adds up to is that we *feel* (in a way that is causally effective) logical normative requirements and conflicts only with regard to our own semantic states and acts. And, of course, purely normative teleological causality works only among semantic states and acts of the same subject.

This is not to deny that we can emotively experience logical normative requirements and conflicts among the beliefs of others, even among statements abstracted from all psychological states and acts; it is only to deny that such felt logical normative requirements and conflicts are causally moving or disturbing to the self in the same way as is experience of the logical normative structure of one's own mind. There are parallels to be pointed out, on one hand, between somatic value sensations of one's own bodily conditions and felt logical normative structures of one's own mind, and, on the other hand, between experiences of the logical and normative structures of beliefs and statements of others and our emotive experiences of the normative structure of external situations in general.

Henry Johnstone has defined a self as something that can harbor a logical contradiction.[6] We often say of a paper or a book that it contains a contradiction, but this is not strictly true. A book, as a physical thing, cannot contain a contradiction, for it does not instantiate statements or propositions; only tokens of words and sentences exist in it. The book that is embodied in a physical book is first and foremost a set of linguistic acts of the author; however, it may come to be regarded as a set of abstract propositions, questions, and the like that may be instantiated in the mental states and acts of anyone. So the contradictions in the book are really contradictions in a mind.

We have contended that perhaps an integrated organism can behaviorally take the content of a semantic state of itself to be existent. In such a case, it would be the organism, not the particular semantic state, that instantiated the proposition. Could an organism instantiate, in this manner, contradictory propositions? That is, could an organism both behaviorally take X, the semantic content of one of its states, to exist and not to exist? Or could an organism behaviorally take the semantic contents of two of its states to exist in a way that would constitute a self-contradictory taking or two contradictory takings? It is not at all clear that a self-contradictory behavioral taking is a possibility. The frog either grabs for the fly with a flick of its tongue or it does not. But could the frog not be surprised by the result of its grab for the fly, if there were no fly? In attributing surprise to the frog, we would be attributing to it an expectation and a perception of the outcome of its behavior, both of which are nonbehavioral, semantic takings. There is no logical contradiction involved in an organism's behaviorally taking X to be F at

t_1 and its behaviorally taking X to be *not-F* at t_2. Two behavioral takings would have to be simultaneous to be contradictory. And it is not clear how this would be possible. Perhaps the organism would stand in quivering muscular tension, unable to act; but, in such a case, there would be no behavioral propositional taking at all, even though we might say that the organism was caught in the dynamic conflict of two normative requirements.

A semantic taking is not something that a biological organism as such can do; it requires a complex, teleologically functioning, unitary system of semantic states and acts. It is only a being with such a concrete system that can instantiate a self-contradictory proposition or two or more logically inconsistent propositions. But it is possible for one who is capable of semantic takings to have a semantic taking that is inconsistent with one's behavioral takings. This would be true of the person who behaviorally took X to be F but was surprised by the outcome.

Johnstone recognizes that the tension between contradictory propositions instantiated in the same self is not purely logical but causal as well; he holds that the tension is felt, that the contradiction not only exists but is present as a problem. This does not seem to be the case in all instances. One can harbor contradictory propositions without a felt dynamic tension. Instantiated propositions, however, have causal as well as logical consequences; they participate teleologically in the generation of other takings. Although inconsistent propositions can be instantiated in a psychological being without felt conflict (provided they are far enough removed from each other in logical space), they are likely to come into *felt* conflict sooner or later by coming into touch with each other through their logical/causal consequences. The person who harbors both may, at some point, be moved to accept some proposition, P, and moved to accept its contradictory, *not-P*, in such a way that the dynamic tension is immediately felt, even though one might never discover the root contradiction that produced the felt problem. Of course, if one becomes aware that two of one's beliefs are contradictory, regardless of how one achieved this awareness, one will feel the normative tension between them as a problem.

The point of these remarks is to show that one can have contradictory beliefs without having a felt problem. We may modify Johnstone's position to accommodate this fact. Accordingly, only a mind can harbor contradictory propositions in such a way that they can become, either directly or through their logical/causal consequences, a felt logical problem.

But, more basically, it seems that only semantic takings can be self-contradictory and that one of any pair of contradictory propositions instantiated in the same being must be a semantic taking; that is, purely behavioral takings, while they may be in conflict and may be self-defeating (as with normative requirements and biological processes in general) do not seem to be capable of being contradictory for reasons already indicated. And semantic takings do not stand alone; they do not occur singly. Only a normatively organized system with some semantic capacity is capable of behavior, for behavior involves a teleological response of the organism as a whole to something semantically present that is existentially external to the effective reach of the organism's own internal normative teleological system. In like manner, only a teleologically organized semantic complex that functions as a whole is capable of semantic takings. Thus a semantic taking is necessarily an internal operation of a dynamic organization of semantic states and acts. Only such a structure can harbor logically inconsistent states and acts.

A mind, however it has come to be, is a complex system of semantic states and acts with a causally effective normative structure. It is a teleological system that is self-corrective and creative through an inner dynamic that works toward coherence and completeness. The peculiar normative requirements inherent in a mind are more or less effective, either directly or through being felt by a higher-level awareness, in bringing about what they require. It is in this way that the mind dislodges or blocks semantic states and acts and generates new ones.

The normative requirements inherent in a mind are, at least in part, grounded in, and pertain to, the logical structure of its semantic states and acts. A semantic taking is a taking by virtue of its logical form; and, by virtue of what it is, it ought to be correct, it ought to be true. If it is not, it is a mistake; it is a failure as a taking. If a semantic taking is self-inconsistent, it is inherently a failure by virtue of its logical form. So a semantic taking ought to be self-consistent and true. Both are required for its success. Furthermore, a semantic taking ought to be consistent with all the other semantic takings in the semantic system that generates it, for otherwise the whole complex would be self-inconsistent and in trouble; it would be in error somewhere.

Beings capable of only simple behavioral takings are not bothered by logical inconsistencies or unintelligible things and events. These are problems only for beings capable of semantic takings, for beings with a mind, for beings who operate under the imperative to be consistent and correct in one's semantic takings. A semantic taking, unlike a simple behavioral taking, places its content in what is semantically taken to be the world. And in order for one to place a semantic content in the world, one has to have a conception of the world into which it will fit. So beings capable of semantic takings, minded beings, are under twin governing imperatives: the imperative to be consistent and correct in one's takings and to render intelligible whatever semantic content one takes to obtain in the world—to understand how it fits into the world. These two correlative and interdependent imperatives drive minded beings toward a unified self and toward a unified world-view. The two cannot be separated. A mind struggling toward self-consistency and correctness in its takings must also struggle toward a unified world-view; for assurance of self-consistency and correctness in one's takings is not possible without assurance of a unified world. A chaotic or unordered world would be one in which nothing would be intelligible. If there were no limits to what semantic contents could be located in the world, there would be no meaning to correctness in one's takings. Takings could not be simply subject to logical error, for they could not be inconsistent if they were not correct or incorrect vis-à-vis the world. And if there were no meaning to correctness in one's takings, there would be no such thing as a taking, for a taking is precisely something that is either correct or a mistake.

There are, of course, psychological states and acts that are not semantic takings, but not as many as some people think; for there are more modes of taking than we are accustomed to acknowledge. For instance, we have thoughts that do not take something to obtain in the world, thoughts that only entertain some fact or normative requirement as a possibility. Yet there is a taking involved, namely, the fact or requirement is taken to be a possibility; and the fact or requirement may, under further consideration, be rejected as a possibility, either for purely logical reasons or because it is taken to be inconsistent with other beliefs about the constitution of the world. Again, a fact may be taken as probably the case or it may be taken as unlikely. A novelist may have an idea of a sequence of events and take them to be a possible or fitting episode in a story. Even feelings, desires, and intentions involve takings: To feel embarrassed is to take something one has done, or some state one is in, to be unfitting or degrading to oneself. To desire something is to "subscribe" to the imperative for it to be, which is to take it to be such that it would be good if it were the case. To fear something is to take it to be something that is bad in some way. To be a fearful person, to live in fear but without clearly defined fears, is to take the world to be untrustworthy, to expect undertakings and situations in general to turn out badly.

Rationality and the Unconscious

We do, of course, think of, or imagine, things without a taking in any mode. Some ideas and images of things just seem to occur; they well up from within, sometimes with external stimulation, but sometimes apparently from inner resources alone. Some of these ideas and images seem to be idle thoughts or reveries; some are part of the productive work of the mind. "Many artists, philosophers, and even scientists," Carl Jung says, "owe some of their best ideas to inspirations that appear suddenly from the unconscious. The ability to reach a rich vein of such material and to translate it effectively into philosophy, literature, music, or scientific discovery is one of the hallmarks of what is commonly called genius."[7]

What Jung calls "the unconscious" is just that, all of the semantic states and acts of a person of which one does not have self-knowledge and thus are not available to one's reflective awareness. This semantic mass is productive of new semantic states and acts, some of which, but not all, are at the conscious level. The ideas and images that come to us "out of the blue" must be generated in this manner. But we have reason to believe that unconscious semantic states and acts are generated in this manner as well. At times, after having been in a quandary about what to believe or to do about something, we simply find that we have made up our mind about it. We have suggested that the causality involved in this productive process is teleological—that it consists of causally effective normative requirements grounded in the logical structure of the mind, or of normative requirements grounded in other features inherent in the semantic states and acts that make up the mind, or of normative requirements grounded in the semantic contents of the psychological states and acts that constitute the mind.

We do not mean to rule out non-teleological causality. Some ideas and images may be generated by simple association, for instance. But even those generated in this manner may have been generated by a feeling that they *belonged* together or *fitted* together. In any case, it seems reasonable that not all processes of the mind that generate ideas and images and takings involve causally effective normative requirements grounded in the logical structures of the mind. Perhaps no one ever thought this was the case. In sleep, for instance, psychic forces gain uncensored expression or development in the imagery of dreams; in reverie, they may develop into undisciplined and undirected fantasies; indeed, in a thoroughly relaxed, unfocused state of consciousness, images may appear that seem strange and inexplicable, not as one's imaginings in daydream fantasies, but as unauthored images. These kinds of images can be reported appropriately only as occurrences.

All of these "subterranean" semantic forces are at work behind or under the centered, focused semantic states and acts of which we have self-knowledge and on which we can reflect. They can come to fruition directly in overt action, but more often, in a well-constituted and well-functioning self, they bear upon action through conscious thought and decision. Some people seem to think that the extent of irrationality is measured by the extent of the influence of these forces in conscious thought, decision, and action. And the influence of these forces in the conscious life of everyone is enormous; in fact, these forces seem to be the source of much of the psychic energy of the self. So some conclude that human beings are basically irrational; that rationality is superficial and largely ineffective in human life.

This is the wrong way to think about the role of rationality. The unconscious semantic states and acts of an organism come to consciousness when they become sufficiently integrated to generate centered semantic takings; and this integration consists of coherence. Inconsistency among the semantic states and acts of the complex makes for division and hampers centered acts. So the inherent natural dynamics of even the unconscious is toward rationality; when the inner dynamics of the unconscious is otherwise, a pathological condition exists, and its inner forces are destructive to the self.

It seems reasonable to think of consciousness, not only as a further development and extension of the semantic powers of the self, but as a way of fulfilling the need, or the requirement, of the complex of unconscious semantic states and acts for greater rationality in their own realm. Rationality, properly understood, is a way of perfecting selfhood. It is repressive and damaging only when distorted, perverted, or abused—a situation that is not infrequent. The correction is not more irrationality, but better rationality.

Many of those who minimize rationality and emphasize the "irrational" forces of the mind have a rather restricted conception of rationality. Forces at work in the depths of one's psyche often find their completion only in overt expression. Often, while listening to others speak on a subject, for example, we may have dim feelings of an inner struggle going on just below the threshold of consciousness that prompts us to speak, but we do not know exactly what the struggle is until we speak or give it expression in some form. Something is going on that requires an expression for completion. We can, of course, let the feeling or thought come to completion at the conscious level in silent thought or imagination without overt expression. But we are all limited in this capacity. Our feelings and thoughts mature more fully and accurately in speech, writing, or some form of expression.

Of course some think that there are forms of conscious action and expression that are not subject to rational assessment and control. This is more a matter of how we categorize some types of action and expression than how we think of rationality. Whatever is subject to rational appraisal has to have the appropriate categorial structure. If feelings and emotions, for instance, are not thought of as having a semantic and logical dimension, they are not thought of as subject to rational and epistemic appraisals; but if they are thought of as not only subject to being reported and described but as subject to being *expressed* in language or symbol, as being coherent or incoherent with other feelings and emotions and beliefs, and as being warranted or not with regard to the reality of the situation, then they are regarded as subject to rational appraisal.

The issue about the extent of the rationality of the human mind is not a question about the extent to which the generative processes of the mind are reasoning processes; it is rather a question about the extent to which the expressions and actions of the self, however they are generated, are subject to, and responsive to, critical review and assessment. It is a matter of the extent to which reason (the reflective, critical powers of the self) is in command—the extent to which reason can govern and regulate the self, regardless of the sources of the energy of the self. Irrationality is a matter of either the extent to which the expressions and actions of one cannot be brought into compliance with one's own reason, or the extent to which one's reason is perverted in its work so that it is not self-correctable because of systematic error in its critical judgments. The first form of irrationality is a lack of integrity of the self; the second form is a matter of the derangement of the rational faculties themselves. Derangement may be caused by physiological conditions; by bondage to certain psychic forces so that they control the verdicts of reason rather than being under its governance; or by deeply embedded false assumptions, usually part of one's cultural perspective, that shape one's critical judgments but are themselves beyond the scope of one's effective critical review.

The imperative to be consistent and correct in all our semantic takings, under which we find ourselves as thinking beings, is not a matter of choice; it is not a conditional imperative; it binds us categorically. It is presupposed by all of our takings and by all of our centered acts, including even our most fundamental choices. The imperative is grounded in the very nature of our semantic states and acts, in their inherent logical structure. The imperative is a constitutional principle of the human mind. It is not simply an instinct or psychological drive; it is a responsibility. It is something to which we hold ourselves and others accountable. We fault ourselves when we do not comply with it, for failure to comply with the imperative results in failure in the non-complying activities and those based on them. Inability to govern one's semantic and other activities in terms of the principle affects one's status as a person; it is regarded as a serious defect at the core of one's being. This is why we cannot regard a mental illness that affects one's rationality in the same way as we regard bodily illness that does not

impair or derange the mind. Even death does not impair one's standing as a person, but the loss of rationality or derangement of one's
rational powers does jeopardize one's status as a person; it compromises one's right to self-governance.

We feel differently about the derangement of one's mind from the
way we feel about the impairment of one's rational powers, for derangement is a perversion of rationality while impairment is simply loss
of it in some degree or totally. And we feel even more differently about
those who, with all their rational powers intact, allow their wants and
wishes to shape their beliefs, and who allow their impulses or short-
term interests to determine their behavior. We hold such people responsible for their lack of integrity, for we believe they are capable of
being rational. We blame them in a way in which we do not blame those
with a deranged mind or with a loss of reason; and they blame themselves and lose their self-respect in a way in which the deranged or
mentally impaired do not.

Some claim that the symbols and stories of religion and of tribal and
national consciousness are immune to rational criticism. Such claims
are grounded in a restricted view of the semantic and knowledge-yielding powers of the mind and thus in a restricted view of the scope of
rational and epistemic appraisal. As we achieve a more ordered world
by limiting it to what is knowable on the basis of a restricted view of the
knowledge-yielding powers of the human mind, the more we have to
regard various sectors of the culture as exempt from rational criticism
and correction. We have contended throughout this work that the
whole semantic culture, including all that we typically embrace under
the term "ideology," is a logical web that struggles toward coherence
and correctness. The stories and symbols of a religion or of a political
"ideology" may be inconsistent within themselves; they may be inconsistent most clearly with the developing ethics and metaphysics of the culture; they may be inconsistent even with the empirical findings of science and history and have to be reinterpreted in light of developments
in these areas. Theology and normative social and political thought, as
well as philosophy of religion and social and political philosophy, attempt to formulate the conceptual truth-claims embodied in these stories and symbols and to reconcile them with the other truth-claims in
the culture.[8]

The human mind cannot be content with logical inconsistencies
wherever they appear in the culture; it struggles toward consistency,
coherence, and correctness. The important question is whether there
are dimensions of the culture, such as religion and political "ideology,"
that are not part of the logical web. If they are all part of the logical
web, as we have argued, there is no basis for the condemnation of ra-

tionality or for the praise of "the irrational" that we hear from some cults, ideologues, and romantics. Irrationality, properly conceived, is always alien and destructive to the self; it is never something to be praised or condoned. It is a disease of the self.

Whatever goes on in the wells of the unconscious, whatever assumptions and commitments that lie in the depths of the mind, when they come to fruition in personal acts (in centered acts of the self), they are, if the mind is functioning normally, under the governance of our reflective, critical powers in that they are subject to, and correctable by, critical review.

Ethics and Selfhood

Although human persons (for simplicity, we may speak of human persons and persons interchangeably) bear many descriptions, they are, above all, moral beings. This is the most basic, comprehensive, and philosophically revealing thing we can say about them. Their actions are subject to moral appraisal; and, just as professional evaluations of one's work as a surgeon bears on the evaluation of one as a surgeon, moral appraisals of one's actions reflect on one as a person—how one, presumed to have normal, mature powers, performs or is disposed to perform as a person.

To judge what one does in a way that implies that one is insane, stupid, or generally incompetent (or the contrary) reflects on one as a person also; but such judgments pertain to one's powers as a person. These are not moral matters, unless the level of adequacy of the powers in question is, or has been, in the power of the person and the present condition is, to some extent, a matter of one's own doing.

In saying that one is suffering from weakness of will, we are judging one's character; we are charging that there is a gap between one's intellectual morality and one's effective morality—a gap between the judgments one makes when one's desires and passions are quiet and when they are in full force. Character is a matter of how one judges and acts in the heat of action, not how one judges in the calm and cool of the morning after.

The morally weak person is often said to have a lack of willpower. But this is different from lack of intelligence—inability to comprehend a situation, inadequate power of self- and present-transcendence, or the like. A person with a morally weak will lacks self-discipline that is within the range of his or her powers. Such persons do not effectively use their powers of comprehension, self- and present-transcendence, and critical judgment; rather they allow the immediate appearance of fact or value to dictate action that is contrary to what their own considered judgment would be. When we take the abilities for comprehension, critical judgment, and self-discipline to be absent, we do not consider the person to be morally weak but defective in some other way.

Some might say that to judge the acts of one in a way that implies that one is wicked is to make a moral judgment that calls into question one's powers of moral judgment. And, if we are to believe Aristotle, they are right. The wicked, in contrast with the morally weak, according to Aristotle, are incapable of correct moral judgments. They may be strictly self-disciplined in following their own best judgments, but they are systematically in error in their judgments of what is morally right. Nevertheless, the perverted condition of the wicked, their inability to make correct moral judgments, according to Aristotle, is a product of their own actions. Hence, moral judgments that imply wickedness in the Aristotelian sense reflect on how one uses, or has used, one's powers rather than solely on the adequacy of one's powers as such.

Moral appraisals, unlike the appraisals of one's powers, presuppose that one's powers are within the normal range; they pertain to how one has developed and used one's powers in fulfilling the responsibilities of personhood. While recognizing that the conditions of one's upbringing and socialization influence one's development and actions and may provide one with excuses in some situations, moral appraisals of persons and their actions presuppose that they have critical self-evaluative and self-corrective powers and thus are morally responsible for their own moral character and their own actions.

Hence, moral discourse has a unique logical connection with person talk. The intellectual fortunes of the two stand or fall together. Moral skepticism and nihilism challenge the concept of a person, and, indeed, personhood itself, for the concept of a person is internal to, and constitutive of, persons. Also, the restructuring of our thought about human beings and their behavior along certain scientific lines is a threat to both persons and moral discourse about persons, for according to a widely accepted scientific way of categorizing human beings and their behavior, human beings are not moral agents with freedom and dignity and their behavior is not subject to rational and moral appraisal. This is why philosophical error in our cultural ways of thinking about persons and morality can be so disastrous.

It is a fact that generally human beings more or less define and live lives of their own. We do this because we are not merely psychological beings, but rational beings; we have minds and characters. We extend our elementary psychological powers (such as sensory awareness, desires, and emotions) by the development and use of language and symbol systems. And with these enhanced semantic powers, we develop self- and present-transcendence. With awareness of the logical structure of our primary psychological states and acts, critical powers emerge. We are disturbed by inconsistencies within the web of our experiences and beliefs and we seek coherence and correctness. In this manner, we become self-correcting and creative.

But it is not simply a fact that human beings, for the most part, define and live lives of their own. Persons, according to moral discourse, are beings who *have a life of their own to live.* There is no moral truth more universally accepted. Not to recognize that a person has a life of one's own to live is the highest insult. To think scientifically of persons and their behavior as causally produced by evolutionary and environmental conditions is to deny their personhood; it is to think of them as things. To treat people merely as tools, or instruments, or commodities is to treat them as things. To regard one as a slave or pet is to deny one's personhood. To exercise power over others by whatever means so that they cannot live their own lives is to injure, to cripple, or to hobble them as persons. To the extent one is in the power of others as an instrument of their will, one is not a moral agent but an extension of the others who exercise power over one. But to the extent one subjects oneself to the will of another or to the extent one has the power to liberate oneself, one must bear responsibility for one's condition and for what one does.

Talk about the life of a human being is fundamentally different from talk about the life of a tiger. The life of a particular tiger is, for the most part, the life of *the* tiger. It is largely genetically and environmentally programed. Although tigers are psychological beings, they do not have minds and characters. And there is no intentional, rational structure that gives the life of a tiger an internal unity and identity. So tigers do not have lives to live in the sense that human beings do.

Living a life, in the human way, is not simply existing biologically between birth and death; it is not simply suffering or enduring a sequence of events; nor is it a succession of responses, pursuits, projects, or lived episodes. Living a life is a matter of setting and pursuing one's own goals, under the guidance of one's own experiences, beliefs, and critical judgments, in such a way that there is a progression from one's lived past, through one's lived present, to one's anticipated future—a progression that is subject to rational appraisal and for which one is responsible.

A human life is not an anthology of short stories; it is more like a novel. It has an intentional structure that embraces a life plan, a life story, and a life-style; all of which are caught up in one's normative self-image and sense of identity.

Living a life demands that one's experiences, relationships, and activities be meaningful. And the conditions of their meaningfulness are much like the conditions of the meaningfulness of words, sentences, and paragraphs. Words become meaningful only in sentences, sentences become really meaningful only within a wider text, and a set of sentences or paragraphs or chapters require an even wider text for their full meaning. Even a book requires a culture in which it is embedded. In like manner, experiences and acts have to be integrated into the life one is living in order for them to be meaningful. And the life one is living has to be integrated into a wider context of meaning as well. Fragmentariness, disconnectedness, or lack of integrity in life robs the individual experiences, relationships, activities, and the whole life of meaning. People who have no well-formed life plan may be quite confused, disoriented, and unable to make up their minds; or they may be quite ambiguous and live incoherently, with first one identity and then another according to circumstances or companions.

We do not construct a life plan and then live it. We develop it in our experiences and choices as we mature and as we go along in life. Sometimes, of course, one may engage in radical self-review and deliberately make a life-reconstituting decision. Some people even undergo rather sudden radicalization or conversion under the impact of some dramatic experience and emerge with a sense of being a new self with a new life to live. But however one's life plan is formed, it becomes embedded in one's normative self-concept and becomes an integral part of one's character. It is, however, never beyond the limits of critical review and revision.

One may not be able to talk clearly and accurately about the life one is living, but one is aware of it in many ways. One cannot live a life without direction, review, foresight, and criticism from a position of present- and self-transcendence. Some sense of one's overall life plan has to feature in one's response to a given event. Otherwise the response would be more or less arbitrary or hardly a *response* at all, only an effect of the given event. This is the plea sometimes made for a quick reaction, grounded in suddenly aroused emotion. The more deliberate an act is the more it is thought to fit into one's life plan, and thus the more it is taken to be one's own. Also, one's life plan is revealed in what one considers as options for oneself, in one's choices, in one's sense of success or failure, in one's regrets and satisfactions, in one's morale or depression, in one's self-esteem or lack of it, in one's aspirations and expectations, and the like.

One's life story embraces all one does or suffers that has or takes on meaning in one's life. Here one's life plan is essential, for it is the major generator of meaning in one's life; it is the plot of one's life story. When one's life plan, or some significant component of it, dissolves or suddenly collapses, as in the case of the death or divorce of a life partner, everything may seem flat and meaningless until a new or an amended life plan takes shape. Lack of a fruitful life plan is the primary source of boredom, disinterestedness, meaninglessness, lack of self-esteem, and even depression and suicide.

Enhancement of meaning can be achieved by embedding one's life story in a larger story. This is often accomplished by joining one's life with another, and identifying with the life of a family, an institution, or a historical community. Some religions seek to enlarge and to reinforce the meaning in life by embedding the life plans of individuals and of nations in a divine plan for human history and, indeed, for the whole universe. Anyone with full human powers cannot but relate the life one is living to the universe as one understands it and thereby form a basic attitude toward oneself as a human being in the world. The more one's life is understood as part of a larger context of meaning the more meaningful everything in one's life becomes. Isolated individual life plans and life stories, without reinforcement of shared lives and identification with some institution or historical community, are very thin and fragile things. And the more one's life plan is limited, the more one's self-image and identity contract and the less meaningful one's life and one's experiences and activities become.

A person's life-style is the form of the life one is living; it expresses the identity and spirit of the self. One's life-style is revealed in one's likes and dislikes in personal dress and grooming, in selection of personal possessions, in the arrangement and decoration of one's personal space, in the organization and management of one's activities and affairs, in one's social relationships, and in whatever one enjoys or is comfortable with in one's personal bearing and manner. Style is important in literature and all the arts; it is even more important in life. Refinement of style in art comes with perfection of skill and mastery of material. In like manner, refinement of one's life-style comes with self-mastery and perfection of one's way of life.

It is not easy to say what is needed to give a novel aesthetic excellence and to make it a great work of art, but in some sense we all know. We are concerned with the grace of verbal expressions as we are with the grace of movements in a dance. And grace has to do with style, with the dominance of spirit over matter. To the extent the resistance of the material in a work of art is overcome and meaning dominates and resides in it unrestrained, the work has aesthetic excellence. And of course we have to look to the meaning embodied in a work of art in order to judge its greatness. Art is revelatory. We find revealed in it the meaning of human experiences and interpretations of human existence. The more profound the revelation, the greater the art.

The beauty and greatness of a life, likewise, has to do with the dominance of spirit over matter and circumstance and the interpretation of human existence that it embodies. The greater the interpretation of what it is to be human in the circumstances of one's existence, the greater the life. A hero is one who gives, in one's own person, an interpretation of a certain kind of human being. A hero in football, for example, is one who gives, in one's own person, an interpretation of a football player at (or near) perfection. A "saint" is a kind of hero of the moral life; he or she is one who gives, in one's own person, an interpretation of humanity at (or near) perfection. A "Christ" is one who renders in human form an interpretation of the divine. The character God in religious stories is an interpretation of Being at perfection.

Although one cannot live a life without some awareness of its plan, story, and style, there are, of course, different degrees of such awareness. Some think that there can be too much self-awareness; they think that it can turn people into readers and analysts of their own lives to such an extent that they are weakened in living them. They agree with Shakespeare's Hamlet: "Thus conscience does make cowards of us all;/ And thus the native hue of resolution/ Is sicklied o'er with the pale cast of thought. . . ." Too much analysis of, and thought about, one's life can lead to an abandonment of the command post as agent. We can, of course, live reflectively and deliberately from within the command post. Although circumstances often demand immediate actions, immediate responses can be informed and rationally justified on the part of those who have learned to live reflectively and critically. A fuller awareness of the life one is living from the vantage point of oneself as agent should be better than any lower level of consciousness, for one would be freer and more in charge of one's own life, and the life one lived would be more authentically one's own. As the Player King in *Hamlet* said, "What to ourselves in passion we propose,/ The passion ending, doth the purpose lose." But what the reflective, critical agent proposes, even in the urgency of an immediate situation, is framed by the life one is living and has the backing of the stable critical self.

But what is it *to have* a life to live? This is not simply a factual matter. If it were, some people would not have a life to live and that would be simply a fact about them. Neither is it merely an analytic truth that persons factually have a life to live; in this case if one did not factually have a life to live, one simply would not be a person. Indeed, some persons do not factually have a life to live, as in situations where one lacks the powers to comprehend one's situation, to review the past, to plan for the future, to accept responsibility, and the like. In short, one does not factually have a life to live if one lacks the powers to define a life for oneself and to live it. For some people, such a lack is only a matter of immaturity and, therefore, not a fault or privation; for some, the deficiency is the result of physical injury, disease, or aging; for some, it is a privation grounded in genetic defect; and for some, it may be the result of cultural privation or social injury. The controlling fact is that human beings, by their nature, *ought* to have these powers; or, what amounts to the same thing, they are beings who have these powers in a *normal, mature* state.

A person, however, may actually have these powers, and, in this respect, be normal and mature, and yet fail to have factually a life to live in any significant sense. This would be true for those whose choices were so coerced over a long period of time that they, in effect, had lost the agency of, and thus the responsibility for, "their" actions. It would also be true to some extent of those who fail, without coercion, to have a life that hangs together and projects into the future with an internal unity. We say of some people that their lives are messed up, that they haven't gotten their act together, that they aren't going anywhere, that for them life is just one thing after another.

The point is that one *has* a life to live even if one *factually* does not have a life to live. And the question at issue is: What is it *to have* a life to live in this sense? It is a normative matter. A person is a being who, by one's nature, *ought* to define and to live a life of one's own. As the holder of an office has the responsibilities of the office, a person has the responsibility to define and to live a life of one's own. The emphasis here is on *responsibility*. It is not merely that people have an inclination to live by their own deliberation and decision and tend to resist being yoked to the will of another; nor is it simply a fact that they develop patterns of behavior and make plans. People feel themselves to be under an imperative to define and to live their own lives; they feel that it is proper and fitting for them to do so; that it is improper or not fitting for them not to do so; they feel pride and self-esteem in doing so, and self-contempt in not doing so; they feel indignant at those who would not allow them to do so—that those who deny them the opportunity to define and to live their own lives violate their personhood. In like manner, people feel contempt for those who have the opportunity but do not define and live their own lives; and they feel indignation at those who prevent others from defining and living their own lives. If such feelings and judgments are not universal, they tend to appear with heightened consciousness and the advancement of humankind.

In short, it is a summary judgment of human experience that a human person is a being who is, by virtue of the kind of being one is and by virtue of the normative self-concept one has in a normal mature state, under an imperative to define and to live a life of one's own.

One's normative self-concept as a person is peculiar, as previously remarked, in that it is not simply of and about oneself, but, indeed, constitutive of oneself. One could not be a fully functioning human being without the normative conception of oneself as a person. One's powers of self-criticism and self-direction would be impossible without it. An imperative grounded in one's selfhood in this manner and operative through being known and under the guidance of knowledge and critical judgment is just what we mean by a responsibility.

A human being with the requisite powers knows oneself to be under the imperative to define and to live a life of one's own by virtue of the fact that it is presupposed by one's personal experiences, deliberations, and acts. The imperative is the basic a priori principle grounded in one's normative self-concept and thus in one's selfhood. It is not open to one to consider any alternative to the principle, for any such deliberation would presuppose it. The principle cannot be reasoned to from more basic commitments, for such reasoning would presuppose it. One cannot validly contract away the responsibility by agreeing to make oneself a slave of another, for such a contract would be logically inconsistent with its own presuppositions. So every person with the requisite powers must acknowledge, on pain of self-inconsistency, that one is under the imperative to define and to live a life of one's own.

The status of this principle is similar to what Alan Gewirth calls "the dialectical principle of generic consistency."[9] For him, a rational agent, on pain of self-contradiction, has to accept such a principle in the sense that one cannot logically reject it; but Gewirth thinks that its logical undeniability does not establish its truth. He reasons to the principle in assertoric form on the grounds that one ought to do whatever one logically must acknowledge that one ought to do.

For Gewirth, ethics is without ontology. He regards his assertoric principle of generic consistency as an analytic moral truth. If he should acknowledge that the value judgments that agents must acknowledge as agents—the value judgments that constitute the subjective normative structure of agency—make truth-claims and have truth-values, it would jeopardize his value-free ontology. Having established what he regards as the supreme, analytic moral principle of generic consistency ("Every agent ought to act in accord with the generic rights of his recipients [those affected by his acts] as well as of himself"[10]), he argues that we reason from it as a premise (when conjoined with factual premises about situations) to contingent moral truths that guide our actions.[11]

From our point of view, this approach is misguided by his unexamined naturalistic assumptions. We hold that the value judgments people make in lived experience and in deliberating their actions have truth-values and can be confirmed or disconfirmed. So rational agents are justified in concluding that a normative principle is true if it is presupposed by their valuations and deliberations in such a way that they cannot consistently deny it. Such a principle is not analytic in the narrow sense that its negation would be simply self-contradictory by virtue of its own terms; but it is analytic in the sense that the negation of it would do logical violence to the system of categorial concepts and principles that is essential to personal agency. The principle is, or so we claim, an a priori, categorial, normative principle of rational agency. It is in this respect similar to the a priori causal principle of our descriptive/explanatory conceptual system: "Every event has a cause." While a Kantian may have logical room to raise skeptical questions about whether the a priori causal principle and others of its kind are metaphysically true of the world (a skepticism which this work has tried to defuse), there is no logical room to doubt that the categorial principles of rational agency are true of the subjectivity of rational agents. Whatever is an a priori normative principle of rational agency is a formulation of, and is true of, the normative structure of selfhood. It makes no sense to say that the human mind imposes *its* categories and categorial principles on *itself* in experiencing, thinking, reasoning, deliberating, deciding, and living in such a way that we cannot know the real structure of the human mind itself. What we find in our reflective categorial analysis of the experiences and activities of the self is simply the categorial structure of the experiences and activities of the self, for these experiences and activities are inherent structures of meaning with their own categorial and logical aspects. So the categorial structures we find in our subjectivity by reflective analysis are the constitutive structures of our subjectivity itself.

Each human being with more or less normal, mature powers knows, through one's normative self-concept, that one is under the imperative to define and to live a life of one's own; we know a priori that all persons with the powers of rational agency have this responsibility; and we know that others have this responsibility in knowing, through our experiences of them and our interactions with them, that they are rational agents.

The Form of a Moral Life

Granted that people have the responsibility to define and to live their own lives, does it matter what kind of life one lives as long as it is one's own? Are there any guidelines? Clearly some life plans lead to wrecked lives; some keep those who try to live them in trouble and make for frustrated and unhappy lives; some seem to be successfully lived but fail to make for happy lives or to win moral approval; and some seem to make for happy lives and to gain moral approval. These facts suggest that life plans are, in a sense, life hypotheses to be tested in the living of them. We seem to learn something about how to live in the living of our own lives, in knowing others, and in studying biographies. Playwrights and novelists define and test life hypotheses in the development of characters in imaginative living; and, to the extent they are successful, they instruct us all about various life plans and what it is to live them.

This suggests that there is an "empirical" dimension in testing life hypotheses. And there is such a dimension; but there is also, as we observed previously, an a priori dimension to our normative self-concepts and thus to life criticism. We need to consider both aspects, but the a priori has the first claim on our attention at this point.

What is it for one's life to be genuinely one's own? Is it enough for it to be defined by one's own decisions? Or must it be one that stands justified under one's own critical powers? A life that did not have one's approval under critical judgment would be one to which one was not fully committed; it would be one with which one did not fully identify; it would be one in which one was not fully in control; in a very important sense, it would not be one's life. Thus, in order for a life to be fully one's own, it must be a life that would stand justified under one's rational and moral criticism; that is, it would have to be a life that one judged to be worthy of one as a human being and as the individual one was. This is a second a priori principle, or an amendment to the first.

It seems clear that normative requirements grounded in one's individuality or in the particular situations in which one lives would have to be known empirically by moral responses to the comprehended facts. Is it also the case that, in further appraising our lives as worthy of ourselves as human beings after they have been judged to be genuinely our own, we must depend entirely on our moral responses to the comprehended facts about ourselves and the circumstances of our existence? Or are there further a priori imperatives grounded in one's selfhood as a human person, requirements that are presupposed in life criticism and in living a life? If so, would such principles constitute a kind of master life plan, a skeletal plan, that anyone's life plan would have to embrace in order to make possible a well-lived, happy life that would be worthy of one and merit rational and moral approval?

The imperative to define and to live a life that is genuinely one's own cannot be the only a priori imperative in the normative structure of selfhood, for being justified under rational and moral criticism presupposes other imperatives. Simple rational criticism reveals the formal requirements that one's life plan must meet: Namely, it must be coherent, comprehensive (a plan for one's whole life), and realistic (possible for one in terms of the individual one is and the circumstances of one's

existence). Any life plan that does not meet these minimum rational
requirements, which are sometimes known as the imperatives of prudence, will give rise to frustration and failure in the living of it. Furthermore, such a plan is morally defective, for it is one that is unworthy
of one as a human being with normal, mature powers. It is a moral
obligation to be rational in this sense. Although prudence may not be
one of the highest moral virtues, it is a basic moral virtue nonetheless.

But there are other a priori requirements presupposed in rational
and moral criticism. Personhood, we have insisted, is defined in terms
of a responsibility. Earlier we spoke of a concept defined in this manner as an "office" concept in order to distinguish it from a functional
concept. It is in this sense that we are entitled to speak of personhood
as an office. Human beings, humanistically conceived, are by their nature holders of this office. It is a natural office, for it is not a social
artifact; it is not created or constructed by society; nor are human beings appointed or elected to the office; nor can they resign or be dismissed from it. Human beings hold the office of personhood by virtue
of their nature. Even in their immaturity they are destined by their
inherent normative structure to develop the requisite powers and to
have the responsibility to define and to live a life of their own. Of
course individuals may be thwarted in their development and may
never come to have the requisite powers in an actualized form; and,
therefore, they may never have the actual responsibility. But since human beings are defined by their inherent normative structure, they are
titular persons even if they never acquire the requisite powers and the
actual defining responsibility of personhood.

Part of the normative structure of any office are certain rights
grounded in the defining responsibility of the office. The rights inherent in an office are the freedoms and means the officeholder must
possess in order to have the opportunity to fulfill the responsibility of
the office. Lack of the necessary freedom or means for fulfilling a responsibility nullifies the responsibility. And when the responsibility of
an office changes, the rights of the office change along with it; if the
responsibility ceases to obtain, the rights grounded in it are dissolved.
In other words, the responsibilities of a position and the rights that go
with it are strictly correlative. They are logically connected. Talk about
the rights of an office is meaningless if divorced from the responsibilities of the office. And one cannot have the responsibility of an
office without having the rights grounded in it. Any claim to the responsibility of an office without the correlative rights is null and void
for reasons of logic. Of course the circumstances in which an officeholder operates may be a factor in determining what the rights of
the office are. For example, the president of the United States may

have the right to do things in a national emergency that he or she would not have the right to do under normal conditions. But even so, the responsibilities of the office determine what the rights are under the circumstances.

Much the same is true with our talk about human rights. It is the *responsibility* to define and to live a life of one's own that would be worthy of one as a human being that grounds human rights. Those who do not recognize such a responsibility as inherent in the normative structure of selfhood have a serious problem with the concept of human rights. This is why human rights have been intellectually problematic in our modern culture. Jeremy Bentham said that talk about natural human rights was "rhetorical nonsense";[12] and Alasdair MacIntyre said recently that belief in natural human rights "is one with belief in witches and in unicorns."[13] Most of those who have tried to validate the concept of human rights from within the reigning assumptions of our culture have had difficulties.[14]

One of the major difficulties in moral philosophy in the modern age has been an impoverished conception of humankind and personhood. We have, for the most part, brought to moral philosophy views and assumptions about what it is to be a human being that have been formed in, or under the influence of, the sciences. When this is the case, it is not surprising that we have difficulty in understanding morality and how it is grounded in what we are. Morality itself, as previously remarked, should be a primary resource in the development of our philosophical understanding of what it is to be a human person. From within a fully humanistic view of human beings and personhood, the problems of moral philosophy are not so intractable.

Human rights, then, are the rights pertaining to the natural, inalienable office of personhood that human beings occupy by their nature. We have to distinguish between one's *normatively having* and *actually having* the responsibility to define and to live a life of one's own that would be worthy of one as a human being and as the individual one is. The former, as already indicated, is a matter of being the kind of individual who ought to develop, or ought to have, the requisite powers and ought to have the responsibility at the appropriate stage of maturity, whether or not one ever actually has the powers and the responsibility. One actually has the responsibility only when one actually has the requisite semantic and critical powers to fulfill the responsibility.

Some of our basic human rights are dependent on the actual possession of the defining responsibility, but some are not. Children, for example, do not have the right to decide important matters about their lives in the manner of normal adults. The same is true for severely retarded or impaired adults. But clearly some basic human rights pertain to immature and mentally defective persons. Children, for instance, have a right to the conditions of well-being and education that would make it possible for them to become well-functioning persons in their more mature years. And retarded and impaired human beings have a right to the conditions of their well-being and of the development of which they are capable. These rights are grounded in their normative constitution. Those who locate the grounds for human rights and the moral imperatives in only personhood and not in human nature as well have a problem when it comes to the rights of the immature and the seriously impaired.

One cannot be a well-functioning, mature person without recognition of the fact that one is a person and thus that one has the responsibility to define and to live a worthy life of one's own, and that one has the moral rights grounded in this responsibility. Moral rights are not simply what one is free to do without normative restraints. Thomas Hobbes's so-called natural rights were just such liberties; they were not moral rights in any significant sense, for they did not impose normative limits and requirements on others. So one cannot be a reflective person without recognizing that other human beings have the same human rights as oneself and that their rights impose normative limits on others, including oneself.

One whose life plan lacks respect for other persons and their rights and ignores the normative limits they impose on oneself is both logically and morally at fault. Such a life plan is inconsistent, for it presupposes one's own responsibility as a person to define and to live one's own life and *the rights inherent in this responsibility*, and these presuppositions entail that other persons have the same rights that impose normative limits on oneself. And so, if one's life plan does not take proper account of the normative limits imposed on oneself by the rights of others, it is inconsistent with its own presuppositions. The moral fault lies in the fact that lack of respect for the rights of others shows one's lack of commitment to, or unwillingness to accept and to execute faithfully, one's most fundamental and defining responsibility as a person. In other words, for one to define and to live one's own life in a way that does not respect the basic responsibility and rights of others does violence not only to them but to oneself. Such a life cannot be authentically one's own; it cannot be worthy of one, for it cannot be justified under one's own rational and moral criticism.

The Goal of a Moral Life

But does being authentically one's own, and thus approved under one's own rational and moral criticism, require more of one's life plan than coherence, comprehensiveness, realism, and compatibility with the basic responsibility and rights of other persons? In other words, does the master plan provide some positive content, some generalized goal, that every life plan should include? Is there anything presupposed in moral criticism about the goal of life other than to live in a manner that is beyond reproach relative to the restraints we have already considered?

First of all, do the rights of others impose on us not only normative limits but also positive requirements? The issue is not whether persons by virtue of special relationships or arrangements have obligations to provide for, and to assist, others in securing and protecting their rights. The question is whether the rights of others as human beings, without regard to special relationships, impose normative requirements on those who are in a position to help when their rights are endangered. Although the claim that no person should violate the rights of others in living one's own life is less controversial than the claim that the rights of a person impose positive requirements on others, it is widely agreed that, paraphrasing John Locke, as everyone is bound to try to secure and to protect one's own rights, everyone, insofar as one is in a position to do so, and one's own rights come not in competition, ought to assist others in securing and protecting their human rights when they are in jeopardy.[15] And it is also widely agreed that a generalized version of this principle is binding; namely, that every person ought to work for, and to support, a social order that would, insofar as possible, provide the necessary support and protective systems for oneself and others to have the opportunity to live lives that would be worthy of them as human beings and as the individuals they are.

The moral sentiments and judgments of civilized people certainly support the claim that we are morally obligated in these ways. But are they a priori requirements grounded in the normative structure of selfhood? Are they principles that are presupposed in living a life and in life criticism? A convincing case can be made for the claim that the responsibility to define and to live a life of one's own that would be worthy of one entails these responsibilities. Certainly one has the responsibility to try to secure and to protect one's own basic rights. Not to do so would be to fail to fulfill one's defining responsibility. In trying to secure and to protect one's interests one can be strictly partisan, but the matter is different with one's basic rights. One cannot divorce the security and protection of one's own human rights from the security and protection of the rights of others. An attack on, or threat to, the rights of one endangers the rights of others. We all recognize that a violent attack by a person or group on the life of another is not only a violation of the right to life of that individual but a threat to the security of others. Since we are all subject to the fortunes of change, when the right to life of one is threatened by poverty, the right to the conditions of existence of all is insecure. The only rational way to try to secure and to protect the rights of anyone, including one's own, is to try to secure and to protect the rights of all. Although people can and must be partisan with regard to interests, they cannot rationally be partisan with regard to human rights. If nations would turn away from trying to defend their national interests with military force and try to defend only their basic national rights in this manner, perhaps we could build a just world order—for each nation, in defending its own rights, would be defending the rights of other nations as well. Certainly neither an individual person nor a nation can rationally defend its own basic rights by violating the rights of others. Therefore, inherent in one's basic responsibility to live a worthy human life is the responsibility to assist, when one's assistance is needed and can be given, in trying to secure and to protect the rights of other individuals as well as one's own; and, since one's own rights and the rights of others cannot be secured by individual actions alone, the defining responsibility of personhood entails the responsibility to work for, and to support, a social order that would provide the necessary support and protective systems for individuals to have the opportunity to live lives worthy of their humanity and their individuality.

This much, then, is included in the skeleton life plan that must be incorporated in, and be basic to, any life plan that is worthy of one as a human being: It must be a life plan of one's own that is coherent, comprehensive, and realistic; it must take account of the human rights of others—it must embrace the commitment not to violate the rights of others and to come to the assistance of others when their human rights are in jeopardy and one's assistance is needed and possible without a greater threat to oneself; furthermore, it must embrace the commitment to support, and to work with others for, a just social order that would provide, insofar as possible, the necessary support and protective systems to give each person in the society the opportunity to define and to live a life that would be worthy of one's humanity and individuality.

Being justified under rational and moral criticism embraces more than meeting these a priori normative requirements of selfhood; it includes being justified in terms of the normative requirements that impinge on one in the concrete situations in which one lives as determined by critically assessed value experiences in those situations. In other words, ethics is not just a matter of a priori moral judgments and empirical knowledge of the facts. As in other areas of knowledge, there are both a priori and empirical aspects. In ethics as elsewhere, the a priori dimension is basic and provides the framework for empirical inquiry and thought; but we have to rely on our critically assessed value experiences to discover what life is worthy of us as the individuals we are and what we morally ought to do in the concrete situations in which we live.

Principles of Life Criticism

Classical philosophers attempted to provide a defensible philosophical account of the world, a metaphysics; this, in our terminology, is an account of the a priori categorial structure of the world. Some have sought to discredit philosophy in this sense as armchair science; they have thought of it as in competition with, and to be replaced by, empirical science. It is true that the rise of modern science went against the establishment metaphysics of the time, but the establishment metaphysics was replaced by a new metaphysics, namely, modern naturalism, not by empirical science itself. But the new metaphysics was presupposed by, and provided the categorial framework for, the empirical sciences.

Classical moral philosophy, like metaphysics, deals with the a priori categorial framework of morality. Part of its task is to formulate the a priori normative principles inherent in the categorial framework of morality. But often these a priori normative principles have been misunderstood. Many philosophers have regarded them as providing the normative premises with which we conjoin factual beliefs about concrete situations in order to reach our ordinary moral judgments about specific human actions. In other words, they regard all moral knowledge about particular actions as deductive. But these a priori normative principles are presuppositions, not premises, of our ordinary moral experiences and judgments about what we ought to do or whether what we do is right. The relationship between these a priori principles and ordinary morality is parallel with that between metaphysical principles and the empirical sciences.[16] But no doubt the a priori dimension of ethics still looms large in our ethical thinking as metaphysics did in our thinking about the world before the development of the empirical sciences in the modern era.

Philosophers who acknowledge that there is a basic master plan for a human life presupposed in moral criticism of our lives have divided, for the most part, into two broad categories: those who think that the master plan pertains to the constitution of one's self and to the worthy life for a human being, and those who think that it provides principles of decision-making in terms of what is to be achieved through action. Those in the first group emphasize virtue. Plato talked about ethics as concerned with the proper organization and functioning of the soul; Aristotle spoke of the activity of the soul in accordance with virtue; the classical Stoics thought of the good person as one who understands and accepts reality with tranquility, for they believed that reality, except in the case of human subjectivity, is always the way it ought to be; Christians think of the good person as loving and caring—as one who is moved and guided by devotion to what is of highest worth; Kant thought of the good person as one with good will—a will determined by respect for the moral law. In other words, classical virtue ethicists emphasized the proper organization of selfhood according to its own inherent normative structure.[17] We may call the second group utilitarians—those who think that moral appraisals presuppose the imperative to maximize values through the effects of action. Bentham, for example, held that the principle of utility is the principle presupposed by the meaning of our moral terms and by our moral appraisals of our actions.[18] The emphasis in the first group is on what a person ought to be and the kind of life one ought to live; the emphasis in the second group is on how one judges which actions are right and what one ought to do.

Clearly the two positions are intimately related. Being a certain kind of person involves being disposed to judge actions in certain ways; and judging one's actions in terms of the maximization of values, however conceived, involves being a certain kind of person. But there are important differences. The utilitarian conceives the self and defines the moral point of view so that there is a genuine problem about why one should be moral. Those who emphasize virtue and define morality in terms of what one ought to be and the kind of life one ought to live as a person locate the moral point of view in the self in such a way that there cannot be a separation between the authentic point of view of the self and the moral point of view. The person who does not develop and accept the moral perspective is, according to this view, either undeveloped as a human person or perverted and self-alienated.

Utilitarianism, at least in its modern form, is a theory of ethics from within a general philosophical perspective that cuts the foundations from under the moral-being approach. A theory of knowledge that rejects value realism in the ontological sense, as most versions of modern empiricism do, gives rise to views of the self and world that make some form of utilitarianism seem plausible for those who acknowledge some form of objectivity for value judgments. But for a value realist who recognizes ontological normative structures, a sufficiently rich conception of selfhood becomes available and even compelling for the moral point of view to be anchored in one's identity as a person. According to such a view, moral appraisals are understood as being concerned with how well one is constituted and how well one performs as a person. And so concern with being justified under moral criticism and meriting moral praise will be seen as concern with being fully oneself as a human person. On this view, happiness will be regarded, not as a life free from pain and full of pleasure, not in terms of external power or possessions, not even in terms of the effects of one's actions on the world; rather, happiness will be regarded as perception of one's moral health, a sense of one's well-being and well-living as a person.

From this viewpoint, then, morality, according to its a priori categorial framework, is concerned with human development and the moral health of persons. By extension, this includes social development and the moral health of institutions and society as well, for, as we shall see in the next chapter, the development and moral health of persons cannot be separated from the development and moral health of society.

We have been talking about the life plan presupposed in moral appraisals, not the ends of action from the perspective of decision-making. In confronting a concrete problem, one does not ask, "What action in this situation would tend to perfect my being and support the human enterprise?" One would ask, however, "What should I do here and now? What does this situation require of me?" Some might say that the utilitarian formula ("Of all the options, choose the one that has the best predictable consequences for all affected") comes in at this point and provides the answer. But how do we evaluate the consequences? And why does the set of consequences judged best for all impose an overriding requirement on me in the given situation? In many situations this would seem to be a pale responsibility in comparison with the special responsibilities we bear to certain individuals, including ourselves. Rule utilitarians try to meet this objection by saying that one should do in the given situation what would maximize values, if the maxim of the action were to become the general practice for those in similar situations. This is more plausible than act utilitarianism, but it seems to be fatally flawed, for it would make human rights and justice dependent on empirically assessed utility rather than being part of the framework in terms of which we calculate utility. There is nothing in the principle that would preclude, for example, the possibility of the moral rightness of a general practice of officials of the state, under some limited set of circumstances, punishing a person whom they knew to be innocent to appease a dangerous public outraged by a heinous crime. Yet to judge as right such treatment of a person known to be innocent seems to do violence to the categorial framework of morality.

In discovering what a given situation requires of an individual, we must, it seems, rely on what informed, morally sensitive persons would judge that the situation required of him or her—what they would judge in terms of their critically assessed moral responses to the comprehended facts of the case; for coherence of judgments on the part of informed, morally sensitive persons is the most reliable test of moral truth in concrete situations. Of course there is a body of moral wisdom (including a priori moral truths and a set of more or less consensus moral judgments derived from critically assessed experiences in the past) that bears on such cases, and it is helpful; but such wisdom is rarely sufficient to yield a responsible judgment about a concrete situation without critically assessed moral responses to the comprehended facts of the individual case. This is the empirical side of morality; it is what does the work of morality in lived experience. Many reject this position because of the way they understand the categorial nature of emotive responses to comprehended facts; but, if our epistemic analysis of emotive experience is correct, this is not a valid objection; for critical assessment of such experiences can yield epistemically justified and true moral judgments about the objective normative structure of the situation, especially what the concrete situation normatively requires of the given individual as a human being and as the particular individual he or she is.

Conclusion

In this chapter, we have considered what it is to be a human person. We have concluded that *person* is a humanistic categorial concept; and that human beings must be conceived in terms of the humanistic categories of meaning, logic, normativity, and personhood. Yet we have maintained that human beings, humanistically conceived, constitute a natural kind. We have argued that human beings have a mind—an organized set of semantic states and acts, with a transcending center, that is self-critical, self-correcting, and creative under an inherent governing imperative to be consistent and correct. Furthermore, we have maintained that human beings, as persons, have a natural social office that is constituted by (1) the responsibility to define and to live a life of one's own that would be worthy of one as a human being and as the individual one is and (2) the rights that are grounded in this responsibility, namely, the freedoms and conditions of well-being that are necessary for one to have an opportunity to fulfill the defining responsibility of the office. The epistemic self with its governing imperative is not distinct from the moral self with its governing imperative. The epistemic self is the self organized under the imperatives to be consistent and correct in experience and belief and to render intelligible whatever is taken to be real, whereas the moral self is the self organized under the imperative to define and to live a life that would be worthy of one as a human being and as the individual one is. The self organized for living, the moral self, is the more inclusive; but it is based on and requires the epistemic self. And the imperative that defines the epistemic self is subsidary to the moral imperative, for knowledge and understanding are imperative for beings engaged in living a life.

This account of human persons has significant implications for a philosophical account of social reality. And no philosophical account of human persons can be complete without an account of the social world in which human persons have their being. This brings us to our next topic: the nature of social reality and the normative structure of society.

CHAPTER 7

Persons and the Normative Structure of Society

In the last chapter, we contended that a human person is one who, by virtue of one's nature, ought to develop one's knowledge-yielding and critical powers and to define and to live a life of one's own, under the guidance of one's own beliefs and critical judgments, that would be worthy of one in terms of one's humanity and individuality. We further concluded that this defining responsibility of personhood grounds one's human rights—the conditions of well-being and the freedoms that are necessary for one to have an opportunity to fulfill the primary responsibility of personhood. This means that persons with normal, mature powers are responsible for their own lives and for their own beliefs and judgments.

The Individual and Society

Of course everyone is heavily dependent on others and the culture for the development of one's knowledge-yielding and critical powers, for one's self-concept, and for most of one's knowledge and wisdom. Yet, with developed learning and critical powers, one should not be content to allow others to define one's identity and to do one's thinking; one should not be the product of other people's choices or enslaved to one's culture; rather, through the use of one's own critical powers, one should liberate oneself as much as possible by gaining mastery of one's own identity and life. This does not mean that one should reject one's identity and belief/precept system that were formed under cultural conditioning and tutelage; but it does mean that, insofar as possible, one should justify these matters to one's self through criticism or else reconstruct them in justifiable ways. Of course self-criticism is possible

227

only from within a constituted self with an extensive belief/precept system already in place. Nevertheless, critical self-examination can liberate one to a considerable extent from the social and cultural process that generated one's first identity and provided one with a supply of cultural capital with which to begin one's life enterprise. This is what freedom means in the tradition of classical liberal individualism. This is the objective of liberal education.

Liberal individualism is under attack today. It is charged with being destructive of both the moral self and the social order. According to widely shared assumptions, individuals, left to their own critical and knowledge-yielding powers in defining and living their lives, have no guidelines but their own wants and preferences; and wants and preferences are regarded as natural occurrences, devoid of validity conditions. Accordingly, liberated individuals tend to suffer a severe identity crisis, and the social bonds that make society possible tend to dissolve. All relationships are regarded as contractual; but, from within the widely accepted value subjectivism, contracts are binding only so long as the wants and preferences of the contracting parties dictate. Any party to a contract may abrogate it whenever one thinks that it is to one's advantage to do so.

Rationality, on this view, is regarded as inherently prudential, with the ends of behavior set by desires and preferences. Rights come to be regarded as liberties—things one is free to do without normative limits. Without justifiable social limits on behavior, it follows that one should be left free to do as one pleases. It is often added, of course, that one's freedom should be consistent with the same freedom for others, but even this limit on one's behavior can have no basis within moral subjectivism other than a prudential contract. The efforts of society to channel, or to restrain, behavior beyond the protection of individuals from interference with their liberties are regarded as being without justification, for each person must choose one's own values and the kind of life one is to live. This is the way conservative critics tend to characterize all liberals.

Some liberals try to construct a prudential contract theory of morality that would support an enduring social order. However, morality conceived in this way fails to provide the motivational force to restrain antisocial behavior dictated by immediate feelings and passions and nearsighted self-interests; and it is too weak to compel the behavior needed to sustain a viable social order. Only strong moral emotions grounded in one's identity, in one's normative self-concept, seem strong enough for the twofold task. And these emotions are weakened or perverted for individuals whose normative self-concept and moral identity have been weakened or perverted.

For these reasons, there are powerful voices that condemn liberal individualism. There is a new emphasis on the primacy of society. Many conservatives, sharing the basic value subjectivism of latter-day liberals, think that society, not the individual person, should be the source of the values by which we live. Unlike subjectivistic liberals, they do not regard the traditional morality as something for the individual to overcome. Indeed, they take society and its established ways to be the standard of what is right. The historically evolved social structure, according to some, embodies the values of the historical community and thus is good as it is. In the same way the evolved biological structure of a species is the standard of normalcy for members of the species, the historically evolved traditions and social structures of a society are taken to define normality for that society. These traditions and social structures are said to be no more subject to ethical criticism and reform than the natural biological structure of human beings is subject to criticism and technological reconstruction. Persons who fit into the society are taken to be as they should be. Behavior that fits in with the society's ways is right; behavior that is socially deviant or disruptive of the established ways is morally wrong. Whereas liberalism (in its traditional form) emphasizes an ethics of individual rights and the common good that leads to social criticism and reform, conservativism emphasizes an ethics of virtue and personal reform. The virtues on which conservatives concentrate are those dispositions of mind and heart that prepare individuals for their roles in society. The function of government, conservatives say, is to protect the society, not to reform it. They are more disposed toward government regulation of the private lives of individuals than regulation of the institutions of the society. Of course conservatives are not against undoing social reforms of liberal governments that haven't yet come to be regarded as products of the lathe of history.

The subjectivistic conservative shares with the right- and left-wing totalitarians the view that individuals have to be trained by social conditioning to fit them into the society's ways of doing things. They have to be conditioned so that they, in effect, develop a second nature: The customary and institutionalized ways of behavior (or a pattern of behavior dictated by a revolutionary totalitarian government) are internalized by the socialization process to form a set of habits of the mind and heart that are, in many respects, similar to a set of instincts. These virtues are grounded in one's socially determined self-concept similar to the way in which instincts are grounded in an animal's biological nature. Once the socialization process has taken effect in individuals, they act from inner motivation within the established ways of the society; they feel self-fulfillment in conforming to the ways of the society, and violence to their own identity in acting contrary to the ways of the society. Unlike that of the liberal individualist, the conservative ideal is not for the individual to liberate oneself from one's socially and culturally determined identity by gaining self-mastery of one's self-constituting beliefs and precepts through critical self-examination; rather the ideal is for the individual to accept one's socially and culturally determined identity and way of life as beyond critical reconstruction.

Critics are correct in holding that *subjectivistic* liberal individualism tends to generate a personal identity crisis and to erode the social order; but the corrective, we contend, does not lie in conservatism in the subjectivistic mode, which tends to distort and to enslave the individual, to relativize morality to particular historical communities, to deny the pathological conditions the culture and society may be suffering, and to foreclose the possibility of a just world order. The fault with subjectivistic liberal individualism, according to our analysis, lies not in liberal individualism as such but in the widespread moral subjectivism shared by many latter-day liberals and conservatives.

From within moral subjectivism, the effort to liberate the self and to achieve self-mastery leaves the self, with its socially formed identity deconstructed, only a mass of feelings, impulses, desires, and preferences; and these motivational forces, devoid of validity-conditions, are taken to be subject to being organized only on the basis of cost/benefit analysis for maximum self-satisfaction of the individual. The proper corrective, we contend, is not the new conservative "socialism" but moral realism. The inherent normative structure of the individual, as we argued in the last chapter, embraces a basic life plan for all human beings that demarcates the human from the inhuman in life-styles and human behavior. This basic life plan, defined by the presuppositions of rational and moral criticism, is to be filled out in detail by each individual, not on the basis of one's wants and preferences as such, but on the basis of one's confirmed beliefs and critical judgments about oneself and the conditions of one's existence—these beliefs and judgments being infused with cultural knowledge and wisdom and with the counsel and criticism of others.

There is, according to moral realism, an inherent normative structure of society. It is grounded in the normative structure of human beings, not the other way around. A society ought to provide the protective and support systems necessary for its members to have an opportunity to define and to live lives worthy of them as human beings and as the individuals they are. This "ought" captures the basic normative structure of every society, which provides a universal society plan in much the same way that the basic normative structure of human lives (as defined by the presuppositions of rational and moral criticism) provides a basic life plan for all human beings. And in the same way individuals have to fill out the details of their life plan according to their individuality and circumstances, each society has to fill out the details of its social structure according to its history and circumstances. So a wide variety of institutional and other social structures for a society can be justified. Nevertheless, by virtue of their common normative structure, all societies are subject to being objectively appraised as well developed or undeveloped, as well formed or deformed, and as healthy and well functioning or as sick and malfunctioning.

The basic normative structure of a society is grounded in, and generated from, the rights and responsibilities that pertain to the natural office of personhood. The first responsibility of a society is to protect and to support the human rights of all its members. This is a matter of basic justice. It stems from the responsibility of individuals to respect the rights of others and, if in a position to do so, to assist them when their rights are in jeopardy. The second responsibility, which overlaps with the first, is to provide the institutions and social conditions that make it possible for human beings to flourish—to develop their powers and to fulfill their responsibilities as human beings and as the individuals they are. This is the promotion of the common good. Some societies may not be able to provide such protective and support systems for its members; but, to the extent a society cannot, it is not a well-developed society. To the extent a society can provide these systems but does not, it is morally at fault as a society. The moral guilt is borne by the members of the society proportionately to their responsibility for the decisions and actions of the society.

Objective liberals, liberals who accept semantic and value realism, do not think of the individual as a social atom. It is commonplace, in fact, to say that human persons are *social* beings. The position taken by the last chapter gives this truism a special meaning. Human beings, as we argued in Chapter 6, are, by their nature, persons. They are normatively constituted so that, even from conception, they ought to come to have, in their maturity, the requisite semantic and critical powers and the responsibility of personhood—the responsibility of defining and living a life of their own that would pass muster under rational and moral criticism. They have, by virtue of their nature, the rights that are grounded in this responsibility—in their immaturity, they have a right to the conditions of well-being that would make it possible for them to develop the requisite powers of personhood, and, in their maturity, they have a right to the freedoms and the conditions of well-being that would make it possible for them to fulfill the defining responsibility of personhood. These rights are not simply liberties in the Hobbesian sense (merely the absence of normative restraints), but fully *moral* rights in that they impose normative limits and requirements on others. In other words, personhood is a natural, inalienable office for human beings; it is neither chosen by one nor assigned to one by society; nor can one resign from it or be dismissed from it.

Human beings can mature as persons only in a social and cultural community. They have to be socially and culturally generated and sustained. Yet human beings generate and sustain the society and the culture. (Of course the society and the culture are not two distinct things. Perhaps we should speak of a "cultural society"—one that is based on, and embodies, a culture.) This sounds like a paradox. The reality is that human beings actualize their normative potentiality as persons only in and through the generation of a cultural society. Human beings, prior to their generation of a cultural society, could not actualize their personhood; and they could not generate a cultural community without actualizing their personhood proportionately. The two processes are not distinct; they are two dimensions of the same process. Neither could advance without an advancement in the other. Personhood and cultural community are inextricably bound together.

A society is not a complex organization of atomic individuals. It is more like an organism than like a mechanism. Members of a society do not have an independent identity; unlike the god who appeared to Moses in the wilderness, they cannot identify themselves simply as the I AM nor as an I AM. The answer to the question about who one is must locate one in a social structure. Social relationships enter into the very constitution of one's being as a person; they are internalized in one's self-concept. One feels, and is, incomplete as a person if one does not know who one's parents were or where one came from. Amnesia victims are incomplete as persons and do not know who they are until they regain self-knowledge of their past identifying relationships. One discovers one's identity not so much by what one is prepared to say with the pronoun "I" as what one is prepared to say with "we." "We" locates one in a family, a community, an institution, a nation, a civilization, and so forth. No human being is a mere I. If one were, one could not say "I"; this inability would not be simply the lack of a language but lack of the kind of internality that would make it possible for one to say "I."

Persons are peculiar beings in that they are constituted by their subjectivity; and their subjectivity develops and flourishes in the manner of a person only in intersubjective relationships. Persons are the dynamic, critical, and creative nodes in an intersubjective cultural matrix. To the extent they do not critically justify to themselves their own semantic states and acts, they are at the mercy of the dynamics of the intersubjective cultural web; they let themselves down and the cultural community as well. To the extent they gain self-mastery of their own subjectivity, they become a more dynamic, critical, and creative point in the intersubjective cultural field. Cultural liberation does not cut one out of the cultural web; it only converts one from a passive to an active partner in the cultural community.

We identify more readily with others who share our culture, especially with those who speak our language, have lived where we have lived, attended the schools we attended, know some of the people we know, and have shared in some of our experiences. We are lonely and feel incomplete and diminished in our own being when we are cut off from others, especially from those with whom we have shared our lives. The more distant others are from us in experience and culture, the more alien they seem to us. We care more about those who are closer to us in experience and culture, for they are more a part of our selves.

The culture of a historical community not only enters into and shapes the subjectivity of the people and is modified and developed further by the critical, reconstructive, and creative participation of individuals and groups; it is embodied in the institutions and social structures of the society. To the extent the social order embodies the culture that structures the subjectivity of the people, the people will embrace the social order and feel at home in it; to the extent the culture that structures the subjectivity of the people (or a subclass of the people) is different from that embodied in the social order, the people (or the subclass) will feel alienated in the society. A well-ordered society is one in which the people, without manipulation or coercion by external sanctions, live and work comfortably within the social order, feel at home in it, and draw strength from it.

So a society is not simply a collection of individuals with independent identities. It is a complex social structure in which people live and have their being. It consists of persons, systems of offices (various institutions), and systems of institutions (the educational, health-care, economic, governmental, religious, and other systems). The whole society, insofar as it is *a* society, is a more or less self-sustaining and self-governing system of all the systems of offices. Each system has its functions. Each office is constituted by a set of responsibilities and the correlative powers, rights, and liberties. In the functions, responsibilities, rights, liberties, and traditional ways of the office structure, the social order embodies the culture.

When the assumptions, beliefs, and values embodied in a social structure come to be progressively questioned and rejected by the people, the social order gives way and may collapse. Those in positions of power who continue to identify with the old social order may try to sustain it by force for a while, but in time a social order that embodies

the emerging culture will replace it. This may be accomplished by revolution or by social reform in an evolutionary way. Those who try to
sustain an old social order, as well as those who try to impose a new
societal blue print, are prone to try to control the culture as a way to
manage the social order. A society that is committed to a free culture—
a culture that develops through education and through the free and
open exercise of the critical and creative powers of the people—must
institutionalize social reform; otherwise a gap will emerge between the
developing culture and the social structure, and the people will become
alienated from the institutions of the society. This can result in open
and violent revolution.

Personhood is the basic and paramount office of the whole social
structure. It is a natural office. Personhood is, of course, defined in
each culture and social structure, but how a particular culture and social order defines it is subject to criticism and reconstruction by an epistemic appeal to the inherent normative structure of human persons.
Hence the natural office of personhood is universal; it is common to all
societies. Some would say that it is the only natural office, that all other
offices are constituted by a conventional division of responsibilities.
Others, however, argue for additional natural offices such as man,
woman, husband, wife, mother, father, son, daughter, and maybe
others; they also argue that the family, constituted by these offices, is a
natural institution. A case can be made for these claims. There is a
natural division of responsibilities and rights in procreation; and there
are responsibilities and rights grounded in the natural relationships involved in procreation and in caring for the young. Families with similarities in the internal division of responsibilities appear in all (or
nearly all) known societies. Nevertheless, some argue that there are no
inherent responsibilities or rights grounded in sex as such. According
to this view, *male* and *female* are not social but purely biological concepts. Those who hold this view claim that where manhood and womanhood are social offices, they are so by social convention and should
be abolished for they tend to exploit women. Whatever stand one takes
on these offices, personhood remains the basic natural office in any
society. All other offices, whether natural or conventional, are subordi-
nate to, and must accommodate, the office of personhood.

While the parallel between a society and an organism is striking,
there is an important difference. In an organism, the functions of the
organs are to serve the needs of the organism; indeed, the organs are
conceived in terms of the parts they play in the organism. They have
different functions and are of different value according to the importance of their function to the whole. If a part becomes a hindrance
rather than an aid to the whole, it may be removed for the sake of the

organism, which is the important thing. In contrast to an organism, all the basic elements of a social system have a common position: the inalienable office of personhood, which is defined in terms of responsibilities grounded in the inherent nature of human beings, not in the nature of the society of which they are members. The conventional offices of a society, which may be regarded as more analogous to the organs of an organism than the office of personhood, are occupied by individuals whose primary office is that of personhood. These offices are judged, not only in terms of their service to the society as a whole, but also in terms of the effects they have on the persons who hold them. Furthermore, the normative structure of society is grounded in, and is a function of, the normative structure of persons. And the society is judged by how well it serves the needs of its members, not the other way around.

There are, of course, "socialists" who take an organic view of society. Some hold that the most powerful state with the most advanced culture is the highest achievement of God (or ultimate reality, however conceived). Accordingly, individual human beings are defined by the differentiated offices they are selected for by the society. Thus the normative structure and status of individuals are defined by the normative structure of the society; the worth of individuals is determined by their functions in the society and how well they fulfill them. It follows that human beings have no inherent rights that impose normative limits and requirements on the society; those who are a hindrance to, or a drag on, the society are eliminable for the good of the society.

The analysis of personhood in Chapter 6 counters such a "socialist" position. According to our view, the first line of criticism of any alienable office in a society pertains to its compatibility with the office of personhood. The basic question to ask, in the moral appraisal of such an office, is whether a person can hold the office and function well in it without being compromised, corrupted, perverted, or stunted as a human being. The second question pertains to how well the office serves the larger society or the common good.

It is not at all clear how an office that failed to pass the first test could be redeemed under the second. Consider the position of a slave. The office is fundamentally incompatible with that of personhood. One cannot be a good slave and also fulfill one's responsibility as a person to define and to live a life of one's own that would be worthy of one as a human being. This is the final and decisive moral argument against slavery, regardless of how much social and cultural good an institution of slavery might make possible. This is the kind of argument the women's movement directs against the traditional office of womanhood, defined in such a way that women are supposed to be wives, mothers, and caring and nurturing support persons and workers in general for family and community betterment. Women liberationists insist that the office of womanhood understood in this manner, as in the case of slavery, is incompatible with the office of personhood; furthermore, they contend that, as in the case against slavery, the incompatibility point brings the argument to an end, regardless of how beneficial the office might be for the family and for the society. The pacifist makes a similar argument against the office of the soldier. Whether or not we accept these particular arguments, if we grant the incompatibility thesis, the moral argument is over in each case.

No doubt good can be done by morally corrupting offices, but the question is whether the good that results can redeem the acts, the agent, and the office. If the good results should morally redeem the acts and if the agent should fully comprehend and accept this fact, the acts would not be morally compromising or corrupting. They would not be contrary to the agent's primary responsibility as a person. Nevertheless, performing the acts might have damaging psychological effects on one; it might be even dehumanizing in some way. Accepting such effects on oneself in order to fulfill an important responsibility even could be morally praiseworthy. Consider the mother who accepts and works at a dreary, servile, dehumanizing job to support her family; or the soldiers who are psychologically damaged and dehumanized by the acts of war in their efforts to defend their country against the invading army of an aggressor. Morally corrupting or perverting official acts are those that are not morally redeemable by good intentions or good results. Consider the father who becomes a hit man for a crime syndicate in order to support his family. Such unredeemable acts are typically those that violate the rights of others or one's moral responsibilities to others in some way.

Often, no doubt, the responsibility of a society to achieve some common good may override and thus nullify some of the antecedent rights of some individuals. Consider, for example, how a community's need for a public water source may override some local property-owners' right to keep their property for their own purposes. Even if the responsibility of the community's government to provide the needed water supply and the property-owners' responsibility to support the community's efforts to fulfill its responsibilities nullify the rights of the private owners to keep their property for their own use, they do not nullify the right of the property owners to a fair price for their property. After all, property rights in land are grounded in conventional arrangements, which are made on the basis of both the rights of individuals and the common good. The same reasoning does not apply to basic human rights. They are not grounded in social arrangements and cannot be canceled by social rearrangements. Human rights cannot be nullified by public need or public responsibility, except under extraordinary conditions in which the exercise of certain rights might endanger more basic rights; for example, a society might be justified under certain conditions in curtailing temporarily the exercise of such rights as the freedom of movement, assembly, or speech for the sake of protecting the more basic human right to physical security. If the actual situation did not limit one's freedom rights, the society would not be justified in imposing restrictions on freedom for the sake of a less demanding public good.

The fundamental point is that the responsibilities and rights of persons as such impose normative limits on what the responsibilities and rights of the offices they hold in society can be. In other words, the offices of a society, unlike the organs of an organism, are not to be judged solely in terms of their service to the whole of which they are a part. Indeed, judgments about the common good or the good of the society must be made from within an orientation that begins with respect for basic human rights. The common good cannot be promoted by violation of human rights; and the violation of the human rights of some cannot be simply counted as part of the cost of some public good. Human rights, unless overridden by more basic human rights in the situation, veto actions that would violate them, regardless of what the beneficial consequences of the actions might be. The common good cannot be achieved except within the limits of human rights and justice for all. A good that is based on a violation of the human rights of anyone is a partisan good, not a common good.

The Normative Structure of Society

The implications of the normative structure of personhood for the normative structure of society need to be spelled out more fully. Human rights are connected to the office of personhood; they are grounded in the constitutive responsibility of the office—the responsibility to define and to live a life of one's own that would be worthy of one as a human being and as the individual one is. Human rights are the conditions that one must enjoy if one is to have an opportunity to fulfill the defining responsibility of personhood and for which someone or society collectively has a responsibility to allow, to protect, or to provide. The qualification is essential, because the necessary conditions for one to become or to be a functioning person do not simply translate into rights. These conditions have to be ones that could be provided and for which somebody or society collectively has a responsibility to provide; or they have to be ones with which others could interfere but for which others have a responsibility not to do so. We might say that people who were suffering with coronary artery disease in 1960 needed bypass surgery, but they did not have a right to have the operation because it could not have been provided then. A person living in some remote part of the world today with coronary artery disease may need bypass surgery (that is, it may be a necessary condition in order for such a person to survive), but there may be no one or no society with the responsibility to provide it. Under these conditions, we would not say that one had a right to the surgery. Rights impose responsibilities on others: the responsibility to provide some benefit or opportunity, the responsibility of noninterference, or the responsibility of protection. We cannot assess what one's rights are in a situation independently of assessing what the responsibilities of others are; nor can we assess the responsibilities of people in a situation independently of assessing the rights of the people involved. We can assess neither the rights nor the responsibilities that obtain in a situation without assessing what can be done.

Human rights divide into two groups: (1) welfare rights—the conditions of one's existence and well-being that one must have in order to develop and to sustain the powers necessary to fulfill the responsibility of the office of personhood and for which some others or society collectively bear responsibility in some way, and (2) freedom rights—the freedoms one must enjoy in order to have the opportunity to fulfill the basic responsibility of the office and for which others have an obligation not to interfere with and to help provide for and to protect.

The primary welfare rights pertain to the necessary conditions of life, health, comfort, security, education, and personal freedom and dignity. These conditions are not in and of themselves rights. They become rights, as already indicated, only insofar as they are possible in a situation and a person's need for them imposes a requirement on somebody or the society collectively to provide them, to protect them, or not to interfere with them. So the specific contents of welfare rights vary greatly from time to time and place to place. The last person in the world, or a last survivor on an island whose existence was unknown to the rest of the world, would have no welfare rights, for there would be no one upon whom such a person's needs would impose a requirement. Of course we might say that one in such a situation has welfare rights in that one's needs would impose normative restraints and requirements on others if there were any appropriately situated. But there does not seem to be much point in extending the concept in this manner. We think that everyone in our society today has a right to the kind of housing, health care, education, information, culture, work, and work conditions and benefits that no society before modern times could have provided. Only in modern societies, for example, could the young be supported for thirteen to twenty or more years of schooling before entering the work force full time and the old for ten to twenty or more years in retirement. We think that people in our society have a right to certain conditions of personal freedom such as mail service, access to a telephone, access to a library, means of transportation, a level of income that enables one to live with some dignity, and the like that were not available in earlier societies and still are not available in many. We think that one has a right to a free culture—to a culture that has stood the test of open and free examination and criticism and in which the self-corrective processes are still at work, rather than being subject to, and manipulated by, a culture that is controlled by some interest group or power structure. For the most part, only in modern times has the idea been entertained that a culture could be critically developed and reconstructed.

We need to distinguish between the welfare rights people have in a society in which these rights are not acknowledged and no social arrangements have been made to meet them, and the welfare rights people have in a society in which they are acknowledged and arrangements exist to provide for them. A society may be slow to acknowledge its responsibilities in this regard. But presumably, when a society makes arrangements to provide certain welfare benefits for its people, it acknowledges that it has a responsibility to provide them and even that the people had a prior right to them. We argue about the responsibilities of related individuals, institutions, and the society at large in meeting human needs. Presumably there is something to argue about and about which an opinion is correct or incorrect. So basically social arrangements do not create welfare rights; but once social arrangements are in place for dealing with certain kinds of human needs and for fulfilling the responsibilities of society related to them, the arrangements define certain welfare rights and who or what agency has the responsibility to provide for them. No doubt welfare rights often exceed those that have been acknowledged and for which arrangements have been instituted. For instance, it is widely recognized that many people in the United States today have rights to housing and health care for which there are no satisfactory arrangements. These rights may impose requirements on certain individuals, families, or voluntary institutions until the society collectively makes arrangements to assume its responsibility in this regard. Once welfare rights have been explicitly defined and social arrangements made to provide for them, some individuals may have rights under these definitions and arrangements that they would not have had otherwise. But to the extent welfare rights (as distinct from procedural rights) are created by such definitions and arrangements, the definitions and arrangements are subject to being faulted.

Since welfare rights are those conditions of well-being that one must have in order to develop and to sustain the requisite powers for actually having and carrying out the responsibilities of the office of personhood, they, unlike freedom rights, pertain to one in one's immaturity as well as in one's mature years. It is a highly controversial matter in our culture about the level of maturity at which the welfare rights obtain. This controversy is a product of the controversy about the nature of personhood and the ground of human rights. For those who accept our position on these matters, there is no room for further controversy about when welfare rights come into force. The normative structure of the individual is present from conception. The fertilized human egg is an individual entity that ought to develop into a fully mature human being. If it does not, something will have gone awry along the way. It is in the process of becoming a mature human being from the beginning. So it is an immature human being from conception. There is no nonarbitrary line that can be drawn at any point in the maturation process at which we can say that welfare rights become operative.

If we were to choose the point at which the organ structure was complete and the familiar human physical form was existentially present for the emergence of welfare rights, we would be taking human rights to be grounded in that particular existential structure; yet there is nothing to indicate that the human normative structure was not present and being progressively realized prior to this point. If we were to choose the point of viability, the point at which the fetus could survive outside the womb by the exercise of its own systems, we might be considering the fetus prior to this point as an extension of the mother's body and thus not as an individual human being with its own normative structure; or we might be considering the right of the mother to control her own body as overriding any rights that the unborn child might have by virtue of its own normative structure.

The first alternative of the last statement seems to be clearly false. Although the fertilized egg, under natural conditions, needs the mother's body for its continued existence and development, it is an independent human being with its own inherent normative structure from the beginning. It is not a part of the mother's body. At no point in its development does the mother's body come to have two heads, four hands, four feet, and so forth. The mother's body is host to the fetus in a way in which her body is not host to any part of itself. The maturation of the child after birth is a continuation of the maturation process that began at conception. The second alternative is more arguable. Certainly there is justification for the claim that a normal mature woman has the responsibility and right to control her own body. But this does not mean that she is at liberty to control her body without regard to the normative limits and requirements imposed on her by the presence of others. Rather, she has the responsibility to control her body in a way that would be justified under rational and moral criticism. So the right to control her body does not in itself justify her decision to have an abortion. It only justifies the claim that she is the one to make the decision so long as she makes it responsibly, with proper regard for all the normative factors involved, including whatever welfare rights her unborn child may have.

That the fetus needs its mother's body as host does not in itself establish that it has a right to her body; whether the fetus has a right to her body as a necessary condition for its continued development depends on whether its need imposes an overriding responsibility on the woman to make her body available in this manner. Clearly she does not have that responsibility if it would cost her her own life. Some think that a woman would not have any responsibility for the fetus if she were not responsible in any way for her pregnancy, as in the case of rape. Others counter that, if one found an abandoned infant in an alley, one would have a responsibility to make arrangements for its welfare; in like manner, they claim that the woman has a responsibility to provide for the fetus in her womb regardless of her responsibility for its being there. If a woman should conduct her sexual life in a careless manner and became pregnant, she would obviously have a responsibility for the fetus. It would seem that she would have a responsibility even if she acted responsibly but became pregnant by accident, for in other areas we are held responsible for the accidental consequences of our actions. In all these cases, the important question would be whether the responsibility the woman had for the fetus outweighed other responsibilities she had that would have to be foregone if she met her responsibility to the fetus. Under any of these conditions, the matter of abortion is a weighty moral issue.

The central question about abortion for public policy is whether the unborn have rights from conception that should be given legal protection by the society. In other words, does a woman have the authority to make the decision about whether to have an abortion, regardless of whether she makes a justified or an unjustified decision? Is she the one to make the decision as to whether some other responsibility she has overrides her responsibility to make her body available for the development of the fetus? It is clearly her decision to make unless the society vests that authority elsewhere. The important question is whether the society would violate her right to make the decision if it should vest the authority elsewhere or if it should outlaw abortions or limit them to certain special conditions.

The main argument against either making abortions illegal or vesting the authority to authorize an abortion in some agency of the state is the lack of consensus in our society on the metaphysical issues on which the moral questions turn. We cannot prohibit by law behavior that a large portion of the informed and conscientious people of the society do not judge to be wrong, especially if they are not prepared to accept a contrary verdict by the government as tolerable. When the societal decision procedure reaches a contrary moral judgment on an issue that is grounded in a metaphysical position that is not widely shared in the society, those who do not share the metaphysical position cannot accept the moral judgment as possibly correct in any straightforward way. For a society to try to enforce laws on people in this manner only discredits the institution of law and undermines the authority of the government, for such laws can be enforced only by the police power of the state. That is the situation most Western societies are in with regard to abortion. So there is no viable option in these societies but to leave the authority to make the decision to abort or not to abort a pregnancy to the pregnant woman and her doctor.

Those who disagree with abortion should be free to express their disagreement, but they should focus on the underlying metaphysical issues. They should not morally condemn the women who have the abortions or the abortionists as murderers, for if their metaphysics does not allow them to acknowledge that the human fetus is a person, their acts cannot have the requisite intention to be murder. Indeed, it is not clear how a woman who has an abortion on the belief that the fetus is not a person can be morally at fault. How can one be morally at fault for holding a metaphysical position, especially if it is a widely shared position that the advanced culture and educational institutions of one's society foster? We excuse people for actions based on miscomprehension of the simple facts of the situation; we even excuse them for actions based on controversial views about the facts of the situation. It seems more reasonable to excuse them for their miscomprehension of, or their controversial views about, the metaphysical facts of the situation.

On the basis of the humanistic metaphysics put forward in this work, the fetus, as previously observed, is a human person from conception and progresses through many stages before it reaches full maturity and comes to have the full array of human responsibilities and human rights. The more the potential has been actualized the greater the perfection of the individual and, in this sense, the greater worth of the person. People have quite a different emotional response to an early miscarriage than they to do to the death of an infant; they have quite different moral responses to an induced early abortion than to an infanticide. This is partly because the idea that a fertilized egg or a few-weeks-old fetus is a human person is an intellectually comprehended fact; it does not engage the emotions in the way of a perceptually recognizable human being with the familiar human physical form. And, too, fertilized human eggs and very young human fetuses usually do not occupy much of a recognized place in social space. They have not become deeply intertwined with the lives of others. Their death might be experienced as a disappointment but not as so great a loss as the death of a child who had come to occupy a place in a family. So it is not at all surprising that people find it difficult to become concerned about the rights of such beings. Nonetheless, we do make moral judgments on the basis of intellectually comprehended facts as well as perceptually comprehendible situations. And it seems clear intellectually that, if the humanistic metaphysics presented here is correct, a human being from conception has the normative nature, however minimally actualized, in which human welfare rights are grounded; it is the same normative nature at conception as at birth or at any later period. Even though the emotional intensity of judgments based on such an intellectual comprehension may be less than those based on a perceptually recognizable human being, their validity is not.

It might be argued that the closer an individual is in the maturation process to having the requisite powers and the responsibilities of personhood, the more welfare rights one has. On this basis we would have to say that the one-year-old child has a greater claim to welfare rights than the infant, that the two-year-old child has a greater claim than the one-year-old, and so on. But few of us would want to acknowledge that the older has the greater claim. If the degree of maturation does not hold here, why should it hold in the prenatal period?

There is less controversy in our society about the welfare rights of the seriously impaired than about abortion. It is not clear why this should be so, unless it is that people tend to take the presence of the perceptually recognizable human form as the defining characteristic of a human being and that we widely acknowledge that the basic right of human beings is the right to life. Both of these claims are questionable. We have contended that the defining characteristic of a human being is the presence of the human normative structure, not the existential presence of the human form. And we have argued that the basic right of a human being is to have a life of one's own. If this is so, the right to biological life is secondary; it is a right as a necessary condition for having a life of one's own. With the seriously and irreversibly impaired, biological life may be possible in the absence of any possibility of a life to be lived. Thus the usual ground for the right to biological life no longer obtains. This puts into question whether, under these conditions, one has a right to biological life and to the conditions necessary for sustaining it. It seems much clearer that even the most immature human fetus has a right to biological life and to its necessary conditions than it is that an impaired human being, with no chance of a human life of any kind, has a right to the conditions of its continued existence—for the immature fetus has the prospect of developing the requisite powers and coming to have a life to live.

This is not to suggest that such seriously impaired people do not have rights. Persons have a right to be taken care of in their sickness and disabilities. They have the right to be treated humanely even in a state of total, irreversible impairment of their human powers; indeed, they have a right to have their bodily remains disposed of in a respectful manner. There seems to be no validity-condition, however, for the claim that those for whom all human life is gone beyond recovery have a right to the necessary conditions for their continued biological existence, especially when it is at the cost of great sacrifices on the part of others.

Even if the most seriously and irreversibly impaired do not have a right to the necessary conditions for their continued existence, it does not follow that people should be free to dispose of them at their discretion. There is wisdom in our traditional position of letting nature take its course in such matters. Our primary responsibility in these situations is to make that course as easy and as free of suffering as possible for such persons and to preserve the humanity and integrity of those responsible for their care. We would create many new problems, problems for which we are poorly prepared to handle, if we should bring the matter of when to end our own lives or those of others into the realm of decision.

The basic freedom right of every human being, with sufficient knowledge-yielding and critical powers, is the right to define and to live a life of one's own that is worthy of one's humanity and individuality. This is simply the constitutive responsibility of personhood viewed from the perspective of the normative limits and requirements it imposes on others. It is widely recognized that for anyone (a parent, a lover, a slave owner, a state, or whomever) to deny a person the freedom to define and to live a life of one's own when one has the requisite powers to do so in a responsible manner is to violate one's personhood in the most fundamental way.

The right to the freedom to define a life of one's own that would be worthy of one's humanity and individuality entails other freedom rights: the right to the opportunity to develop one's knowledge-yielding and critical powers and to acquire the knowledge and the skills required for the life one defines for oneself; the freedom of inquiry, thought, and expression; the freedom of association and assembly; the freedom of movement; the freedom to work and to benefit from the fruits of one's labor; the freedom to choose one's occupation; the freedom, within the factual limits of one's ability and circumstances and the normative limits imposed by the existence of other persons and the environment, to acquire and to use the resources for living the life one justifiably defines for oneself; the freedom to participate in the social and political decisions that affect one's life; the freedom of religion— the freedom to form one's own understanding of, and attitudes toward, oneself and others as human-beings-in-the-world and to choose how one will promote one's own and others' life morale and spiritual well-being; the right to privacy—the right to a realm in which one is free to be and to act with a shield from public scrutiny; and more.

The conditions of well-being and the freedoms that are necessary for one actually to have (as distinct from normatively having) the defining responsibility of personhood and the opportunity to fulfill it are rights in that they impose normative limits and requirements on the behavior of others. It is wrong for anyone to interfere with any of these conditions of well-being and freedoms of another, except under some conditions in defense of a similar right of oneself or of others. The conditions under which a person's human rights impose positive requirements on other individuals and the extent of those requirements are more controversial. But there is considerable agreement that the human rights of individuals obligate their society, insofar as it is able, to provide adequate protective and support systems for the rights of all. Indeed, as previously remarked, the basic function of a society is to provide a way of organizing human relationships and activities so that, insofar as possible, the life and health of each individual is protected and supported, education and work are available for all according to their abilities, a free culture and the material resources are available for the essential needs of all, and the basic freedom rights are protected and supported.

After the basic rights of all the people have been provided for in an acceptable manner, a society has the responsibility, insofar as possible, to promote the common good further by providing the conditions under which the people can flourish in living their lives. But supporting and protecting basic rights has precedence over providing the further conditions required for flourishing. Everyone has an obligation to work for and to support a social order that provides such support and protection for the basic welfare and freedom rights of its members.

The responsibility to support the collective efforts of the society in providing the general conditions for human flourishing over and above providing support and protection for basic rights is of a different order. Individuals have a responsibility to support efforts to provide for the basic rights of all even when it involves sacrifice. But it is not as clear that individuals have the same kind of responsibility to make personal sacrifices to support the society in its efforts to make human flourishing possible. Support of the society in its effort to provide for the basic rights of its people is an extension of the responsibility of individuals, when they are in a position to do so, to assist others whose rights are in jeopardy; but individuals do not have the same kind of responsibility to assist others in their efforts to advance themselves. So do individuals have a responsibility to support the society in its efforts to provide the conditions for a higher level of general well-being? And, if so, in what is that responsibility grounded?

It is difficult, of course, to draw a sharp line between these two kinds of societal efforts. Most of the time a society has to support general conditions for flourishing in order to be able to provide support and protection for basic rights. A society culturally and materially impoverished cannot provide for the rights of its people. And of course the rights of the people expand according to the ability of the society to provide for their needs. Consider how the rights of people for education and medical care have expanded with advances in the economy and medical science. So the theoretical distinction between societal provisions for basic rights and for the conditions for flourishing may not be clearly drawn in dealing with practical problems. Nevertheless the common good does seem to impose limits and requirements on individuals over and above those imposed by the rights of individuals. We recognize normative limits on what private parties can do for their own benefit at the expense of the society even when no individual rights are violated. This is at least part of the reason for zoning laws, restrictions on land use, appearance commissions, protection of the environment, and the like. We also recognize requirements imposed on people by the common good. This is certainly part of the reason for government support for education, research, the arts, economic growth, and so on.

The question is not "Whether?" but "Why?": Why is detriment to, or advancement of, the common good a moral reason that all should acknowledge and be moved by? Of course many people sustain a prudential loss from anything that is injurious to the common good and many people benefit prudentially by anything that advances the common good. But the question concerns why these are moral issues. Presumably a person has a responsibility to support some efforts to promote the common good even when there will be no prudential advantage to him or her in doing so. How and why does the common good, over and above support for, and protection of, basic human rights, impose moral limits and requirements on individuals in this way?

If neighbors have helped one with some improvement projects on one's home, then one has an obligation to assist them when the occasion arises. If one's neighbors have foregone a development of their property because it would have damaged the value of one's own, then one has an obligation to consider how the use of one's property would affect theirs. In other words, consideration, cooperation, and support from others obligate one to reciprocate. But what about the neighbors' original considerate, cooperative, and supportive acts, which were not done in reciprocation? Were there no moral reasons for these?

Perhaps the neighbor had other considerate, cooperative, and supportive neighbors and such neighborly conduct had become a way of life; it had come to define the role of a neighbor—to be one of the criteria of a good neighbor. And no doubt good neighbors make for a good neighborhood. It follows that those who benefit from living in a neighborhood already made good in this manner have an obligation to be good neighbors themselves. And so a member of the community might have an obligation to be considerate, cooperative, and supportive of a particular neighbor without these acts being reciprocations to prior acts on the part of that person.

This line of reasoning can be extended from being a good neighbor to being a good citizen of a city, of a state or province, and of a country—even to being a good planetary citizen. But we have a greater responsibility for promoting the common good of our own country than we do for promoting the common good of the whole world in its present condition, for we are integrated and organized for mutual consideration and support as a country in a way in which the world is not at this time. We have obligations to citizens of our country that we do not have to citizens of other countries; and we have obligations to the common good of our country that we do not have to the common good of other countries. These are obligations grounded in our shared way of life from which we all stand to benefit much as the obligation of the neighbor to be neighborly is grounded in the shared way of life that makes for a good neighborhood.

Although the office of citizen of the world is not well defined at the present time, all people have human rights that impose normative limits and requirements on others under certain conditions; and obviously there is a common good in which all peoples of the world share and for which we all have responsibilities to protect and to promote. So the office of planetary citizenship is being defined in the normative structure of human existence even though it is not yet well constituted in the institutional structure of the world.

The obligations of neighbor and citizen are moral in that the office of personhood requires one to accept and to fulfill, to the best of one's ability, the responsibilities of being a neighbor and of being a citizen insofar as they are consistent with the responsibilities of personhood. To fault one as a neighbor or as a citizen is to fault one as a person as well. One who shirks one's responsibilities as a neighbor or as a citizen fails in one's responsibilities as a person. Hence neighbor and citizen obligations are moral obligations. To the extent one benefits from a shared way of life one is obligated to support it so long as this obligation is compatible with the other responsibilities of personhood. There is no moral room for free-riders who actually are able to do their part.

Furthermore, the responsibility of a person to define and to live a life that is worthy of oneself both as a human being and as the individual one is entails the responsibility to strive for the perfection of one's own rendition of what it is to be a human being under the circumstances of one's existence. Although this responsibility of a person to strive for a higher-quality life may not require other individuals to assist one in one's efforts at the expense of the quality of their own lives (especially when the quality of their lives may be lower than one's own), individuals do have a responsibility to support collective efforts to enable all members of the society to realize higher levels of their potential and thus to elevate the general quality of life in their society.

The first responsibility of a society is to provide the conditions that make it possible for all with the requisite powers to reach the threshold of a human life; but beyond this, a society has the responsibility, relative to its ability, to provide, in an equitable manner, the conditions that make possible human flourishing. Although a society would not be able to fulfill the first responsibility without some success with the second, there is an independent ground for the second. Indeed, a society would have a responsibility to keep on struggling to advance the quality of human life even if all its members had reached the threshold. Of course the threshold itself is elevated with the advancement of the society. And the struggle for the upper limits of human perfection is endless. The responsibility for individuals to support the society in its efforts for human advancement is grounded in the responsibility of each to live a life that would stand justified under rational and moral approval. A life that did not have built into it support for the society's efforts toward human advancement would not merit such approval.

In a well-ordered capitalist society, contrary to popular belief, the government, in taxing people and corporations, is not taking *their* money; it is only collecting the society's share of the wealth and productivity of individuals and corporations. In spending the money collected to secure the rights of the people and to promote the common good in other ways, the government is spending the society's money. The government is no more spending the money of the individuals who paid the taxes than a landlord, in spending money collected as rent, is spending the money of the tenants. Of course there is this difference: the tax revenues belong to the people collectively. If the landlord were a cooperative of the tenants, the two situations would be more parallel. Citizens have a voice in how the government spends money, not because it is their money they paid in taxes, but because of their citizenship and the collective ownership of the social wealth of the society.

It is a myth that only the private sector in a capitalist society produces wealth. It is, however, widely believed. A former editor of *The Wall Street Journal* once remarked that everyone on the public payroll was a social parasite. If we should take away everything that the society does collectively through local, state, and national governments, what would our gross national product be? Consider the productive role of government and public agencies through education; the preservation, advancement, and availability of our cultural capital; a standard and more or less stable monetary system; regulation of our activities and settlement of disputes; security and safety in many forms and at all levels; roads and bridges and other aids to transportation and communication; public health services and other forms of health care; protection of the environment; promotion and protection of our interest in the world at large; and on and on. Without these, we would not be a functioning society at all. So a society collectively owns the common wealth of the society and has a share in all the productivity of the individuals, partnerships, and corporations operating in the society—a share proportionate to its contribution to their productivity. The primary justification for a progressive income tax is not the variable ability of taxpayers to pay but rather the fact that, in general, the larger incomes are progressively more dependent on the resources of the society; and, consequently, a proportionately larger share of the larger incomes belongs to the society.

Social Organization

Although there is a universal normative structure for society grounded in the normative structure of personhood and human nature with respect to which any society can be judged to be well-developed or undeveloped, well-formed or malformed, and healthy or unhealthy, there is more than one way of organizing a good society, just as there is more than one way of defining and living a good life. But there are bad ways also, even wrong ways. The history and circumstances of a particular society are important factors in determining how the society should be organized, in the same way the particularities of an individual person are important factors in determining what kind of a life one should live. A social organization that is good for an advanced society may not be good for less developed societies and vice versa. But the basic normative structure is constant, for it is grounded in personhood, the common factor in all societies. A society ought to provide, insofar as it is able, the necessary protective and support systems for individuals to have an opportunity to define and to live lives worthy of their humanity and their individuality.

The institutional structure of a society is to it what character is to the individual. An individual may give intellectual assent to a set of normative principles for conduct without living by them. For such principles to be effective in living one's life, they must be written in one's heart, so to speak; they must inform one's character; they must be the organizing and governing principles of one's emotive and volitional life. In like manner, a society may subscribe, in a sense, to a normative culture without living by it. In order for the normative culture to be effective in organizing and governing the life of the society, it must be embodied in the institutional structure of the society. The United States, for example, subscribed to a culture of freedom and equality for nearly two centuries while allowing an institutional structure of slavery or segregation and second-class citizenship for blacks. Just as the character of an individual determines one's behavior in ordinary situations, the institutional structure of a society determines its actual behavior in ordinary situations. And just as intellectual commitment to normative principles provides a basis for judging and trying to rework one's character, the normative culture of a society provides the basis for judging and modifying or reconstituting its institutional structure. It was the traditional American commitment to human rights that was invoked in the abolition of slavery and racial segregation and in the attack on racial and sexual discrimination.

Radical revolutionaries, contrary to reformers, reject the prevailing culture as well as the existing social structure. They seek to deconstruct the existing society and to create a new social order in terms of a new or radically different culture. Although gaps may develop between the emerging culture and the existing social structure in a healthy, well-ordered society so that social reform is necessary on a more or less continuing basis, there is no place in such a society for radical revolutionaries. They have a place only in seriously deformed or desperately sick societies. But there is always a problem about the confirmation of the culture of radical revolutionaries. In the very nature of the case, the culture in terms of which they operate lacks a wide consensus in the society, and this culture has not been tested in institutional form in the particular circumstances of the society.

The family, no doubt, is the basic institution. It is an all-purpose institution based on relationships between mates and their offspring, forebears, and other forms of kinship. Institutions with specialized functions develop to supplement or to replace the family in meeting human needs. For the purposes of this study, we shall divide specialized institutions into cultural, economic, and governmental groups, and consider the basic normative structure of the institutions within each group—that is, the form they ought to have and the principles by which they are to be judged.

Cultural Institutions

Our culture is our most important capital. We, as persons, are generated by it. Without the language and symbol systems and the accumulated knowledge and wisdom of the historical community that gave us spiritual birth and identity, we would not be functioning persons but relatively helpless creatures. Without the enhancement of our semantic and logical powers that the culture provides we would not be intellectual, moral, artistic, and religious beings; we would not have a life to live in the human sense, but rather we would exist in interaction with the immediate environment; we would not have our social capital—the complex social structures that support us and make possible extensive cooperative projects across space and through time; we would not have technology to extend our physical and mental powers. Each individual or small group, having extremely limited selfhood and little intersubjectivity, would be largely at the mercy of the physical and ecological environment.

So our cultural institutions are of the first importance. All other institutions and enterprises depend on their success in the preservation and advancement of the culture and in the preparation of people for access to and use of it.

There is an old proverb to the effect that fish are the last creatures to discover water. Although everyone operates in a culture and would not be human without it, relatively few people become aware of the culture in which they live and have their being, and even fewer understand its powers and riches and the conditions of its overall healthy development.

A truth long recognized is that community life, even the existence of a harmonious, cooperative society, requires that a considerable set of beliefs and attitudes be held in common by all or most of the people of the society. For the greater part of human history, it was believed that a cultural consensus was possible only if there were institutions endowed with the authority to define and to teach a fixed belief/precept system and with the power to root out subversive ideas.

Under this system, from early childhood each one is put through a process of psychological and social conditioning that is supposed to, and usually does, result in more or less blind acceptance of the authorized opinions and attitudes. Furthermore, the individual is so conditioned that a psychological block is created against any doubts or questions. Consider authoritarian religious institutions. The religion of a culture integrates the meaning, values, and beliefs of the culture and anchors them in a conception of ultimate reality. Some religions teach that the greatest sin of all is to doubt any of the authorized beliefs or to take a critical attitude toward them. Unhesitating credulity is praised as the highest virtue. If one does come to doubt, instead of being given reasons to support the authorized opinions or being encouraged to engage in inquiry to discover the truth for oneself, one is punished for one's offense. Hence, both cultural slavery and forceful restraint are employed to assure common acceptance of established beliefs and sentiments.

It is not difficult to stir people to fight and even to die for liberty when deprivation of it occurs by open and flagrant imposition of the will of another. We adjust to natural events and reformulate our desires in light of our knowledge of changing circumstances without feeling any constraint or loss of liberty. But few, if any, ever knowingly yield to the will of another under duress without resentment and a desire for freedom. We resent this imposition because it compromises our status as persons. One can suffer no greater injury. Many have judged it better to die as a person than to live without the status of a person.

Throughout history most people who have successfully controlled and used others as means to their own ends have sought to rob slavery of its sting by shaping the beliefs, desires, and feelings of their victims through the culture so that the victims would do from inner motivation what their masters wanted them to do. The victims of cultural slavery may be completely unaware of their servitude and, consequently, harbor no resentment of their bonds and entertain no desire for their freedom.

The discovery of culture and the way it is grounded in human powers and how it can be advanced by human effort constitutes the greatest leap forward the human race has ever made. Although there had been glimmers of these truths about culture in earlier civilizations, especially in the Greek Enlightenment of the sixth to the fourth centuries B.C., it was not until the Renaissance and the Enlightenment of modern Western civilization that the full force of the discovery of culture and its potential for development by human effort began to be realized. Once it was accepted that the culture was the foundation of all human activity and that it could be understood and further developed by human effort, people began to realize that human knowledge-yielding and critical powers should be cultivated and unleashed.

The democratic revolution of the eighteenth century is often considered to have been primarily a revolution against political tyranny and the despotic monarchs of the time. But it went much deeper. It was a revolt against the cultural slavery that accompanied and undergirded the political tyranny. The people's woes were not attributed directly and solely to individual tyrants, but rather to the historically evolved social institutions and the culture that sustained them. These institutions and the culture they embodied distorted persons and stunted their critical powers. Some such persons were made into lords and kings who imposed their will on the masses and were led to believe that in doing so they were fulfilling a divine appointment. Anyone who dared to tamper with the existing conditions under which those in high places enjoyed power and privilege while the masses suffered hardships and degradation of their human dignity was thought to be shaking the order of the universe in defiance of the will of God.

Even those who were the greatest victims of this state of affairs were induced by the culture to accept it as their divinely appointed lot and that, in some way beyond their understanding, it was right. Thus they were brought not only to resign themselves to their fate but to approve it. In this way, even the inner life, the heart and mind, was controlled by the culture. The people, for the most part, were compliant with the will of those in positions of power without feeling oppressed. So they suffered their servitude and revered their masters.

Liberation from cultural slavery is a far more difficult task than the overthrow of tyrants. But the leaders of the Enlightenment realized that the right to live one's own life according to one's own beliefs and judgments entailed not only the right to freedom of action but also the right to freedom from cultural slavery. Furthermore, they realized what communist countries are only now coming to realize—that cultural, social, and economic progress depend on inner and outer freedom and on the educational development of the knowledge-yielding and critical powers of the people. A society that does not make a major educational effort to develop and to use the knowledge-yielding, critical, and creative powers of its people is neglecting its greatest resource. A society that attempts to control the culture by restraining inquiry and criticism condemns itself to stagnation and decline.

Freedom of inquiry, thought, and expression from external restraints and internal manipulation enjoys a twofold justification. In the first place, to distort the culture by restriction or manipulation is to deny the people the opportunity to be self-directing, responsible persons and thus violate their basic right as human beings. If one is to be free and responsible, one's knowledge-yielding and critical powers must be *well* developed and one must be free, within the limits of moral responsibility, to investigate any subject and to arrive at, and to publish, independent conclusions. In the second place, in the words of John Stuart Mill, "The peculiar evil of silencing the expression of an opinion is, that it is robbing the human race; posterity as well as the existing generation; those who dissent from the opinion, still more than those who hold it. If the opinion is right, they are deprived of the opportunity of exchanging error for truth; if wrong, they lose, what is almost as great a benefit, the clearer perception and livelier impression of truth, produced by its collision with error."[1] We cannot afford to have opinion protected from criticism, for, as Mill says, "The beliefs which we have most warrant for, have no safeguard to rest on but a standing invitation to the whole world to prove them unfounded."[2]

Objective liberalism believes that a free forum of ideas will result in sufficient common beliefs and attitudes for social solidarity and community life. And, furthermore, it believes that the beliefs that win the competition in the free forum will be the most reliable. If unreliable beliefs win, their victory can be only temporary, for the only way an idea can hold its own within a free society of inquiring minds is for it to be grounded in reality. As the founders of the American republic realized, even the most outrageous ideas must not be repressed so long as reason is free to combat error.

Once the possibility of objectivity in belief and judgment is in doubt, the rationale for a free culture is in jeopardy; one could no longer defend free inquiry and debate as a necessary condition for progress. Indeed, if the culture were not objective, cultural freedom would no longer be possible, for one could not liberate oneself from the culture in which one was generated by gaining mastery of it through criticism. And a common culture would have to be the result of either historical forces or the manipulation of some power structure.

Everyone begins in a state of cultural slavery, for one has to be culturally generated and must reach a certain level of maturity before one's critical powers develop and the liberation process can begin. But one can and should be educated for freedom rather than trained and conditioned for cultural slavery. One should not be taught anything but what has withstood critical testing and what is expected to withstand one's critical examination in later life. A human being ought to be acculturated in terms of a culture that has been freely and critically developed. And a human being ought to be educated in a way that develops one's knowledge-yielding and critical powers so that one can gain self-mastery and freedom in one's mature years. Any society with an uncritical, historically evolved culture enslaves its people. Any society with a controlled, manipulated culture violates the basic rights of all its citizens, especially its children, for they are set on life's course with a severe handicap and with their powers of self-correction undeveloped or impaired.

There are religious groups in our society who hold that their basic religious culture is beyond human criticism and that even in public education their children should not be taught contrary beliefs or a critical approach to what their religion advocates. Religion, like all other areas of the culture, must be held accountable to rational criticism. It is logically webbed to the other sectors of the culture; and, in a progressive culture, logical tensions develop that raise questions about the religious belief system as well as about the other sectors. If the religion is to survive, it must either control the whole culture or submit to rational criticism and reconstruction along with the rest of the culture. The first way chokes the engine of progress and stagnates the whole culture. Furthermore, it violates the rights of all the people by denying them the opportunity to fulfill their primary responsibility as persons. Many theologians, including Thomas Aquinas, have recognized that religion cannot stand in opposition to rationally defensible truth without self-destruction. This is not to deny that religious claims may have epistemic weight of their own in the struggle for coherence within the culture, but the struggle for coherence must be a rational process if the freedom of the culture is to be preserved. If any area of the culture is protected by a power structure so that it is exempt from criticism and reconstruction, the struggle for coherence ceases to be a rational process. The freedom of the culture must be preserved if the rights of the people are to be protected and if human progress is to be possible.

It is important, of course, for education to proceed with wisdom and a judicious concern for the personal well-being of the students. The culture in terms of which one's identity as a person is first formed should not be brought into question until one is sufficiently mature and properly educated to handle deep logical difficulties in a constructive manner. If one's identity-forming culture is challenged before one has the personal strength and the critical resources with which to handle it, the challenge may be psychologically and morally destructive. The primary difficulty with public schools and religious and ethnic subcultures is that children are subjected to contrary and competing identity-forming cultures at an early age. Adherents of the subcultures are likely to think of the culture of the public schools as simply the ethnic culture of the dominant group in the society. And sometimes this may be the case. But hopefully the culture of our public schools, and even the culture of most of our independent schools, is the culture that has withstood the most severe rational tests over time and will likely withstand the students' critical self-examination in their mature years. The right of children to be nurtured in such a culture may be in conflict with the right of parents to bring up their children in their own subculture. We have not yet found a satisfactory way to solve this problem in a way that protects the right of such parents to rear their children in their own culture and the right of their children to a rationally tested culture. Indeed, there may not be a rational societal solution to the problem without a rational cultural resolution that eliminates the problem.

Even if cultural objectivity is theoretically possible, and and it is to some extent, it is not easy to achieve objectivity. No one ever achieves it completely. We are all provincial, for we are all culturally generated. And we all have our individual prejudices and biases. Nevertheless, by virtue of our critical powers, we can achieve a measure of objectivity step by step and transcend our biases and prejudices by either justifying them or rationally reconstructing them. Perhaps no one ever completely transcends his or her personal prejudices and the provincial perspective of his or her origins, but people from many provinces can reach higher plateaus from which they share a common perspective and can reason together to common conclusions on many matters. Only those who share a plateau and can reason together from common ground can live together freely and peacefully in a politically organized society. A state that is not united by a common culture can be held together and made to work only by force. And a government that tries to act beyond the limits of reasoned agreements can do so only on the basis of force.

The people living within the established boundaries of a state may not be able to achieve a sufficient rational consensus to make a free society possible. This seems to be the case in many parts of the world today. Nevertheless, a free society, based on a free culture, is an ideal toward which all societies should strive and by which all societies should be judged.

There are, as previously observed, two ways in which a culture may not be free; namely, it may have been generated by historical forces without being subjected to critical evaluation in the process or it may have been controlled and manipulated to serve some end other than truth. In both cases, the freedom of the culture, or lack of it, is a matter of degree. No culture totally lacks historical determination and none is totally free from manipulation and control. On these counts, modern Western culture is, perhaps, the freest in human history. But there is a sense in which a culture can be relatively free and rational and yet not objective to the same extent. It may be, as we have claimed,[3] that modern Western culture is deranged by virtue of false philosophical assumptions about the nature and grounds of knowledge and the metaphysical structure of the world; yet these assumptions have been reasoned about and debated throughout the modern period and, for the most part, they have been given the approval of reason. Nevertheless, we contend that the culture and the way reason works in the culture have been unduly shaped by the dominant values of the culture.

Perhaps this is an instance of historical determinism after all, but it is quite different from the kind of uncritical evolutionary historical process just mentioned. In the first place, what is determined by the values of the culture is the basic conceptual system in terms of which knowledge is defined and sought rather than simply beliefs and precepts; and, in the second place, as already remarked, this framework has been much criticized and debated. However, this critical examination, according to our thesis, has operated, for the most part, within the modern mind so that it has tended to validate the modern assumptions geared to our materialistic values and has not probed deep enough to expose the distorting bias within the foundations of the modern mind. A fully objective culture is not simply one that is free from manipulation and control and that has been rationally developed and critically assessed; it is one that reflects the whole spectrum of human interests, materialistic and humanistic, and is grounded in, and held accountable to, the whole range of our semantic, knowledge-yielding, and critical powers.

In a society in which the culture is manipulated and controlled, regardless of the end for which it is done, the subjectivity and behavior of the people are manipulated and controlled. In a traditional society, one that allows its culture to develop as it will under the influence of historical forces without rational criticism and reconstruction in the process, the people are in cultural bondage. In a society in which the culture becomes hitched to some special set of interests even without deliberate intent, reason itself may become perverted and lose its corrective and liberating power. A free and objective culture is a necessary condition for a well-developed, well-formed, and healthy society.

In our society, the culture and our cultural institutions are increasingly geared to economic growth. This means an emphasis in research and in education on science and technology, economics, and the cul-

ture of management and cost/benefit analysis. It is not only that the
humanities and the arts suffer from lack of attention and support; our
deep assumptions about our knowledge-yielding and critical powers,
the culture, and the world are shaped by this emphasis so that the way
in which we understand and critically assess the culture becomes perverted and our self-corrective powers mislead us. The result is that we
have a culture that gives us great power over things but one that makes
for weakness and misdirection in the development and governance of
persons, institutions, and society from within. This is the Faustian bar-
gain that modern Western civilization has made.

A well-formed, healthy society must place a high priority on the preservation, transmission, self-correction, and advancement of the culture. It must give special attention to its cultural institutions; it must
protect their freedom and provide them with the necessary resources
to do their work, for everything else in the society depends on their
success. The sciences are important for the knowledge they yield and
the power they give us over things through technology. The humanities and the fine arts are important for the knowledge and wisdom
they provide and the significance they have in the inner development
and self-correction of the culture as a whole and in the inner development, enrichment, empowerment, and governance of persons, institutions, and society.

Economic Institutions

An economic system consists of the ways a society organizes and man-
ages the production and distribution of goods and services. In earlier
societies, the economic dimension was not clearly differentiated. The
family and the community as a network of families were the chief economic institutions, but they had humanistic functions as well. Only in
modern times has the economic system become clearly differentiable so
that economics could become a specialized discipline. We are now in
danger of everything's being embraced within the economic sector and
brought under the rationality of the economic process. In response to
this development, socialists incorporate the economic sector into the
political system.

The free enterprise system is characterized by private ownership of
property, the profit motive, and the competitive market price mechanism. It also involves the division of labor, the supporting bourgeois
ethos, and, in modern forms, the application of science, technology,
and industrialization.

The free enterprise system developed as an integral part of our
modern Western civilization. The shift in priorities in the early modern

period from humanistic concerns to materialistic values not only re-sulted in a shift in our culture-generating attitude toward the world but transformed the earlier humanistic society with an economic dimension into an economic system with a tangential humanistic dimension. The emerging culture in early modern times not only released people to pursue their own wants; it set them to transforming the world through work for private gain as a moral responsibility. In other words, the culture was transformed so that humanistic values reinforced a way of life in which each was preoccupied with enhancing his or her own eco-nomic power as a generalized means and even as an end in itself. In this manner, maximum human effort and ingenuity were generated for the economic enterprise. The achieving society was created.

The kind of knowledge that is important from within this orienta-tion is that which will direct and guide action in making and controlling things. So, as we observed in the opening chapter, modern science was developed and the conceptions of knowledge and reality were trans-formed.

The era of social revolution was inaugurated. Our institutions and social structures were subjected to continual change. Just as all areas of the culture had to adjust to the new developing science, all social struc-tures had to yield to the expanding needs of the new developing eco-nomic institutions, for they, like science, served the dominant values of the culture.

Of course the free enterprise system is not the only way of organiz-ing a scientific, technological, industrial civilization; but it is the form within which it first developed, and perhaps it was the only form in which it could have come into being. The necessary knowledge, cre-ativity, and human energy may not have been possible within any other system. Once scientific/technological industrialism is developed, it can be transplanted into other economic and social structures, but that is a different matter.

Everyone has to admit that the free enterprise economic system, with its supporting bourgeois culture, has been very successful in in-creasing productivity, in improving the material conditions of our exis-tence, and in enhancing the quality of life in many important respects. There are, however, other kinds of considerations that must be taken into account in the evaluation of the free enterprise system. These include the following questions: (1) Can a developed free enterprise, scientific, technological, industrial system sustain itself in a healthy condition? (2) Even if it is (or can be) self-sustaining, how well does it respond to and meet the economic needs of the society? (3) Are there any alternatives that would better serve the functions for which an eco-nomic system exists? (4) How healthy are the culture and social struc-

tures it requires and generates? and (5) How well does the whole economic, cultural, and social system meet the full spectrum of human
needs, including our humanistic requirements?

Whether a highly developed free enterprise system can sustain itself
in a healthy state is a question for the economists. We will consider only
some of the more obvious difficulties that have been recognized.

The engine of the free enterprise system is the morally reinforced
drive for private gain, and the regulator is the price mechanism of the
competitive market. Decision-making is broken down, individualized,
and simplified. Individual agents make their decisions on the basis of
their own economic goals and the knowledge available to them. Thus
the knowledge required for rational decision and successful action is
limited and more attainable. The great goals of social welfare and the
common good, which often, if not always, outreach the capacity for
knowledge and rational decision, are left to the unseen guiding hand of
the free, competitive market. According to the classical theory, the
market will keep the whole system working for the common good without its being deliberately sought by anyone. Furthermore, the free market, according to the theory, will assure a more or less just distribution
of income, for the income of each person will be proportionate to his
or her contribution to the society.

Critics maintain that the system is highly unstable and self-destructive. Left unto itself, they say, the competitive market will be destroyed
by monopolistic developments; and, without the unseen guiding hand
of the competitive market, the system loses it moral legitimacy, for it no
longer serves the common good and no longer achieves a just distribution of income.

Even if monopolistic tendencies should be restrained by governmental action, critics maintain that the inner dynamics of the system is
such that it will move through cycles of boom and bust. When the economy is expanding, the economy needs the savings of the community to
invest, and there is fuller employment. But interest rates, left to the
money market, will go higher and higher until the expansion slows and
recession sets in. The total income of the society drops and the demand
declines. Production is cut back, unemployment rises, and total income
drops further. At some point interest rates are supposed to reach a
sufficiently low point to trigger a new period of expansion. However,
Keynesian economists contend that there is no automatic mechanism to
reverse the economy, for at the bottom of a recession income could be
so reduced that there would not be sufficient savings to finance a new
expansion period. The economy could sit in recession with the expansion and contraction cycle broken. This, John Maynard Keynes maintained, was what happened in the great depression of the 1930s. The

only remedy at this point, he argued, was for the government to pump in investment capital to get the economy moving again. The cure, however, has the side effect of inflation; and the only cure for inflation seems to be measures that bring on another recession. Some think that the government must regulate the economy all the time by manipulating the flow of investment capital to keep the system working in anything like a healthy manner.

Apart from the fact that the free enterprise system, without a helping hand from the government, does not seem to be self-sustaining, how well does it respond to and meet the economic needs of the society? Consider these points. First of all, the system responds to demand, not to needs as such. Needs can be registered in the system as demand only when backed by something with exchange value. And whims and fancies backed by exchange value can be as readily converted into demand as can vital needs. One of the virtues of the system is that it leaves to the individual the ordering of priorities among one's needs and whims, provided one has the means to translate some portion of them into effective demand in the market. But there is nothing in the system as such to assure that one will have sufficient exchange value to register even one's vital needs in the market. The system by itself does not assure full employment opportunity. And there are always people who, for various reasons, are unemployable and lacking in other assets. In the more advanced technological societies, the percentage of the economically dispossessed is higher than in more primitive economies. In this respect, even a well-functioning free enterprise system—one that functions well according to its own inner logic—would have to be aided by some external controls and actions to make it fully responsible to the common good. In fact, some contend that an advanced technological society should provide a guaranteed minimum income to assure that the basic economic needs of all would be met.

Furthermore, it does not seem that, in an advanced technological society, the free market distributes income proportionate to contributions made. So much of the productivity of a given time period has to be assigned to the cultural and social heritage on which no one can stake out private claims of ownership. In the production of economic goods, the workers and the owners of the investment capital and the means of production share in the rewards, and rightly so, for they all contribute to the production. But what about the contribution of the common cultural and social capital? Who receives its share? If left to the market distribution system, it would be divided up among the consumers and the various participants in the production, service, and marketing system. But what about those who do not contribute to the process for whatever reason, derive no income from it, and do not

receive the benefits of a consumer? (Of course there may be none who
fully meet this description in our society, but there would be if we re-
lied solely on the market system for the distribution of income.) Do
they not share in the collective ownership of the cultural and social
capital and thereby merit a share of its rewards? Herein lies a legitimate basis for a guaranteed minimum income as the fair share of those
who are not able to contribute otherwise to the productive process.

Another difficulty with the free enterprise system is that, in an advanced technological society, the total cost of production and consumption is not reflected in the price set by the free market. Consider the
cost of our production and consumption in terms of adverse effects on
the environment and on people. The society has to find an extramarket
mechanism for assessing and assigning this cost.

And there are areas in which a competitive market system does not
make sense, as in the case of certain utilities. There are those services
that most everyone will agree should be provided by government agencies or private nonprofit institutions, for they are more or less indispensable but would not be provided effectively by the free enterprise
system.

So it seems that an advanced free market economy is unstable and
tends to develop in such a way that it loses its moral legitimacy. The
free competitive market, left to its own ways, does not perform its regu-
latory function adequately to keep the economy healthy and geared to
the common good. The unseen guiding hand has to be aided or replaced by a direct concern for human need, justice, and the common
good.

The state socialist would have the government take over the ownership of the instruments of production and distribution and have it plan
and manage the economy in terms of the common good. There are
serious difficulties with this approach. Here, without elaboration, are
some of the major criticisms: (1) Socialism, with its central planning,
necessitates an irrational decision-making process, for it demands decisions for which the requisite information and wisdom cannot be provided. (2) While the system relies on, and appeals directly to, the social
and moral sentiments of individuals, which are not by nature the main-
springs of human action, it sets private self-interest against the system
and thus invites obstruction. (3) The system seems to require a public
consensus and constant moral motivation in a way that makes a controlled culture and an official ideology mandatory. (4) Cultural freedom and individual freedom rights appear to be counterproductive in
the system. Even when the system works at its best, the total effect of
this approach is likely to be the sacrifice of individual autonomy for the

sake of measurable collective good. (5) Socialism fuses and concentrates economic and political power and thereby eliminates the checks and balances inherent in multiple centers of each and thereby invites abuse. (6) It is not a system that puts a premium on criticism, creativity, experimentation, and bold new ventures; rather it tends toward stagnation.

In short, if these criticisms are true (and there is much to support them), a centralized socialist state is a malformed society that is doomed to malfunction, for it is based on a misunderstanding of the inherent normative nature of both the individual person and the social order. The primary responsibility of the individual is to define and to live one's own life within certain normative limits and constraints. The primary responsibility of society is to provide the necessary protective and support systems for individuals in living their own lives. Accordingly, the primary dynamism of the society must be located in individual initiative and under individual direction in living worthy and meaningful lives. But socialism locates the primary initiative and direction in a centralized bureaucracy in building a good society. Regardless of what economic security and social benefits a socialist society may provide, the result is not a good society, for the system tends not only toward stagnation but toward the obstruction of individuals' efforts to live worthy lives of their own, especially through the society's tendency to manipulate the culture and to control its members lives.

Some form of controlled market economy seems to be needed. The governments of capitalist countries presently attempt a great deal of control of their economic systems through tax policies, subsidies, regulations, government spending, and control of the money supply. And communist regimes have collapsed in many places because of economic stagnation and repression. Perhaps what we need is an effective two-level system: a free enterprise market economy under a more coordinated and effective meta-control system that would study and plan the economy in broad outlines in light of social needs, equitable distribution of income, and the common good in general. It would manage the free enterprise system by controlling the environment within which economic decisions were made for private reasons. The meta-control system should be subject to governmental oversight and control, but it should be buffeted from raw political forces. Those in charge of the meta-control system should be governed by a concern to assure that the free enterprise sector of the economy worked effectively in meeting the real needs of the society. Such a modified free enterprise system, geared to human values by a rational meta-control system, should enjoy much of the freedom, ingenuity, vitality, and efficiency of the free enterprise system and the real advantages of planning and working for the common good under socialism without the major disadvantages of either.

But even such a system would have to be supplemented with a system of not-for-profit institutions to meet needs that could not be well served by the for-profit institutions. We now have a vast array of religious, cultural, educational, research, civic, health-care, and recreational institutions in this category. Some are public and some are independent institutions. Institutions of this type should have a greater role in society; and they should have a greater share of the society's resources.

Not-for-profit institutions geared to human and societal needs are animated by a different set of values than the for-profit institutions. Those who work in the former should share in the values of those institutions. If such institutions had greater prominence in the society, in addition to the primary good they achieved, their values would be a counterbalance to the values that govern the for-profit sector of the economy. A society organized along these lines, having a strong not-for-profit sector and a for-profit sector under a meta-control system that kept it geared to human values and societal needs, should make for a more balanced civilization, free from the pathological distortions caused by overemphasis on the materialistic values of the for-profit economy. Such a reorganization of society, however, would itself require a major shift in our dominant cultural values.

In Chapter 1, we discussed the shift in the West toward materialistic values in early modern history, the new orientation toward the world it produced, and the impact of this on our culture and society. It has produced marvelous advances in science and technology and improvements in the material conditions of our existence. The advancement of medical science and the improvement of economic conditions have greatly lowered the mortality rate. Scientific agriculture has made urbanization and industrialization possible. The harnessing of physical energy through science and technology has replaced muscle power and is now replacing mental power. Educational opportunities and cultural resources have been made available to the masses. We have exceeded in so many ways the fondest hopes of the Enlightenment apostles of progress. Yet we are becoming increasingly aware that what we have achieved is no utopia.

In seeking to impose our will on our environment, we have recognized only its factual structures; indeed we have denied that others exist. Yet there is a sense in which the terrarium seems to have an inherent normative structure of its own. It can be said to be well and healthy or sick and dying. There are natural processes that work to restore and to maintain its health. But exploitation of the environment for our own purposes, without regard for the normative structure of the biosphere and the requirements and restraints that it imposes on us, may result in the death of our planet.

There are two ways in which we may respond to our environmental crisis: We may see these dangers to the environment as simply further factual limitations on our will to be overcome and mastered by still more advances in science and technology; or we may reorient ourselves toward the world in such a way that we recognize ourselves as having a normative place with normative limits and that we must live in a continuing symbiotic relationship with other living things within the value structure of the terrarium. This, of course, would not exclude the continuing advancement of science and technology nor its desirability, but it would affect how we used the manipulatory power science and technology make available. We would, in some respects, submit to and accept the requirements of our environment and cooperate in their fulfillment; in other respects we would continue to overcome and to master the purely factual limitations on our will. But our basic relationship with, and response to, the world about us would be quite different.

This new orientation might prove to be of significance for the human spirit as well as for the continued existence of humankind; for our modern stance toward the world and the civilization it has generated not only threaten the biosphere but promise to destroy the cultural and social conditions that support the human spirit. Alexander Solzhenitsyn, in his *Letter to the Soviet Leaders*,[4] wrote: "All that endless progress ['dinned into our heads by the dreamers of the Enlightenment'] turned out to be an insane, ill-considered, furious dash into a blind alley. . . . [I]t is not 'convergence' that faces us and the Western world now, but total renewal and reconstruction in both East and West, for both are in the same impasse." "Bearing in mind," he says, "the state of people's morals, their spiritual condition and their relations with society, all the *material* achievements we trumpet so proudly are petty and worthless."[5]

Neither we nor the Soviets can go back. Nor should we abandon our needs that lend themselves to being satisfied by science and technology. They are important, but it is a mistake to give them such priority that they distort our culture and social structures in such a way that our distinctively humanistic needs are starved. It would be equally wrong to allow our humanistic needs to dominate our culture and society so that we would be ravished by material poverty. In that case, neither set of needs would be met. What we need, of course, is the proper balance which will generate a civilization grounded in the full spectrum of human experience, responsive to all the requirements grounded in, and impinging on, us as human beings, and underwritten by a unifying intellectual vision of humankind and the world.

Political Institutions

A complex society, even a family, needs ways to establish and to clarify rules, to enforce them, to settle disputes, and to make collective decisions. In short, a society, to the extent it is *a* society, regardless of its size, needs some form of government.

A government is not just a power structure that makes decisions and imposes its will on the people by force. Hijackers of a ship or of a country can do that, provided they have enough force. The difference between a dictating power structure and a government is that a government has authority; that is, a government has the responsibility and the right to make decisions for the society on certain kinds of matters, and the members of the society are obligated to comply with them; furthermore, the government has the responsibility to enforce compliance on the part of those who do not comply otherwise. Whenever a government acts in such a manner that the only reason the people have to comply with its "laws" or commands is the imposed sanctions of the government, the government is without authority; it is only a power structure and the people are free (indeed, ought) to oppose it as best they can.

There are two important issues with respect to the authority of government: the nature and ground of the authority and the compatibility of the authority of government with the autonomy of the individual.

We speak of authority in two distinct but related senses. One pertains to beliefs or knowledge, which we may call "epistemic" authority; the other pertains to decisions or actions, which we may call "moral" authority. With regard to the first, we may speak of a person as an authority on some subject. What this involves can be put succinctly, for there is no particular problem about it. To be an authority on a subject is to be in a position to know about it, or in a somewhat stronger sense, to be one whose business it is to know about such things, and to have credentials such that others less privileged in relevant ways are justified in accepting one's views on the subject, indeed ought to accept one's views, even if they are contrary to their own. It is irrational of one to persist in one's own ill-founded beliefs about a matter in the face of contrary beliefs of a genuine authority on the subject. The rational thing to do, if one is not an authority on a given subject, is to defer to the beliefs of those who are; for one who is not knowledgeable in a given field cannot have any better ground for a belief in that area than that of its being the belief of one who is knowledgeable about such matters, especially of one whose business it is to know about such things. This, in no way, involves shirking one's responsibility for one's own thoughts. It is simply a matter of the responsible way of weighing evidence or reasons for beliefs in the process of making up one's mind on the subject.

Authority in the area of decision and action is more complex. There is, of course, the kind of authority just mentioned—the authority of experts on skills, of such people as marriage counselors, consulting engineers, economic advisers, and the like. The only difference is that such authority concerns know-how or what to do rather than knowledge of facts or what to believe. But as in the case of belief, in addition to any arguments one who is an authority may give in support of one's advice, the fact that one gave the advice counts in favor of the advice given and others may be justified in deferring to the authority's superior wisdom. The judgment of an authority is at least partially self-warranting. This is not unlike the way in which the fact that a normal person has a given perceptual experience counts for the veridicality of the experience. The layperson who does not know or cannot evaluate the reasons of the authority has two kinds of reasons for accepting the authority's view or advice: (1) Knowing one to be an authority in the field, the layperson knows that there probably are good reasons for his or her view or advice; and (2) the layperson knows that the authority has been led to his or her position by assessing the relevant reasons that bear on the issue.

The kind of authority that is peculiar in the area of decision and action—the area of moral authority—concerns the responsibility or right to decide or to act in a way that commits others accordingly or obligates others to commit themselves accordingly.

A word about decision and action. An action is the fulfillment of, or an effort to fulfill, an accepted imperative. The action itself is properly described only in terms of the intention that informs (structures) it. A decision, the formation of an intention, is the acceptance of an imperative to do something much as the formation of a belief is the acceptance of a proposition. One can form a belief from one's own experience and thought or by simply accepting a statement of another person. One may be rationally justified either way. The fact that so and so made the statement may be a good reason for believing it, especially if the person is an authority in the field. The same is true in the case of a decision. One can reach a decision on the basis of one's own experience and thought, on the basis of the counsel of another, or on the basis of what one is told to do by someone who has authority over one. Any of these approaches could be rationally justified.

A person in a position of authority may have the responsibility or the right not only to decide what another is to do or not to do but actually, in some cases, to act for them as well—for example, a mother for her child, an officer of an organization for the organization, and so forth.

To have moral authority, then, is to have an office or position constituted by certain responsibilities and rights that involves making decisions that obligate certain others (at least *prima facie*) to accept and to comply with them regardless of what their personal decisions about the matters in question would have been otherwise. In the very nature of the case, the voice of authority is at least *prima facie* overriding for those subject to or obligated by the authority. Furthermore, the authority, or some other agency whose function it is, has a responsibility to enforce compliance. Such is the case with the parent, the teacher, the supervisor, the judge, the legislative body, the head of state, and so forth.

Our primary concern is with the rationale for moral authority. How can one be obligated by the decision of another in this way? Is a structure of authority in society compatible with the primary office of personhood? Does the nature of personhood force us to accept some form of anarchism? Or have we been wrong about the office of personhood? These questions focus on the central problem in political philosophy: the authority of government versus the autonomy of the individual.

No one simply as a human being has authority over another. This is the doctrine of the equality of human beings. Each has the responsibility and the right to define and to live a life of one's own under the guidance and governance of one's own knowledge-yielding and critical powers. Authority of a person over another is always with respect to some special office or position. The authority of a parent with respect to a minor child, for example, is not simply grounded in a biological fact but in an office defined by certain responsibilities and rights—an office that one may, under some conditions, voluntarily relinquish, and one from which one can be dismissed. Competence to fulfill the responsibilities and to exercise the rights of the office is assumed. The parent has the responsibility and the right to decide for the child and the child is subject to, and is obligated to obey, the parent in those areas in which the child is incompetent to decide for oneself. As a child matures and becomes more capable of responsible self-direction, the authority of the parent diminishes accordingly until the office becomes purely honorary.

It is clear that one important factor in both the authority of the parent and the obligation of the child to obey is that the parent is in a better position to know what ought to be done. Even though one as a child may not comprehend one's parents' reasons, one may be justified in believing that one's parents have good reasons for what they ask of one; furthermore, the fact that the parents, on the basis of whatever reasons they have, made the decision in question counts in favor of the decision; and because it is the business of the parents, by virtue of their office, to make such decisions, it ought to be obeyed by the child, unless there are very strong counter-reasons available to the child. Therefore, from the child's point of view, the rational thing for one to do in most cases, even without taking into account penalties for disobedience, is to accept and to act on the decisions of one's parents. If a parent should establish a pattern of irresponsible decisions, his or her authority would thereby be dissolved.

Much of what pertains to the authority of a parent is true of the whole structure of authority. The supervisor, the teacher, the police officer, the judge, the legislative body, to name a few, hold offices constituted by responsibilities and rights that involve making decisions that certain others have obligations to accept and to act on; and, in the case of inexcusable disobedience, the authority in question, or some agency, has the responsibility to enforce compliance by imposed sanctions. If the offices that exercise authority are wisely constituted and if the general competence of office holders is maintained, then those subject to the authority of a particular office have good reasons to comply with the authority in question quite apart from whatever penalties there may be for disobedience.

The penalties serve two functions. The first is educational. They point out, in clearly recognizable terms, the importance of compliance. The second function is to give those persons who are not responsive to the primary reasons for compliance a reason that will move them.

The authority of an office within an organization committed to a limited goal like that of an educational institution or a business firm is itself limited. The offices of the organization are constituted by a division of functions required for achieving the specific objectives of the organization. Some of these offices will have the responsibility or the right to make decisions for others to execute. It may be assumed that, in a well-managed organization, responsibility for decision-making is assigned on the basis of relevant knowledge and competence. The maximum penalty for those who are subject to the decisions made and who fail to act on them is expulsion. One makes oneself subject to the structure of authority in the organization and one is free to escape from it, even though it may be inconvenient or costly to do so.

Political authority is significantly different. The objective of a polity is nothing less than that of the moral enterprise itself, at least as far as life within the society is concerned. The function of a government is twofold: (1) to regulate private and public pursuits for the purpose of securing the rights of individuals and assuring justice for all; and (2) to be the agency of the society for collective action in pursuit of the com-

mon good. Thus *bona fide* government, government with authority, is
the moral voice and arm of the people. Herein lies its peculiar authority. The government of a state, insofar as it is the moral voice and
agency of the society, has authority over individual and group interests.
Whenever the government of a society becomes the voice and arm of
some faction or special interest group, it ceases to have authority and
becomes only a power structure and should be dealt with as such. We
mark this distinction by speaking of *de facto* and *de jure* governments.

The voice of *de jure* government has authority not only over individuals and groups in that it obligates them; the official judgments of the
government have a kind of authority vis-à-vis the judgments of individuals or special interest groups. Here we have to distinguish between
one's independent moral judgment about a matter and one's judgment
in light of the fact that there is a law or policy of government about it.
One's independent judgment in a given situation might be that one
ought to do act *A*; but, taking into account that there is a law against it,
one might conclude that one ought not to do *A*; and one might reach
this conclusion without taking into account the penalty for breaking the
law. Epistemic authority is a factor. Under a government with authority, the existence of the law prohibiting the act indicates that a body of
people whose business it is to consider such matters has found reasons
that convinced its members that such actions were wrong to such an
extent that they should be prohibited by law. This brings additional
considerations into the picture that one must weight in making up
one's own mind on the matter; and these considerations may be sufficient to call into question, or to reverse, one's prior judgment. Even if,
after careful consideration, one's first judgment remains unshaken and
one is supported in it by the responsible judgment of many others, the
law still has priority over one's judgment and should be so recognized,
for it is the official moral voice of the society, which, presumably, has
been formed by a procedure of which the members of the society approve.

This is not to say that one should never, on the basis of one's own
judgment, act contrary to the law. It does mean, however, that the one
who feels that there are compelling reasons in a particular situation for
one to go against the law must accept the responsibility of justifying
one's action in a court or accept the penalty under the law. Nor does it
rule out civil disobedience as a way of protest and reform. If a person is
informed and rationally convinced that one's government has made a
grievous error of great magnitude, and if other means of protest and
correction have been exhausted or are unavailable, one may justifiably
protest by disobedience and acceptance of the penalty involved to call
attention to the reasons that already exist for correcting the govern-

mental position. This is just as proper as violating a law in order to get a court case to test the constitutionality of the law itself.

However, one cannot forcibly resist the government without denying its authority or acknowledging the criminality of one's action. The right of rebellion holds only with regard to a *de facto* government. Only if one's government were systematically and grossly unjust and all established procedures for correction had been exhausted would one be justified in confronting it with force. Under such circumstances, however, one might even be obligated to do so.

Each person, in judging and making decisions, has to operate from within one's own perspective, defined by one's assumptions, beliefs, attitudes, and experiences. One's decisions and actions may be rationally justified within one's perspective without the perspective itself being defensible. Therefore, we have to distinguish between subjective and objective justification. The first is internal justification only; the second includes justification of one's perspective. The latter is very difficult. Any correction of one's perspective has to be made from within. One's perspective can be more or less free of internal contradictions; it can make for genuine dialectical exchanges with others who have different perspectives; it can be self-corrective, creative, progressive, and open to growth; it may enable one to draw on and to utilize more or less of the resources within oneself and the resources of the human community; it may make for a fulfilling life; it may make for a life that wins approval or admiration from others; and so forth. No one has a right to be as sure of the justification of one's perspective as of the internal justification of particular judgments and decisions, for there is always the possibility of an undetected bias that may distort one's judgment. Given the conflict of perspectives, there is reason for each person to accept the perspective of responsible government, especially in a free, enlightened, democratic society; for the perspective of such a government on an issue, having been generated by a dialectical clash of many perspectives, is likely to be more inclusive and one in which people of different perspectives can concur.

Revolution is a rational option only when a large number of people, on the basis of their own perspectives, become rationally convinced that the perspective of the government is partial and biased so that its decisions and actions are systematically perverted. This is a difficult conclusion to defend, for the perspective of the government calls into question the correctness of their contrary perspectives in the same way their perspectives cast doubt on the perspective of the government. Something of a wide public consensus has to emerge against the perspective of the government to make revolution a rational option. But if such a wide consensus should develop in a democratic society, a revolution would not be necessary, for the perspective of the government would be changed by the emerging public consensus. One of the merits of democracy is that it, in effect, institutionalizes revolution.

A well-formed and well-functioning government is not incompatible with the autonomy of rational persons, for the individuals subject to the authority of such a government have good reasons, quite apart from any penalties that might be involved, to comply with its require-ments. Freedom would be compromised only if the rational, informed person would have to take into account the penalties in order to find a reason for compliance. Thus ideally the coercive force of government would be used only against those who grossly fail to do the morally right thing for the right reasons. The informed, rational person, acting from one's own deliberations, would never feel the external restraint of governmental authority; nor would one's beliefs and inner motivations be manipulated or shaped by indoctrination or propaganda. Through knowledge and critical judgment one can be free under authority; and without knowledge and critical judgment one cannot be free at all. Of course, perfect rationality is never achieved either by the government or by the individual citizens. Therefore, perfect freedom under gov-ernment is never achieved. But freedom can be extended by improving the rationality of both the government and the citizens.

A government has authority to the extent it is the moral voice and arm of the society. It has to provide the institutional structure for the formation of societal moral judgments on issues of common concern, and it must be the agent for the implementation of those judgments. When a government acts without the backing of a societal moral judg-ment, it undermines its own authority.

Even in a well-organized society, a societal moral judgment may not be possible on some issues of wide concern—for example, the issue of abortion in the United States at the present time. There are deep dif-ferences in metaphysical beliefs about whether the fetus is a person with human rights; therefore, some think that abortion is murder and some think that it is not. The metaphysics of many is such that they cannot even entertain the idea that abortion might be murder, for they think that such a judgment is based on a superstition. Many serious-minded, conscientious, reflective people would evade a law that prohib-ited it and feel justified in doing so. Any law for which the government has to rely solely on the coercive power of the state to obtain compli-ance on the part of a sizable number of well-informed, conscientious citizens tends to discredit the institution of law and the authority of the government. On such matters, a state should not legislate—not even if a majority of the people approve it. The laws of a state should be justi-fiable by and large to the informed, reflective, conscientious people who have to live under them. To the extent the laws of a society do not meet this test, the society becomes a police state.

The cultures of "a society" defined by geographical boundaries may be such that a common moral voice is not possible on many issues, if any. If no moral consensus is possible, no government with authority is possible; if a moral consensus is possible on only a limited set of issues, a government with authority must be limited accordingly. Of course a country with only a geographical definition may have to subdivide into two or more countries in order to have governments with authority. The best that some societies may be able to do is to establish a government committed to working toward the development of a sufficient moral consensus to endow the government with authority. Such a commitment and effort toward that end may, in itself, lend some legitimacy to a government for a period of time. But a government committed to imposing the voice of a faction on the whole society is nothing more than a power structure; it cannot obligate the people by its legislation and policies. This is the case whether the factional government acts deliberately to promote the interest of a faction at the expense of others or whether it enacts the moral voice of a faction in disagreement with the moral voice of another faction.

It is often said that a government should be responsive to, and act on, the will of the people. Perhaps there is an interpretation of "the will of the people" in terms of which this claim can be justified. The issue turns on whether it is possible for the will of the people to be different from the moral voice of the people. It is more plausible that the will of the people and the moral voice of the people coincide on purely domestic issues, for presumably "the people" could not have a unitary will on many domestic problems except from within a moral perspective that respected the rights and legitimate interests of all. It is conceivable, however, that all the people of a society could concur in a governmental action on a domestic problem on the basis of the self-interest of each, without anyone's endorsing the action for moral reasons. In such a situation, there might be a will of the people about the matter that was not the moral judgment of the people. Indeed, it might be something that a genuine societal moral judgment would condemn. Consider an action from which all would stand to benefit in the short run, but at the ruinous expense of the next generation. And of course there is nothing to assure that the will of the people on an international issue would be identical with a societal moral judgment on the matter. The point is that it is not enough for a government to be the agent of the will of the people; it must be the instrument of the moral will of the people. Whatever a government does for whatever reason, it must be such that it can be morally justified to the informed, reflective, conscientious people of the society. The people have to be able to say of their government's actions, for the most part, "This is what *we* did," with self-respect and self-approval. Whenever a government establishes a pattern of behavior that the people cannot embrace in this manner, it loses its authority.

It is a rather common belief in democratic societies that only a constitutional democracy has genuine authority. But the distinction between the will and the moral voice of the people could jeopardize that article of democratic faith. It seems possible that an undemocratic government could embody the values of a culture and reach decisions that the people would recognize as expressions of, or at least as congruent with, their moral judgments in such a way that they would identify with the government and give it their moral support. This would seem to be sufficient to invest the government with moral authority. Of course if the government, or a power structure favored by the government, should manipulate the culture to obtain that support, it would undermine whatever validity the government gained from that popular support.

Even though there may be other forms of government with authority, there can be little doubt that a democratic government in an enlightened society that has constitutional restraints on the government to protect the rights of individuals is the best way to assure the authority of the government and to protect the autonomy of the individual. Democratic governments, however, are quite vulnerable to corruption by advertising techniques, governmental propaganda, special interest politics, and bargained agreements rather than government by public debate and reasoned agreements about justice and the common good. So there is nothing to guarantee that a democratic government will be the moral voice and arm of the people. Democratic governments can, and often do, lack moral authority. The moral authority of the government and the protection of the autonomy of the individual have to be worked at constantly even in the best of societies. The exercise of power by any effective government is likely to exceed its authority. Every government needs built-in checks and balances; and the people need to be ever alert to the misuse of power in government.

Conclusion

Metaphysically speaking, social reality, whether that of a person or that of a social structure, involves the categorial dimensions of fact, value, and meaning. There is the existential and factual dimension at several different levels, including the physical, the psychological, the personal, and the societal; but what is distinctive about social reality at all levels are the dimensions of normativity and meaning. The whole matrix of requirements, responsibilities, rights, and offices that make up a society is a complex normative structure. And all social structures have a dimension of meaning. Simple societies, such as those of gorillas, involve, and are dependent on, the psychological states and acts of the members of the society; simpler societies, such as those of ant colonies and bee hives, are dependent on even more primitive forms of the psychological, perhaps the more or less purely instinctual. But these are all semantic in nature or have a semantic dimension. In a human society, the semantic dimension is greatly extended by the culture. In fact, it is the cultural dimension that makes the human society so distinctive. An office, for example, is constituted by responsibilities that have to be known in order for them to be had and they can be carried out only under the guidance of knowledge and critical judgment.

Of course persons are essential components of a human society. They are the constituent elements of the social structure. They constitute the basic offices and are the principal holders of the other offices. They give substance and energy to the whole system. Without them the social order is an abstraction; it lacks concreteness and vitality. Nevertheless, a society does not collapse into the collection of persons who populate and animate it. What is sayable about a society cannot be reduced, without loss of meaning, to statements about its members and what they do. A society has a history, a story, that is not simply the sum of the biographies of all who are and have been members of the society; a society has an institutional structure that cannot be reduced to the patterns of behavior of the members of the society; a society embodies its culture in its institutional structure in a way that is not identical with the embodiment of the culture in the lives of the members of the society; a society has responsibilities and rights and relationships that cannot be broken down into the responsibilities, rights, and relationships of past, present, and future members of the society; a society does things that are uniquely its acts, not just a set of acts of individuals; and so forth. Of course nothing is true of a society without correlated truths about people, but not all the truths about society are identical with their correlated truths about people.

The social order is internal to the persons involved in it in such a way that they cannot be extracted from it and maintain their identity. Much of their subjectivity and normative structure, including their self-image, which is involved in their identity, semantically contains the social structure within it. In this respect, the reality and identity of human beings depend on the objective reality of the social order. Social reality, whether that of a person, an institution, or a society, is not dependent on knowledge of it in the manner claimed by epistemological idealists, but it does involve subjectivity, including meaning and knowledge, in its very essence.

A society comes into being, grows, and lives with an inner dynamics of its own. It has an internal normative structure with respect to which it may be judged to be more developed or less developed, well formed or malformed, healthy or sick. It has the capacity to correct and to heal itself by its own internal processes. A society is a peculiar being with a life and history of its own.

Societies may develop in different ways. We find wide differences in institutional structures. But all societies share the basic office of personhood and the same overall functions. The office of personhood, with its inherent responsibilities and rights, provides the basic normative structure that defines what constitutes a well-developed, well-formed, healthy society. The good society is (1) one that provides the necessary conditions and ample opportunities for all the people to develop their abilities and to find social positions through which they can live lives of their own that are worthy of them both as human beings and as the particular individuals they are; (2) one that provides adequate support for, and respects the dignity of, the disabled and the dispossessed; and (3) one that provides the conditions and the encouragement for the people, in living their own lives, to advance the culture and the social order in ways that enhance the human potential and advance the quality of life, not only for the present generation but for generations to come.

There are a number of ways in which a social order can be malformed. The basic moral judgment to be made on any office or position, as previously remarked, is on whether the person who holds it must fail to fulfill one's primary responsibility as a person in order to fulfill the responsibilities of the office. The worst form of this is where one has to be morally corrupt (or at least has to perform morally wrong acts) in order to carry out the responsibilities of the office. Few would deny, for instance, that Nazi Germany, with its extermination camps, had offices that no human being could hold and function well in without malfunctioning as a person. Any office that commits the officeholder to ends unworthy of a human being is a form of prostitution; and the social order that embraces it is, to that extent, malformed and immoral, regardless of how much good it may generate.

An office or position may be incompatible with personhood without committing one to inhuman ends. The responsibilities of the office, although legitimate in themselves, may be such that they make it virtually impossible for holders of the office to live lives worthy of human beings. This is the indictment that social critics made of early industrial societies. It is the charge that some have made about migrant farm workers in the United States. It is the charge made by some feminists about the traditional office of womanhood. Whether or not these charges are valid, a social order that contains offices or positions that are dehumanizing for those who hold them is, to that extent, malformed.

Offices or positions that are neither inherently immoral nor dehumanizing may thwart particular holders of them in their efforts to define and to live lives worthy of them as the particular individuals they are. The minimally acceptable office for a person is a position that will neither pervert nor thwart one either as a human being or as the individual one is. The ideal position for one is a position through which one can fulfill, at least in part, both one's humanity and one's individuality. This is the difference between a job by which one makes a living and a position that is an integral part of one's life. In the latter kind of position, unlike the first, one expresses and fulfills one's self in one's work. To the extent a society does not provide the opportunity for its members, according to their abilities, to find an office or set of offices through which they can make a living and have a self-fulfilling life, it is inadequate. To the extent a society excludes a class of its members from offices or positions worthy of them for reasons that have nothing to do with their ability or personal worthiness, it is malformed.

A social order may become deformed in a variety of ways: by an ideology that falsely defines the function of society, such as, for example, a racist or militarist culture; by an inverted order of priorities that distorts the culture and social order, such as a materialistic value system; by institutional dysfunction so that the institutions fail to meet the needs of the people; by social lag so that a gap develops between the developing culture and the social structure, rendering the social order obsolete and the people alienated from it; and so forth. A society may appear to be well organized and efficient when in fact it is in pursuit of some unnatural end and the people are locked into positions and structures that hobble, choke, thwart, or pervert them as persons and as the particular individuals they are; or a society may appear to be well organized and well functioning when, in fact, the culture is stagnant and human advancement has been stopped.

A social order may malfunction for many reasons. It may be underdeveloped, malformed, too rigid, or too soft; it may be obsolete, in a state of decay and disintegration, without legitimacy for lack of a shared culture that binds the people and social order together; its people may lack an adequate intellectual vision of humankind and the world to sustain it; and so on.

It is the responsibility of the people through the government and other institutions, but primarily the government, to monitor the social order and to assure, insofar as possible, that it is well developed, well formed, and well functioning.

Personhood, then, if the basic philosophical position of this work is correct, provides a set of universal functions and a normative structure common to all societies; and all societies are subject to being judged on the basis of this inherent normative structure which they share. There are, of course, alternative ways in which societies may fulfill these functions and meet these normative requirements.

CHAPTER 8

Toward a Humanistic World-View

It is now time for review and for reflection on whether the understanding we have gained and the conclusions we have found compelling offer a solution to the problem with which we began. What we called, in Chapter 1, "*the* modern problem" is the human identity crisis in the modern age. It was occasioned by the elimination of the distinctively humanistic concepts in terms of which we define our identity as persons and organize and live our lives from the descriptive/explanatory conceptual system in terms of which we define the world.

Summing Up

We have rejected, for compelling reasons, the three most popular ways of trying to solve the fissure in modern Western culture between the humanistic and the scientific dimensions of the culture: (1) the reductionism of those who would trim the humanistic dimension of the culture to its absolutely indispensable elements and try to validate the minimal version on the basis of a naturalistic epistemology and metaphysics; (2) a subjectivistic, relativistic, "historicist" theory of the humanistic dimension of the culture, joined with a realistic theory of science and its naturalistic world-view; and (3) the completely subjectivistic, relativistic, "historicist" theory of the whole culture, including science, with multiple world-views, if any. We have dared to argue for what Ernest Gellner calls "the great illusion of the Enlightenment": that the culture can be integrated from within a humanistic perspective and that a rational humanistic world-view is possible. We are well aware of the modern arguments against this enterprise, but we have argued for it by challenging the underlying assumptions of the modern mind,

279

assumptions that we contend limit and systematically distort reason in its work. We cannot achieve an integration of the culture and a humanistic world-view without deep cultural therapy that gets beneath, critically exposes, and corrects these deranging assumptions.[2]

Although the humanities themselves are subject to perversion within the modern perspective, and there are good reasons to think that they have been distorted, they are capable of deep criticism and reconstruction of the culture by examining the social character, the structure of feeling, and the cultural mind of the age. As we argued in Chapter 2, the structure of feeling of a culture, especially as revealed in its literature and art, when properly analyzed and interpreted by the humanities, gives the verdict of lived experience on the social character of the culture—the personal and social forms and identities and the way of life the culture generates. But the structure of feeling only reflects favorably or unfavorably on the culture and society; as bodily feelings indicate whether our bodily conditions are good or bad, lived experience judges whether the personal and social identities and the forms of life the culture generates are good or bad. The rise in negative life attitudes over time indicates that something is wrong in the culture, but it does not reveal what is wrong. Philosophical analysis and criticism of the cultural mind is necessary for a more specific diagnosis of the trouble.

The cultural mind consists of a set of organizing and governing ideas and assumptions about the constitutional principles and powers of the human mind and the categorial structure of the world. These epistemological and metaphysical assumptions determine how we understand and interpret the different sectors of the culture; indeed, they have considerable influence on how we use the powers of the human mind in developing the culture, especially in criticizing and reconstructing it. False philosophical assumptions about the constitutional principles and powers of the human mind or about the categorial structure of the world would have perverting effects on the culture; those who were generated by the culture and operated within it would be systematically thwarted in their efforts to know and to cope with reality and to live meaningful and worthwhile lives. The correct diagnosis of a deranged cultural mind would consist in locating the false epistemological and metaphysical assumptions that were perverting the culture and, through it, distorting the social order and the lives of the people. Cultural therapy would consist, not only in the diagnosis of the trouble, but in correcting the false assumptions and reconstructing the cultural and social order and the lives of the people accordingly. This is not something that can be done easily or quickly. It might take generations. Individuals, however, can reconstruct their own thinking and their own lives and they can teach and influence others. Over time this process could work a cultural and social change; but the existing cultural and social order always has great inertia. Furthermore, there are always those with vested interests in the existing cultural and social order who resist change. Nevertheless, ongoing philosophical exploration and criticism of the cultural mind and its implications for the culture in general is essential for cultural health and progress, regardless of whether such criticism confirms the cultural mind or finds it to be in perverting error. It requires time, but philosophical therapy for a deranged cultural mind can be fruitful. Success for individuals alone is sufficient to justify the effort.

Trouble in the epistemological and metaphysical assumptions that constitute the cultural mind shows itself in certain kinds of logical difficulties in the culture—inconsistencies and incongruences that challenge, not just the truth of certain statements, but also whether a certain use of a sentence states what it seems to state, or has the logical form it seems to have, or even whether it can be used to make a truth-claim at all. These philosophical questions about discourse are also metaphysical questions about whether some apparent or supposed subject matter of the discourse is real or whether the subject matter has the categorial form it seems, or is assumed, to have. But in the same way our assumptions or views about the semantic and knowledge-yielding powers of the human mind and the categorial structure of the world give rise to questions about what seems to be the case with regard to various modes of discourse and the categorial structure of their subject matters, the apparent meaning and form of those areas of discourse and the apparent categorial form of the subject matters in question give rise to questions about the epistemological and metaphysical assumptions and views that put them in question. Philosophical investigation of the problem must not focus on only the area of discourse or apparent subject matter in question; it must examine the other side of the logical tension, the assumptions or views that gave rise to the skeptical questions in the first place. These may be simply assumptions or beliefs; or they may be the presuppositions of a universe of discourse. If they are assumptions or beliefs, they may be simply false and can be altered or abandoned without any deep cultural change. But if they are presuppositions of a universe of discourse and if they are inconsistent with the actual presuppositions of another universe of discourse, the culture is in deep trouble. Radical cultural reconstruction may be necessary.

Philosophy attempts to articulate the governing epistemological and metaphysical assumptions of the culture; and it subjects these assumptions to rigorous tests by fresh philosophical investigations of the se-

mantic and knowledge-yielding powers of the human mind and by an
analysis of the categorial structures of the subject matter of the various
sectors of the culture in light of the conclusions reached about our
semantic and knowledge-yielding powers. The semantic and epistemic
powers of the mind are discovered by a categorial analysis of the various modes of experience and thought that are candidates for epistemic
encounters to determine whether they have the appropriate categorial
structure for data-gathering and for funding language with meaning.
The categorial structure of a mode of experience or thought, as with
any other subject matter, is revealed by a philosophical analysis of the
language we use to report and to describe it and by a consideration of
what it makes sense to say and what it does not make sense to say about
it.

Given confirmed views about what our semantic and epistemic
powers are, we explore the categorial structure of the subject matter of
the various sectors of discourse by considering what, in light of our
views about the semantic and epistemic powers of the mind, it is possible for us to mean and what it is not possible for us to mean about any
apparent subject matter. Any tentative set of epistemological and metaphysical conclusions must be further tested by interpreting the whole
culture in terms of them to see if further philosophical perplexities
would be generated; that is, to see whether inconsistencies between the
epistemological and metaphysical claims and the presuppositions of the
various universes of discourse would be revealed. When inconsistences
do appear, philosophers must either revise their philosophical theory
or arrive at some interpretation or theory about the area of the culture
in question that would alleviate the logical difficulty. The happiest result of such a test would be for the philosophical theory to be found to
be fully consistent with the presuppositions of all areas of the culture
without having to discredit or radically reinterpret any universe of discourse. If no philosophical theory can be found in terms of which all
areas of the culture can be accepted for what they appear to be, the
philosopher has an obligation to try to determine which area or areas
must yield; that is, which area or areas must be philosophically reinterpreted (or perhaps even discredited as superstition) to achieve a coherent set of presuppositions of the culture as a whole.

What is central and most basic in the philosophical enterprise are the
assumptions and views about the semantic and knowledge-yielding
powers of the human mind. Among the fundamental questions of philosophy are: What is it to be able to mean and to know items, features,
and structures of the world? What modes of experience provide us
with semantic and epistemic access to items, features, and structures of
the world? By what powers or acts are we able to break out of the

intralinguistic circle of definition and to establish (or to grasp) ties between linguistic expressions and items, features, and structures of the world? In other words, what experiences can be synonymous with a linguistic expression? Is this true of only sensory experiences? If other modes of experience have the requisite categorial structure and power, which are they?

Even though epistemological questions are very basic in philosophy, they are interdependent with metaphysical questions. We cannot proceed without probing into such metaphysical issues as the nature of meaning and of the thinking self as well as the categorial structure of various modes of experience and thought. And we cannot pursue any of these matters without being involved to some extent in the philosophy of culture. Philosophy is a systematic discipline. There are very few, if any, philosophical questions that stand alone so that they can be investigated successfully with disregard of other philosophical issues.

We have argued that the semantic and knowledge-yielding powers of the human mind are broader than have been acknowledged in our scientific/technological age; specifically, that our affective/conative experiences, perceptual understanding (including expression perception), and reflective awareness, as well as sensory experience (somatic and external), are modes of epistemic encounter and thus are capable of funding language with meaning and of gathering data about an independent reality. With this broader semantic and epistemic base, the distinctively modern strictures on the philosophical analysis of humanistic discourse are considerably relaxed. The language of meaning, subjectivity, normativity, personhood, and social phenomena can be analyzed in its own terms; it does not have to be interpreted in tortured ways so that it will square with modern empiricist theories of knowledge and naturalistic metaphysics based on modern science as the paradigm of knowledge. In fact, the primary realities we know are ourselves and others as well as cultural and social phenomena. Any philosophical theory that does not square with this dimension of knowledge and reality cannot be valid.

We have argued (mostly in the first two books of this trilogy, but the results are summarized in Chapter 2 and 3 of this work) for a realistic theory of value language, with "ought" as the basic value concept. Accordingly, something is good or bad according to whether it is something that ought to be or whether it is the way it ought to be. Normativity, what we capture in "ought" talk, is a requiredness, a mode of constitution, that holds in things or situations. For example, X's being F requires that X be G, or, situation S requires that there be an x that would be G. We state such things by saying, in the first case, "X, being F, ought to be G"; and, in the second example, "Situation S's being what it is, there ought to be an x that would be G." We know normative structures, as has been argued here, through critically assessed affective/conative experiences and thought grounded therein.

Meaning, too, we have contended, is a mode of constitution. An experience, for example, has something semantically, but inexistentially, in it. Semantic intentionality, according to our theory, is the nature of subjectivity—the mental. We have self-knowledge and reflective awareness of some of our own subjective states and acts; and we have expression-perception or perceptual understanding of other subject matters with an inherent structure of meaning.

However, to accept such a humanistic theory of meaning, value, selfhood, and the social world is to run headlong into conflict not only with philosophical assumptions and beliefs derived from modern science, but with the world-view of modern science itself. The problem is deep within the culture.

We have concluded that the burden of the logical tension between the two areas of the culture must fall on modern science, not on the humanities and the culture of lived experience, for the humanistic culture itself is presupposed by science. Scientists have to think humanistically about their problems, experiences, theories, and themselves in doing science. In other words, the conflict is not just between the humanistic dimension of the culture and modern science; it is within the presuppositions of modern science themselves. Scientific naturalism not only generates unsolvable problems about the humanistic dimension of the culture; it is self-destructive, for it does not allow sufficient room to make philosophical sense of scientific knowledge and naturalistic metaphysics.

Modern science, like other areas of the culture, presupposes the constitutional principles of the human mind; but it is also an area of the culture that was built on revolutionary ways of investigating, categorizing, and theorizing about its subject matter. These new ways involved presuppositions about the knowledge-yielding powers of the human mind and the categorial structure of the world. These special presuppositions of science are in conflict with the basic presuppositions of human culture—the constitutional principles of the human mind. The world that scientific thought defines is a world in which science itself would be impossible. Since there is no such internal difficulty within the humanistic perspective, it seems clear that we have to relieve the tension between the scientific and the humanistic views of human beings and the social world on terms favorable to the humanistic view rather than on naturalistic terms.

Science, of course, is a great human achievement. By concentrating on the existential and factual constitution of things, it has had amazing success in ordering sensory data and in providing us with knowledge that enables us to manipulate and to control things through their existential and factual dimension. As an intellectual enterprise, however, the scientific approach is less objective than the humanistic approach in some important respects. The scientific conceptual system and methodology are under the influence (indeed, control) of a limited set of human interests, namely, our materialistic needs (those that lend themselves to being satisfied by manipulatory action on the conditions of our existence). This influence shows itself in the test that science imposes on itself to the effect that its theories must provide the kind of understanding that, in principle, would enable us to remake our environment and to manipulate and to control things. Furthermore, science is based on a limited set of our knowledge-yielding and data-gathering powers; and, consequently, it employs a limited set of categories in defining its world-view and in describing and explaining its subject matter. These limitations show themselves most clearly in the extension of the scientific method and categorial system to human behavior and social and cultural phenomena. But the limitations become evident in other areas when we try to render intelligible human existence and the whole array of human phenomena in a world otherwise conceptualized in scientific terms.

A human being, according to the humanistic view, is not an individual differentiated from nonhuman things by certain kinds of properties; but rather a human being, or so we have contended, is a kind of substance defined by its categorial modes of constitution. As argued in Chapter 3, a material substance is a concrete individual constituted existentially, factually, and causally (the causality engaging only existential and factual structures) so that it resists disintegration. Of course strict empiricists have trouble with the notion of a causal structure that involves natural necessity. But what is important for our purposes is that a purely material substance does not have a normative or semantic mode of constitution; it does not have anything either normatively or semantically in it; it has no internality in either of these senses. Regardless of whether there are any purely material substances, human beings are not material substances. They are constituted existentially, factually, normatively, semantically, and causally; and the inner causal dynamics of the individual engages all these modes of constitution.

Human beings whose normative potentiality is actualized beyond a certain point are constituted logically and morally as well. This is what sets them apart from other psychological beings. Their semantic powers are enhanced to the point that their semantic states and acts become a dynamic system integrated under a normative self-concept as a person; they think and live under rational and moral imperatives.

Human beings have minds and lives as well as bodies. They are human persons. A mind is an integration of semantic states and acts under the inherent rational imperative to be coherent and correct in experience and thought. An actualized person is an integration of experiences, thoughts, and actions under the inherent moral imperative to define and to live a life of one's own that would be worthy of one both as the kind of being, and as the individual, one is. But experiences, thoughts, actions, and lives require a bodily dimension and draw their energy from it. Whether or not we accept the Christian trinitarian view of God, it seems that we must accept a trinitarian view of human beings: body, mind, and person, but one substance. Only incarnated minds and persons are real.

A society, according to our humanistic view, is an integrated system of offices with its own inherent normative structure. It has its own inner dynamics by which it develops and sustains its identity through time and works to maintain its health. The basic office in the social structure is that of personhood, which is a natural, inalienable office for human beings. Other offices, which are held (for the most part) by persons, are conventional, with several possible exceptions such as manhood, womanhood, fatherhood, motherhood, and the like. But a society has an inherent normative structure, which is grounded in the normative structure of persons, with respect to which it is under-developed or more or less well developed, well formed or malformed, well functioning or malfunctioning. In a well-formed and healthy society, the culture that generates the people and shapes their subjectivity is embodied in the institutions and social structure of the society; it unifies the people and enables them to identify with the social order and to feel at home in it. When the culture embodied in the institutions and the social order in general is different from the culture that structures the consciousness of the people, especially the younger generation, the people become alienated from the social order. Under such conditions, either the culture or the social order has to be reformed. Since the culture should be allowed to develop freely under the critical and creative powers of the people, social reform is necessary.

In Chapter 7, we spoke of the ways in which a society is both like and unlike an organism. The centrality and importance of persons in a society is what makes it unlike an organism. The well-being of the whole is judged by how well it meets the needs of its components. But in a very real sense, a society is a living substance—a peculiar one, to be sure, but a living substance nonetheless. It is not simply a collection of people. The members of the society are webbed together by a shared culture, social relationships, offices, and institutional structures that not only bind the members together but enter into their individual identities. A society endures and undergoes changes in a way that transcends its individual members. Talk about a society cannot be paraphrased, without undergoing loss in sayable content, into talk about individual persons. And much of what we say about persons involves uneliminable talk about society or aspects of it. Of course, a society without persons is an abstraction; it lacks substance and vitality. A social order can be embodied only in a set of people who internalize it. The mortar that builds a society out of persons is not something external and material; it is a structure of meaning and normativity. Without recognizing the reality of meaning and normativity, we see society only as a collection of human beings in interaction with one another in certain ways. But from within the perspective of realistic humanism, we seem compelled to acknowledge that a society is a substance, even though a peculiar one. It is a social substance. It is not something to which we have epistemic access through sensory observation; like a person, its internality is what is important about it. Only its extensional aspect is open to sensory observation—its territory, its physical structures, and the bodies of its people. However important these are, they do not constitute a society.

Liberal individualists recoil from such a view on the grounds that a society is likely to be taken to be a superior being before whom human beings have only limited rights at best and for the sake of whom individuals can be justifiably sacrificed. But if the normative structure of society is grounded in the normative structure of personhood and if society exists, and should be structured, to provide the necessary protective and support systems for individual human beings to have an opportunity to fulfill their inherent normative nature, then such a view of society should be no threat to the individual.

A Humanistic World-View

The big question we have to face up to is this: If we must accept such a full-fledged humanistic view of persons and the social world, what kind of world-view must we have in order to make the existence of persons and society intelligible? How can we integrate the humanistic categories of persons and the social world into a unified world-view so that we can place ourselves, our culture, and the social order in the world in a way that makes the human phenomenon intelligible without having to mutilate ourselves and our cultural and social world? From our philosophical explorations, it seems clear that the naturalistic world-view will not do. Human beings are diminished or even destroyed in being intellectually processed to fit into the naturalistically defined world. This is not simply an intellectual matter, for we are beings who are constituted in our actuality by our self-understanding. When there is logical tension

between our cognition and human identity, the fault must lie with our
way of thinking, for our human identity is presupposed by thinking
itself. We must conceive the world in sufficiently rich categorial terms
to make sense of the human phenomenon in all of its manifest categorial richness.

What does this entail? It certainly means that the modern scientific
conceptual system, insofar as it remains faithful to its traditional restraints, is not adequate for biological, psychological, personal, and social subject matters; and, furthermore, it means that, with regard to
persons and human societies, it may be worse than inadequate—it may
actually pervert the subject matter in its existence, not only in our comprehension of it. It seems clear that the conceptual system in terms of
which we understand these areas must include the categories of normativity and meaning as well as those of existence and factuality and a
category of causality that embraces all these dimensions. But what
about the sub-biological realm? Is a purely naturalistic categorial system
adequate to describe it? If so, can we make sense of the existence of the
categorially enriched biological, psychological, personal, and social phenomena in an otherwise naturalistic world?

The argument seems to be solid for the claim that we cannot eliminate the categories of normativity, semantic intentionality, and teleological causality from our descriptive/explanatory conceptual system
and that, therefore, we cannot eliminate them from our metaphysics.
Some who agree with this, or at least part of the thesis, hold that the
categorially enriched human territory is an oasis in an otherwise naturalistic desert. Joseph Margolis, for example, admits that we have to
acknowledge semantic intentionality (the mental) as an ontological category; but he holds that it must be regarded as an emergent feature in
an otherwise materialistic universe.[3] Given the soundness of our argument thus far, the emergent thesis seems to be the only alternative to a
full-fledged humanistic world-view—that is, a world-view in which ultimate reality is conceived in humanistic categories.

Contrary to the view held by Margolis, if the biological, psychological, personal, and social realms emerge in an otherwise materialistic
universe, normative as well as semantic structures must be emergent.
Many have felt that this is not a possible solution. There are intellectual
tensions, widely felt, that tend to drive those who believe in the categorial richness of the biological and the human realms to conceive the
world as categorially richer through and through in order to make biological and human existence intelligible. The same intellectual tensions
tend to drive those who accept a materialistic view of the sub-biological
realms toward a reduction of our thought about biological and human
beings to materialistic terms.

Since most contemporary philosophers seem to be untroubled with the view that value language is ontologically neutral but are still nervous about the language of meaning and the mental, we shall focus on whether the existence of beings with a mental dimension can be made intelligible in an otherwise materialistic universe or whether, in such a world, they would have to remain a mystery—an ontological dangler. The question here concerns not the ontological neutrality of the language of meaning (and the language of normativity), but whether a naturalistic theoretical conceptual system is adequate to explain a subject matter that must be conceptualized in humanistic categories.

In Chapters 3 and 4, we characterized psychological states and acts as discrete, with their identity and unity constituted by an inherent structure of meaning with a logical form. But exactly how discrete and atomistic are psychological states and acts? Could there be only one psychological state or act in the world? Could even a particular animal, human or otherwise, have only one discrete psychological state or act? Could a given human being have a first one? In other words, what kind of a context does a psychological state or act require? Could one occur in a purely physico-chemical context? Or in a purely physico-chemical and biological context? If so, what does this imply about such a context? And could there be just one or a first biological state in an otherwise physical and chemical world? If so, what does this say about the physical and the chemical world? Or must we look at these questions only in terms of what they force us to say about the nature of psychological and biological states? That is, must we conceive biological and psychological states in such a way that they are, or could be, at home in an otherwise physico-chemical environment? If we are right about the fundamentals, the latter alternative is not a viable option.

Many would agree that we cannot make sense of the claim that there might have been only one statement (in the form of a linguistic act) in the world, for a statement presupposes the resources of a language in a holistic sense. Perhaps we can make sense of the development of language within the context of prelinguistic psychological states and acts, for language and the psychological are categorially similar. Both involve semantic and logical structures. There are prelinguistic "takings" and "mistakings"; there are even expressions of them. Linguistic statements seem to be only a more sophisticated version of the same thing. But could there be a world otherwise devoid of structures of meaning that contained one and only one discrete psychological state? Can an object O be semantically present in state S, where S is the first and only state in the whole universe with a semantic content? Is such a semantic singularity conceivable? Or must any semantic state be embedded in a semantic system of some kind?

Some philosophers, especially classical British empiricists, have thought of sensations as atomic in this manner. Each was conceived as a singular occurrence capable of standing by itself. But it was an unstable idea. When the sensation of red, for instance, was conceived as the semantic presence of red, what was red semantically present in or to? Was it simply the time marked by its presence, the occurrence itself? Or was there a subject? If so, what was its nature? And just what was semantically present? The universal redness? A red object? If a red object, what was the object? The region of subjective space delineated by the color, a sense datum? Or a patch of objective space? How could the distinction between subjective and objective space be drawn in such a world? Or did the alleged semantic presence of red collapse, as Hume contended, into the existence of a red something that did not in any way transcend the sensation?

It is widely accepted that, for language-in-use, sentences are more basic than words and phrases; that, in an important sense, words and phrases are abstractions from sentences. In a somewhat similar way, it seems plausible to hold that semantic presences occur primarily in perceptions and desires or some prototypes of these. If this is so, the occurrence of sheer semantic presences would be derivative from perception and desire, or perhaps even from appearings. In the order of being, not necessarily in the order of thought, perceptions (and perhaps desires as well) are turned into appearings by reflective, critical withholding of the *taking* factor. Perhaps appearings are turned into sheer semantic presences by a further withholding. An appearing is an *appearing to be*; it involves the distinction between semantic presence and being. Perhaps the occurrence of a sheer semantic presence is an appearing that does not have any reference to being. This would make *semantic presence* a "thinner" concept than appearing, but it does not necessarily make semantic presence more basic in the order of being. While, in the order of reflective criticism and analysis, we move from taking to be, to appearing to be, to sheer semantic presence, it is not clear that, in the order of being, there is a reverse progression from semantic presence, to appearing to be, to taking to be. This was the mistake of the British empiricists. They thought we moved in our psychological activities from semantic presences (sensations) to appearings-to-be to takings-to-be; and they tried to provide an epistemic justification for the progression and could not. In other words, the efforts of British empiricists toward psychological atomism were not very promising. They ended in incoherence.

Can psychological atomism within a realistic conception of the world be more successful? Here perhaps some of the above questions can be answered. When *O* is semantically present in *S*, *S* is a state of a biological organism and O is a physical entity—something, let us say, that physically touches the organism. (This would be the most primitive case.) The psychological state is the organism's *feeling O*. *O* is present to the organism, not simply existentially present with it. (Such a state is not presumed to be a conscious state, or, in other words, a self-aware state.) Can there be such an occurrence in the world for the first time? And could there have been only one such state and no more? If we knew or postulated that such a state occurred at the level of an organism with regard to an object in its environment, how could we know that such states did not occur in cells in their relations to objects in their environment? Or even in atoms in molecules or subatomic particles in atoms? If they require some complex organization, then what must be the nature of that organization? Could it be purely existential and factual? If a first simple psychological state existed in a world otherwise devoid of inherent structures of meaning, would it be intelligible? Or would it be a surd, an ontological dangler?

The point of this line of questioning is to reflect on the intelligibility of psychological atomism. If the psychological (or at least inherent structures of meaning) is categorially distinct as we have claimed, is psychological atomism intelligible? There are reasons for thinking that it is not. The psychological states and acts that we know in an experiential way, whether our own or those of others, are very complex and systemic. They occur within a psychological system and seem to be functions of the system. The system is not simply the product of its parts; it is holistic in that there are no atomic psychological states that could maintain their unity and identity apart from the system. If this is so, how can we justify atomism in our theoretical psychology?

The thought that psychological states and acts may be required conditions for the fulfillment of biological needs suggests that there might be a normative teleological explanation of the existence of semantic states and acts. It is true that the normative seems more akin to the semantic than the factual. Both are intentional structures. Could it be that the primitive or protoform of the semantic is the normative? Could it be that the semantic is somehow a complex of the normative? Perhaps the most primitive form of the psychological is desire, a normative requirement of an x that is such that the X is not only normatively present in the requirement but is semantically present in the organism *as the content of the normative state*; that is, perhaps X is semantically present in the organism *as something normatively required by the condition of the organism*. Could this be the form that a normative requirement grounded in a limited condition of an organism takes when its satisfaction becomes a requirement of the whole organism in a way that bids for the energy of the whole for its fulfillment? In other words, are psychological states and acts complex higher-level normative structures? Or do psychological states and acts *emerge* out of such complex higher-level normative structures?

There are compelling reasons for the claim that there is a categorial distinction between the normative and the semantic. Although normative structures are intentionalistic, semantic states and acts are *of* or *about* something in a unique way. The language of meaning cannot be paraphrased in the language of normativity and value. Semantic states and acts are not only reportable in language; they are, in principle, expressible in language and may be synonymous with other semantic states and acts. Normative structures, although reportable, are not expressible in this manner; and it makes no sense to talk about two such structures being synonymous. Furthermore, unlike normative and value structures, semantic states and acts come in a variety of logical forms in much the same way as sentences do, and they stand in logical relationships to one another. Furthermore, they are subject to semantic and logical appraisals. For these reasons, if no others, we cannot identify semantic intentionality with normative intentionality or reduce the language of meaning to the language of value.

Perhaps psychological states and acts are forms that meaning takes, somewhat as linguistic states and acts are forms that psychological states and acts take. So even if there were a first psychological state or act, there might not be a first state or act constituted by an inherent structure of meaning. Meaning does seem to be more basic than the psychological. We talk generally about genetic *codes* and *information* at the biological level. And we talk about *signals* and the *information* they bear in teleological systems. Where an end is internal to a causal process, as it seems to be in organisms, facts or events giving rise to changes in the process that keep it oriented toward its inherent end are spoken of as signals; and signals are events that bear information. Could it be that all meaning language at the prepsychological level is metaphorical? Or is it either analogical or literal semantic talk? If it is either of the latter, we would be justified in saying that there is meaning or a prototype of meaning that is not psychological. Perhaps psychological states and acts are complexes of meaning that occur only in normative teleological systems that must take account of facts and events external to the inner normative teleological causality of the system.

In any case, the psychological states and acts that we know are all in one psychological system or another. They do not appear singly in deserts of factuality, not even singly in oases of factuality, normativity, and perhaps meaning, such as in biological organisms. Psychological atomism (and even semantic atomism, if this should be understood as being more basic), as a strategy of analysis, has to yield at some point to a systemic approach that transcends extensional interaction of atomic elements. Psychological states and acts are always part of a system that involves essentially inherent structures of meaning. And as single identifiable psychological states and acts, they are dependent in *what* they are on the system of which they are a part. Are they also dependent in *that* they are on the system of which they are essentially a part? That is the question.

There is an intimate connection between the psychological and the biological. In fact, the psychological seems to be supervenient on the biological. The psychological, as we know it, appears only within biological systems that have to "negotiate" a complex relationship with an external environment. In fact, it seems that the psychological dimension appears in biological organisms that *need* it for their self-sustaining operations. In other words, it appears that the psychological is an extension of the biological under the constraint of normative requirements.

Of course it might be said, from within a wider perspective, that the biological exists as a necessary condition for the existence of the psychological, especially for the more complex psychological systems. This is suggested (if not meant) by the so-called anthropic principle.[4] It seems incredible to many that the complex structures of personal, social, and cultural realities exist as a condition for the continued existence of human beings as biological organisms. From our perspective, we feel compelled to think of our bodies and their well-being as a condition for our personal lives. But from within the biological realm, we can locate specific needs for which psychological states and acts are necessary conditions of their satisfaction. For example, in certain types of organisms, desire, perception, and intentional action seem to be necessary powers for the satisfaction of the organisms' need for food and water and for propagation of the species. The biological is not so much a condition for the satisfaction of psychological needs as for the existence of psychological states and acts of any kind. And there are no obvious conditions in the total context of our existence that might normatively require the psychological and thus the biological as a condition for the existence of the psychological. If there is a normative requirement in the structure of the universe for which the existence of human beings is a fulfillment, as the anthropic principle suggests, it is not grounded in some locatable set of conditions; rather it must be grounded in the wholeness of things or in the ground of the universe. This would imply that in some way the universe, in generating beings in whom the psychological or rational dimension was dominant, was fulfilling itself—fulfilling needs or requirements inherent in *its* nature, not the needs or requirements grounded in some local beings or situations.

Atomism in general seems to have limits, even in the physical sciences. So does factual atomism of the kind advocated by Russell, the early Wittgenstein, and Carnap. In scientific theory, atomism is a half-way house; at more basic levels, field concepts play a significant role and the alleged basic elements are identified and understood in terms of their environment. An extensional world of atomic facts, a world of complete contingency, is unintelligible; for each fact would have only conjunctive relationships with other facts and there could be no explanation of why anything was as it was rather than otherwise.

Scientists accept what seems to be a holistic turn within their own theory at the point where they talk about elements that have no identity apart from their environment. But we have to question whether such a move makes sense within the categories of existence and factuality. When we turn away from atomism to holism, we turn away from extensionality and accept internality. And the internality of holism involves the category of normative intentionality, if not that of semantic intentionality.

No atomistic theory can provide an adequate explanation of any subject matter that involves an inherent structure of either meaning or normativity, for such structures connect elements internally with others. It seems that our theoretical language must be as rich categorially as the language we use to describe the subject matter being explained.

In fact, we may question the coherence of atomism in its fundamentals. Essential to the position is the claim that there are basic elements with self-contained identities and inherent laws of behavior so that all of their relationships with other entities are extensional. The problem here is the concept of law. What is it to have a lawlike nature or identity? Is not the concept of an inherent law of an atom an intentional concept? Does not such a law connect the atom internally, in its identity, with its environment? Is not the notion of a self-contained atom having only extensional relations with its environment an incoherent concept?

Law was originally a normative concept. It made sense to talk about a law's being "obeyed" or "disobeyed"; a law could be deviated from without the law itself being put in question. Also the *nature* or *identity* of something was conceived as normative. An individual could have various degrees of actuality that were also degrees of perfection. When we eliminated normative concepts from our scientific descriptive/explanatory conceptual system, we came to think of laws extensionally and to think of the nature of things in terms of extensional laws. This made the very notion of an inherent nature or identity problematic; and we came to think of the nature and identity of things as relative to our pragmatically formed classificatory systems.

Yet in our atomism, we think of atoms as self-contained elements, each with its own identity and *inherent law*, and we think of the laws of interaction of atoms as extensional and derivative from the inherent laws of the interacting elements. Clearly realistic atomism is inconsistent with empiricism and extensionalism, for it holds on to non-extensional notions of the identity and inherent laws of atoms.

David Bohm speaks of basic elements that are supposed to be *autonomous* in that they are subject to laws inherent in themselves.[5] Any such basic elements would be *heteronomous* as well in that they would be subject to laws of interaction with other things as well as to the laws inherent in themselves, but the laws of interaction would be derivative from the laws inherent in the individual interacting elements. Heteronomous elements, he says, are subject to analytic descriptions; they can be "loosened from above" by techniques of analysis and described in their singularity and interaction with other elements.

"However, in sufficiently broad contexts," Bohm contends, "such analytic descriptions cease to be adequate. What is then called for is *holonomy*, i.e., the law of the whole." "'The law of the whole,'" he says, "will generally include the possibility of describing the 'loosening' of aspects from each other, so that they will be relatively autonomous in limited contexts (as well as the possibility of describing the interactions of these aspects in a system of heteronomy). However," he continues, "any form of relative autonomy (and heteronomy) is ultimately limited by holonomy, so that in a broad enough context such forms are seen to be merely aspects, relevated in the holomovement, rather than disjoint and separately existent things in interaction." Indeed, each whole that is discerned, he contends, turns out to be an aspect of a larger whole. This implies, he says, "that the total law of the undefinable and immeasurable holomovement could never be known or specified or put into words. Rather, such a law has necessarily to be regarded as *implicit*."[6] It is the law of the whole that he regards as the *implicate order*, which he contends is *enfolded* in the explicate order that can be revealed by analysis.

So atomism in general seems to be the product of a strategy of analysis that can take us only so far; in the end it yields to some form of holism. There seem to be no system-neutral basic elements out of which all systems are constituted. It seems that a theoretical language limited to the categories of existence and factuality would be adequate for an explanation of epistemically primary realities with a complex categorial structure of fact, value, and meaning only if the value and meaning dimensions were in some sense emergent from the organization of categorially simpler elements. We talk about emergent properties in the physical sciences. A certain organization of subatomic particles, for example, gives rise to oxygen and hydrogen atoms, which have properties quite different from any possessed by the subatomic particles. And, in turn, a certain organization of oxygen and hydrogen atoms gives rise to water, which has properties quite different from the properties of oxygen and hydrogen atoms. Emergentists think that we can account for normativity and meaning in a similar way.

This does not seem to be a promising approach. We can explain the properties of water in terms of the properties of the atoms involved, and we can explain the properties of the atoms in terms of the properties of the subatomic particles of which they are composed. Indeed, that is the whole point of the atomic and subatomic theories. If they did not provide explanations of this kind, they would be inadequate as scientific theories. But if normativity and meaning are emergent states or structures, it is not at all clear what would constitute an explanation of them in a way parallel with scientific explanations of the so-called emergent properties in the physical realm. Consider, for example, what we may call the emergence of sensory experience, or, more specifically, auditory experience. We may talk in general terms about sound waves, an organic transducer that converts sound waves into neural and cerebral (perhaps electrical) impulses, and then the emergence at some point of an auditory experience. What is this last step? Is there some transducer that makes another conversion of energy from one form to another? Or is the auditory experience something that cannot be explained in terms of neural and cerebral impulses and a transducer in any way similar to the way the ear transforms sound waves into the neural and cerebral impulses? The transition here, if the semantic theory of the mental is correct, is more like the transformation of patterned sound waves into sentences. The auditory experience seems to be a semantic dimension of a neural and cerebral process, not something into which the neural and cerebral processes are transformed. No observation and study of the neural and cerebral processes in a scientific way would discover the transformation, to say nothing about how the transformation occurs. A wholly different categorial dimension is involved, that of subjectivity or meaning, with its logical properties. We cannot even conceive of what it would be like to explain the semantic and normative dimensions of persons in terms of their purely factual constitution.

Meaning and normativity, if our analysis is correct, are not properties of something that emerge from the organization of simpler things with different properties. They are themselves modes of constitution somewhat parallel with the factual constitution of things. We can give no explanation of why things are constituted factually, that is, why there are particulars and why they exemplify properties. The most we can do is to answer why some given particulars exist and why they exemplify the properties they do. It seems as though we are just as helpless when faced with the question of why there is such a structure as the inexistential presence of one thing in another in either the normative or the semantic mode. We can, of course, say something about why a given thing ought to have some particular property and why a given person has some particular thing in mind at a given time. We are at a loss to explain why the world has the categorial structure that it has. This is so basic a matter that there is nothing that could constitute such an explanation.

Even if we should hold that the world could exist with only a factual constitution, and that, indeed, it did exist for aeons as a purely physical universe before normative and meaning structures came into being, we would have to maintain that the value and meaning structures were just as inexplicable as existence and factuality. So to hold that normativity and meaning are in some way emergent within what was antecedently a purely existentially and factually constituted world would be to hold that their emergence was a transcendental mystery—a mystery for which there could be no possible explanation. Such a view of the world would be most perplexing. It would project unintelligibility into the midst of developments in the history of the universe, rather than only in its foundations. There would be fewer mysteries (there would not be the mystery about why normativity and semantic intentionality appear where and when they do) if we postulated categorial dimensions of value and meaning as well as existence and factuality throughout reality. Reduction of mystery is always at least some warrant for a theory.

Even with a categorially enriched, humanistic theoretical conceptual system, we could grasp and understand only what Bohm calls "the explicate order," even though it would not be the atomic explicate order he had in mind. We would have to say that the world transcended the reality manifested in our categories. The implicate order cannot be turned into an explicate order without residue. Whatever reality we brought into our theoretical grasp would leave intimations of transcending reality. There is reason to believe that any conceptual system, if pushed far enough, would be found to be inadequate. This seems to follow not only from human limitations, but from the limits of intelligibility itself.

Nevertheless, the reality that is enfolded in the explicate order as comprehended in our most adequate categorial system must be such as to make possible all that is knowable to us by all of our epistemic powers. When our categories cannot be reduced to some basic set such as those of existence and factuality, we have to assume that what is basic has to be rich enough in its ontological structure to make possible the way reality comes structured in the whole range of human experience and thought.

Theorizing within a humanistic categorial system would not be atomistic in nature; it would have to be holistic, for the central humanistic categories would commit us to an internality of the candidates for basic elements. Perhaps self-sustaining organizations of energy (causal power) at any level have a holistic structure that involves normative and semantic dimensions. And perhaps such holistic units are embedded in larger holistic structures that involve normative and semantic dimensions.

This would imply that modern scientific theory, insofar as it remained faithful to its established methodology and assumptions about the knowledge-yielding powers of the human mind, was condemned to being conceptually limited so that it could grasp neither all the dimensions nor the full context of its subject matter, even though it might be able to guide us with remarkable success in our efforts to manipulate the factual dimension of things. If there were other categorial dimensions to the subject matter of science, alterations in the factual structures might work changes in the other dimensions as well. But where the other dimensions were more prominent, the greater the limitations would be on the scientific and technological approaches. This is what seems to be progressively the case with biological, behavioral, personal, and social phenomena.

Religion, Theology, and Ultimate Reality

Even with a broader humanistic conceptual system, we would not be able to bring the whole of reality within our conceptual grasp. As previously observed, there seems to be limits to intelligibility in any conceptual system. Regardless of how far we extend the realm of the intelligible, regardless of how much we are able to encompass within any explicate order, there will always remain an implicate order beyond the reach of our conceptual grasp.

In theology, the conceptualization of the unconditioned ground of everything as God is an attempt to extend the categories of a humanistically conceived explicate order beyond the explicate order to what is ultimate in the order of being. It has long been recognized, even by theologians, that this effort cannot succeed in any straightforward sense; that it tries to accomplish the impossible; that it tries to convert the elusive, transcendent implicate order into the top level of a human-istically conceived explicate order.

Of course talk about God had a much humbler origin. Early people experienced mystery wherever it occurred as numinous—as something that bore on their identity and well-being and thus engaged their higher emotions. People tended to feel themselves to be at issue in nearly everything that was out of the ordinary, for whatever disturbed their familiar world disturbed their sense of identity and place. For example, the Hebrew people, wandering in the wilderness after their escape from Egypt, saw a constant cloud in the sky in the day and a pillar of fire at night. They saw them as guides leading them to the promised land. In following the cloud and the pillar of fire, they came to Mt. Sinai, where they encountered what sounds to modern ears, from the biblical description, to have been an erupting volcano; but to them the awesome power in the mountain was the god of the desert, who had led them out of Egypt and to this place. Ever since the Hebrew people have connected the founding of their law and their peculiar covenant with Yahweh, their god, with the mysterious power they experienced in the fiery, smoking, roaring, quaking mountain. It was common for primitive people to take a religious approach to the strange and unknown.

The most commonly recognized form of theology today is what is known as sacred theology. It takes its departure from within an estab-lished religion. It attempts to interpret, to develop, to defend, and to show the cultural relevance of the belief system embodied in the sacred literature, symbols, rituals, and creeds of the religion. It typically ac-cepts these beliefs as given—as the residue of the "revelations" about ultimate matters in the lived experience of the historical community that have been built into the identity and way of life of the people. Sacred theology tries to reconcile this belief system of the religion with the accepted truths in other sectors of the culture. When religious be-liefs are seriously challenged by developments in other sectors of the culture, theologians usually reinterpret the religious beliefs rather than reject them as false. Saving their truth is more important to the religion than preserving an established interpretation. In the same way the Constitution of the United States lives through reinterpretation by the courts, religions, especially in progressive societies, live by reinterpreta-tion of their belief system. Of course there are always controversies between the strict constructionists (fundamentalists) and the reinterpre-ters (the neo-orthodox).

In addition to sacred theology, there is the religious thinking that went into the development of established religions and that continues to go on both within and independently of established religions. By "religious thinking" we mean thinking in response to religious concern. And by "religious concern" we mean concern about one's basic identity and place in the scheme of things in a way that bears on the ultimate meaningfulness and worthwhileness of one's life and of the human enterprise. The fundamental religious problem is whether "life is a tale told by an idiot, full of sound and fury, signifying nothing." The basic religious need is assurance of a worthy identity, the possibility of a meaningful and worthwhile life, and a fitting place in a hospitable and supportive world that makes sense of human existence and of the meaning and values we discover in living our lives. So religious theology tries to understand what is going on in our lives, in our history, and in the world in a way that will help us primarily with our religious problems. When the focus is on ordinary problems, the religious concern is always in the background; it exercises control over the questions asked and how they are answered.

Religious thinking of this kind is called "religious" theology to differentiate it from both sacred theology and what has traditionally been known as "natural" theology. Of course sacred theology is religious, but it is authoritarian in a way in which religious theology is not; that is, it begins with, and accepts accountability to, a sacred authoritarian source, whether a bible or a tradition. Religious theology looks to experience and insight in trying to make sense of human experience and reality under a governing religious concern. It may, or may not, understand the experience and insight on which it depends as authoritative "revelations."

Primitive people thought of the forces at work in their environment and in themselves as forces working for good or for evil. They were conceived as spirit forces or as value-oriented impersonal forces (what cultural anthropologists call "mana" forces). We still have remnants of this way of talking in our ordinary language. We still talk about "waiting for the spirit to move us" or not being "in the spirit" to do something; we also talk about a person's being "a little demon," about "beating the devil out of a person," about "having good luck" or "bad luck," about something's "being fated," about astrological powers and signs of the zodiac, and so on. People of some religions still talk about "being filled with the Holy Spirit," "being protected by guardian angels," "being overcome by the devil," and the like. These ways of talking are remnants of a way of trying to make sense of the forces at work in and around human beings and the way they bear upon people in living their lives. This was primitive religious theology. It was thoroughly empirical and about contingent matters.

As people developed a more complex organization of society and discerned more connectedness and order in their world, they came to think of ever greater and more unified forces at work in the world until they came to think in terms of a unitary numinous power behind all things. Some conceived this power as God and some as an ultimate impersonal mana power such as Brahman or the Tao. Both were operating from within a humanistic way of thinking about the dynamics of the universe. It was only when religious theology became more sophisticated that it came to ask philosophical questions about God and to develop philosophical arguments about God's nature and existence.

Natural theology is a more purely intellectual enterprise from within the humanistic perspective. It is not tied to any religious tradition; nor is it explicitly governed by religious concerns. It seeks to solve intellectual problems within a humanistic framework of thought, without being closely tied to governing religious interests. Nevertheless, it stands to the whole complex of humanistic needs, including religious needs, much as science stands to our materialistic needs. What is usually thought of as natural theology is the part of a humanistic metaphysics that attempts to push philosophical understanding of the world to its limits; but, as suggested in *Philosophy and the Modern Mind*,[7] we might think of any systematic search in humanistic categories for an understanding of reality as natural theology. If so, we would recognize an empirical as well as a philosophical part of natural theology.

Natural theology in its classical forms has been connected with, and influenced by, religious and sacred theology. It borrowed the name "God" for ultimate reality from religious theology; but it has been recognized all along that the God of natural theology is not the God of religion. Although the God of natural theology has been identified with the religious God, without being clothed in the literary language of religion, this God does not engage the religious emotions of people and does not meet their religious needs. Our concern here is with the "God" of natural theology: what, from within a humanistic metaphysics, we can reasonably say about ultimate reality, if by "ultimate reality" we mean what is beyond the categorial structure of the world. As we shall see, we cannot say much.

The classical arguments for the existence of God were, for the most part, efforts to explain the categorial structure of the world. Thomas Aquinas, in his arguments for the existence of God, reasoned from what he recognized as five basic features of the world (his version of what we would call categorial structures): motion (the reduction of potentiality to actuality), causation (the order of efficient causes), contingency (the existence of things that might not have been and may not be at some time in the future), a hierarchy of beings (the gradation of things according to worth, goodness, perfection), and normative structures and processes (the ends in nature). He reasoned that the ground of motion must be an unmoved mover; that is, within his framework of thought, he maintained that the reductions of potentiality to actuality that go on in the world would be intelligible only if there were something with no unactualized potentiality that in some sense started and sustained the process of actualization of potentialities. In like manner, he reasoned that the order of efficient causation would not be intelligible without an uncaused cause; that the contingency of things in the world would not be intelligible without a being who had necessary (noncontingent) existence; that the gradations of beings according to worth would not be intelligible unless there was a supreme, perfect being; and that the normative structure of things (the ends in natural processes) would not make sense unless there was an intelligence behind them—that (in our terms) normative teleology requires rational teleology for intelligibility. So he concluded that the ground of each of these basic features of the world is what everyone calls "God." In sum, God is said to be an unmoved, uncaused, necessary, perfect, intelligent being. In other words, God is a being with complete self-sufficiency and perfection. For Aquinas, only a being so conceived is the final question-stopper; only an explanation in terms of such a being ends the intellectual quest for intelligibility.

Unlike modern thought that attempts to explain the "higher" in terms of the "lower" (or the more complex in terms of the simpler), Aquinas assumed that, in a value-saturated world, the explanation of something had to be in terms of something of equal or higher value. Descartes formulated this principle in his argument for the existence of God this way: There must be as much reality in the cause as in the effect. Within classical metaphysics, this meant that there must be as much perfection in the cause as in the effect. Aquinas said that the ultimate cause in each genera is the highest of its kind; his example: In the class of hot things, fire, the cause of warmth in things, is the hottest. So the ultimate cause of all things must be being at perfection, at complete actuality, with no unactualized normative potentiality.

In each of his arguments, Aquinas is arguing to the more perfect or highest of its kind as ultimate cause. He reasons from moved movers to an unmoved mover, from caused causes to an uncaused cause, from contingent beings to a noncontingent being, from higher and lower beings to a supreme being, and (in our language) from normative ends in nature to something with rational ends (semantic ends intelligently arranged), which he thought of as a more perfect teleological being. A moved mover, a caused cause, a contingent being, a less than perfect being, and something with a nonrational end in its nature are all dependent beings. They stand in need of explanation. So, in this framework of thought, the search for intelligibility leads ineluctably to a supreme, perfect being as the ultimate explanation of all that is inherently incomplete, less than perfect, and dependent in its existence.

Kant, in his peculiar way, argued for the God-belief (but not for the existence of God) as a basis for the intelligibility of moral life.

Anselm argued that our concept of God as a supreme being (a being greater than which cannot be conceived) entails that God is a noncontingent being—that is, God is a being that cannot not exist, for if God could not exist, then, even if God did exist, God would be a dependent being and thus not the greatest being that could be conceived.

All of these arguments appeal to God (or the God-belief) as a question-stopper in the search for intelligibility. It seems that the questions are stopped not by final intelligibility but by unintelligibility. Although, unlike Kant, we have argued that the categorial structures we attribute to things are real features in the world, we cannot treat them like noncategorial features. They are not susceptible to explanation in terms of something that gives rise to them or as something in which they are grounded in some way in the order of being. There is no explanation of normative potentiality and actuality in a being that has no unactualized potentiality; there is no explanation of causality in an uncaused cause; there is no explanation of existence in a being with noncontingent existence; and so forth. The God-hypothesis does not explain the categorial structures of selfhood and the world, for God is conceived as a being who shares in the categorial structure to be explained.

The world with its categorial structure is not something that exists and stands in need of explanation in any way like things in the world. It is helpful to consider how questions of existence arise. Things inexistentially present in experience, thought, or discourse may or may not be existentially in the world. So we ask about objects of experience, thought, or discourse whether they exist—whether things in the mind are in the world also. Thus mind and world are related concepts. Talk about the existence of the world is peculiar. The world is that in which things can and do exist. How can the world itself exist? And how can it not exist? Are these sensible questions?

Obviously the world does not exist in the sense of having location in the world. But we do talk about the world; and, when we do, we may ask if what our language is about (its object) is independent of the language. And it seems that we must say that it is. But what does this independence amount to? It is not like saying that the pen in my hand is independent of our thought about it. For the pen to be independent of our thought about it is for it to exist in the sense of having space-time location. The world is independent of our talk about it in some other sense. It is that in which things exist. It is the arena of existence.

The logic of "world" is much like the logic of "space." In fact, what one takes the world to be is a function of the kinds of things one takes to exist. If one admits the existence of only purely physical things, then one's world is the physical space-time continuum. If one admits the existence of numbers, platonic forms, and so forth, one's world embraces timeless logical space. If one admits the existence of persons, one's world must embrace social space and a peculiar time that embraces past-present-future physical time in a living present.

What is it for physical space to exist? Does it amount to more than the existence of physical objects? If there were no physical objects, would there be space? Kant's thought experiment in which we can think away all the objects in physical space seems to suggest the affirmative. Then, it seems that the sentence "Physical space exists" means no more than that it is possible that there are physical objects—it is possible that the objects of sensory perception and of physical-object language have independent existence.

If this line of thought is correct, "The world exists" means that knowledge is possible—that it is possible that the objects of experience and thought exist.

One's world has an a priori, categorial structure because the structure of experience, thought, and language delimits the possible (the conceivable) and thereby delimits the world as we can know it. There is no distinction between the actual world and the possible world except with respect to contingencies. The only way we can talk about alternative possible worlds, other than with respect to contingencies, is relative to alternative beings with different constitutional principles of mind.

If this is what is involved in saying that the world exists, then is its denial possible? Is the existence of the world with its categorial structure logically contingent? The statement "I do not exist now" does not formulate a logical possibility. "I might not have been" not only formulates a possibility; it states a truth. But it seems that neither "The world does not exist" nor "The world might not have existed" formulates a logical possibility. The statements do violence to themselves in what they say. Their presuppositions are inconsistent with what they assert. The conditions for the meaningfulness of these statements guarantee their falsity. They are necessarily false. So it seems that we must conclude that "The world exists" is a necessary truth. *World* is a categorial concept.

The issue raised by the question "Why is there something rather than nothing?" is not why there is a world, but why there is anything in it. This is not a matter of the possibility of the existence of things, but of the actual existence of things. The question is meaningful only if it is possible for there to be nothing. The statement "There is nothing" does not formulate a logical possibility. The statement or thought itself refutes what it asserts, for it itself exists. Furthermore, its presuppositions, the conditions of its meaningfulness, are inconsistent with what it claims. It is inconceivable that there could be the distinction between the inexistential presence of an object and the existence of an object unless something existed. Even the statement "There might have been nothing" presupposes the distinction and, therefore, the existence of something. We cannot genuinely entertain an empty world as a possibility. Even the annihilation of everything, if that should be consistently thinkable, would not leave us with an empty world. It would be, if anything, the end of the world—the end of time, at least. But even that is not a clear, well-formed thought. So the question "Why is there something rather than nothing?" is not a genuine question.

Yet these are bothersome quasi questions. They seem to present a problem, but not one that we can clearly formulate. In asking them, we are trying to reach beyond the edge of meaningful discourse. Are we up against the limits of reality or just up against the limits of thought as defined by the constitutional principles and powers of the human mind?

In this work, we have argued that the a priori character of our knowledge of the categorial structure of the world is a function of the fact that our categorial concepts are grounded in the constitutional principles of the human mind so that we cannot consistently conceive of the basic structure of the world as otherwise. Yet we have argued for a realistic interpretation of the categories. Nevertheless, we have contended that we are not warranted in concluding that the necessity involved in our a priori knowledge of the categorial structure of the world (this is not to be confused with "natural" necessity) cannot be taken to reflect a metaphysical necessity in the nature of things. So it seems that the real structures in the world grasped in our a priori knowledge of the categorial structure of the world may be in need of explanation for complete intelligibility, but, by the very nature of human knowledge, any such explanation is forever beyond our reach. The best we can do is to conclude that the transcending implicate order that is enfolded in our explicate order (our humanly categorized world order) must be such as to make our explicate order possible, for we know that the explicate order with its categorial structure obtains.

The argument that the categorial structure of our explicate order of the world is humanistic rather than naturalistic may be taken as an argument for a theistic view of the world, for the basic implications of the traditional religious belief in the existence of God are that human life is meaningful and worthwhile and that the dynamics of the universe work for the realization of what is good. But the humanistic categorial structure of the world is the limit in our intellectual quest for intelligibility; it is the ultimate in the order of knowledge, even though it may not be ultimate in the order of being. Nevertheless, there are intimations and troublesome quasi questions that drive us to try to go beyond these limits. We seem compelled to hold that there is an unknown, what David Bohm called a transcending implicate order, that is enfolded in, and makes possible, our categorially structured explicate order, whether it is naturalistically or humanistically conceived. But the nature and character of this implicate order must remain for us a mystery; all we can know about it is that it must be such that it makes possible our structured world, including ourselves and social and cultural phenomena.

Insofar as our explicate order is defined by the humanistic conceptual system, the implicate order may be an appropriate subject matter of some form of nondiscursive, artistic, mythical, or symbolic approach as in religion. This approach may yield congenial supplements to the humanistic approach to intelligibility; but they are not compatible with naturalism, for they presuppose a humanistic categorial structure in their subject matter.

Religion begins from within the thick of life. The story is the most natural form of discourse for lived experience; and poetry, art, and symbol are the most adequate modes of expression of our rich life-and-death experiences. In like manner, the story, poetry, art, and symbol are the natural modes of discourse and expression in religion. Religion attempts to extend the life story of individuals, the historical story of a people and their way of life, and, indeed, the historical story of humankind to incorporate the universe and what is ultimate. In the biblical story, for example, what is ultimate in the order of being appears as God, the leading character in the comprehensive story of the universe; the creation of the humanistically categorially structured universe is an event in the story; and the history of humankind, including the life story of each human being, is an integral part of the larger story. In this way, religion presents the world and all that transcends it as a text within which the life story of each person and the history of humankind are meaningful. The language of the story is the language of persons and society; it has its primary use in the personal and social realms. It is given an extended use in trying to encompass all of reality and to integrate our human lives and history and the fragmentary meaning and values we have found into a unified world story that makes sense. This literary way of seeking intelligibility is in sharp contrast with the abstract intellectual quest, whether in a naturalistic or a humanistic conceptual system.

There is every reason to believe that the literary, poetic approach does garner important truths about human life and the social world, even truths that are not available to the abstract discursive approach; and, indeed, there are reasons for believing that the literary, poetic approach may yield important truths about the larger world as well. The character God in the biblical story, for example, may be a symbol through which we can extend human experience and insight into the ultimate in the order of being. Religious language and symbols may make possible experiences that will provide some measure of confirmation for the insights that the language and symbols make possible. The language and theory of science extend scientific experience. Why would it not be the same here?

The truths of literature, poetry, and religion may defy translation into the language of abstract, discursive thought, but certainly the prospect is better for an abstract humanistic conceptual system than for a naturalistic one. Sacred theology tries to do this. It remains, of course, an important issue whether the God of theological conceptualization, as well as the God of religious stories, is a symbol that symbolizes an implicate order that transcends our conceptual grasp. Nevertheless, the symbol may have a measure of adequacy as indicated by its integrative and enriching power for the whole range of human experience. The theoretical belief in God, however, remains largely the belief that somehow the categorial structure of persons and society reflects something about the nature of ultimate reality, even though what is ultimate in the order of being cannot be brought within our categorial grasp.

Although it would be affected in important ways, there are no compelling reasons why science could not adjust to, and even thrive within, a dominant humanistic cultural perspective and a humanistic worldview. Unless it modified its own conceptual system and methodology, no doubt science, in such a cultural context, would lose some of its prestige and some of its own inner motive power; for it could no longer be regarded as working toward a comprehensive and complete understanding of the nature of things. It would have to regard itself as concerned with one dimension of things from within a limited perspective in the service of practical needs. It would no longer occupy center stage in our intellectual quest. But the intellectual problems in the particular scientific disciplines would be enough of a challenge, along with the practical benefits through technology, to keep science, even as it is, a thriving enterprise.

What seems solid is that it is only from within the humanistic perspective and in terms of a humanistic world-view that we can resolve the deep intellectual tensions that have rent our modern civilization and given rise to our human identity crisis. Human beings, whose identity is defined in terms of their normative self-concept as persons and as the individual social beings they are, need not be estranged or threatened in a humanistically categorized world. Rather, from within a humanistic framework of thought, the intellectual search for intelligibility should underwrite and reinforce the human quest for meaningful and worthwhile lives in a supportive and moral social order. Even the ultimate mysteries could be humanized in the literary and poetic language and artistic symbols of religion with intellectual respectability and support. From within the humanistic approach, and in no other way, human beings, the culture, and the world can be made whole again.

NOTES

CHAPTER 1

1. Marcel Proust, *The Past Recaptured* (1927); quoted in Saul Bellow, "The Nobel Lecture," *The American Scholar* 46, no. 3 (Summer 1977): 321.
2. Robert Nisbet, *History of the Idea of Progress* (New York: Basic Books, 1980), p. 383.
3. Ibid., p. 317.
4. Marshall Berman, *All That Is Solid Melts into Air* (New York: Simon and Schuster, 1982), p. 345.
5. Friedrich Wilhelm Nietzsche, *The Gay Science*, trans. Walter Kaufmann (New York: Random House, Vintage Books, 1974).
6. C. S. Lewis, *The Abolition of Man* (New York: Macmillan, 1947).
7. Robert Bellah et al., *Habits of the Heart* (Berkeley: University of California Press, 1985).
8. Ibid., p. 46.
9. Alexander Solzhenitsyn, "The Exhausted West," *Harvard Magazine* 80, no. 6 (July–August 1978), pp. 21–26.
10. Daniel Bell, *The Cultural Contradictions of Capitalism* (New York: Basic Books, 1976).
11. Roberto Unger, *Knowledge and Politics* (New York: Free Press, 1975).
12. Alasdair MacIntyre, *After Virtue* (Notre Dame, Ind.: University of Notre Dame Press, 1981).
13. See especially my *Philosophy and the Modern Mind* (Chapel Hill: University of North Carolina Press, 1975; reprinted, Lanham, Md.: University Press of America, 1985).

CHAPTER 2

1. Raymond Williams, *The Long Revolution* (New York: Harper Torchbooks, 1966), pp. 47–48.

2. E. M. Adams, *Philosophy and the Modern Mind* (Chapel Hill: University of North Carolina Press, 1975; reprinted, Lanham, Md.: University Press of America, 1985), p. 11.

3. Ibid., pp. 10–19, 29–55.

4. Ludwig Wittgenstein, *Philosophical Investigations*, trans. G. E. M. Anscombe (New York: Macmillan, 1953), p. 79e (para. 194).

5. Ibid., pp. 47e, 49e (paras. 109, 124).

6. Gilbert Ryle, *Dilemmas* (Cambridge, Eng.: Cambridge University Press, 1956).

7. Nelson Goodman, *Ways of World-Making* (Indianapolis: Hackett, 1978), p. 6.

8. Ibid., p. 21.

9. Ibid., p. 129.

10. Ibid.

11. Ibid., p. 17.

12. Ibid.

13. See Nelson Goodman, *Of Mind and Other Matters* (Cambridge, Mass.: Harvard University Press, 1984), pp. 30–31.

14. John J. McDermott, *Streams of Experience: Reflections on the History and Philosophy of American Culture* (Amherst: University of Massachusetts Press, 1986).

15. Ibid., p. 25.

16. Ibid.

17. Ibid., p. 50.

18. Ibid., p. 57.

19. Richard Rorty, *Philosophy and the Mirror of Nature* (Princeton, N.J.: Princeton University Press, 1979), p. 317.

20. Henry Johnstone, *Philosophy and Argument* (University Park: Pennsylvania State University Press, 1959).

21. Alan Gewirth, *Reason and Morality* (Chicago: University of Chicago Press, 1978).

22. See R. B. Perry, *General Theory of Value* (New York: Longmans, Green and Co., 1926).

23. G. E. Moore, *Principia Ethica* (Cambridge, Eng.: Cambridge University Press, 1903).

24. G. E. Moore, in his reply to Charles Stevenson in Paul Arthur Schilpp, ed., *The Philosophy of G. E. Moore* (Evanston and Chicago: Northwestern University Press, 1942), p. 554.

25. Everett W. Hall, *What Is Value?* (London: Routledge & Kegan Paul, 1952).

26. E. M. Adams, "The Nature of Ought," *Philosophical Studies* 7 no. 3 (April 1956): 36–42; "'Ought' Again," *Philosophical Studies* 8, no. 6 (December 1957): pp. 86–89; "Mr. Hall's Analysis of 'Ought'," *Journal of Philosophy* 55 (January 1958): 73–75; *Ethical Naturalism and the Modern World-View* (Chapel Hill: University of North Carolina Press, 1960; reprinted, Westport, Conn: Greenwood Press, 1973), pp. 107–21.

27. C. I. Lewis, *An Analysis of Knowledge and Valuation* (Lasalle, Ill.: Open Court, 1946), pp. 211–23.

28. Adams, *Ethical Naturalism*, pp. 120–21.
29. Stephen Toulmin, *An Examination of the Place of Reason in Ethics* (Cambridge, Eng.: Cambridge University Press, 1950).
30. Kurt Baier, *The Moral Point of View* (Ithaca, N.Y.: Cornell University Press, 1958).
31. Gewirth, *Reason and Morality.*
32. See William Frankena, *Thinking about Morality* (Ann Arbor: University of Michigan Press, 1980); David Gautheir, *Morals by Agreement* (Oxford, Eng.: Clarendon Press, 1986); R. M. Hare, *The Language of Morals* (Oxford, Eng.: Clarendon Press, 1951); Friedrich Hayek, *Law, Legislation and Liberty*, vol. 1, *Rules and Order* (Chicago: University of Chicago Press, 1973); Alasdair MacIntyre, *After Virtue* (Notre Dame, Ind.: University of Notre Dame Press); John Rawls, *A Theory of Justice* (Cambridge, Mass.: Harvard University Press, 1971); Jean-Paul Sartre, *Existentialism and Humanism*, trans. Philip Mariet (London: Methuen, 1948).
33. See Adams, *Ethical Naturalism* pp. 153–206, and *Philosophy and the Modern Mind*, pp. 106–38.

CHAPTER 3

1. E. M. Adams, *Philosophy and the Modern Mind* (Chapel Hill: University of North Carolina Press, 1975; reprinted, Lanham, Md.: University Press of America, 1985), p. 173.
2. Ibid., p. 176.
3. To say this does not mean that all indefinable terms are categorial. Consider color words, for example. There are other conditions to be met; a concept must be connected with the constitutional principles of the mind to be categorial.
4. See Jay F. Rosenberg, *Linguistic Representation* (Boston: D. Reidel, 1974), ch. 2, "A Mentalistic Theory."
5. Wilfrid Sellars, "Mental Events," *Philosophical Studies* 39 (1981): 328.
6. Ibid., p. 329.
7. Ibid., p. 331.
8. An excellent guide to the present literature and positions held on the subject is given by J. A. Fodor in "Fodor's Guide to Mental Representation: The Intelligent Auntie's Vade-Mecum," *Mind* 94, no. 373 (January 1985): 76–100.
9. Ibid., p. 85.
10. Ibid.
11. See Hartry Field, "Tarski's Theory of Truth," *Journal of Philosophy* 64, no. 13 (1972): 347–75; also in Mark Platts, ed., *Reference, Truth and Reality* (London: Routledge & Kegan Paul, 1980), pp. 83–110.
12. Fodor, "Fodor's Guide," p. 86.
13. Sellars, "Mental Events," p. 336.
14. Ibid., p. 337.
15. Sellars, "Mental Events," p.337.
16. Ibid., p. 338.
17. Ibid., p. 337.

18. N. J. Block and J. A. Fodor, "What Psychological States Are Not," *Philosophical Review* 81 (1972): 165; also in Ned Block, ed., *Readings in Philosophy of Psychology* (Cambridge, Mass.: Harvard University Press, 1980), vol. 1, p. 245.

19. See H. P. Grice, "Meaning," *Philosophical Review* 66, no. 3 (July 1957): 377–88; "Utterer's Meaning, Sentence-Meaning, and Word-Meaning," *Foundations of Language* 4 (1968): 1–18; and "Utterer's Meaning and Intention," *Philosophical Review* 78, no. 2 (April 1969): 147–77.

20. Sellars, "Mental Events," p. 326.

21. Sydney Shoemaker, "Functionalism and Qualia," in Block, *Readings in Philosophy of Psychology*, vol. 1, p. 264.

22. Ibid., p. 252.

23. J. A. Fodor, *Representations* (Cambridge, Mass.: MIT Press, 1981), ch. 7.

24. Sellars, "Mental Events," p. 337.

25. Hilary Putnam, "Philosophy and Our Mental Life," in his *Mind, Language and Reality: Philosophical Papers* (Cambridge, Eng.: Cambridge University Press, 1975), vol. 2, pp. 291–303.

26. See my *Ethical Naturalism and the Modern World-View* (Chapel Hill: University of North Carolina Press, 1960; reprinted, Westport, Conn.: Greenwood Press, 1973); also my *Philosophy and the Modern Mind* (Chapel Hill: University of North Carolina Press, 1975; reprinted Lanham, Md.: University Press of America, 1985), chs. 4 and 5.

27. The fact that I quantify over properties does not mean that I take properties to exist in a Platonic sense. I hold that we may quantify over whatever has an independent status, whether semantic, normative, or existential, so that it can be picked out or located in discourse.

28. See especially my *Ethical Naturalism and the Modern World-View*, ch. 7.

29. See my *Philosophy and the Modern Mind*, chs. 6–7.

30. See especially ibid., pp. 150–57, and 194–201.

CHAPTER 4

1. The distinction intended is this: When a term is applied to a referent that has only some of its defining characteristics, for the purpose of making a revealing comparison with the ordinary referents of the term, it is being used *metaphorically*; when a term is applied to something that literally has none of the defining characteristics of the term but is taken to have some characteristics that are to it what the defining characteristics of the term are to the ordinary referents of the term, for the purpose of giving some kind of conceptual shape to the object, the term is being used with analogical meaning.

2. We need to keep in mind the distinction between the need for semantic concepts in the language in which we report and describe the primary realities we know and the need for such concepts in our theoretical or mythical language. Here we are talking about only the need for semantic concepts in our reporting and descriptive language of the primary realities we know.

3. Alvin I. Goldman, *Epistemology and Cognition* (Cambridge, Mass.: Harvard University Press, 1986).

4. Ibid., p. 16.

5. Ibid., pp. 16–17.

6. Ibid., p. 103.

7. Ibid., p. 115.

8. Ibid., p. 106.

9. Ibid., p. 66.

10. John Rawls, *A Theory of Justice* (Cambridge, Mass.: Harvard University Press, 1971), pp. 20–21, 46–51.

11. Goldman, *Epistemology*, p. 66.

12. Many philosophers have claimed, and I agree, that well-formed statements and the facts (and I would include normative requirements, necessities, etc.) they assert share a common form. But usually we consider a form to be *logical* by virtue of its connection with structures of meaning. When the same abstract form that is instantiated in a structure of meaning is part of the structure of a non-semantic fact, we consider it as part of the metaphysical structure of the fact. Of course we could generalize the concept of the logical and extend it to the kind of abstract form in question regardless of whether it was instantiated in structures of meaning or in the structure of non-semantic facts. This seems to have been the position of Russell, the early Wittgenstein, Suzanne Langer, and H. M. Sheffer, to name just a few. But this tends to blur the distinction between logic and metaphysics.

13. See especially E. M. Adams, "Linguistic Analysis and Epistemic Encounters," *Philosophy and Phenomenological Research* 34, no. 3 (March 1974): 404–14; or *Philosophy and the Modern Mind*, ch. 3.

14. Norman Malcolm, "Knowledge and Belief," in his *Knowledge and Certainty* (Englewood Cliffs, N.J.: Prentice-Hall, 1963).

15. For a detailed argument for this point, see my *Philosophy and the Modern Mind* (Chapel Hill: University of North Carolina Press, 1960; reprinted, Lanham, Md.: University Press of America, 1985), pp. 42–47, 139–201.

16. This statement needs qualification. Belief in a false theory can both justify and explain why one got a matter right. Certainly people got many things right on the basis of their belief in the Ptolemaic theory. But when this is the case, the true theory has to be able to explain why people were able to get some things right on the basis of the false theory.

17. Consider Thomas Nagel, *The View from Nowhere* (New York: Oxford University Press, 1986).

18. For a critical discussion of reductive phenomenalism, see my "The Inadequacy of Phenomenalism," *Philosophy and Phenomenological Research* 20, no. 1 (September 1959): 93–102.

19. For a critical discussion of C. I. Lewis's position, see my "C. I. Lewis and the Inconsistent Triad of Modern Empiricism," in Paul Arthur Schilpp, ed., *The Philosophy of C. I. Lewis*, vol. 13 of *Library of Living Philosophers* (La Salle, Ill.: Open Court, 1968), pp. 377–93.

20. See my "Perception and the Language of Appearing," *Journal of Philosophy* vol. 55, no. 16 (July 1958): 683–90.

21. See Bertrand Russell, *My Philosophical Development* (New York: Simon and Schuster, 1959), pp. 22–27.

22. See Wilfrid Sellars, *Science, Perception and Reality* (New York: Humanities Press, 1963), pp. 91–95.

23. Ibid., p. 99.
24. Nagel, *View from Nowhere*, p. 101.

CHAPTER 5

1. The position I am summarizing here is developed in my *Philosophy and the Modern Mind*, (Chapel Hill: University of North Carolina Press, 1975; reprinted, Lanham, Md.: University Press of America, 1985), pp. 65–72.
2. Ibid., passim.
3. See my "Mind and the Language of Psychology," *Ratio* 9, no. 2 (December 1967): 122–39; "The Scientific and the Humanistic Images of Man-in-the-World," *Man and World* 4, no. 2 (May 1971): 174–92; "Skinner on Freedom and Dignity," *Southern Journal of Philosophy* 10 (Spring–Summer 1973), 111–19; "Human Substance," *Review of Metaphysics* 39 (June 1986): 633–52; and especially *Philosophy and the Modern Mind*, pp. 139–201.
4. See especially my *Ethical Naturalism and the Modern World-View* (Chapel Hill: University of North Carolina Press, 1960; reprinted, Westport, Conn.: Greenwood Press, 1973), chs. 5 and 6; and *Philosophy and the Modern Mind*, ch. 5.

CHAPTER 6

1. See Ernest Nagel, "Logic without Ontology" in Y. K. Krikorian, ed., *Naturalism and the Human Spirit* (New York: Columbia University Press, 1944).
2. Donald C. Williams, *The Ground of Induction* (Cambridge, Mass.: Harvard University Press, 1947), p. 26.
3. For a recent sophisticated argument for the thesis that what can be imagined is possible and for mind/body dualism, see W. D. Hart, *The Engines of the Soul* (Cambridge, Eng.: Cambridge University Press, 1988).
4. In some of M. C. Escher's works, impossible spacial structures are depicted so that they look real. See *The Graphic Work of M. C. Escher*, trans. John E. Bringham, rev. ed. (New York: Gramercy, 1984).
5. Williams, *Ground of Induction*, p. 30.
6. Henry W. Johnstone, *The Problem of the Self* (University Park: Pennsylvania State University Press, 1970).
7. Carl G. Jung, "Approaching the Unconscious," in *Man and His Symbols*, ed. Carl G. Jung (New York: Dell, 1968), p. 25.
8. See my "The Accountability of Religious Discourse," *International Journal for Philosophy of Religion* 18 (1985): 3–17.
9. Alan Gewirth, *Reason and Morality* (Chicago: University of Chicago Press, 1978).
10. Ibid., p. 150.
11. For a fuller criticism of this position, see my "The Subjective Normative Structure of Agency," in *Gewirth's Ethical Rationalism*, ed. Edward Regis, Jr. (Chicago: University of Chicago Press, 1984), pp. 8–22.
12. Jeremy Bentham, "Anarchical Fallacies," reprinted in A. I. Melden, ed., *Human Rights* (Belmont, Calif.: Wadsworth Publishing Co., 1970), pp. 28–39.

13. Alasdair MacIntyre, *After Virtue* (Notre Dame, Ind.: University of Notre Dame Press, 1981), p. 67.

14. For a discussion of some recent theories of human rights, see my "The Ground of Human Rights," *American Philosophical Quarterly* 19, no. 2 (April 1982): 191–94.

15. See John Locke, *Second Treatise of Government* (1690), ch.2, para. 6.

16. For a fuller discussion of this point, see my "Classical Moral Philosophy and Metaphysics," *Ethics* 74, no. 2 (January 1964): 97–110.

17. Some might object to the inclusion of Kant in this school of thought. The reason for doing so is that Kant thought that a good person is one whose will is rational; and he thought that a purely rational will has a form imposed by reason in somewhat the way as judgment has a form imposed by the understanding. So a moral person is one who wills and acts in accordance with the requirements of one's constitution as a rational agent.

18. See Jeremy Bentham, *An Introduction to the Principles of Morals and Legislation* (1789), ch. 1, para. 12.

CHAPTER 7

1. John Stuart Mill, "On Liberty," in E. A. Burtt, ed., *English Philosophers from Bacon to Mill* (New York: Modern Library, 1939), p. 961.

2. Ibid., p. 965.

3. See my *Philosophy and the Modern Mind* (Chapel Hill: University of North Carolina Press, 1975; reprinted, Lanham, Md.: University Press of America, 1985).

4. Alexander Solzhenitsyn, *Letter to the Soviet Leaders*, trans. Hilary Sternberg (New York: Harper and Row, 1974), p. 21.

5. Ibid., pp. 34–35.

CHAPTER 8

1. Ernest Gellner, *Legitimation of Belief* (Cambridge, Eng.: Cambridge University Press, 1974), p. 194.

2. For my efforts toward this end, see my *Ethical Naturalism and the Modern World-View* (Chapel Hill: University of North Carolina Press, 1960; reprinted, Westport, Conn.: Greenwood Press, 1973) and my *Philosophy and the Modern Mind* (Chapel Hill: University of North Carolina Press, 1975; reprinted, Lanham, Md.: University Press of America, 1985).

3. Joseph Margolis, *Persons and Minds* (Boston: D. Reidel, 1978) and *Culture and Cultural Entities* (Boston: D. Reidel, 1984).

4. See John D. Barrow and Frank J. Tipler, *The Anthropic Cosmological Principle* (New York: Oxford University Press, 1986).

5. See David Bohm, *Wholeness and the Implicate Order* (London: Routledge & Kegan Paul, ARK Paperbacks, 1983), pp. 156–57.

6. Ibid.

7. Adams, *Philosophy and the Modern Mind*, p. 216.

INDEX

state of and new orientation for modern, 264–65

Wickedness, in contrast with moral weakness, 208

Will: of person, 115; weakness of, 115, 207–8

Williams, Donald, 192, 196

Williams, Raymond, 21

Wittgenstein, Ludwig, 25, 27, 40, 207

Womanhood, moral criticism of traditional office of, 235–36

Words and ideas, pragmatic theory of, 67

World: basic constitution of, 27, 28, 31; a priori categorial structure of, 304–6; contents of, 108–9; existence of, 303–5; disenchantment of, 10; logic of concept of, 304; modern struggle for objective view of, 119–26; normative structure as dimension of, 110; unified under descriptive/explanatory conceptual system, 3, 51

World-view: humanistic, 4, 287–308; naturalistic, 13, 77; non-naturalistic, 4; religious, 4. *See also* Conceptual system; Perspectives